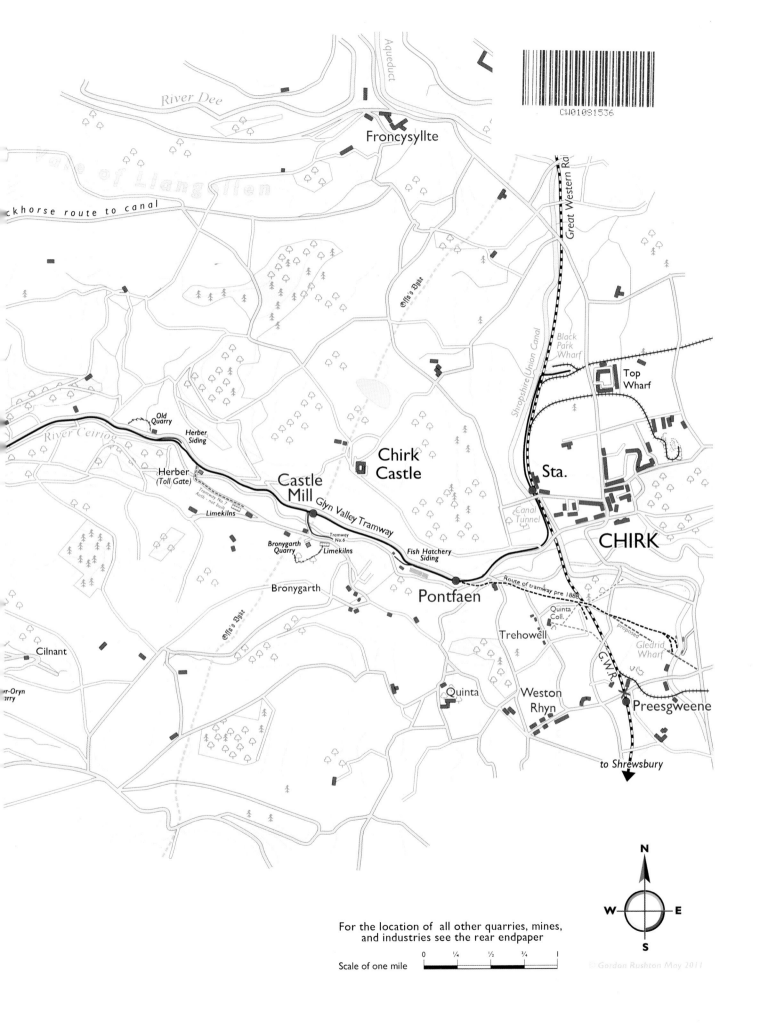

Rails
to
Glyn Ceiriog

PO Box 85, Chester CH4 9ZH
United Kingdom

*SIR THEODORE crossing the road at Pontfaen and about to enter Baddy's Wood
on route to Chirk with a mixed train.*

©Philip D. Hawkins

Rails
to
Glyn Ceiriog

by
John Milner
and
Beryl Williams

The History of the Glyn Valley Tramway

Part 1

Its Background History, Conception
and Battle for Survival

1857–1903

THE INDUSTRIAL HISTORY OF THE CEIRIOG VALLEY – VOLUME 2

Cyflwyniad
Dedication

Dewi Parry Jones

and

David Llewellyn Davies

Long-standing friends and
devoted historians of
the Ceiriog Valley

Disclaimer and Copyright

Every effort has been made to ensure that all the information in this publication is accurate at the date of going to press. All notes, reports and captions have been carefully checked, are believed to be correct and are published in good faith. Neither the Publisher nor the Authors accept any liability for any loss, misrepresentation, or any form of damage arising owing to any reason however caused from any information in this publication. Likewise, every effort has been made to correctly attribute copyright or ownership of photographs and illustrations, and the appropriate permissions have been sought by the Authors where possible. All digital images used in this book are the copyright of Ceiriog Press, unless otherwise attributed. Should any reader be aggrieved by any incorrect credit or statement then he/she should contact the Publisher, when action will be taken to address the issue or, where possible, to rectify any errors in future editions.

Warning

Anyone who is inspired by this book to go and start exploring the remains of the tramway, old quarry or mine workings of the Ceiriog Valley should be aware of the fact that they are to a large extent located on private land. Access to areas away from the limits of a public footpath, where one exists, should first have the owner's/mineral rights owner's permission, as well as permission from other landowners should their land have to be crossed to gain access. Some of these sites are extremely dangerous, with hidden and unprotected ventilation shafts, unstable tips and rock faces. They should be treated with great respect and any visitor should be fully aware of the safety precautions required.

Cledrau
i
Lyn Ceiriog

gan

John Milner

a

Beryl Williams

Hanes Tramffordd y Glyn

Rhan 1

Ei hanes cefndirol, y Cysyniad a'r

frwydr i oroesi

1857–1903

ISBN: 978-1-900622-14-1 (Hardback)

British Library Cataloguing in Publication Data

A catalogue record for this book
is available from the British Library
Catalogue Reference No. 385.5'0942937-dc22

Publishing, Typesetting and Design by:
Ceiriog Press, PO Box 85,
Chester CH4 9ZH

Special Graphics by:
Ashley Milner and John Milner

Maps by:
Gordon Rushton and John Milner

Printed by:
The Amadeus Press,
Cleckheaton BD19 4TQ

Published *in Wales*

Ceiriog Press is an imprint of RailRomances Publishing

Cydnabyddiaethau
Acknowledgements

A book of this nature would not be possible without the assistance of other persons, both officials and private individuals. During the preparation of this book, everyone has been only too willing to assist.

Special mention must be made of the assistance given by David Llewellyn Davies, Eric Lloyd MBE, the late James I. C. Boyd and the late S.H.P. Higgins, all of whom over the years have conducted a great deal of research into the history of the Glyn Valley Tramway. On the research side, my thanks are due to my good friend, the late Alistair Lamberton, for his painstaking work, on my behalf, in searching the Beyer Peacock Company records in the late 1950s, at a time when they were unsorted and uncatalogued.

Special thanks go to the local inhabitants of the Ceiriog Valley, and ex-employees of the GVT company in the early years of my research and too numerous to mention, but whose hospitality and assistance is greatly appreciated. Sadly, few of the GVT employees have lived long enough to see this work completed. Of special mention are: Rona Bates, Ned Beale, Bryan Butler, Sydney and Theodore Davies, Lawrence Evans, Graham Greasley (Chirk History Group), John Griffiths (Ruabon), Heather and Tom Hughes, John Hughes (John Hughes journal), Gwilym Hughes, Neville Hurdsman, Angela James, Robert Jones, Anne Jones and her late husband, Dewi, Miss Einwen Jones, His Honour Judge Geoffrey Kilfoil, Eddie Lambert, Mr & Mrs Mottram, David Norman, Ven. Bill Pritchard, John White (Surrey), Bill Williams and Bob Yates.

Without photographs a book of this nature would be inadequate. The assistance of all those individuals who have supplied photographic material is gratefully acknowledged. To name but a few: Harry Arnold (Waterways Images Ltd), John Amlot, Dennis Bishop, Keith Buckle, Crosse Wyatt Verney & Ayre, Mark Hignett, Peter Johnson, Jane Kennedy (Oakwood Press), David Mitchell (Talyllyn Railway), Andrew Neale, Bob Pearman, Garth Tilt, Verna Palmer, Dr. Ann Pulsford, Ian L. Wright and Sian Williams and Edward A. Wilson.

Of the official institutions, acknowledgement is given to the staff of Shropshire County Archives, Flintshire County Archives, Denbighshire County Archives, the late Beyer Peacock & Co., Metropolitan-Cammell Carriage & Wagon Co. Ltd. and Powell Duffryn Ltd., Cartographics, Canal Maps Archive, English Heritage, Institution of Civil Engineers, Gwynedd Archives Services, Llangollen Museum, National Library of Wales, National Railway Museum, Ceiriog Memorial Institute, Oswestry Public Library, Companies Registration Office, British Museum, British Library, House of Lords Record Office, Narrow Gauge Railway Museum Trust, National Archives (Kew), North Devon Record Office, Royal Commission on the Ancient and Historical Monuments of Wales, the Science Museum, Stephenson Locomotive Society, The New Glyn Valley Tramway & Industrial Heritage Trust, The Waterways Trust (in particular Caroline Jones, Archivist), Welsh Railways Research Circle (in particular Tony Miller and Nigel Nicholson), Jonathan Gorman (Wrexham Museum) and Esther Williams (Wrexham County Archivist). Acknowledgement is also given to the Chirk & Ceiriog Valley Partnership for its donation towards costs.

John Bate (Talyllyn Railway) has, in his usual impeccable manner, provided constructive comments and suggestions on various topics in the book. The collaboration of Allan Baker on W.G. Bagnall topics and Andy Cuckson on the Snailbeach District Railways history has been gratefully received and is mentioned in more detail in the Introduction.

The book has been greatly enhanced by the presence of some outstanding artwork by Philip Hawkins, who has generously and freely allowed it to be used in this book. Likewise, artist Jonathan Clay has similarly enabled the use of his artwork.

A quality book without a quality printer is a wasted effort, so my appreciation and thanks go to Richard Cook and David Crosland of Amadeus Press, who have been very patient with my demands, having been involved in the printing of all but one of my books since 1984, and not forgetting Patrick Roberts for undertaking the proofreading and Esther Hitchcock for her editorial assistance.

Last but not least, I am deeply indebted to my co-author, Beryl Williams, for all her diligent work on research and editing, to Gordon Rushton for his painstaking and outstanding work on the maps and to Ashley Milner for his exceptional work on technical drawings. Their involvement as part of the 'team' is explained in more detail in the Introduction.

To all who have assisted, past and present, however small or large their contributions may have been, I offer my sincere thanks.

Cronoleg ddethol
Selected Chronology

1529	Tŷ Draw Slate Quarry at work.
c1740	Tŷ Draw Slate Quarry closed.
1750	Wynne Slate Quarry reputed to have been started by John Wynne.
1769	*Steam engine patented by James Watt.*
1770	Bronygarth limekilns built.
c1790	Chwarel Ucha Slate Quarry (Cambrian) opened.
1801	Chirk aqueduct opened.
1805	Pontcysyllte aqueduct opened.
1818	Wem & Bronygarth Turnpike Trust took over the existing toll road to Bronygarth.
1820s	Upper Chirk Bank Colliery waggonway built.
1837	*Queen Victoria's accession to the throne.*
1847	SUR&C Co.'s canals leased to the LNWR Co.
1848	Chirk viaduct completed in September 1848.
c1850	Henry Dennis moved to North Wales from Cornwall.
1851	*First train ran in British India.*
1854	3rd August: Cambrian Slate Co. registered.
1856	Act passed for a new road to Llanarmon DC.
1857	Dennis & Glennie, Ruabon, partnership formed.
1857	First proposal to build a tramway down valley.
1858	Timber-built spans of Chirk viaduct replaced.
1858	5th January: Cambrian Slate Co. authorised to raise capital to build a tramway.
1860	Plans for Wem & Bronygarth Turnpike Trust to build Quarry Road in Glyn Ceiriog.
1860	Wem & Bronygarth Road Act 1860 passed and the first sod cut at Glyn Ceiriog 19th August.
1863	W&BRT turnpike road to Chirk completed.
1863	*First London underground railway opened.*
1865	Glyn Valley Railway Bill (withdrawn 1866).
1866	August: Ellesmere & Glyn Valley Railway Act 1866.
1868	Henry Dennis tramway proposal for E&GVR Co.
1869	Ellesmere & Glyn Valley Railway Act 1869.
1870	*The Tramways Act 1870 given Royal assent.*
1870	*Glyn Valley Tramway Act 1870.*
1870	22nd July: Cambrian Slate Quarries sold.
1871	28th June: SUR&C Co. agreed to operate the GVT.
1871	August: Quinta Tramway under construction.
1872	March: First GVT shareholders' meeting.
1872	8th June: New Cambrian Slate Co. Ltd registered.
1872	Patent Gunpowder Co. Ltd registered.
1873	*Glyn Valley Tramway opened.*
1873	Cambrian incline built to connect the quarry to the GVT.
1874	January: Granite discovered during construction of leat to gunpowder works.
1874	Glyn Ceiriog Granite Co. opened Hendre Quarry.
1874	*22nd April: GVT horse-drawn passenger service started.*
1874	GVT/GWR interchange sidings built at Quinta.
1874	June: F.W. Webb asked to design a locomotive for the GVT.
1874	June: Proposal to connect the GVT to Ifton-Rhyn Collieries.
1874	6th November: First plans to extend GVT to Hendre Quarry.
1874	19th December: Accident on Pontfaen bridge and passengers thrown into river.
1877	January: Introduction of steam power discussed.
1878	11th March: Road trustees agreed to use of steam locomotives.
1878	May: Proposal for GWR/GVT passenger interchange at Trehowell.
1878	*Glyn Valley Tramway (Nantyr Extension) Act 1878 (use of steam not included in the Act).*
1879	*June: Powers introduced for trial use of steam operation of tramways.*
1879	14th July: Wynne Slate Quarry Co. Ltd placed into liquidation.
1879	29th October: Jebb proposal for re-routing GVT.
1879	*December 28th: Tay Railway Bridge disaster.*
1880	Preesgweene Colliery proposal for tramway to join GVT at Gledrid Wharf.
1880	Abandoned gunpowder works site taken over by Hendre Quarry.
1881	*23rd July: Start of 5-day trial with W.G. Bagnall & Co. steam locomotive 'Tunis'.*
1881	August: Road authorities consent to use of steam locomotives on the GVT.
1881	23rd August: Ceiriog Granite Co. restructured to enable it to operate the GVT.
1881	1st September: Ceiriog Granite Co. Ltd took over GVT operation from the SUR&C Co.
1881	November: Legal control of W&BT Trust road passed to Llangollen Highway Board.
1882	6th March: New Cambrian Slate Co. Ltd placed into liquidation.
1883	12th March: Pant Glâs Slate & Slab Company Ltd registered.
1883	*23rd December: BoT approved use of steam.*
1884	Locomotive 'Rattlesnake' at work at Trehowell Colliery.
1885	6th May: Parliamentary Committee sat for Glyn Valley Tramway Bill 1885.

1885	July: Production restarted at Wynne Slate Quarry by Pant Glâs Slate & Slab Co. Ltd.
1885	*31st July: Glyn Valley Tramway Act 1885 gained Royal assent.*
1886	George and Francis Rooper took over the Cambrian Quarry.
1886	*31st March: GVT closed to passenger traffic.*
1886	Incline built from the Wynne Slate Quarry to connect with the Glyn Valley Tramway.
1887	*Work started on the conversion of the GVT to steam power.*
1887	*June 21st: Queen Victoria's Jubilee.*
1887	Autumn: Snailbeach locomotive 'Fernhill' arrived on loan to the GVT.
1887	October: GWR interchange sidings installed at Chirk for the new GVT station.
1888	January: Snailbeach locomotive 'Belmont' arrived on loan to the GVT and 'Fernhill' returned.
1888	Spring: Extension built from Chirk station to the canal interchange at Black Park Wharf.
1888	17th October: Locomotive 'Sir Theodore' arrived.
1888	Autumn: Landslide on Pontfaen–Chirk road.
1888	*Glyn Valley Tramway converted to steam power.*
1889	April: Locomotive 'Dennis' arrived on GVT.
1889	April: 'Belmont' returned to Snailbeach.
1889	*GVT extension to Hendre Quarry completed.*
1889	July: Black Park basin goods interchange in use.
1889	GVT installed access for Lower Pandy chinastone quarry which was reopened by CG Company.
1889	Pandy spur and coalyard built.
1889	Quinta Colliery and Brickworks closed and Pontfaen–Gledrid horse track lifted.
1889	*Queen Victoria visited North Wales.*
1889	20th December: agreement for CG Co. to build culvert for leat under GVT at Pandy.
1890	4th March: Francis Rooper negotiated with the GVT for a loading facility at Coed-y-Glyn quarry.
1891	*16th March: GVT reopened for passenger traffic.*
1892	March: Locomotive 'Glyn' arrived on GVT.
1892	Chirk, Pontfadog, Dolywern & Glyn Ceiriog waiting rooms built.
1893	GVT Pandy spur connected to the Teirw Hill Roadstone Quarry line.
1898	*March: GVT started to carry the Royal Mail.*
1900	Lilleshall locomotive purchased by CG Co.
1901	*22nd January: Queen Victoria died.*
1901	Chirk Fish Hatchery built and siding installed.
1902	Short GVT siding built to serve a new CG Co. quarry at Upper Pandy.
1903	26th October: Part of Cambrian Quarry incline washed away.
1905	'Sir Theodore' on loan to Snailbeach Dist. Rlys.
1905	New tippler and chute built at canal-side granite wharf at Black Park.
1905	3rd December: George Rooper died aged 93 years.
1906	24th June: Henry Dennis died aged 81 years.
1907	CG Co. built a line from Pandy to a tarmacadam plant being constructed at Lower Pandy quarry.
1909	18th August: Sir Theodore Martin died aged 92 years.
1910	Glyn Quarries Co. Ltd registered to take over Wynne, Cambrian and Coed-y-Glyn quarries.
1910	Underground horse haulage at Cambrian Quarry replaced by oil-fired Bagnall locomotive.
1911	14th March: Glyn Silica Co. incorporated to work Craig-y-Pandy and Coed-y-Glyn quarries.
1914	*4th August: World War I started.*
1918	*11th November: World War I ended.*
1920	'Sir Theodore' returned to Beyer Peacock & Co. for new boiler and overhaul.
1921	August: Baldwin locomotive arrived on the GVT.
1921	The GWR Co. urged to take over the GVT.
1923	Proposal by Warrington Corporation to flood the upper reaches of the Ceiriog Valley.
1926	The Ceiriog Granite Co. started using road transport.
1929	Cambrian Quarry purchased a 'Planet' petrol locomotive.
1929	13th August: BQC Ltd purchased the Ceiriog Granite Co.
1931	Traffic Commissioner granted licence for bus services to Llanarmon.
1932	30th September: GVT passenger service reduced to one train each way per day.
1933	*6th April: Last passenger train on the GVT.*
1935	*6th July: Glyn Valley Tramway closed.*
1935	22nd August: GVT Co. registered as a limited company.
1936	2nd October: Cambrian Quarry purchased its incline from the GVT Company.
1937	*GVT Company liquidated.*
1939	3rd September: Francis Rooper died aged 83 years.
1939	*3rd September: World War II started.*
1945	*7th May: World War II (Europe) ended.*
1947	March: Cambrian Quarries officially declared abandoned.
1947	12th September: Glyn Quarries Ltd placed into liquidation.
1948	14th July: Cambrian Quarry assets sold at auction.
1953	Hendre Quarry closed.
2003	18th February: Pontfadog and Dolywern waiting rooms granted Grade II listed building status
2003	7th August: Glyn Ceiriog engine shed granted Grade II listed building status.

Rhagair

Foreword

Part 1 of "*Rails to Glyn Ceiriog*" is an admirable tour de force of assiduous research presented in high-quality form by an author and publisher who has pursued his chosen subject with dedication for over 50 years, joined and assisted during recent years by his fellow researcher and author, Beryl Williams, who shares John Milner's exacting standards and together they have presented something in which they are entitled to take considerable pride.

This work deserves to rank as the most comprehensive history of the trials and tribulations – and some successes – of a minor Welsh narrow-gauge rail system so far published and should share bookshelves alongside classic works of highly respected authors in this field such as Rolt and Boyd (and the author's own widely acclaimed "*Slates from Glyn Ceiriog*" published by him three years ago).

John Milner's latest publication is the first part of the second volume in his ambitious "*Industrial History of the Ceiriog Valley*" project which, on completion, is destined to furnish the definitive reference work on both the Glyn Valley Tramway *and* the industries of the valley for the foreseeable future.

The authors have achieved not only a fine balance between rail and canal history, but also social and biographical accounts together with a general background history of the valley. The book makes, in addition, an important contribution to recording the era of the Shropshire Union Railways & Canal Company in building and operating the tramway. It provides a significant account relating to the canal at the valley's border with England, especially since that location forms a part of the wider area recently designated a World Heritage Site centred, of course, on Telford's astonishing aqueduct at Pontcysyllte.

The result is a thorough and integrated work which will cater to all readers' aspirations to extend their knowledge, understanding and appreciation of the aspects covered in this volume and will serve to herald far and wide the wealth and varied riches to be discovered throughout this truly beautiful and still very Welsh valley and its surrounding mountains and moorland, which enclose its soul.

For the residents of our valley and their now scattered families and descendants it will provide a soundly researched and, very importantly these days, an authenticated historical perspective and base from which can be developed the exhibition displays for their new heritage centre in the heart of the G.V.T. country, namely in the village of Glyn itself.

"*Absque labore nihil*" (Dim heb ymdrech – nothing without striving) – my old Ruabon Grammar School coat of arms' motto may perhaps have some aptness in describing the authors' path to publication: the visiting of sites far and near, the photographing of physical and engineering features some of them hardly discernible to the amateur eye, the trawling of Record Offices and museums locally, nationally and cross-border, the obtaining of permissions to use and/or copy documents, plans, deeds, correspondence and other items (which today's researchers will attest to, is an increasingly and alarmingly expensive ordeal in the face of the 'make everything subject to the highest price the market can get away with' economic philosophy) and the myriad tasks inherent in a project such as this.

I wish this book the success it fully merits.

His Honour Judge Geoffrey E. Kilfoil M.A. (Oxon)

President – Neuadd Goffa Ceiriog (Ceiriog Memorial Institute Hall)
President – The New Glyn Valley Tramway & Industrial Heritage Trust – Y Dram
Vice President – Cymdeithas Hanes Hen Sir Ddinbych (Historical Society of the old Shire of Denbigh)

Cyflwyniad
Introduction

Bloody battles, between the English and the Welsh; the beautiful and inspiring landscape of outstanding beauty, gouged out by the activities of the human hand to generate wealth for English industrial barons, one of whom was a personal friend of Queen Victoria, leaving vast spoil heaps for future generations to 'enjoy'; the location of some of the early north–south road, canal and railway routes, including some spectacular engineering feats; a place of extraordinary geological interest; the birthplace of some of Wales' most famous poets and home to a one-time Lord Mayor of the nation's capital.

In 1923, ex-Prime Minister Lloyd George stayed at the Queen's Hotel, Dolywern, when he visited the Ceiriog Valley to see for himself why there was such strong condemnation of the Warrington Corporation Water Bill 1923, by the inhabitants of the valley including Sir Alfred T. Davies, Permanent Welsh Secretary to the Board of Education, and his influential supporters. He concluded that the valley was *'Darn bach o nefoedd ar y ddaear'* – *'A little bit of Heaven on Earth'*, and indeed it is.

Croeso i Ddyffryn Ceiriog!
Welcome to the Ceiriog Valley!

Today, in the 21st century, evidence of the industrial activities of the Ceiriog Valley has all but disappeared, the quarries, mines and other works having long ceased operation and being now reclaimed by nature. Once again, it is a place of tranquillity and outstanding natural beauty; it is likely to remain so, unless further exploited in the guise of progress or the development of tourism for the masses.

My own journey of adventure down 'memory lane' in the Ceiriog Valley has been a long and extraordinary one – to date some 58 years! During this time, I have had the pleasure of meeting many residents, from all walks of life, with stories to tell; all keen to welcome me into their homes and willing to share their memories of earlier days and 'tales' passed down from former generations, who had earned their living by working in the mines and quarries or on the tramway that served them.

Having been born and spent my schooldays in Oswestry, Shropshire, home of the headquarters of the Cambrian Railways, and with a grandfather who was a retired Cambrian engine driver, it is only natural that, from a very early age, I developed a keen interest in railways. I was encouraged by Henry Jones, the then Librarian at Oswestry Library, to delve into local industrial history and that I did with great zeal. While, on Saturday afternoons, all the other boys were pursuing their quest to become another Denis Compton, I was off on my bike exploring some long-forgotten tramway, quarry, colliery or brickworks, only to find myself standing outside the headmaster's study on a Monday morning to explain my absence from the Saturday afternoon sports field! In the early 1950s, my grandfather told me about the 'little railway' that used to run from Chirk to Glyn Ceiriog and my mother used to relate stories about the Sunday School treats up the valley on the 'tram'. My interest was aroused and I set out with determination to explore and find out all that I could about the Glyn Valley Tramway; undoubtedly to the relief of the staff of the Cambrian Railway Works and the locomotive sheds at Oswestry, who had previously received my attention.

Regular visits to one-time employees of the Glyn Valley Tramway Company, and much time spent further afield, began to unveil a fascinating story of a railway, which, like so many others, struggled for its survival from the very day it was first proposed. Political, legal and financial battles persisted throughout its existence. Contacts in the valley directed me to the ex-secretary of the GVT Co. who, despite my immature years, proved to be very friendly, helpful and patient with my many requests for information. Imagine my delight when I was presented with old timetables, photographs, and even a sample of the material used for re-upholstering the First Class carriage. As the story was unveiled, the tranquil Ceiriog Valley came to life. I began to hear in my imagination, above the noise of the waters of the River Ceiriog, the beat of the tram engine in the distance, with the unmistakable rattle of its train of granite or slate wagons never, of course, to appear in sight. To this day, some 76 years since the last train trundled down the valley with its load, I can still let my imagination run wild; but, to the unknowing visitor, the Ceiriog Valley today is simply a peaceful

Railway historians James I.C. Boyd (left) and Lewis Cozens on the platform of the GVT station at Chirk c1949, during one of their exploratory trips to the tramway.

Courtesy: The late J.I.C. Boyd

haven with little trace of its former industries and is much sought after as a place of retirement and for such leisure activities as trout fishing, pony trekking, walking and outward bound activities.

The Glyn Valley Tramway, unlike its contemporaries in Wales, only attracted the attention of the press on the odd occasion and was little known outside the locality, but through the diligence of a few railway historians a great amount of its history has been unearthed over the years. In the 1960s, I acquired a large cache of the GVT Co.'s records, including virtually all the Agreements and drawings for the acquisition of land, which provided a wealth of new material, although much of it made little sense at the time because related documents were missing. However, diligent and relentless research by my co-author, Beryl Williams, has pieced together this documentation with the result that it has been possible to write a much more informative account of the early years of the tramway.

One of the earliest descriptions of the GVT in its steam era was written by railway historian H. Fayle and published in the *Railway Magazine* (No.64) for October 1902. Over the years, various other authors contributed articles to magazines, but it was James I.C. Boyd who recorded the first brief historical account of the tramway in his book *Narrow Gauge Rails in Mid-Wales*, published in 1952. I first met him in 1954 when I was but a young lad of 18, finding my feet as a junior member with the Talyllyn Railway Preservation Society, founded in 1951. I well remember walking with him along the track near to Dolgoch station, when I duly announced that I was going to write a book on the Glyn Valley Tramway. With a smile on his face, his only response was: 'Oh yes!'. It was his friendship, encouragement and advice that inspired the decision to write my original GVT history, eventually released in 1984. By the time my book was published I understood exactly what he was thinking on that day, 30 years earlier, as we walked the track together. He had already been down this route and knew that it was not to be an easy task, contrary to what I thought at the time – but I was not to be defeated! In March 1949, James Boyd had offered to pass his GVT records over to Selwyn H.P. Higgins, who had also conducted a lot of local research into the GVT, with the intention of writing a book, and to drop his own plan of having a GVT chapter in what was to become his *Narrow Gauge Rails in Mid Wales* book. However, Selwyn Higgins ventured off to work on another book, *The Wantage Tramway* (Abbey Press 1958), although he did collaborate with me on GVT issues right up to his final years. After both James Boyd's and Pearce Higgins' deaths, their GVT research records were passed into my custody.

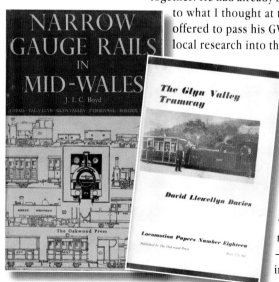

The third exceptional author, having a profound knowledge of the valley as a whole, is David Llewellyn Davies, who has always been a prolific researcher into all aspects of the history of the Ceiriog Valley, and he was the first to delve deeper into the annals of the GVT Company. The result was a booklet, *The Glyn Valley Tramway* (The Oakwood Press 1962 – Revised 1991). As a good friend, he too has been of valuable assistance in my work and has also entrusted me with the custody of his GVT records.

During the 1960s, I had done much research into the various quarries and mines that generated the traffic for the GVT. However, at that time, the publishers that I approached deemed that the book should be based solely on the tramway and should not include the industries that formed part of the social and economic life of the Valley, as they had no place in a 'railway' book. My viewpoint was that these industries were, indeed, the very reason for the tramway in the first place – I was ahead of my time! When the book was eventually published in 1984, the then publisher still considered this to be the case. However, disappointing as it was at the time, this decision left me with unpublished manuscripts that now form the foundation of my present series on the *Industrial History of the Ceiriog Valley*.

It was C.R. Clinker who, in his Presidential address to the Railway and Canal Historical Society in 1961, said, '*One cannot effectively study an individual railway or canal in isolation, but it must be seen in its social, economic and geographical context*' and how right he was! In contrast to the many railway enthusiasts who write about their beloved subject in great detail, without considering external factors, I have always deemed the circumstances under which a railway has been built and operated to be of the utmost importance to the readers' understanding of events, the outcomes of which are almost always dependent on the prevailing conditions. For this reason, I have included much background information that, hitherto, may have been unavailable to readers, in particular to those researching their family history.

Twenty-seven years ago, my history of the tramway concluded with the words: '*Hopefully, this work will form the base for future historians who wish to research particular aspects of the subject ... it is only part of the industrial history of the Ceiriog Valley, the history of the quarries, mines and other industries being, as yet, virtually untouched.*' Nobody took up this challenge, other than myself, ably assisted in more recent years with equal enthusiasm by Beryl Williams, with the target of producing a complete industrial history of the Ceiriog Valley; bearing in mind the immortal words of evangelist St. James: '*Be ye doers of the word and not hearers only.*'

Having spent so many years researching the history of the GVT, the dilemma that I now faced, was one of far too much information on some topics and not enough on others. Being forever mindful of railway historian James I.C. Boyd's comment, when my 1984 GVT book was published, that it was '*much more than this little line ever deserved*', it was a question of deciding whether to simply summarise events and produce a low-cost publication, or continue researching in order to produce a more complete and well-illustrated, albeit large and expensive, series for prosperity. In the interest of producing a definitive history for future generations, I opted for the publication of *The Industrial History of the Ceiriog Valley* in several volumes. The first volume of the series, *Slates from Glyn Ceiriog*, was published in 2008.

'Amser dyn yw ei gynysgaeth'

'A man's time is his endowment'

Monument in Bala to T.E. Ellis, MP for Merioneth.

Designated Volume II of *The Industrial History of the Ceiriog Valley*, this book, *Rails to Glyn Ceiriog Part 1*, covers the background and birth of the Glyn Valley Tramway, the pioneers responsible for its development and details of other local tramways. It describes the construction of the horse tramway, its operation under the Shropshire Union Railways & Canal Company and then the Ceiriog Granite Company, its reconstruction and the building of the deviation to Chirk and its extension to Hendre in 1887, its conversion to steam operation, the re-introduction of the passenger service in 1891 and the working of the line up to 1903. Part 2 relates the remainder of the story up to its closure in 1935 and the liquidation of the GVT Co. in 1937. Included are details and new drawings of the locomotives and rolling stock, and also the route and buildings, with appendices giving particulars of employees, traffic figures and other items likely to be of interest to the reader.

This book has been written at the same time as a new history, '*Lead Down, Coal Up – The Snailbeach District Railways*' by Andy Cuckson (RCL Publications). There are various overlapping areas in the history of both railways, and to ensure that good, factual works appear in print, Andy Cuckson and I have co-operated fully, with a free exchange of information at all times, while writing our respective books. Likewise, there is also a similar overlap in *'Bagnalls of Stafford'* by Allan C. Baker and T.D. Allen Civil (The Phyllis Rampton Narrow Gauge Railway Trust), and Allan Baker and I have also co-operated fully with a free exchange of information regarding the 1881 steam trials on the GVT. Such co-operation has given me a better understanding of the GVT's short periods of involvement with these two companies and has enabled me to include details of these that may not have been otherwise available.

John Milner and Beryl Williams outside the restored GVT waiting room at Pontfadog in 2010.

Photo: Mandy Connor
© John Milner 2010

Acknowledgements are listed elsewhere, but it must be iterated that without the assistance so freely given by local inhabitants, ex-employees and people too numerous to mention, a work of this nature would not be possible. Special mention must also be made of my wife, Beryl, who, over the past fifty years, has been very patient, with her home sometimes resembling and smelling like the archive room of some long-forgotten solicitor's office!

As with my first volume in this ongoing work, *'Slates from Glyn Ceiriog'*, I have been fortunate to have been accompanied on this project over the past six years by my co-author, Beryl Williams, who has not only been an exceptional and dedicated companion, but has a professional approach to the subject, bringing fresh air to my own work. One task that she has undertaken has been to sort and analyse boxes of GVT Co. legal records that I obtained from the company's liquidator in the 1960s; a monumental job that has taken hundreds, if not thousands, of hours to complete and one for which I have never been able to afford the time. The result is that numerous missing links in the story of the GVT have come to light and what in the past has been speculation, has been either verified or disproved. Without her enthusiasm, encouragement, dedication and editorial support my work would have been so much the poorer.

A book of this nature, without good-quality maps, would be akin to a drawer without a handle. In this respect, my good friend Gordon Rushton has excelled himself with the large-scale detailed maps that he has produced for this book. This kind of work is very time consuming, but he has willingly and enthusiastically managed to fit it into his already busy commercial schedule. He has suffered my constant demands for quality and seemingly endless amendments in the search for accuracy, but he has more than obliged – although not always in silence! Special mention must be made of Ashley Milner, who has toiled over the technical drawings for both parts of this work. Although only one of his drawings appears in this book, Part 2 will reveal work that is a joy to behold. Without such a team, small as it is, a work of this magnitude and quality would not be possible.

The aim of this series is to bring together, for the first time, the best and most interesting of the photographic and documentary material collected. Hopefully, this first part of *Rails to Glyn Ceiriog* will be a major contribution to the comprehensive history of GVT's early days as a horse tramway and its subsequent conversion to steam, and readers will share some of the enjoyments and surprises that it has given to me over the years. Despite the extensive research there are still many questions left unanswered, which may inspire others to pursue their own lines of research to fill in some of the gaps and help complete the story.

John Milner
June 2011

Sylw'r cyd-awdur
Co-author's Comment

It has been my privilege and a joy to work with John to bring this book to fruition. Some six years ago, I joined him on his *'journey of adventure'*, which has taken me to the reading rooms of far-flung archives and libraries, as well as into numerous nooks and crannies in the Ceiriog valley landscape – always with a notebook at hand and usually with a tape measure as well!

John has set himself very high standards indeed. He must be admired for his dogged determination to locate the original documents, in order to establish the true facts of the story, and for his insistence on the subsequent rigorous checking and cross-checking of material to ensure the accuracy of our interpretation. As an established specialist publisher of high-quality books, his skills and expertise have enabled him to embark on the production of this lavishly illustrated series and, in that capacity, he alone is responsible for the design of the book, the choice of illustrations and the setting out of every page in preparation for printing. My main contribution as co-author has been to support John in searching out and interpreting original documents and, where appropriate, incorporating the new information into the draft text; I take no credit for the illustrations or the presentation.

The natural beauty of the Ceiriog Valley is appreciated by residents and visitors alike; the unfolding of the history of its industrial past must add a new dimension to an understanding of what now lies hidden but not yet completely forgotten. Undertaking this research has been like starting to assemble a jig-saw puzzle of infinite size, not knowing where to find the pieces or, indeed, whether they still exist. As a result the picture that John and I present can never be complete but the *'journey of adventure'*, although sometimes difficult and frequently frustrating, has been very rewarding and exciting, especially when yet another piece of the jig-saw was seen to be falling into place!

CBWilliams

Beryl Williams
June 2011

Finally, a little food for thought. We are all familiar with the French high-speed train, *Train à Grande Vitesse* or *TGV* for short. Dr Martin Barnes corresponded with the author recently saying:

'I was musing on the way back from Paris on Eurostar about how the French language puts nouns before adjectives, yet they talk about **TGV** *when, by their own rules, it ought to be* **TVG**. *If they did it the proper English way, it would be* **GVT**'!

Cynnwys
Contents

Monetary values are quoted in pre-decimal currency and all units are British Imperial.
For conversion tables see Appendix 1

Chapter 1

The Background and Birth
of the Tramway

The River Ceiriog flows eastwards from the Berwyn Mountains in northeast Wales through seventeen miles of picturesque valley, eventually to emerge into the Dee Valley where it joins the River Dee, the last four miles or so forming the boundary between England and Wales. Tranquil and picturesque it may seem today but, during the past 800 years or more, this deep and fertile valley, sandwiched between the River Dee to the north and the River Tanat to the south, has been the scene of bloody battles and much industrial exploitation.

In 1165, the valley beneath Chirk Castle, which stands guarding its entrance, was the scene of the celebrated Battle of Crogen fought between Owain Gwynedd, Prince of North Wales, and Henry II's vast army that had been assembled at Oswestry to 'once and for all' suppress the Welsh. Chirk Castle was at that time known as Castell Crogen, its Welsh name. Henry II and his army were well and truly defeated by the Welsh with a great loss of men and equipment; the area below the castle is still known as Adwy'r Beddau – *'The pass of the graves of the men who were slain here.'* Today, the Ceiriog Valley still retains its Welsh culture despite a large influx of English inhabitants since the nineteenth century.

The Chirk Castle Estate still embraces most of the land on the northern side of the valley though, at one time, it had engulfed much more of the locality so, not surprisingly, the owners had a big influence upon developments in the valley and the surrounding areas. In the early 1800s, the estate extended as far as Llanymynech in the south and to Froncysyllte in the north, including many industrial concerns, some of which were leased out and paid royalties on their output to the estate. Successive monarchs had granted Chirk Castle to a multitude of owners until, in 1595, Sir Thomas Myddelton (1550–1631) purchased it from Lord St. John of Bletsoe for the sum of £5,000. Sir Thomas became an Alderman of the City of London and, in 1614, was elected its Lord Mayor – no mean achievement for a person who started life as an apprentice to a London grocer! Sir Thomas was an entrepreneur, with his finger in many pies, a merchant adventurer, universal banker and moneylender, adviser to Parliament and he was also the owner of extensive estates elsewhere in England and Wales. In 1630, he financed the translation of the first portable Bible in Welsh. When he died, on 12th August 1631, all his Welsh estates passed to his Parliamentarian son General Sir Thomas Myddelton, Knt (1586–1666) who, during the Civil War temporarily lost Chirk Castle to the Royalists. However, in a bizarre twist of events, he switched his allegiance from the Parliamentarians to the Royalists gaining the King's favour, along with the restoration of the Chirk Castle Estate to the Myddelton family. The estate passed down from General Sir Thomas Myddelton, directly to his grandson Sir Thomas Myddelton 2nd Bt (1651–1684), through a line of Myddeltons to Richard Myddelton (1726–1795) and then to his son, another Richard Myddelton (1764–1796), who died

The coat of arms of the Myddelton family, with its red 'bloody' hand, on the famous Chirk Castle gates. The motto reads 'I triumph in the truth'.

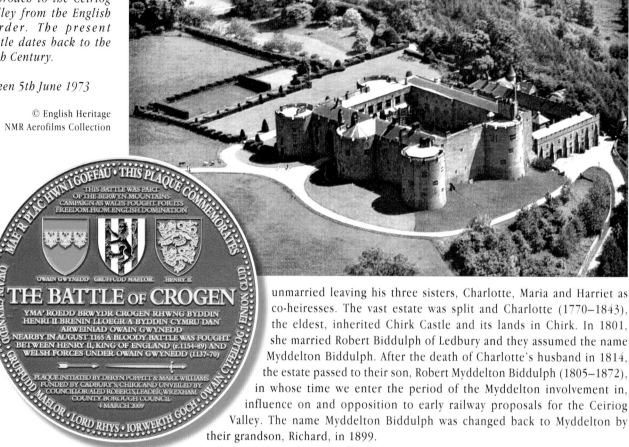

unmarried leaving his three sisters, Charlotte, Maria and Harriet as co-heiresses. The vast estate was split and Charlotte (1770–1843), the eldest, inherited Chirk Castle and its lands in Chirk. In 1801, she married Robert Biddulph of Ledbury and they assumed the name Myddelton Biddulph. After the death of Charlotte's husband in 1814, the estate passed to their son, Robert Myddelton Biddulph (1805–1872), in whose time we enter the period of the Myddelton involvement in, influence on and opposition to early railway proposals for the Ceiriog Valley. The name Myddelton Biddulph was changed back to Myddelton by their grandson, Richard, in 1899.

The Berwyn Mountains are rich in a range of commercially exploitable rocks and minerals, including slate, granite, chinastone, lead, silica and limestone, and at the east end of the valley there are extensive deposits of coal. As early as the 1500s, before the time of the Myddelton family, Chirk Castle Estate records contain entries regarding the purchase of 4,000 slates at 2s. 6d. per thousand (which are believed to have been quarried at Tŷ Draw, Llansantffraid Glyn Ceiriog) and the haulage of local coal for the '*lyne kylne*' (limekiln). By the 1630s, the Myddeltons were digging coal from drift mines and bell-pits in the Black Park area and had interests in the iron industry in Ruabon, Bersham and Birmingham. They also acquired an existing charcoal-fired furnace on the side of the Morlas Brook, a small tributary of the River Ceiriog, to convert iron ore into pig iron to be sent to the nearby water-powered forge that they had built on the banks of the River Ceiriog at Pont-y-Blew. The iron forged here was not predominantly for local use, but destined to be sent to the River Severn at Montford Bridge to be transported to the Midlands.

After the death of Sir Thomas Myddelton in 1666, the industrialisation of the area continued but slowly. The ownership of Chirk Castle Estate stayed with the Myddeltons, but they gradually reduced their direct involvement by leasing out many of the enterprises. Although the Morlas Furnace was out of use by 1670, the forge at Pont-y-Blew continued working for another two hundred years; the iron industry survived in the area at Brymbo, near Wrexham, until 1990, when the last furnaces were closed and the plant sold to China. Numerous small coal pits were sunk in the Chirk locality, on both sides of the Ceiriog, and it is recorded in a series of accounts covering the years 1681–1694 that the average annual output from the Chirk Castle Colliery was 3,500 wagonloads of coal, mainly for use at local forges and for coking to make it suitable for drying malt on the Chirk Castle Estate. Coal continued to be mined in this area until the late 1960s, when Ifton Colliery, on the English side of the Ceiriog, was closed. Since 1920, the underground workings at Ifton had been connected to those at Brynkinalt Colliery at Chirk, on the Welsh side and, later, by a tunnel to a shaft at Black Park Colliery, which had been closed in 1949.

Despite the close proximity of the developing areas of Shropshire, Denbighshire, Cheshire and the Port of Liverpool, the Ceiriog Valley, to the west of Chirk, remained almost dormant until the middle of the nineteenth century, except for the substantial limekilns built at Bronygarth in 1770 and some small-scale quarrying of slate around Glyn Ceiriog. In 1849, another industry that had become well-established in the valley was mentioned by Samuel Lewis in his '*Topographical Dictionary of Wales*', where he described Glyn Ceiriog as being of 2,274 acres with 572 inhabitants and continued:

> '*The village occupies a low and very retired situation, entirely encompassed by lofty hills. The parish contains slate of excellent quality, of which some extensive quarries are worked for profit. The manufacture of flannel is carried on to a considerable extent; and on the stream of the Ceiriog are two fulling mills, with large bleaching grounds attached.*'

In the early days, the only means of transporting merchandise in and out of the valley had been by pack-horse, there being no proper roads. The situation should have improved from 1800 with the arrival of the Ellesmere Canal, at the Chirk end of the valley, which provided a link, via the extensive canal network, to the Midlands, Cheshire and areas beyond, but for the time being this canal was of little use as a transport route to outside markets because there was no road, suitable for carts, down the valley to Chirk.

The Ellesmere Canal, as planned, had been intended to unite the River Severn at Shrewsbury and the River Dee at Chester, with a branch to a wharf, to be known as Ellesmere Port, with locks down to the tidal River Mersey. Although the plan to continue the route north from Pontcysyllte to Chester, and south from Weston Wharf (at Weston Lullingfield in rural Shropshire) to Shrewsbury, was abandoned, a canal was built eastwards from Welsh Frankton, completing the route to Ellesmere Port by utilising the existing Chester Canal, with which the Ellesmere Canal was amalgamated in 1813; another canal through Llanymynech made a junction with the Montgomery Canal. Following further amalgamations over the years, in 1846 the Ellesmere & Chester Canal became part of the Shropshire Union Railways & Canal Co.'s network, which in the following year was leased to the London & North Western Railway Co. in perpetuity. As a result of a 1922 regrouping of railways, the LNWR was amalgamated with the London, Midland & Scottish Railway Co. and, as part of a much

An early engraving by R.K. Penson, illustrating a logging operation in progress at Chirk Castle.

Collection: John Milner

larger network, the canal at Chirk became designated the Pontcysyllte Branch, but today is usually known as the Llangollen Canal.

The chosen route for the canal required two massive engineering projects to carry the canal across the full width of the deep valleys of the Rivers Ceiriog and Dee. At the time of the passing of the Ellesmere Canal Act, in April 1793, the owner of Chirk Castle, Richard Myddelton, although otherwise very supportive of the building of the canal through the district, strongly objected to the canal spoiling the rural atmosphere of his estate, especially the construction of the *'embankment of earth, which would shut up the view of the valley',* which was planned to carry the canal high across the wide expanse of meadow between the bridges at Chirk and Pontfaen. This objection was heeded and the original proposals eventually modified to his satisfaction. First of all, the route of the canal across the valley was moved upstream and, in August 1793, William Turner was requested by the Ellesmere Canal Co. to prepare plans and estimates for an aqueduct at Pontfaen. Crossing the valley here was a logical decision, as the valley narrows considerably, although it would still have entailed extensive construction work on embankments to form the approaches to the proposed aqueduct on either side of the valley.

However, in October that year, Thomas Telford, then Surveyor of Public Works for Shropshire, was appointed as part-time *'General Agent, Surveyor, Engineer, Architect and Overlooker of Works'* for the canal, under William Jessop, the company's Principal Engineer, at a salary of £300 a year. The appointment of contractors was delayed for two months to enable Jessop and Telford to work together and critically reconsider every detail of the plans for the aqueducts. After many revisions of design and reversions of decisions, plans were finalised for two spectacular structures, although not of the same design, which would carry the Ellesmere Canal in troughs supported by a series of stone pillars or piers, high across the two valleys at the same contour level, without the use of locks. The designs were revolutionary because puddled clay did not have to be used to make the troughs watertight as was usual, which considerably reduced the weight that had to be supported by the stonework beneath.

Aqueduc

Designed by Thomas Telford and William Jessop.
10 arches of 40ft span, 70ft high and with a 710ft-long trough.
Foundation stone laid 1796.
Masonry finished 1800.
Opened 1801.

Chirk Aqueduct, built to carry the Ellesmere Canal over the Ceiriog Valley at Chirk, under construction in 1799. Pencil drawing by Sir Richard Colt Hoare.

Llyfrgell Genedlaethol Cymru
The National Library of Wales
Drawing Vol.35 No.3

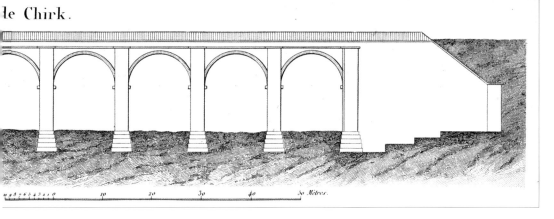

Side elevation of Chirk Aqueduct drawn by the French engineer, Charles Dupin, in 1825.

Collection: John Milner

A view of the aqueduct from Chirk Bridge in 1802, showing the surface activity around the 300ft-deep colliery shafts, believed to have been sunk by Arthur Davies in 1801. All this equipment was destroyed, and the underground workings flooded out, when the canal burst through its bank in December 1816.

Drawn by Hendrick Frans de Cort, 1802.

By 1796, the foundation stone for Chirk Aqueduct had been laid, not near Pontfaen, but closer to Chirk Bridge, and work had started on the construction of ten substantial stone arches, each of 40ft span, which would carry the canal 70ft above the valley in a 700ft-long trough. The bottom of the trough was formed from overlapping iron plates bolted together, the joints made watertight with Welsh flannel and the sides built of hard bricks, laid in Parker's Cement and faced with close-fitting ashlar masonry. The stone for the masonry had been quarried locally and the lime for the mortar brought from the Vron Lime Kilns at Froncysyllte, three miles away. The masonry work was finished by 1800 and the aqueduct opened in 1801. Jessop had originally proposed a structure similar to the Pontcysyllte Aqueduct, which had been started on 25th July 1795, the foundation stone being laid by Richard Myddelton MP. This aqueduct is over 1,000ft long with 18 slender stone pillars supporting an iron trough 120ft above the river, and was not opened until 26th November 1805.

At the north end of the Chirk Aqueduct, the canal immediately plunged into a 460-yard long tunnel, to emerge into a deep cutting, which left the landscape visually unchanged and the roads of the Chirk Castle Estate intact. The spoil from this mile-long excavation was transported north to form the massive southern approach embankment to the Pontcysyllte Aqueduct across the valley of the River Dee.

The arrival of the canal at Chirk did not immediately provide an accessible transport route from the valley for the output from the developing industries. The aqueduct, at 70ft above the river, was too high for the canal to be reached from the valley floor; to the north, after emerging from its tunnel, the canal was in a mile-long deep cutting and, to the south, it was clinging high up, close to the escarpment on the Chirk Bank side, although room enough was found to build a small warehouse with a crane, which was still being used for unloading grain in 1901, and a small stable.

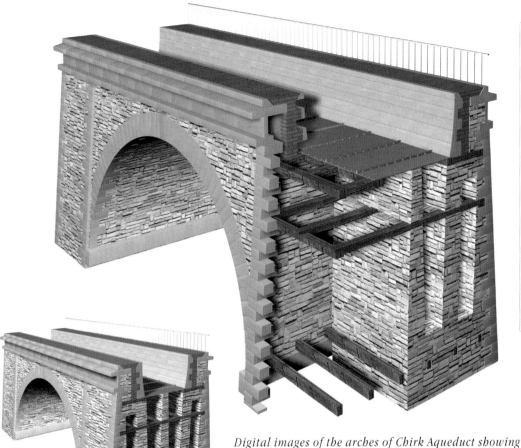

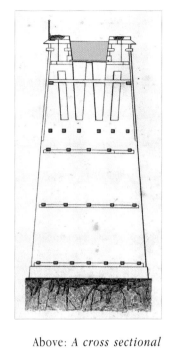

Above: *A cross sectional drawing of one of the Chirk Aqueduct columns, showing the extent of the arch spandrels and reinforcing struts. Drawn by the French engineer, Charles Dupin, in 1825.*

Collection: John Milner

Digital images of the arches of Chirk Aqueduct showing their construction, with the reinforcing struts and hollow spandrels. They clearly show the original arrangement of the trough, with the single iron baseplate flanked by brick and stone sides. Iron side plates were added in 1869.

© Crown copyright: RCAHMW
Licence No.: RCPL2/3/34/015

The Chirk Aqueduct in the 1820s, viewed from the old Chirk road, stands like a majestic gateway to the Ceiriog Valley. Note that the colliery site is now just green pasture land. On the left is the Bridge Inn and, in the distance to the right is a house, Min-y-waen (Telford Lodge), believed to have been built by Telford as an office and living accommodation for key personnel.

Drawn by H. Gastineau.
Engraved by T. Barber.

Collection: John Milner

In the mid-1840s railways were developing at a rapid rate all over the country and they were generally perceived as a threat by the canal companies; this was the age of 'railway mania'. The canal companies could see that their canals, which up to then had held a monopoly for the mass conveyance of goods, would now be shadowed by railways offering a faster and more efficient service.

Before 1845, the canal companies had been, under their constitution, permitted only to build canals and collect tolls for the use thereof. In 1845, with the fierce competition from the newly formed railway companies, Parliament allowed them to become carriers in their own right and, if they so decided, also to operate railways. In 1846, the year in which it was formed, the Shropshire Union Railways & Canal Company, in its right as a railway company, possessed powers to build railways as well as canals, and also to convert its canals into railways. These powers enabled it to obtain an Act *'for the conversion of canals including the Montgomery Canal into a railway'*. The Llangollen Canal, the Ellesmere to Nantwich section of the Ellesmere & Chester Canal and the Shrewsbury Canal were to stay intact, but the conversions of the other canals were not made and the company's powers to do so expired in 1852. The possibility was further considered in 1855 but, again, no action was taken. However, it raised its head again in 1874 (see chapter 3), this time specifically in connection with the building of the Glyn Valley Tramway and developments at Ifton Rhyn Collieries.

The SUR&C Co.'s canals and their operation were leased to the London & North Western Railway Co. in 1847, and administered by a joint committee from the SUR&C Co. offices in Chester. The LNWR Co. used the canal company to undermine its opponents, its canals being in the territory of the GWR and the Cambrian Railways, both great rivals of the LNWR. The use of the SUR&C Co. by the LNWR Co. in this manner had the effect of guaranteeing the survival of the canal through Chirk, whereas in other areas the canal companies were being taken over by the railway companies, and their canals promptly closed down.

William Jessop
1745–1814

The Principal Engineer of the Ellesmere Canal Company with whom Thomas Telford worked closely on the design of the Chirk and Pontcysyllte Aqueducts. Portrait painted by Edwin Williams.

Courtesy: The Institution
of Civil Engineers

Nearly half a century after the building of the aqueduct at Chirk, in the early 1840s, when Henry Robertson (1816–1888) was building the Shrewsbury & Chester Railway, the then owner of Chirk Castle, Col. Robert Myddelton Biddulph, at a public meeting in Oswestry, spoke about the high cost of building the Ceiriog and Dee Viaducts and claimed that the line was uncalled for *'on public grounds'*. He objected to a visible public transport route passing through his estate, saying that the railway *'was personally obnoxious owing to the wanton defacement of my* [his] *lands'*, and that he was confident that both Houses of Parliament would reject the Bill – which they did not. However, the disruption to the Chirk Castle Estate amenities was minimised by carrying the railway across the Ceiriog Valley on a stone viaduct, at a higher level than the canal, and through a 50-yard tunnel, after which it passed over the canal tunnel, so that by the time it reached Chirk station it had changed sides with the canal.

Work had started on the viaduct in early 1847 and, by July of that year, the stone piers had been built to half their final height. However, bad weather and a five-week strike by the contractor's masons, during April and May of 1848, delayed its completion until September 1848. It stands alongside the canal aqueduct and is 846ft long and 100ft in height. Although it had originally been designed to have 16 arches, it was initially built as a 'stand-alone structure' consisting of ten identical arches, each with a span of 45ft. At either end of this 'stand-alone structure' were pedimented abutments containing niches, in line with the ornate architecture of many of the stations and other structures on the Shrewsbury and Chester Railway, and looking as if they were intended to house a sculpture. A highly unusual feature was that the ends of the viaduct

were linked to each side of the valley by wooden-lattice girder construction 'bridges or arches' each with a span of 120ft.

Edward Parry in his *Railway Companion from Chester to Shrewsbury*, published in 1849, explains the reasons for this unusual design:

> *'It was found, however, by the engineer on constructing the river piers that it was necessary, from the nature of the strata, to carry them through a bed of soft sand, about 16 feet below the bed of the river, and that it would have been requisite to found the two piers on the slope of the valley, at a similar depth. From the proximity of the Chirk Aqueduct, and the shaky state of its abutments, this would have been a work of great danger and expense, and the engineer formed the novel and appropriate design of converting the last pier at the foot of the steep bank of the valley into an abutment or bastion pier, and of throwing an arch from the table land above of sufficient span to form as it were a huge gangway to reach the stone viaduct. This has been done with a most pleasing effect, by means of the laminated timber arches of 120 feet span, which are perfect models of constructive carpentry.'*

These wooden spans were replaced, in 1858–59, by three masonry arches at both ends, some four years after the Shrewsbury & Chester Railway had become part of the Great Western Railway.

The first trains ran over the viaduct during the first week of October 1848 and the line was officially opened on the 16th of the month. It is also worthy of note that all the stations on the S&CR were

**Chirk Viaduct
Shrewsbury & Chester
Railway 1848.**

Designed by Henry Robertson and described by Edward Parry, in his Railway Companion from Chester to Shrewsbury, 1849, as an engineering gem with laminated timber end spans of 120 feet span, which are 'perfect models of constructive carpentry'.

Coloured lithograph by
G. Hawkins after G. Pickering.

Science Museum/SSPL

Chirk Aqueduct from the east with Henry Robertson's viaduct beyond. The access holes to the spandrels can just be seen in the centre of the lower part of the arches.

architectural gems when built, attributable to Robertson's architect, Mr T.M. Penson, of Chester, but unfortunately not all have survived, including that at Chirk, initially named Hand Lane station.

By eventually agreeing to allow the railway to cross his land, Col. Myddelton Biddulph ensured that a station was built at Chirk with a long-lasting concession for the owners of Chirk Castle, who were able to request that any train could be stopped there for their convenience. One wonders if this concession still stands?

As we shall see as our story unfolds, Col. Myddelton Biddulph's stubbornness precluded any logical solution for those seeking to promote better transport routes out of the valley. He was opposed to virtually every scheme put forward although, in all probability, they would have been of benefit to his estate and the industries in which he had an interest. Irrational decisions had to be taken, which in the short term proved to be a costly exercise for the promoters and others concerned.

The canal had opened through Chirk in 1801, but it was almost twenty years before any scheme was put forward to improve local transportation in the area. Under the Turnpike Act 1771 a toll road had been built between Bronygarth limekilns and Wem, some 18 miles away, for the purpose of carting agricultural lime to the area it served. The road had been created by widening and repairing existing roads and it had eight tollgates along its length, each of them under the control of the local landowner. Following the passing of an Act of Parliament in 1818, this was taken over by the Wem & Bronygarth Turnpike Trust, although it was of little use to the industries up the valley, because it terminated at the Bronygarth limekilns high above the valley floor.

Although the canal at Chirk made connections with other waterways serving most of the industrial areas of Central England, it had little impact on the sleepy Ceiriog Valley, because without suitable road access up the valley to move goods easily, and like the turnpike road to Bronygarth, this new facility was of little benefit to industry in the valley. In 1840, a meeting was called by interested parties, chaired by Lord Dungannon, who owned land to the east of Chirk, '*to consider a new road to follow the course of the River Ceiriog*', but nothing further appears to have been done. Present at this meeting had been John Wynne[II], of Glyn Ceiriog, who had purchased the Wynne Slate Quarry for the sum of £420 from Charlotte Myddelton Biddulph on 29th September 1829,

Henry Robertson
1816–1888

Chief engineer to the Shrewsbury & Chester Railway Company, who was responsible for the design of the Chirk and Dee Valley Viaducts, and was born at Banff, Scotland, in 1816. He was the third partner in the well-known locomotive builders, Beyer, Peacock & Co., of Manchester.

Collection: John Milner

The River Ceiriog gently flows eastwards under the arches of Chirk Viaduct and Aqueduct, on its way to join up with the River Dee. Now part of a World Heritage Site, the scene has virtually remained unchanged since the 19th century, apart from the trees, which are slowly obliterating the view of these monuments to our early engineers.

© John Milner 2009

Today, the canal is no longer the Ceiriog Valley's lifeline for the transportation of its industrial output, but has found a new lease of life as a popular pleasure location and as a World Heritage Site. High above it, Henry Robertson's viaduct still functions as part of the vital infrastructure carrying the main line from Chester to London. Here the short-lived Wrexham & Shropshire service heads for Marylebone station, London.

© John Milner 2009

[1] See *Slates from Glyn Ceiriog* by John Milner, chapter 2.

probably aware of the development potential of his quarry and anxious for an easy way out of the valley for his slate.[1] It was not until some 50 years later, by which time there was both a road and a tramway down the valley, that this quarry was developed into a fairly substantial slate mine employing up to 80 men.

In 1855, a Bill was presented to Parliament to extend the turnpike road from Bronygarth up the valley to Llanarmon Dyffryn Ceiriog. It was strongly opposed by Col. Myddelton Biddulph, and was redrafted to take into account his objections, becoming the Wem & Bronygarth Road Act 1856. This Act granted the Trustees an initial 21-year toll authorisation and provided for a road from Pandy to Nantyr, to connect with the Nantyr Estate – another part of Col. Myddelton Biddulph's 'empire', for which he wanted a better transport link to the outside world for his timber.

The Road Trustees made little progress until the newly formed Cambrian Slate Company (No.323) began serious development of its slate quarries high up in the valley of Nant Lafar, a small tributary, which joins the River Ceiriog at Glyn Ceiriog. In 1857, they approached this new slate company for financial assistance towards the building of the new road, which would provide a route down the valley to Chirk, giving the company access to the national canal and railway networks. The company agreed to do so, providing that a tramway for its exclusive use could be built alongside the new road. A new Bill was presented in 1857, but Col. Myddelton Biddulph also immediately opposed this. The problem this time was two-fold: the refusal of the Cambrian Slate Co. to agree that the tramway would carry timber from Col. Myddelton Biddulph's Nantyr Estate, on the grounds that it had no intention of carrying non-slate traffic, and the plan to terminate the turnpike road at Preesgweene (Welsh spelling: *Preesgwyn*), south of the Ceiriog, thus bypassing Myddelton Biddulph's Chirk Castle Estate. The slate company had forcefully made the point clear to Col. Myddelton Biddulph, when it stated: '*We will find the money for road and tramway, but will not be carriers; if anyone opposes, we will drop the Bill.*' There was also some other local opposition to the Bill, because of the fear of a Slate Co. monopoly, and it was withdrawn on 5th

Two of the four well-preserved Bronygarth limekilns on the roadside above Castle Mill and, above, a view inside the drawing-hole chamber of one of them. These kilns were the reason for the construction of the Wem & Bronygarth turnpike road in the 1770s.

© John Milner 2009

March 1858. For the first time, an entry appeared in the Cambrian Slate Co.'s accounts of 1858 for '*Parliamentary and other expenses connected with the proposed railway*'.

Following this deadlock, the Cambrian Slate Co. started negotiations with Thomas Barnes, who had recently purchased the Quinta Estate on the south side of the valley, to allow a tramway to be built through his estate, thus enabling an interchange to be made with the Great Western Railway (formerly the Shrewsbury & Chester Railway) at Preesgweene. At the same time, Col. Myddelton Biddulph was arguing a case for running the tramway to the GWR station at Chirk. In October 1859, the Cambrian Slate Co. suggested that the 1856 Wem & Bronygarth Road Act, with its routing to Preesgweene, should be abandoned and a new Act presented, to terminate the tramway at Chirk station.

On 3rd April 1860, a new Wem & Bronygarth Road Act was passed, authorising the same routing as in the 1856 Act for a road up the valley, from its then terminus at Bronygarth limekilns, plus an extension of the road from Herber to Chirk, to satisfy Col. Myddelton Biddulph. There was no mention of a tramway in this Act. This new Act recited that the road trustees had been unable to carry out many of the requirements of the 1856 Act, as they had been unable to raise funds for '*making, completing and maintaining the roads*'. The Cambrian Slate Co. had subscribed £3,000, being half of the capital required, in exchange for the lease of the roads in order to transport its slate out of the valley. Other subscribers included Sir Watkin Williams Wynne (£500), Col. Myddelton Biddulph (£500), Alexander Reid, proprietor and lessor of the Cambrian Slate Quarry (£300), F.R. West, owner of Bronygarth limekilns (£500), and Richard George Jebb of The Lythe, Ellesmere (£100).

Alexander Mackintosh, engineer to the Great Western Railway, prepared the plans and estimates for the new road. The Parliamentary Agent was Theodore Martin, who was later to play an important role in the promotion of the Glyn Valley Tramway.

Details of cutting the first sod for the new road are recorded in the diary of John Hughes, Llwynmawr:

> '*Thursday the 19th August 1860 was fixed upon to turn up the first sod in a field near the New Inn [Glyn Ceiriog]. The turning of the sod was performed by Mrs Myddelton Biddulph of Chirk Castle. She arrived in her carriage on the spot at 2 o'clock p.m. with her younger sons and daughters. The Llangollen band played the "Artillery March", "Love Knot" and*

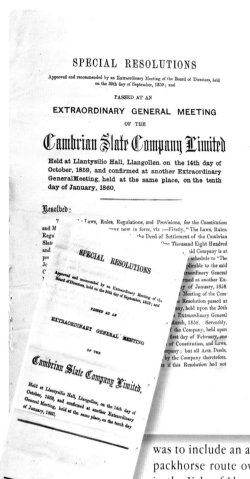

On 10th January 1860 a resolution was passed at an Extraordinary General Meeting of the Cambrian Slate Co. Ltd, held at Llantysilio Hall, Llangollen, to reconstitute the company and give it the right to subscribe to the improvements of roads and/or construct tramways or railways.

the "Conciliation March", etc. The party having alighted, the parson, Mr Lewis, prayed (extempore) in Welsh, and afterwards read an address to Mrs Biddulph. When Mr Reid handed over the spade to Mrs Biddulph who, most navy-like, threw several sods to the barrow, and amidst shouts of hundreds, if not thousands, wheeled down the planks and turning it over, she turned to the people, congratulated them on the certain prospect before them of having a new road from this place to Chirk and Lodge [Weston Rhyn]. Her speech was short, audible, sensible, and to the purpose. Her children also tried their hands at the spade and barrow and several Gentlemen, and several speeches were delivered. Mrs Biddulph retired to the house, and in about half an hour, she and here party returned, preceded by the band over the Bridge. Her way was through Selattyn and Lodge. ... It was a general holiday ... At 4.00 p.m. precisely, dinner was on the table at which about 150, they said, sat. Admittance was 5/- a ticket. This dinner was to do honour to Alexander Reid Esq., as the principal promoter of the New Road.'

Work was started immediately on the road, with tollgates being located at Herber and Glyn Ceiriog, but had ceased by the end of the year because the Trustees had already run out of money. Strangely, no record can be found of there being a tollgate at the Chirk end of the Wem & Bronygarth Turnpike Road, suggesting that tolls were administered from Herber where the plans show the Chirk road gated.

The Cambrian Quarry had six months of slate production in hand, but no means of transporting it out of the valley because the road, which was to include an access road (Quarry Road) from Glyn Ceiriog, had not yet been completed. The packhorse route over the Berwyn Mountains to a wharf on the Ellesmere Canal at Froncysyllte, in the Vale of Llangollen, was slow, arduous and in the winter months impassable. Work at the Cambrian Quarry stopped. A letter, dated April 1861, reported that the new road through the Chirk Castle Estate had been started, but was lying incomplete which, no doubt, did not please Col. Myddelton Biddulph. The problem was that, all the money originally subscribed by the Cambrian Slate Co., Alexander Reid and others had been spent on obtaining the Act and for professional fees, such as surveying. The situation appears to have been further aggravated by the fact that the Trustees *'did not ... seem to pull together'*. One would have thought that with Alexander Reid, one of the Road Trustees, having his own interests in mind, the opposite would have been the case. Eventually, the various parties had to accept a compromise and take out Bonds in the Trust to keep it afloat.

In 1861, the Road Trustees proposed a further Bill, this time:

'To enable the Trustees to grant to the Cambrian Slate Company the Right and Power to lay down, at their expense, the entire length, or portions thereof, a tramway for the exclusive use of the said Slate Company'.

This again raised the alarm and opposition of Col. Myddelton Biddulph and other landowners, who objected strongly on the grounds that a tramway for the exclusive use of the Cambrian Slate Quarry would give it an unfair advantage over quarries in their ownership. The issue became that of the use of the tramway by all, versus the exclusive use by one concern – the Cambrian Slate Company:

'Much heartburning and bickering were the consequences. Attempts were made to induce the Cambrian Slate Company to allow the use of the tramway by the public generally at a moderate maximum rate, but they could not be prevailed upon to consent. The opposition to them was therefore so great that they were compelled to give up the idea of a tramway.'

Despite a petition signed by fifty persons imploring Col. Myddelton Biddulph and his colleagues to let the Bill go through, he used his influence in Parliament with the result that the House of Commons Select Committee concluded that:

'*The Committee did not feel it their duty to pass the preamble of the Bill and therefore in this case could go no further. That the decision of the Committee was based upon Public Grounds, that they had never before been asked to unite railroads, and turnpike roads, and the Committee did not consider it their duty to do so now for the first time.*'

In the face of the overwhelming opposition, the Cambrian Slate Co. withdrew its proposal for a tramway down the valley, at least for the time being.

On 7th July 1862 a further Act, the Wem & Bronygarth Road Act 1862, was passed, authorizing a quarter of a mile extension of the road alongside the Great Western Railway line to Chirk station, but there was no mention here of a tramway. The lease of the roads to the Cambrian Slate Co. was duly annulled by the Act. As lessee, it had been responsible for carrying out repairs to the incomplete road and appears to have been managing the affairs of the Trust as well. At this time the roads were described as being in a condition '*such as to induce, if not necessitate, the public generally to traverse the old road*' – a journey of 13 miles instead of six. Attempts were made at 'metalling' some sections but, by 1865, the Trust had again run out of money and this time discharged all its labourers, resulting in no repair work being carried out at all. It was reported that: '*The road is now impassable and the ruts are so deep that in one of them some time ago a pig was drowned.*' Both Mr Barnes MP and Col. Robert Myddelton Biddulph remonstrated with the Clerk to the Trustees and pressed for the road to be repaired, but both received a negative response.

In 1865, a proposal for a new company with capital of £40,000, entitled 'The Glyn Valley Railway Co.', and backed by the GWR Co., had been put forward principally on behalf of the Cambrian Slate Co., which by this time had become totally disgruntled by the road situation. This was to construct a standard-gauge (4ft 8½in) railway commencing with a junction to the GWR 'Up' line, south of the road bridge at Chirk station, and terminating on the north side of New Road, near the Cross, Glyn Ceiriog. Upon leaving the GWR at Chirk, the line was to immediately turn southwest and enter a 132yd-long tunnel, which was to pass under both the 1767 Chirk Castle coach road and the Chirk–Glyn Ceiriog road, to emerge into the Ceiriog Valley. This would have required an extensive embankment in order to reach the valley floor. At Pontfadog the road was to be realigned in order to allow the railway to clear the river bridge. A Bill entitled 'The Glyn Valley Railway' was deposited in the Private Bill Office of the House of Commons on 23rd December that year and was presented in the 1866 Session of Parliament.

The engineer for the proposed railway was Alexander Mackintosh, Engineer to the GWR, whose estimates showed that the total cost would be £39,987. The promoters included Alexander Reid, Edward Harper, Charles Campbell and Robert Roy, with Theodore Martin again acting as Parliamentary Agent. The Bill gave the new Glyn Valley Railway Co. powers to enter into working arrangements with the Great Western Railway, as well as running rights over the GWR line at Chirk station, including the use of all the facilities.

The original estimate, produced by Alexander Mackintosh, Engineer to the Great Western Railway, and dated 27th December 1865, for the construction of the proposed standard-gauge Glyn Valley Railway from Chirk to Glyn Ceiriog. Notice the mention of the construction of a tunnel, shown in the map over page.

Collection: John Milner

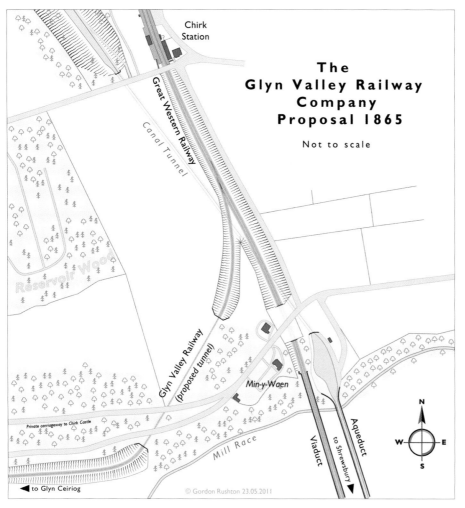

Map, redrawn from the original Plans & Sections, showing the proposed 1865 junction between the Glyn Valley Railway and the GWR at Chirk. It was to pass under the carriageway to Chirk Castle and the Glyn Ceiriog road via a tunnel.

Since 1848, the nearby town of Oswestry had been served by a short branch from Gobowen, on the main Shrewsbury and Chester line, but gradually it became the hub of a network of local railways. In 1855, the Oswestry & Newtown Railway came into being, followed by the Newtown & Machynlleth Railway in 1857 so, with other small companies' lines, the area was connected all the way to the Welsh coast. Another railway, the Oswestry, Ellesmere & Whitchurch Railway (1861), provided links to the east and, in 1864, all these companies were amalgamated to form the Cambrian Railways Company, with its headquarters in Oswestry. It was almost inevitable that this new company would support a counter-proposal to that of the Glyn Valley Railway Co.'s proposed line up the Ceiriog Valley from the GWR at Chirk.

The counter-proposal was put forward in 1865 by a new company, the Ellesmere & Glyn Valley Railway Co., the subscribers to which were Benjamin Piercy, a leading figure in Cambrian Railways' affairs, Lord Hill Trevor, Col. Myddelton Biddulph, Richard Steele Perkins and Richard George Jebb. A Bill was presented to Parliament on the 10th of November that year, which emerged as the Ellesmere & Glyn Valley Railway Act 1866. Benjamin Piercy was the Engineer to the company.

The E&GVR Co. plan was to build a standard-gauge railway from Glyn Ceiriog to connect with the Cambrian Railways at Ellesmere and the GWR at Preesgweene. The 1866 proposal included a line (Railway No.3) from the terminus at Glyn Ceiriog to the Cambrian Quarry. The Brief presented to the House of Commons on behalf of the promoters stated:

> *'This will be a steep line or tramway from Railway No.1 up to various Slate Quarries situate on an elevated position. There is no actual junction shown with Railway No.1 and it would be inconvenient that it should be so because the trucks from the Quarries will come down with considerable force. This line No.3 therefore commences at a separate place from the end of Railway No.1, but within the limits, and so that the trucks may be marshalled and then shunted on to Railway No.1.'*

All a little contradictory, but the promoters probably already knew that any link between the quarry and the proposed standard-gauge railway would have to be via an incline, which would be narrow-gauge; hence the option quoted *'or tramway'* in the brief.

The E&GVR promoters considered that the earlier mentioned Cambrian Slate Co. scheme for the Glyn Valley Railway *'was intended to be a cheap and inferior affair'*, which would probably meet the requirements of the slate company, but not those of the valley in general. They also considered

Reference as may be required for that Purpose. The Railway herein-before referred to and authorized by this Act is,—

A Railway (No. 1.) Twelve Miles and Seven Furlongs or there-abouts in Length, commencing in the Parish of *Ellesmere* in the County of *Salop* by a Junction with the *Cambrian* Railway, and terminating in a Field called *Doltybrith* in the Parish of *Llansaintffraid Glyn Ceiriog* in the County of *Denbigh* :

A Railway (No. 2.) Six Furlongs or thereabouts in Length, commencing in the Parish of *Saint Martin's* and County of *Salop* by a Junction with the *Great Western* Railway, and terminating by a Junction with Railway No. 1. in a Field called *Penylan* otherwise *Penlan Field* in the said Parish of *Saint Martin's* :

A Railway (No. 3.) One Mile and One Furlong or thereabouts in Length, wholly situate in the said Parish of *Llansaintffraid Glyn Ceiriog*, commencing in a Field called *Cae-tan Llwyn*, and terminating on the Slate Bank of the *Cambrian* Slate Company.

ANNO VICESIMO NONO & TRICESIMO

VICTORIÆ REGINÆ.

****

Cap. cccxxxv.

An Act for making a Railway from *Ellesmere* to *Llansaintffraid Glyn Ceiriog*; and for other Purposes. [6th *August* 1866.]

WHEREAS the making and maintaining a Railway from *Ellesmere* to *Llansaintffraid Glyn Ceiriog* in the Counties of *Salop* and *Denbigh* would be of public and local Advantage : And whereas the several Persons in that Behalf in this Act named, with others, are willing at their own Expense to execute the Undertaking : And whereas Plans and Sections showing the Lines and Levels of the Railway and Works by this Act authorized to be made, and the Lands to be taken for the Purposes thereof, and Books of Reference to those Plans containing the Names of the Owners or reputed Owners, Lessees or reputed Lessees, and Occupiers of those Lands, have been deposited with the respective Clerks of the Peace for the Counties of *Salop* and *Denbigh*, and those Plans, Sections, and Books of Reference are in this Act referred to as the deposited Plans, Sections, and Books of Reference : And whereas it is expedient that the Company and the *Great Western* Railway Company, and the *Cambrian* Railway Company (herein-after called the Two Companies), be authorized to enter into Agreements as herein-after provided : And

[*Local*]   57 E   whereas

that the Cambrian Slate Co. was exerting some influence over the Great Western Railway Co., as it had, initially, applied to the GWR Co. for the funding of the new railway. However, in the event, the slate company had been offered only £300 towards expenses!

The Cambrian Slate Co. had by now invested the sum of £8,000 in the Wem & Bronygarth Turnpike Trust, in order to facilitate a means of getting their slate down and out of the valley. As security, they held an equivalent value in Road Trust Bonds, which were now worthless with little prospect of repayment. The Road Trust had run out of money and the Cambrian Slate Company was continually being obliged to carry out repairs to the road at its own expense; the directors had little choice and spent only what the company could afford. Alexander Reid and Charles Townshend, the former a promoter of the Road Trust and the latter a shareholder in the GVR Co., as well as having an interest in the Cambrian Slate Co., approached Robert Piercy, Engineer of the E&GVR Co., with a proposal that the slate company would withdraw its support for the Glyn Valley Railway Bill, leaving the E&GVR Co. to proceed unchallenged, provided that this company would take the slate company's £8,000 in the Road Bonds in exchange for an equivalent fully paid-up shareholding. Subject to the approval of all the E&GVR Co. promoters, agreement was reached to a proposal that the Cambrian Slate Co.'s Bond holding be exchanged for £8,000 of fully paid-up shares in the E&GVR Co. Shortly afterwards the proposition was put before the promoters of the E&GVR, who decidedly rejected the idea of the free issue of shares to the Cambrian Slate Company.

The Glyn Valley Railway Co., became disillusioned when Alexander Reid, who had been the driving force on behalf of the Cambrian Slate Co., died on the 28th February 1866, aged 73. Added to which, there was also continuing opposition from Col. Myddelton Biddulph, who was determined to oppose the Glyn Valley Railway Bill, because the line was to be laid through part of his park, the only possible route to Chirk station; he also made no secret that he had little confidence in the Cambrian Slate Co., which, he said, was unlikely to operate the railway '*in the interests of the public*', because it had not been prepared to operate the tramway as a general carrier.

The promoters of the Glyn Valley Railway withdrew their Bill from Parliament and did not pay the 8% deposit required to legalise the share issue.

The Cambrian Slate Co., as a creditor of the turnpike road trust, now persuaded the latter to petition against the E&GVR Bill on the grounds that it gave the company rights to acquire land owned by the Turnpike Trust; that the railway would '*cross over the said Roads near the Village of Glyn in a most objectionable manner and thereby to interfere with their safe and commodious use*'; and that the proposed railway would deprive the turnpike trust of revenue, resulting in

The preamble of the Ellesmere and Glyn Valley Railway Act, 1866, which received Royal assent on the 6th August that year. This proposal, by the Cambrian Railways Company, was to build a standard-gauge railway up the Ceiriog Valley, starting with a junction to the railway at Ellesmere and terminating at the Cambrian Quarries. A branch was to connect to the GWR at Preesgweene.

Above left: *An extract from the Ellesmere & Glyn Valley Railway Act 1866, listing the three sections of the proposed line.*

Collection: John Milner

it being unable to pay the interest due on Bonds or to complete the road. Another contention was that the E&GVR Co., within its proposal, had the right to reduce the width of the road up to its centre line. It was already a narrow road and this would have made it impassable for wider vehicles. The slate company also considered that the Bill should not be granted unless there was an undertaking that the promoters of the E&GVR Co. would pay off the debts of the Road Trust; in other words relieve the Trust of its debt to the Cambrian Slate Co. which, at the same time, would free the Slate Co. to pursue its own promotion, the Glyn Valley Railway. The E&GVR Company considered that the Cambrian Slate Co. were opposing the Bill 'behind the scenes, if not openly', in its self-interest in order to recoup its initial £8,000 capital vested in the Wem & Bronygarth Turnpike Trust.

The E&GVR Agents for the 1866 Bill, Wyatt & Metcalfe, promptly issued a Notice of Objection stating that: 'The Petition is not bona fide the Petition of the Road Trustees, but of certain individuals who have, at their own expense, petitioned and used the names of the Trustees.' The Notice also stated that the meeting at which the petition was purported to have been signed was held illegally. As a result, the Road Trustees ultimately withdrew their objections to this proposal for a standard-gauge line, but the Great Western Railway Co. then entered the scene and petitioned against the Bill on numerous grounds, which included:

> '... the crossing over and junction with their line will interfere with their property injuriously ... the Junction is objectionable and in an inconvenient place ... the Crossing over the Great Western Line is objectionable and will prevent the Petitioners from improving their undertaking and providing increased accommodation except at increased cost. ... the proposed Railway is uncalled for and unnecessary. ...'

The list of objections presented by the GWR Co. seemed endless. It also considered the whole scheme to be overpriced, badly engineered and ill thought out, devoid of satisfactory financial arrangements and certainly questionable. It also claimed that they already had all the traffic; which was a false statement. All of this was very much a red herring, as the Petition then comes to the real essence of its objection:

> 'Any Railway in the District ought to communicate with the Great Western Railway [i.e. not the Cambrian Railways as proposed] ... the proposed arrangements with the Cambrian [Railways] Company and the Drayton Junction Company are unnecessary and uncalled for. ... they will practically transfer this undertaking [the E&GVR] to the Cambrian and Drayton Junction Companies and direct traffic away from the Great Western Railway.'

The E&GVR Company counter-acted all this by saying that the GWR Co. had a station at Preesgweene, which was far more convenient for servicing the Oswestry district than was Chirk station and that by terminating at Ellesmere, where the line was to connect with the Cambrian Railways, the new railway would serve a thriving agricultural area, and provide opportunities to develop the mineral and flannel trade of the Ceiriog Valley, saying:

> 'The last 6 miles of Railway No.1 is along the Vale of Glyn which is beautifully picturesque and is full of Lime, Slate and Flags. Hydraulic Lime of the fixed quality and also stone for the making of china are also found there. ... There are also 2 Welsh Flannel Mills. ... Other quarries would be opened and worked if this Railway were made.'

The E&GVR Co. further stated that if the connection was made with the GWR at Preesgweene then, 'working in friendly spirit', market trains to Oswestry would produce 'a large traffic in passengers from the Vale of Glyn' for the GWR; but there was no mention of offering them any freight traffic! They then made a very potent point:

> 'If no Junction had been proposed they [the GWR Co.] would have complained of that and they now complain because it is proposed.'

The original Petition lodged with Parliament against the E&GVR 1866 Bill, by the Wem & Bronygarth Turnpike Trustees and which they eventually withdrew.

Courtesy: Mark Hignett

Chirk Mill.

A *Chirk Mill wagon with its team of horses, outside The Hand at Llanarmon Dyffryn Ceiriog at the head of the valley, illustrates the means of transport in the valley in the 1800s. This was not to improve for Llanarmon, as all the railway proposals fell well short of the village. On the right behind the cart is Tyn Llan and the village smithy.*

Courtesy: Sian and
Grant Williams, The West Arms

Chirk Corn Mill was a fairly large concern and just one of many mills along the River Ceiriog.

Collection: Graham Greasley

Ceiriog Valley Railway Proposals
1865–1885

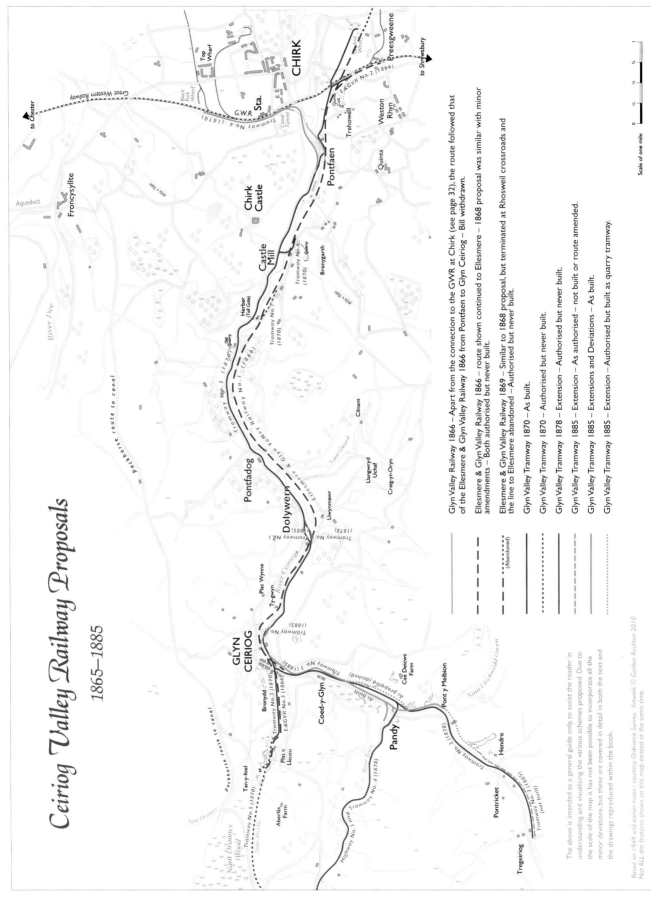

Glyn Valley Railway 1866 – Apart from the connection to the GWR at Chirk (see page 32), the route followed that of the Ellesmere & Glyn Valley Railway 1866 from Pontfaen to Glyn Ceiriog – Bill withdrawn.

Ellesmere & Glyn Valley Railway 1866 – route shown continued to Ellesmere – 1868 proposal was similar with minor amendments – Both authorised but never built.

Ellesmere & Glyn Valley Railway 1869 – Similar to 1868 proposal, but terminated at Rhoswiel crossroads and the line to Ellesmere abandoned – Authorised but never built.

Glyn Valley Tramway 1870 – As built.

Glyn Valley Tramway 1870 – Authorised but never built.

Glyn Valley Tramway 1878 – Extension – Authorised but never built.

Glyn Valley Tramway 1885 – Extension – As authorised – not built or route amended.

Glyn Valley Tramway 1885 – Extensions and Deviations – As built.

Glyn Valley Tramway 1885 – Extension – Authorised but built as quarry tramway.

(Abandoned)

Scale of one mile

The above is intended as a general guide only, to assist the reader in understanding and visualising the various schemes proposed. Due to the scale of the map it has not been possible to incorporate all the minor deviations, but these are covered in detail in both the text and the drawings reproduced within the book.

Based on 1949 and earlier maps: courtesy Ordnance Survey. Artwork © Gordon Rushton 2010
Not ALL the features shown on this map existed at the same time.

The GWR Co. remained the only petitioner against the Bill, but five petitions in favour were presented to Parliament by the '*inhabitants of Ellesmere and neighbourhood; St. Martins and neighbourhood; Vale of Glyn and neighbourhood; Chirk and neighbourhood and the Owners, Lessees & Occupiers on or near the Line*', respectfully signed by Lord Hill-Trevor MP, Col. Myddelton Biddulph and Mr. Barnes MP. The Brief put before the House of Commons was quick to point out that '*not one Landowner or Occupier has petitioned against.*' Not surprising, as in the case of Lord Hill-Trevor and Col. Myddelton Biddulph they were both promoters of the E&GVR Bill along with John Hanton, gentleman and large property owner of Ellesmere, Richard George Jebb, a magistrate of Ellesmere and Mr. R.S. Perkins, a surgeon. Both Lord Trevor and Col. Myddelton Biddulph were prepared to exchange land for shares in the new company. Col. Myddelton Biddulph did not object on this occasion, as the line did not run through his Chirk Castle parkland, as would that of previous proposals; not that it would have made much difference to the visual amenity because any line from the valley to Chirk station would run on the edge of the park and out of sight. Mr. Barnes, Jnr, Mr. Edmund Burke Wood, landowner, barrister and son of the then late Archdeacon Wood, and Lieut.-Col. Lovett, landowner, were all poised to join the Board as directors.

One local industrialist who presented his case to Parliament in favour of the E&GVR was George Morris, Flannel Manufacturer, whose recital in favour of the proposals gives a good insight into the problems facing business people in the valley at the time:

'I hold and work a Flannel Mill at Llantsantffraid Glyn Ceiriog for the making of Welsh Flannels. The water there is peculiarly fitted for the making of Flannels and finishing them none better. There is also plenty of water fall along the Vale so that many more mills may be erected. At present there is only one besides mine.

There is an old disused Flannel Mill still standing on Mr Webster's property. He thought to build a Mill there some years ago and said nothing would pay better, but was deterred by the cost owing to the badness of the roads. About two years ago two Engineers from Chester came to Mr Webster's land with a view to repair the old mill or making a new one. They said it was a beautiful place for a Mill.

The Llangollen Factories would have no advantage over us if we had as good an outlet as they, but our Flannels are not quite the same make as theirs. We pay 4ᵈ per piece of Flannel for carriage to Oswestry and used to pay 3ᵈ per piece for carriage to Chirk, but no one will take them to Chirk for us now owing to the badness of the Roads. Formerly we used to get our wool from Merionethshire and our oil and fullers earth sent to Chirk station. We cannot get it that way now owing to the road. The last time we had any that way I had to lay hold of the rope to keep the load from going over. When I want any more I must either send over the Hill to Llangollen for it or to Oswestry. Either way will be expensive and inconvenient.

The Llangollen Flannel Manufacturers can send their Flannels out cheaper than we can on account of the reduced carriage costs and therefore we are at a disadvantage. Sometime

The list of Petitions from the 1866 Brief to the House of Commons, which illustrates the overwhelming support for the Ellesmere & Glyn Valley Railway proposal, with just one objector – the Great Western Railway Company!

Courtesy: Mark Hignett

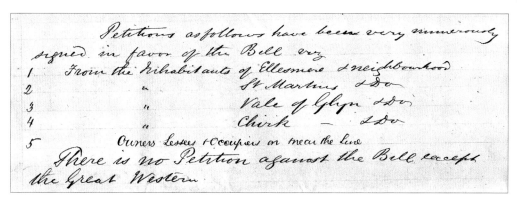

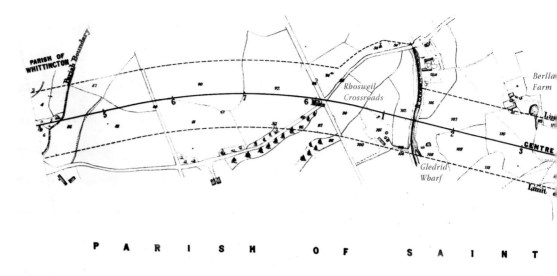

Extract from the Plans & Sections by Robert Piercy for the proposed Ellesmere & Glyn Valley Railway 1866, showing the route through Gledrid and Pontfaen. Railway No.1 was to run from Ellesmere station to Glyn Ceiriog. A branch, Railway No.2, was to make a junction with the GWR near Preesgweene.

Shropshire Archives
Ref: DP 453

ago a person from Messrs Bo.... & Co. of London came to our Factory to buy Flannels. He said it cost him as much to come from Gobowen to Glyn as it did all the way from London to Gobowen. Generally Flannel Drapers will not come to us, but they will do so to Llangollen.

On Mr West's Land and on another property there are large quantities of Chinastone for use in making china. Many years ago the Late Honorable F. West used to send these stones by cart all the way to Staffordshire. Recently Mr. Evans of Talygarth has been negotiating with a person for the sale of the stone for the same purpose. The arrangement was that Mr. Evans was to deliver them to Chirk or Gobowen for 9/- per ton, but he found that the worth of his Team was equal to that and therefore he got nothing for his stones and so he gave it up. Mr. Evans says he has an indefinite large quantity of them, but they will not be got out unless there is a Railway'.

An aide-memoire in favour of the E&GVR had been added to his submission, in pencil, stressing the *'Importance of Oswestry Market.'*

The railway was to be of standard gauge and thirteen miles in length, connecting the Cambrian Railways at Ellesmere with the *'coal, lime, slate, timber, chinastone and flag'* districts along the route and up the Ceiriog Valley. The mention of chinastone indicates that there was already some trading in this mineral taking place between the Ceiriog Valley and the Staffordshire Potteries at that time. The sprat to catch a mackerel, to satisfy and gain the support of the local inhabitants, was the statement that they would now have a rail connection with two market towns, Oswestry and Ellesmere.

Railway No.1 was to run from Ellesmere station (where it would connect with the Cambrian Railways) via Plas Wiggington, Wiggington and St. Martins Moor to Chirk Bank, then along the south bank of the River Ceiriog, to Glyn Ceiriog, although this would have involved the diversion of the river in seven places to accommodate it. From Chirk Bank, another line (Railway No.2) was to run to a junction with the GWR at Preesgweene station (no doubt to Col. Myddelton Biddulph's displeasure). A third line (Railway No.3) was authorized, this being just one mile in length, connecting the station at Glyn Ceiriog with the Cambrian Quarries by a long rope-worked incline, but as no physical connection between the two railways was planned it appears that this section of line was to be of narrow-gauge from the outset, the same as the quarry system.

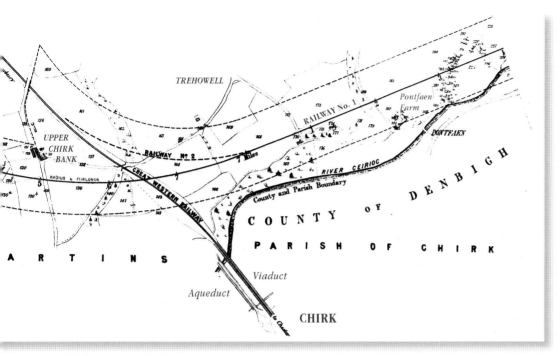

The Parliamentary Brief stated that:

'By means of the Drayton Junction Railway Company (who have running rights over the Cambrian Railway from Bettisfield to Oswestry) and of the friendly relation with the Potteries Junction Railway, Markets will be found in the Potteries, Stafford and in the intermediate Districts. ... By means of the New Lines of The Wrexham Mold & Connahs Quay Railway Company (if sanctioned this Session) from Bettisfield to Sarn Bridge and their Dee Valley Line authorized last year, Slates and Lime will be supplied to the District of Ellesmere, Hanmer and South Cheshire, which greatly need those articles.' [2]

[2] See *'The Wrexham, Mold and Connah's Quay Railway'* by James I.C. Boyd (Oakwood Press 1991)

The station at Glyn Ceiriog was to be situated on the site later occupied by the Glyn Valley Tramway coal yard. Robert Piercy, brother of Benjamin Piercy, who was heavily involved in Cambrian Railways, executed the survey, plans and sections. The Piercy brothers acted jointly as railway engineers constructing the Bishops Castle Railway, the Oswestry, Ellesmere & Whitchurch Railway and many other local undertakings. The Act granted powers to both the GWR and the companies to enter into operating arrangements with the E&GVR Co., but the GWR Co. continued to be suspicious of the intentions of both the E&GVR and the Cambrian Railways companies.

These plans, if they came to fruition, were also likely to have had a serious impact on the turnpike road, especially the engineering works involved in diverting the river in several places in such a narrow valley, so the Wem & Bronygarth Turnpike Trustees must have been very unsure of the effect such a project was going to have on the fabric of their road, their revenue and their plans for the future. The Bill was passed and 'The Ellesmere & Glyn Valley Railway Act 1866' gained Royal Assent on 6th August 1866.

However, tragedy befell the Cambrian Railways Co. because Thomas Savin, who had heavily financed the company's enterprises, had been forced to declare himself bankrupt on 5th February 1866. He had been working the various lines under lease and had ventured into holiday resort and hotel development on the west coast of Wales, all of which failed. Further complications arose as a result of the sensational failure of the Gurney Overend Bank (recently widely quoted as a parallel to the banking crisis of 2008!) leaving the Cambrian Railways on the brink of financial disaster. The proposal was shelved, as the E&GVR Co. was unable to raise the £120,000 required to construct the railway, no doubt assisted by the opposition of the GWR Co., which held a lot of power, but the promoters were not yet defeated, although it was to be another two years before

PARISH OF LLANSAINTFFRAID GLYN CEIRIOG

The Glyn Ceiriog section of the amended proposal by the Ellesmere & Glyn Valley Railway Co. for a standard-gauge railway, 30th November 1868. The railway was to cross the river just below Tal-y-Garth Ucha and enter Glyn Ceiriog on the north side of New Road. It was to cross both New Road and what is now Maybury Avenue to terminate in the field opposite the New Inn. Note the extension of the Limits of Deviation to enable access to hydraulic limestone rock above Tal-y-Garth Ucha. Also shown is the start of the proposed Railway No.3 to the Cambrian Quarries.

Shropshire Archives
Ref: DP 464 IMG16826

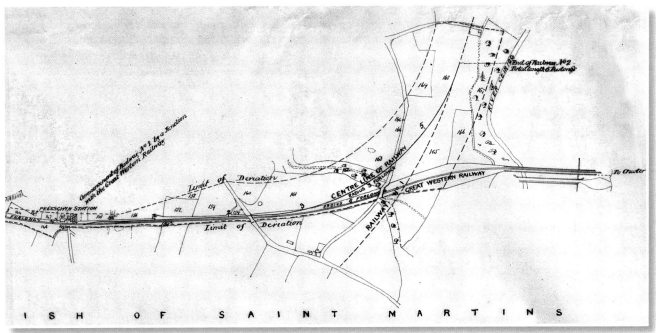

the next proposal was to surface, when an experienced Cornish mining engineer, Henry Dennis, became involved (see chapter 3 for a profile of Henry Dennis).

In 1868, Henry Dennis was engaged by the Ellesmere & Glyn Valley Railway Co. to conduct a survey, this time for a tramway, thus starting the long relationship of the Dennis family with the Ceiriog Valley rail schemes. This new line, for which a set of plans by Dennis & Glennie exist, was to start at the Cambrian Quarry, and end at an interchange station with the GWR line on the east side of Chirk station, alongside the goods yard. The line followed the turnpike road all the way to Chirk station, and it stands without comment to say that the gradients at the Chirk end would have been unworkable if it followed the then existing road. Passing loops or sidings were to be provided at Dolywern, Pontfadog and quarter of a mile east of Tyn-y-Ddol, three miles from Chirk, with a siding at Pontfaen. A short branch at Herber Gate was to have crossed the road bridge over the river to a point in the meadow directly below the Penissa limekilns, which can still be seen on the side of the Herber to Bronygarth road. No more was to be heard of this proposal.

In the same year amended plans, dated 30th November 1868, were made for another standard-gauge line from Ellesmere to Glyn Ceiriog. Railway No.1 of this new proposal was to cross the Shropshire Union Canal just to the south side of Gledrid Wharf, heading northwest for the Ceiriog Valley. After crossing the Quinta–Chirk Bank road on the north side of the cottages at Upper Chirk Bank, it was to pass over the GWR main line north of Trehowell Bridge, run to the south side of Yew Tree Cottages and Pontfaen Farm, to emerge into the Ceiriog Valley proper, passing through the upper portion of Pontfaen Quarry and the nearby cottages, some of which would have had to have been demolished.

From Pontfaen the railway was to continue up the south side of the valley, which would again require the river to be diverted in several places in order to create a suitable route, as was the case with the 1866 Act. At Castle Mill, two diversions of the river were to be made; then, to the west of Herber Gate, the proposed line closely hugged the south side of the valley, because of the steepness of the escarpment, before entering Pontfadog where, yet again, the river was to be realigned to accommodate the railway.

Having left Pontfadog and reaching Dolywern, the railway was to cross the Llwynmawr road, which was to be rerouted to its present location, at a point a little higher up than the later 1888 steam-operated tramway. It was to emerge in the field adjacent to the 1888 tramway yard there,

Part of the Ellesmere & Glyn Valley Railway Co.'s revised standard-gauge proposal of 30th November 1868, showing the route of Railway No.1 from Ellesmere and the branch (Railway No.2) which was to run parallel with the GWR from Quinta Bridge to a junction with the GWR just before Preesgweene station.

Shropshire Archives
Ref: DP 464 IMG16827

Ceiriog Slate . . .

The Wynne slate quarry was well established by 1779, but it was post 1885 before it was seriously developed. The postcard shows the winding wheel for the incline to the underground workings.

Courtesy: Verna Palmer

In Voluntary Liquidation, under the Companies' Act, 1862.

THE CAMBRIAN SLATE COMPANY,
LIMITED.

PARTICULAR OF SALE

Of the Leasehold and other Beneficial Interest of

The Cambrian Slate Company, Limited,

IN THE

CAMBRIAN SLATE QUARRIES,

COMPRISING ALL THE VALUABLE, PRODUCTIVE, AND EXTENSIVE

VEINS, BEDS, AND STRATA OF SLATES AND FLAGS,

Known collectively as "The Cambrian Slate Quarries,"

AND IN THE

OFFICES, SHEDS, WATER SUPPLY, RIGHTS, EASEMENTS, AND INTERESTS

THERETO BELONGING,

Situate at Chwarel-Ucha, in the Parish of Llansaintffraid-Glyn-Ceiriog, in the County of Denbigh,

AND ALSO THE WHOLE OF THE

PLANT AND MACHINERY,

MOVEABLE TOOLS & SIMILAR EFFECTS, & THE STOCK OF SLATES ON THE GROUND,

ALL THE PROPERTY OF THE COMPANY,

Which will be offered for Sale by Auction,

BY MR. THOMAS W. HILL,

(By order of Mr. George Haswell, the Liquidator voluntarily appointed by the Company,) at the

Wynnstay Arms Hotel, in Oswestry,

On Friday, the 22nd of July, 1870, at Three o'clock in the afternoon,

IN ONE OR MORE LOTS, AND SUBJECT TO CONDITIONS.

The Cambrian Slate Quarries have been opened for several years; have produced a large quantity of first-rate Slates, and are capable of great developement. They are situate about 10 miles from Oswestry, and will be upon a Branch of the authorised Ellesmere and Glyn Valley Railway, about to be constructed as a Horse Tramway, under the provisions of a Bill now in Parliament, and by means of which Tramway they will be placed in immediate connection with the Great Western Railway system, and the Shropshire Union Railways and Canals of the London and North Western Railway Company. They are now approached by the Turnpike Roads from Chirk and Oswestry, and Highways from Llangollen and Fron Cysyllte.

The Quarries, Machinery, and Plant are in full working order and condition, and may be inspected at any time upon application at the Works.

The property is held under Leases—originally for 30 years, containing provisions for renewal for a further term of 30 years; which Leases may be inspected at the Offices of the Solicitors, and will be produced at the time of Sale.

These Particulars may be obtained on application at the Offices of the Company, Foregate Street, Chester; or Messrs. Longueville, Jones & Williams, Solicitors, Oswestry; at each of which places Maps of the property may be inspected and all necessary further information obtained.

CHARLES MONK, MACHINE PRINTER, OSWESTRY.

Sale particulars for the Cambrian Slate Company, then in liquidation, which took place at the Wynnstay Arms Hotel, Oswestry, on 22nd July 1870.

Courtesy: Angela James

Rare early photographs of an early gang of slate splitters (bollwr), outside their home-made shelter (waliau) and, below, the mill at the Wynne Quarry with its 30ft diameter overshot waterwheel.

Courtesy: Angela James
and The Quarry 1896

. . . and Flannel

At Glyn Ceiriog, Berwyn Mill (right) was built c1818 and Upper Mill (below) in 1815. They were operated by John Mason and Samuel Edwards. Production continued through various owners until the last flannel was produced in 1951.

Photographs: Ceiriog Press Archive.
Postcard courtesy: Robert Jones

Fulling was carried out in the Ceiriog Valley from the mid-13th century at Melin Deirw, the mill at Pandy (the white building shown below, which later became The Woolpack Inn and is now an Art Glass studio). It is believed to have been the first fulling mill in Wales.

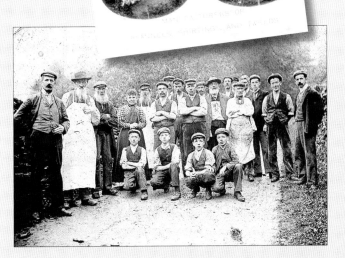

Workers at Upper Mill c1900. Left to right: John Foulks, John Lloyd, Tom Price, Mrs Foulks, Noah Hughes, Evan Evans, Ben Griffiths, Jos Evans, Dafydd Mathews, John Savage, John Mathews, Owen Hughes, Joshua Richards, Jonah Davies, Fred Davies, Albert Foulks, Fred Jones, Thos Foulks, kneeling: Noah Brown, Tom Field, Huw Morris and Tony Austin.

43

from which it was to pass over the Chirk–Glyn Ceiriog road into the fields on the north side and cross the river just below Tal-y-Garth Ucha, in order to avoid the steep outcrop on the approach into Glyn Ceiriog. To the east and alongside Tal-y-Garth Ucha, there was to be a curious extension of the railway's Limits of Deviation extending southwards to embrace nine fields, presumably belonging to Tal-y-Garth Ucha, probably to access the '*hydraulic limestone rock*' at a quarry owned by a David Jones.[3]

[3] The Limits of Deviation are boundaries, shown on the deposited Plans and Sections attached to an Act of Parliament, outside which the railway track or any associated structures must not be built. The engineer had the freedom to alter the route of the line within these boundaries without having to refer back to Parliament.

Railway No.1 was eventually to enter Glyn Ceiriog on the north side of New Road, where the school is today, then cross this road close to where the 1888 engine shed was built, but instead of following the route taken by the 1888 tramway, it was to cross Maybury Avenue at the village end of the terrace and terminate in what is now the playing field.

Railway No.2 was incorporated to connect Railway No.1 with the Great Western Railway at Preesgweene. From a junction with Railway No.1, at a point about halfway between the Pontfaen–Trehowell road and the GWR main line, Railway No.2 was to curve southwards, across the Trehowell–Upper Chirk Bank road (Trehowell Avenue as it is now known) over the site of Quinta and Trehowell Collieries to gently meet up parallel with the GWR, passing under Quinta Bridge and terminating at a junction with the GWR at Preesgweene station.

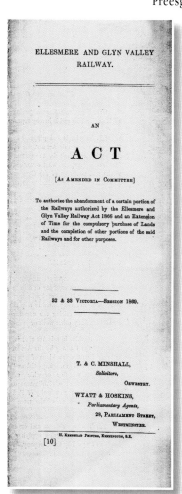

ELLESMERE AND GLYN VALLEY RAILWAY.

AN

A C T

[As Amended in Committee]

To authorize the abandonment of a certain portion of the Railways authorized by the Ellesmere and Glyn Valley Railway Act 1866 and an Extension of Time for the compulsory purchase of Lands and the completion of other portions of the said Railways and for other purposes.

32 & 33 Victoria—Session 1869.

T. & C. MINSHALL,
Solicitors,
Oswestry.

WYATT & HOSKINS,
Parliamentary Agents,
28, Parliament Street,
Westminster.

H. Kershaw Printer, Kennington, S.E.

[10]

The Ellesmere & Glyn Valley Railway Act 1869, which authorized the abandonment of the 1866 proposed line between Chirk Bank and Ellesmere.

Collection: John Milner

Railway No.3 started at the point where Railway No.1 crossed New Road, in Glyn Ceiriog, and was to wind its way up the Nant Lafar Valley to terminate at Chwarel Ucha Quarry (the highest of the Cambrian Quarries). Although not stated in the Plans and Sections, the gradients clearly indicate that most of this section was intended to be an incline; in fact, there was no alternative.

This proposal became yet another failed attempt at providing a transport system for the valley.

During this period of time, the Shropshire Union Railways & Canal Co. was showing great interest in all the various proposals for building a railway up the Ceiriog Valley. As previously related, the SUR&C Co. had the power to operate railways, as well as the right to convert its canals to same, and was keen to benefit from the mooted volume of business that its rivals in the district, the GWR and Cambrian Railways Companies, were so eager to acquire, but it was not yet ready to pounce.

A further Bill was presented to Parliament by the E&GVR Co., but for some unknown reason both the SUR&C Co. and the Cambrian Slate Co. opposed it, although this may have been because they were considering schemes of their own. However, the E&GVR Co. was poised to lease or sell the management of its new line to one of the other operating companies, so on 3rd June 1869, the SUR&C Co. and the Cambrian Slate Co. had second thoughts, and withdrew their objections. This cleared the path for the E&GVR Co. to obtain a further Act, the 'Ellesmere & Glyn Valley Railway Act 1869', which generally incorporated the 1866 one, but authorized the abandonment of the section of line between Chirk Bank and Ellesmere, which was part of Railway No.1 in the 1866 Act, with the exception of the length required to provide a link to the Ellesmere Canal. It also granted an extension of time for completion up to 6th August 1873, a reduction in capital from £120,000 to £25,000 and the right to amend levels and alignments to the route in accordance with the deposited Plans & Sections. The new Act stipulated that transfer facilities for the Ellesmere Canal were to be in place prior to the opening of the railway and the tolls charged to the canal company were to be the same as those afforded to the GWR. The E&GVR Co. was empowered to make the gauge any width between 2ft. and standard-gauge; the mention of 2ft-gauge, along with the somewhat heavy reduction in capital, suggests that narrow-gauge was already in the minds of the promoters at the start.

In November 1869, Messrs Dennis & Glennie produced a revised set of plans for the E&GVR, again loosely based upon the 1866 route. These Plans & Sections retained the word 'railway' in their title, but referred to each individual line to be built as a 'tramway', perhaps paving the way to take advantage of the provisions to be afforded by the Tramways Act, then scheduled to be approved by Parliament in the following year.

The line up the valley was now to start with a connection with the GWR at a point halfway between Trehowell and Quinta Bridges, accessed across the Trehowell/Quinta collieries site, unlike the 1866 route that made a connection with the GWR on the Shrewsbury side of Quinta Bridge. It was then to cross Trehowell Lane to pick up the original 1866 route down to Pontfaen. Had the original 1866 route to the canal been used, an entirely new wharf, between Rhôsweil and a disused coal wharf at Gledrid would have had to have been built, so it was proposed to utilise an existing private 'waggonway' route from Upper Chirk Bank Colliery to this redundant wharf at Gledrid. Connection with the GWR somewhat contradicted its description on the plans as a 'tramway'. However, a proviso was added that, should the railway not be built of standard gauge, enabling a direct connection to be made with the GWR at Preesgweene, sidings had to be provided for an interchange of traffic between the two railways.

Unlike the 1866 route, after running in front of Pontfaen Farm and through Pontfaen Quarry, the line was to now pass through the upper end, rather than middle, of the row of cottages. Instead of continuing up the valley on the south side of the river, it was to cross the field opposite the cottages and bridge the river to join the turnpike road, which it would follow up the valley to Glyn Ceiriog.

This latest scheme for rails to Glyn Ceiriog ended up like the rest, with the E&GVR Co. taking no action to proceed any further. In the meantime, the Cambrian Slate Co. was still struggling on, trying to move its slate out of the valley over inferior roads by horse. However, events elsewhere were about to pave the way forward for the E&GVR Co. to make progress.

Experimental street tramways had been introduced between 1858 and 1861 in London, Liverpool and Birkenhead, but they quickly failed, because the track was laid on top of the roads, which made them impassable by other vehicles! They started to reappear first in Liverpool (1865), then Portsmouth (1868) and London (1870) when grooved rail became available, enabling the track to be laid level with the road, so that other traffic was not impeded in any way. The popularity of the idea spread and, to enable local authorities to introduce grooved rails at street level in their towns and cities, without necessitating the costly process of applying for individual Acts of Parliament, the 'Tramways Act 1870' was brought into being to allow the construction of street tramways to common standards in towns and cities across the country.

Following the failure of the E&GVR Co. to proceed with its railway after the passing of the 1869 Act and the presentation of the Dennis & Glennie scheme, and in light of the possible use of the powers to be provided by the 'Tramways Act', which would enable rails to be laid along the turnpike road, Henry Dennis hastily prepared a further scheme for the E&GVR Co., abandoning part of his original route and surveying a new one, to utilise the turnpike road.

A Bill was presented to Parliament but, having progressed to its final stage, it was put on hold, along with eleven other 'Local and Personal' Acts (all, with the exception of the GVT one, for street tramways), pending the passing of the 'Tramways Act 1870'. This attained Royal Assent on 9th August 1870 and 'The Glyn Valley Tramway Act 1870' was the first to do so on the following day, its preamble being: '*An Act for dissolving the Ellesmere and Glyn Valley Railway Company and re-incorporating the same as the Glyn Valley Tramway Company, with power to construct tramways; and for other purposes.*' However, Clause 3 of the Act stipulated that: '*No part of the Tramway Act 1870, shall apply to this Act*', which is later followed by: '*The Company may use on their tramways carriages with flange wheels, or wheels adapted to run on a grooved rail, and all carriages used on the tramways shall be moved by animal power only,*' which is wording from the 'Tramways Act 1870'. Note the use of the words 'may use', which created a significant loophole for the GVT not to be built with the rails level with the road!

The House of Commons had received only one Petition against the Glyn Valley Tramway Bill 1870. This was from Robert Piercy, Engineer of the Ellesmere & Glyn Valley Railway Co., requesting that the House should not pass the Bill until he had been paid his outstanding dues by the E&GVR Co..

Courtesy: Mark Hignett

45

[33 & 34 VICT.]   *The Glyn Valley Tramway*   [Ch. clxvi.]
                    Act, 1870.

CHAP. clxvi.

An Act for dissolving the Ellesmere and Glyn Valley Railway   A.D. 1870.
Company and re-incorporating the same as "The Glyn
Valley Tramway Company," with power to construct
Tramways; and for other purposes.   [10th August 1870.]

WHEREAS by "The Ellesmere and Glyn Valley Railway Act,   29 & 30 Vict.
1866," (herein-after called "the firstly recited Act,) a Company   c. cccxxxv.
was incorporated by the name of the Ellesmere and Glyn Valley
Railway Company, with power to make and maintain a railway
from Ellesmere to Llansaintffraid Glyn Ceiriog in the counties of
Salop and Denbigh :

And whereas by "The Ellesmere and Glyn Valley Railway Act,   32 & 33 Vict.
1869," (herein-after called the secondly recited Act,) the Company   c. cli.
were empowered to abandon a portion of their undertaking authorised by the firstly recited Act, and further powers were granted to
the said company, and the amount of capital authorised to be raised
by them in shares was reduced from the sum of one hundred and
twenty thousand pounds to the sum of twenty-five thousand pounds,
and the amount of money authorised to be borrowed by them upon
mortgage of their undertaking was reduced from forty thousand
pounds to the sum of eight thousand three hundred pounds :

And whereas the said company have not constructed any part
of the railway by the said Acts authorised, nor acquired any land
for the purposes thereof :

And whereas it is expedient that the said company should be
dissolved, and re-incorporated under another name, and authorised to
construct and maintain the tramways and works herein-after described and authorised, in lieu of the railway and works authorised
by the said recited Acts, with such other powers as are herein-after
granted :

[*Local.-166.*]   A   1

The Glyn Valley Tramway Act, 1870, gained Royal Assent on 10th August 1870, thirteen years after the first proposal to build a tramway up the valley was put forward by the Cambrian Slate Company. After several failed schemes by other promoters, the Ceiriog Valley was within reach of having its transport link to the outside world.

Collection: John Milner

Not surprisingly, Parliament received a petition against the new Act, although from an unexpected quarter. Addressed to '*the Honorable the Lords Spiritual and Temporal of the United Kingdom of Great Britain & Ireland in Parliament Assembled*' it was presented by Robert Piercy, who was the engineer of the Ellesmere and Glyn Valley Railway Co., which was about to be dissolved. He was a creditor of this company, having not yet been paid and being owed '*a large amount*' for his preparation work, which led to the passing of the 1869 E&GVR Act. He had made several applications for payment, but had obtained either an unsatisfactory reply or none at all. After legal proceedings, he had been given some assurances that, once the tramway was constructed, he would receive security for ultimate payment of the debt. Now that the E&GVR Co. was to be dissolved by this new GVT Act, he expressed his concern that there was no provision within it for the proposed new company to offer him any form of security for the debt of the previous company. He argued that the E&GVR Co. had benefited from his money and services and that the House should not pass the Bill until his debt had been settled or provision was made to do so.

The new 1870 GVT Act authorized seven sections of tramways, which was basically a compromise between the proposals of the 1861 Wem & Bronygarth Road Act, the Ellesmere & Glyn Valley Railway Act 1869 and the 1869 Dennis & Glennie scheme, already mentioned.

As authorized by the 1869 Act and adopted by the 1870 Act, the section from Rhôsweil to Ellesmere was abandoned, and Tramway No.1 was to now start adjacent to Telford's Holyhead Road (although provision was made within the Act for crossing it) at Rhôsweil. From there it was to cross the canal on a substantial bridge with a span of not less than 25ft and then the Great Western Railway by means of another one of 28ft. On the opposite side of the latter, it was to connect with Tramways Nos. 2 and 4, in the field owned by Mr & Mrs Edmund Burke Wood. No.2 was to descend towards Pontfaen, cross the lane by Pen-y-lan, run south of Yew Tree cottages, north of Pontfaen farm to Pontfaen itself, and thence across the river to join the turnpike road, which it would follow all the way to Glyn Ceiriog. This first section of Tramway No.2 down to Pontfaen had an average gradient of 1 in 24, which proved in later years to be a big mistake, and was to be extremely troublesome to the company.

Tramway No.4 was to terminate with a 'junction' with the GWR between Trehowell and Quinta bridges, near the site of Trehowell Colliery. Tramway No.3 was to climb up Nant Lafar Valley from a junction with Tramway No.2 to the Cambrian Quarries, via an incline with gradients of 1 in 88, 13, 12, 5, 8 and 9. Tramway No.5, 1½ miles long, was to continue from the end of Tramway No.3 at the Cambrian Quarries, to take advantage of the contour lines and follow a relatively easy route to Nantyr Quarry, owned by Col. Myddelton Biddulph. Also authorized were Tramway No.6, a short siding at Castle Mill to serve the Bronygarth limekilns, and Tramway No.7 to the Penissa limekilns at Herber, which were operated by Richard Steele Perkins.

The interests of the SUR&C Co. were catered for in that the tramway was not to be opened for traffic until a suitable interchange with sidings had been built adjacent to the canal. The Act specified that the GVT Co. had to provide sidings and facilities as requested by the canal company, providing the cost of doing so did not exceed £500; if it did, then the canal company had to pay the difference.

As a result of the tramway being authorized for public use for the carriage of minerals, merchandise and passengers, and not for the exclusive use of the Cambrian Slate Co., the directors of that company, not suprisingly, now wished to have no further financial involvement, having had their fingers burnt by subsidising the turnpike road. While the Cambrian Slate Co. was relieving itself of any further financial involvement, the newly promoted Glyn Valley Tramway Co. had made a rod for its own back by agreeing, in a Memorandum of Agreement attached to the Act, to pay the Trustees of the Wem & Bronygarth Turnpike Trust a minimum annual rent of £150, payable half-yearly, which was to take precedence over any other charges that were likely to be made against the company. It was also agreed therein that the Trustees 'oppose any application to Parliament in the present or any future session for power to work the said tramway by locomotive or other than horse power'.

The authorized capital remained unaltered at £25,000 with three years allowed for completion. The cost for all the engineering and track work was estimated at £14,491, amounting to £560 per mile for the main line and £480 for sidings and spurs. The most expensive part of the whole construction was the incline up to the Cambrian Quarries from Glyn Ceiriog, which was estimated at £2,237. However, the incline was designed as single track only in order to save money but, as events reveal, the New Cambrian Slate Co., which had taken over the operation of the quarries in 1870 (Registered as limited liability company 8th June 1872, No.6347), was having none of this and insisted upon having a conventional double-track incline.[4]

Failing to find local sponsors amongst the landowners, the GVT Co. directors decided to cut their estimates back from £14,491 to £10,000, and approach the SUR&C Co. for financial assistance. Obviously, the SUR&C Co. was interested in the potential trade, as their main competitor was the GWR Co. and, at a meeting of the SUR&C Co. Executive Committee held at Bala on 28th June 1871, it was agreed to provide £5,000 of the capital required, subject to scrutiny of the plans and specifications. It was also subject to agreement that George Robert Jebb, its engineer, should have direct control over the construction of the works, that the balance of capital required could be raised and, finally, that the SUR&C Co. would have the sole right of working the line.

[4] For full details of the Cambrian incline see 'Slates from Glyn Ceiriog' by John Milner.

Part of 1869 Plans & Sections showing the revised route through Pontfaen to join the turnpike road to Glyn Ceiriog. When built, the route was further modified to avoid cutting through the houses and close to the farm. See chapter 5 page 116. A note on this drawings indicated that it was intended to narrow the road by 10ft.

Shropshire Archives
DP592 (Part)

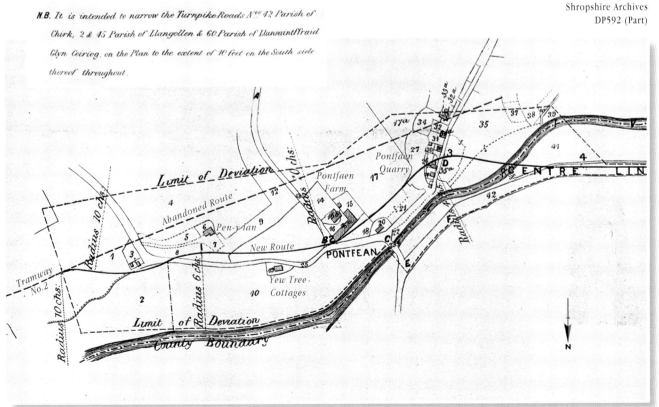

The Act authorized the charging of tolls for the carriage of passengers, minerals and general merchandise, and stated the maximum rate chargeable:

Passengers	2d. per mile
Passengers' luggage not exceeding 60lbs	Free
Hire of Horse and Car	1s. 3d. per mile
Coal, limestone, slate, stone, road mending materials, timber	3d. per ton per mile
Coke, bricks, tiles, manure, sheet/bar/rod iron, heavy castings	4d. per ton per mile
Flour, grain, sugar, earthenware, light castings	5d. per ton per mile
Fish, manufactured goods, wool and other wares	6d. per ton per mile
Iron boiler, cylinder, machinery over 4 ton but under 8 ton	3s. per ton per mile

Thus, after 13 years of proposals and counter-proposals, which followed the Cambrian Slate Company's initial negotiations with the Wem & Bronygarth Turnpike Trustees, to provide a private horse-drawn tramway alongside their proposed new road up the valley to Glyn Ceiriog, the scene was finally set to build a public tramway, which would give all the industries access to the national canal and railway networks, as well as providing a much needed goods and passenger service for the local population.

This concludes the overview of the early industrial activity in the Ceiriog Valley, the story of the ill-founded and aborted schemes that were proposed in a bid to bring a reliable transport system to the valley, as well as the events leading up to the actual building of the Glyn Valley Tramway – all essential to enable a clear understanding of the extraordinary events that were about to unfold in the coming years.

Chapter 2

Other Local Tramways

The Glyn Valley Tramway was not the first tramway to be built in the area. There was a number of private ones that served collieries and brickworks in the immediate vicinity, which were also connected to canal interchanges and, sometimes, to the standard-gauge main line as well. As these were built on private land for their owners' use, they did not have to be sanctioned by an Act of Parliament. Other tramways were proposed, but were never built for one reason or another.

Black Park Colliery Tramway (SJ 298403)

The outcrop of coal at Black Park, on the ridge high above the Dee Valley, had been worked intermittently since the 1500s. By the late 1700s, twenty or so shallow shafts had been sunk and connected to the road at Chirk by a horse-drawn tramway. In 1805 the colliery was leased to Mr T.E. Ward, who embarked upon some twenty years of development, including an extension of this tramway from the road (Upper Wharf) to a canal basin (Bottom Wharf, later known as Black Park Wharf), just off the Ellesmere Canal.

This colliery tramway was typical of its day, the track consisting of 'L' shaped cast iron rails in 3ft lengths weighing about 40lbs, held in place by cast iron chairs fastened to stone blocks. In the 1960s a few of the stone blocks were still visible between Upper and Bottom Wharf.[1]

In 1825, T.E. Ward renewed his lease and continued developments by sinking new shafts at Green Lane in 1832. After the arrival of the Shrewsbury & Chester Railway in 1848, the horse tramway was replaced by a standard-gauge siding from a junction with the main line to the new centre at Green Lane. The building of this siding was one of the conditions imposed by the landowner, Robert Myddelton Biddulph, in the negotiations to allow the railway to be built through his Chirk Castle Estate.

[1] See *Industrial Locomotives of North Wales* by V.J. Bradley. Industrial Railway Society, 1992 and '*A History of the Parish of Chirk*' by C. Neville Hurdsman, Bridge Books, 1996.

Stone sleeper blocks, thought to be from the Black Park Colliery tramway, incorporated into a local building. The unusual rectangular fixing holes were also a feature of those used on the Knowl Hill Brickworks tramway, at Buckley, Flintshire. On the right, the road sign from the 'Top' Wharf at Chirk, interpreted as 'Upper' by the powers that be.

© David Ll. Davies 1960 [Left]
© John Milner 2009 [Right]

49

Brynkinalt Colliery Tramway (SJ 296382)

From about 1840, coal was being mined at Chirk Green on the Brynkinalt Estate and in February 1862, it was proposed to build a railway to connect the colliery with the GWR at Chirk station. The Brynkinalt Coal Co. Ltd stated: '*We could not possibly send more than 600 tons of coal weekly by carts, whereas if we had a branch line we could send 1,000 or 2,000 tons weekly.*' This estimate of output proved to be over-optimistic, but following the sinking of a further shaft in the early 1870s an Agreement, dated 23rd June 1875, was made between Richard Myddelton Biddulph and the Brynkinalt Colliery Co. for the lease of land between the colliery and the GWR station at Chirk, for a period of 21 years at £500 per annum, in order to:

'*... make and maintain a tramway or tramways of the narrow-gauge width ... and to use the same tramway for the purpose of hauling and carrying, with locomotive engines or horses, wagons, trucks and other carriages ... towards the Great Western Railway at or near Chirk station'.*

Royalties were to be paid at the rate of 3d./ton for coal or ironstone, 3 1/2d./ton for slack, 2d./ton for clay and 6d./ton for bricks.

On 5th July 1875, a Covenant was made with the Shrewsbury and Holyhead Road Commissioners for the construction of '*a standard-gauge railway bridge*' under their road at Chirk Green and a further Agreement was made on 24th May 1876, between the GWR Co. and the Brynkinalt Colliery Co., for the establishment of interchange facilities at Chirk station. However, by 1879, the colliery company was in liquidation and, by February 1884, the Agreement had been terminated and these sidings closed.

It appears that for financial reasons the company had opted for a narrow-gauge tramway but by building the standard-gauge bridge, it had the foresight to make provision for an easy conversion to standard gauge, if required. The trackbed of the old tramway was later utilised for a standard-gauge siding from the colliery to the GWR at Chirk station.

A stone tramway sleeper block still visible in the 1960s at Brynkinalt Colliery. Lying alongside is the tell-tale carpenters' ruler that was used by the photographer in many of his photographs.

© David Ll. Davies 1960

Ifton-Rhyn Collieries Tramway (SJ 326375)

To the east of the canal, Ifton-Rhyn Collieries Ltd (7025), registered in 1873, had included in its development Prospectus, the construction of a tramway of 2ft 4in gauge to the canal. Several trial surveys were made and a route eventually agreed with the landowner, Lord Edwin Hill-Trevor. However, Thomas Randolph Mellor, a civil engineer engaged by the directors to report on the company's plans, realised that, if the colliery developed as projected, it needed a connection with the GWR as well as with the canal, so he stressed the '*advisability of obtaining access to the Great Western Railway, by means of an extension of our tramway to a junction with the Glyn [Valley] Tramway on the Holyhead Road*'. This would have given the colliery access via the GVT to the interchange at Trehowell. The GVT (Tramway No.1) was originally intended to continue over the canal in the region of Gledrid to terminate in the field adjacent to the Telford's Holyhead Road, which would have facilitated a connection to Mellor's proposed tramway. Trial surveys were made by Mellor, but it became essential to purchase a piece of land, which lay on the route of the proposed line, whose owner promptly held the colliery company to ransom with the price, so it was abandoned. However, in 1874, he proposed building the line to the canal, initially as 2ft 4in gauge, which would minimise the initial costs, but leaving sufficient land to convert this to standard gauge (4ft 8 1/2in) at a later date and extend it to the Great Western Railway, with the one rail forming half of the new standard-gauge line when built. His report continued:

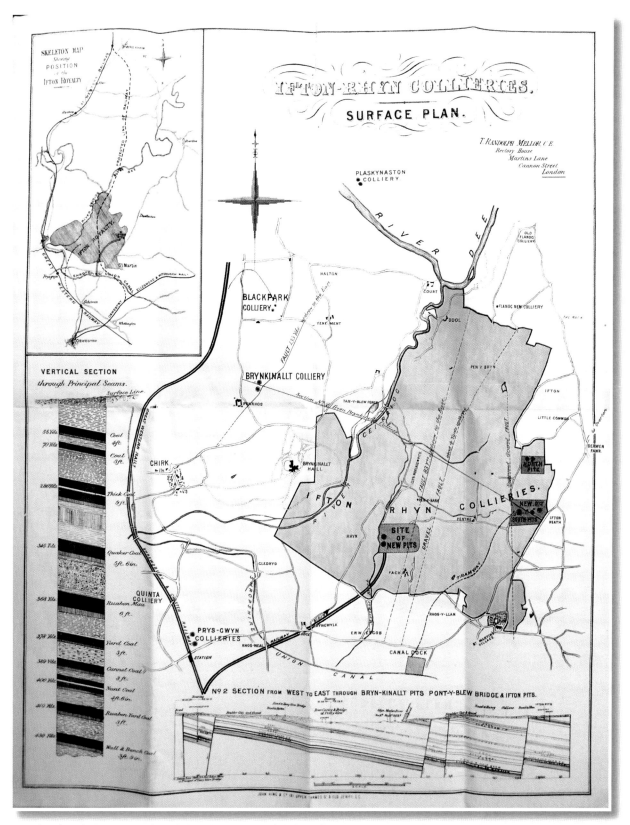

The detailed map produced by Thomas Randolph Mellor C.E. in 1874 illustrates the relationship of the Ifton-Rhyn Collieries to others in the area. Although recommended in his report to the Ifton-Rhyn Company's shareholders, the proposed connection with the GVT at Gledrid is not shown.

Courtesy: Crosse Wyatt Verney & Ayre and North Devon Record Office Ref: 2309B/Z10/5

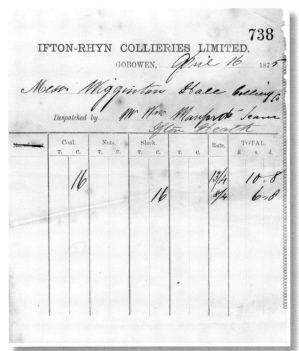

Collection: John Milner

[2] Mellor was referring to a recent suggestion by Jebb, Engineer of the Shropshire Union Canal, that the Llangollen to Weston Wharf length should be converted to a narrow gauge railway and carried on to Wem.

'*... The metals or rails should be about 32lbs to the yard, and the gauge kept 2 feet 4 inches, the same as the Glyn Tramway and the proposed conversion of the canal into a tramway. ... It will always be desirable to keep a third rail on the railway, as far as the canal, so as to be able to avail ourselves of the coal sales that the Glyn Tramway and its proposed extensions will command. ... The proposal of the Shropshire Union Canal Company to convert their canal into a tramway should be kept in view.[2] It appears that any attempt to do so must be strenuously opposed, unless more equal facilities for traffic be afforded.*'

The GVT began making preparations for a junction with this proposed colliery tramway by gaining possession of the strip of land that it required to extend its line from Gledrid Wharf to the crossroads on the Holyhead Road, where the junction with the Ifton-Rhyn line was to be made. The route was to take the same line as the GVT (Tramway No.1), proposed in the 1870 Act, which had been abandoned in favour of road access to Gledrid Wharf via a lift bridge. The tramway extension was to cross the canal by means of '*a substantial bridge of brick, stone, or iron or a combination of each*', with a clear height of 9ft above the canal and towpath, and a navigable width of 20ft. It was to then pass through the Gledrid Brick & Tile Works site, in order to reach the Holyhead Road. These brickworks, and the nearby cottages known as the Coke Oven Cottages, had been built by George Posnett on land that he had leased from Sophia, Viscountess Dungannon, in 1862, for an initial period of 21 years. On 17th October 1873 the GVT Co. paid the Viscountess £10 for the freehold of the narrow strip of land it required and, on 11th September 1874, it gained complete possession when it paid the sum of £83 0s. 6d. to George Posnett for the surrender of his lease, leaving him able to continue to occupy the surrounding land and brickworks with a reduction of one farthing in his annual rent.

The high ambitions of Ifton-Rhyn Collieries Ltd did not come to fruition. By the end of 1874 there were signs that the company was struggling and the next year it went into voluntary liquidation. The extensive colliery tramways were not completed, nor was the GVT extended across the canal and through the brickworks site.

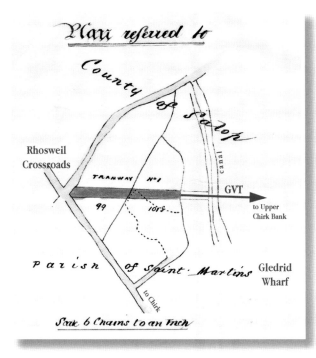

The plan from the Assignment of a strip of land running from the Rhosweil crossroads [now known as Gledrid roundabout] and through the Gledrid Brick & Tile Co. site. The freehold of the strip was acquired by the GVT Co., in October 1873, from the owner Sophie, Viscountess Dungannon, in order to facilitate a connection with the proposed Ifton-Rhyn Colliery Tramway, but the connection never came to fruition.

Collection: John Milner

Preesgweene and Moreton Hall Collieries Tramways (SJ 294363)

To the south of Preesgweene station was Moreton Hall Colliery, on a site that had been split into two when the Shrewsbury & Chester Railway main line was built, leaving one shaft on either side. The colliery was started c1838, amalgamated with the nearby Preesgweene Colliery in 1868, and offered for sale by auction in 1894, but there were no takers and it was duly closed. As well as its own rail connection to the GWR, Moreton Hall Colliery had a short tramway, just over a quarter of a mile long, linking it to a wharf on the curve in the canal where it passes under the Holyhead Road, adjacent to what is now a roadside services site, opposite the Lion Quays complex. In November 1880, Horace Mayhew, a mining engineer from Wigan, submitted proposals to the directors of Preesgweene Colliery Co. for its future development. As part of his proposal he recommended the immediate construction of a tramway from the Preesgweene Colliery to Gledrid Wharf, at a cost of £200, stating that: '*We are now paying 6d. per ton for carting to the canal, and we could tram it down at 2d. per ton*'. This is shown on his drawing dated October 1880 and, although not stated, it would appear that the intention was that this would be of the same gauge as the GVT and was intended to connect with it at Gledrid Wharf, giving the colliery access to a transport route up the valley; this proposed tramway was never built.

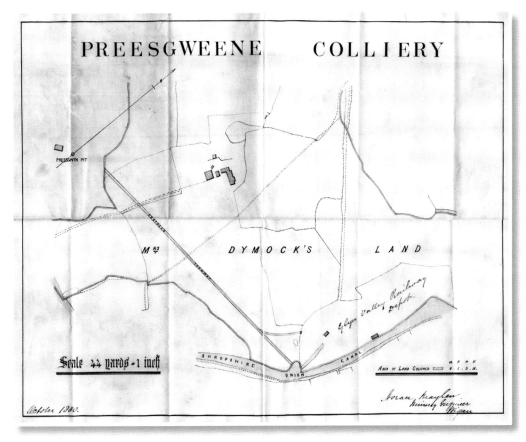

Plan by Horace Mayhew, Mining Engineer, Wigan, dated October 1880, for a proposed tramway from Preesgweene Colliery to Gledrid Wharf, with a link to the GVT. Note that the GVT office and warehouse are shown on the Gledrid Wharf site.

Courtesy: Canal Maps Archive

Chirk Bank Colliery Tramway (SJ 292367)

One of the earliest of these private tramways was built in the 1820s to carry coal from New Pits (Upper Chirk Bank Colliery) down to Gledrid Wharf. This colliery wharf at Gledrid and the tramway from Upper Chirk Bank that served it pre-dated the building of the GVT by some 50 years. The colliery was located opposite the end of Trehowell Lane, on land owned by Thomas Fitzhugh of Plas Power, Wrexham, and at the time the tramway was built, John Pritchard of *Chirk Bank Collieries* was the tenant. Between 1831 and 1839, it was being operated by the Fitzhugh Colliery Company, and appears to have been a fairly substantial concern because, in 1831, advertisements appeared for the recruitment of 70–80 miners and 10–12 boys at somewhat high rates of pay for

Part of an 1829 plan of New Pits (Upper Chirk Bank Colliery) showing the tramway (designated on the plan as a 'Rail Road'), which was built to connect the colliery with the Ellesmere Canal at Gledrid Wharf. This abandoned route to the canal and Gledrid Wharf was eventually adopted for use by the Glyn Valley Tramway, when it was built in 1872.

The tramway sidings are just visible on the inset enlargement of Gledrid Wharf. The dock remains to this day as built and does not appear to have been modified in size.

Coal was being extracted in this area during the 17th/18th century from shallow workings, known as Berllandeg Works.

Some of the features on this plan are still visible today.

Denbighshire Record Office
DD/DM/8241 (Part)

New Pits

South Pit. 5 Feet Coal Level
South Pit. Little Coal Level
North Pit. Six Feet Coal Level

PLAN of CHIRK BANK COLLIERY 1829

the time, of 15s.–18s. per week. Coal is known to have been extracted in this area as early as the 17th/18th century from shallow workings, known as Berllandeg Works. Later, deep collieries were sunk, the earlier of which was Chirk Colliery (1801), which had shafts in the meadow opposite Chirk Mill that were destroyed when it was flooded in 1816, as a result of the canal bursting its banks, and later Chirk Bank Colliery (Old Pit) in c1810, located alongside the canal on the east of Monks Bridge at Chirk Bank, the spoil tip of which can still be witnessed today on the canal bank at the rear of the new houses on Telford's Holyhead road (the original A5).[3]

[3] For further information see *A History of the Parishes of St. Martin's & Weston Rhyn* by C. Neville Hurdsman. Bridge Books 2003.

Gledrid Brickworks Tramway (SJ 298365)

The Gledrid Brick & Tile Works and the Coke Oven Cottages were situated opposite Gledrid Wharf at the point where a lift bridge had been built to provide road access to the wharf facilities. From the brickworks was a short tramway, which terminated alongside the canal. This poses a little mystery, as it is recorded in the GVT weighbills for 1882–1883 that the brickworks despatched 18,000 bricks, by three consignments over a period of several months, to J.G. Briscoe, gunpowder manufacturer of Plâs Garth, Glyn Ceiriog, via the GVT in unnumbered wagons, which was highly unusual, as the weighbills always quoted the GVT wagon numbers. So were the bricks unloaded from brickworks' wagons into carts, on the towpath side of the canal, to be carried the short distance across the lift bridge over the canal, then unloaded from the cart into GVT wagons, which would have been a very laborious affair indeed? Or, is it possible that the brickworks' tramway was the same gauge as the GVT and temporary track was laid across the lift bridge so that brickworks' wagons could pass onto GVT rails and carry the bricks all the way to Glyn Ceiriog? The brickworks' wagons would probably not have had numbers, so was the latter the reason why no numbers were recorded on the GVT weighbills?

An example of a tramway running across a lift bridge, similar to that at Gledrid Wharf, was located on the Llangollen section of the canal at the Pentrefelin Slab & Slate Works (c1845–1895). This carried Henry Dennis' 3ft-gauge Oernant Tramway from the slate quarries up the Horseshoe Pass, over the canal.

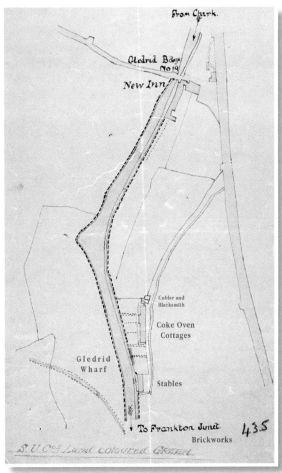

Above: *Shropshire Union Railways & Canal Co. drawing showing a length of canal at Gledrid, with Gledrid Wharf, the GVT, Coke Oven Cottages and the stables.*

Shropshire Archives
IMG16824

Left: *The lift bridge over the canal at Llangollen, carrying Henry Dennis' Oernant Tramway to the Pentrefelin Slate & Slab Works, illustrating how the Gledrid Brickworks Tramway may have used the lift bridge at Gledrid Wharf.*

Courtesy: Langollen Museum

Backing onto the canal and located opposite to Gledrid Wharf are Coke Oven Cottages, which are now known by the less imposing name of Gledrid Terrace. They stand next to the site of an early coke oven, which is shown on the 1838 Tithe map. The original nine cottages were probably built by George Posnett, a gentleman from Ireland, about 1862 when he acquired . . . .

. . . . land from Sophia, Viscountess Dungannon for the development of a brickworks, which became the Gledrid Brick & Tile Works. In 1881, eight of the nine cottages were occupied by coal miners and labourers, with just one inhabited by a family of brickmakers. Stables adjacent to the cottages probably provided livery for canal horses arriving with boats at Gledrid Wharf.

Quinta and Trehowell Collieries Tramways (SJ 288367)

To the south of the River Ceiriog at Chirk was the 3,500-acre Quinta Estate. This was owned by Thomas Barnes of Quinta Hall, Weston Rhyn, who was chairman of the Lancashire & Yorkshire Railway Co., had textile interests in Lancashire and was Liberal MP for Bolton Borough from 1852–1857 and 1861–1868.[4] He was born at Farnworth in Lancashire, in 1812, and moved to Quinta in 1858 upon the completion of his new Gothic style mansion, Quinta Hall. He was a well-respected Congregationalist, and built Quinta chapel also in the Gothic-style and supported it throughout his life, along with a Sunday school, built in 1882. He died on 24th April 1897, leaving the estate to his son, Captain (later Lt. Col.) James Richardson Barnes of *Brookside*, Bronygarth.

Two collieries, Quinta and Trehowell (earliest listing 1860), and a brickworks, the latter making earthenware pipes as well as bricks, had been established on the estate by a previous occupant of Quinta.[5] The bricks from this establishment are distinctive by virtue of their yellow colour and were used in many buildings in the locality. The two collieries were very close together and were linked together by a tramway. Sometime before 1868, the tramway had been extended from Trehowell to enter a tunnel under the southwest approach to Quinta Bridge, emerging to form an interchange with the Great Western Railway, near to the end of a long siding from the Preesgweene station. This siding, stretched all the way from the station to Quinta Bridge, where it ended up at a small interchange wharf, which was difficult to operate, there being no easy means of shunting wagons. To rectify this, the GWR later introduced a slip road between the 'Up' line and the end of the wharf. However, as the Quinta Co. was only too aware, an interchange with the GWR would not suffice on its own and one with the Shropshire Union canal was also essential.

[4] The name *Quinta* is Spanish for country house or seat.

[5] The coal mined in the Chirk area was all part of the Wrexham coalfield. Quinta Colliery had a shallow shaft of 330ft, the first 97ft consisting of glacial debris such as gravel, sand, clay and loam. This was followed by a 5ft seam of coal, a 2ft layer of clay, a 2ft seam of coal, another 2ft layer of clay and then a 4ft seam of coal, and so on for a further seven similar seams until bedrock was reached at 323ft. Trehowell Colliery was similar but neither was easy to work, nor was the quality of the coal as good as that from the deeper Black Park and Brynkinalt Collieries at Chirk.

The solution for the Quinta Colliery Co. had been to build a tramway to the Shropshire Union canal at Chirk Bank, utilising part of an old driveway, which used to connect Quinta Hall with Telford's Holyhead Road between Chirk Bank and Gledrid. The SUR&C Co. Minutes reveal that, in October 1869, an approach was to be made by the canal company to the manager of the Quinta Colliery Co. to ascertain whether the colliery would '*join in putting in a wharf near Chirk Bank*' and to establish how much traffic would be generated for the canal. In June 1871, Mr Alfred Wragge, Secretary, was instructed to arrange with the Quinta Colliery Co. for a wharf to be built at Chirk Bank, and an Agreement was signed on 4th July 1871, being finally approved by the SUR&C Co. Executive Committee that August, at which time Wragge reported that the wharf was already under construction. The Quinta Tramway, as it was known, ran from Quinta Colliery, crossed over the GWR on Trehowell Bridge, and ran down the old drive towards Chirk Bank, crossing the Chirk Bank–Upper Chirk Bank road on a stone-built bridge, with castellated walls, located halfway between the junction with Oaklands Road and the row of terraced cottages near to the canal bridge at Chirk Bank, before passing behind these cottages to a position high above the canal. Here, was located the facility for transshipping coal and bricks into canal narrowboats, via chutes, but therein lay a problem.[6] There was such a drop that coal and bricks would tend to break up, resulting in a lot of waste. Lt. Col. James Richardson Barnes, son of Thomas Barnes, later related, at a Parliamentary Committee examining the 1885 GVT Bill, on 6th May that year:

> '*In the late Quinta Colliery's time there was a tramway made to the canal, to a wharf erected by the Shropshire Union Canal Company, but it was never worked. The shoot for the coal was a very steep one, so it would have broken up the coal considerably in getting it into the barges, and it would not have been a proper one, in my opinion, for the bricks. The line was given up on account of the GVT being made, and the gradients on this were better than those of the private road of my fathers.*'

[6] This may have been a long chute at a steep angle, with no means of controlling the quantity being discharged. The momentum of the coal or bricks dropping into the narrowboats from such a height would not have pleased the boatmen. The SUR&C Co. engineers resolved a similar problem, some 30 years later, when designing a chute arrangement for the GVT at Black Park basin in Chirk.(See *Rails to Glyn Ceiriog* Part 2)

The surviving section of the tunnel that took the Trehowell tramway from the Trehowell Colliery and Brickworks under the road, near Quinta Bridge, to the transshipment wharf alongside the long GWR siding from Preesgweene station.

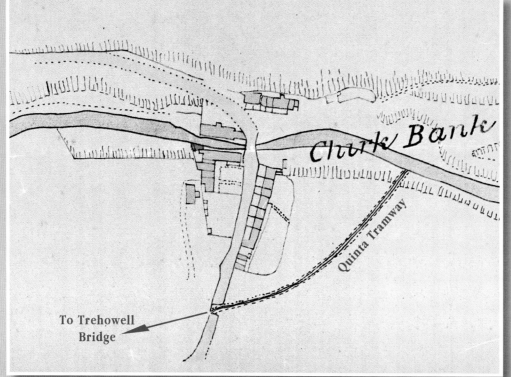

To Trehowell Bridge

Chirk Bank

Quinta Tramway

Above: *Looking down Chirk Bank, the bridge that had carried the Quinta Tramway across the Chirk Bank–Upper Chirk Bank road. Photographed in the early 1960s, this bridge was demolished not long afterwards.*

Collection: John Milner
Ex Late Selwyn H.P. Higgins

Left: *Shropshire Union Railways & Canal Co. plan of Chirk Bank showing the route of the Quinta Tramway to its wharf on the Ellesmere Canal and the location of the bridge in the illustration above.*

Shropshire Archives
IMG 16823

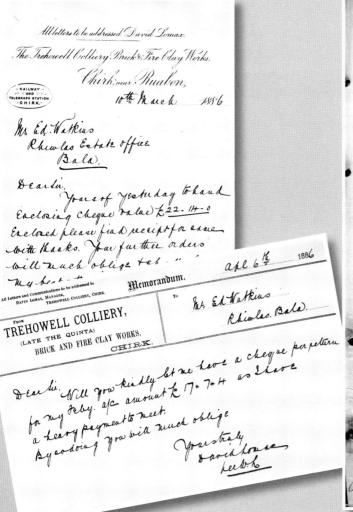

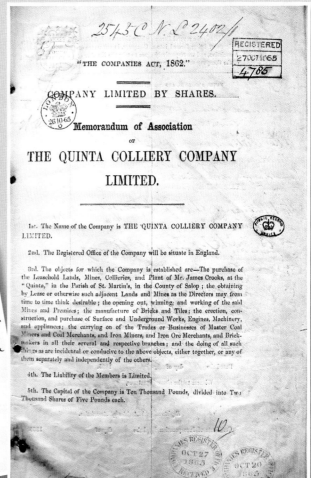

Above left: *Rare examples of Trehowell Colliery & Brickworks letterheads, signed by David Lomax.*

Gwynedd Archives Service
ZDDD2.684.2 & 3

Above right: *The Quinta Colliery Company's 1865 Memorandum of Association.*

National Archives

Left: *The route of the Quinta Tramway, looking from Telford Avenue towards Berwyn Avenue, Chirk Bank, and towards the canal.*
Right: *The route looking back from Telford Avenue towards Trehowell Bridge.*

© John Milner 2009

Thomas Barnes MP
1812–1897

Above: *The east face of Quinta Hall, the imposing residence of Thomas Barnes, built by him in 1858, when he purchased the 3,500-acre Quinta Estate.*

Thomas Barnes was born in 1812 at Farnworth, near Bolton. In 1849 he inherited the family cotton business, became a JP for Lancashire in in 1849, Liberal MP for Bolton (1852–1857 and 1861–1868) and served as chairman of the Lancashire & Yorkshire Railway Co. (1852–1883).

Top: Collection: John Milner
Bottom: Neville Hurdsman

At the same 1885 examination, George Jebb, Engineer of the SUR&C Co., stated that:

'A line was laid out from Mr. Barnes' colliery to the canal beginning at the GWR and going to the canal just under Chirk Bank. The canal company put in a very good wharf especially for Mr Barnes' traffic, but for some reason or other it has never been used. We went to great expense, £100–150, besides the chute for loading coal. The rails may have been taken up. This line was in existence when the GVT line opened.'

David Lomax told the committee that he had been lessee of the Trehowell Colliery, as well as the brick and *'fire clay'* works, since 1868, and that he employed 250 men and lads. At this time (1885) his daily output was 50 tons of coal fetching 8s. 4d. per ton at the pithead, having dropped from 250 tons per day. He also stated that 30–40 tons of fire clay per day were being raised.

Thomas Barnes, knowing the intentions of the GVT company to build a tramway to the canal, which was to run very close to his Quinta and Trehowell collieries, with a GWR interchange on his land, it does appear to be a little odd that he decided to build his own at this time. With his tramway to run entirely on his own land for his own use, he did not require Parliamentary sanction in order to build it and, as the SUR&C Co. was prepared to contribute towards the cost of building an interchange facility exclusive to him, with nothing certain about the future of the GVT, this proposition probably sounded very attractive.

The Hendre Quarry Tramway (SJ 191346)

In late 1873, good-quality granite was accidently found by a local contractor, Elias Griffith of Chirk, on land close to Hendre Farm, owned by Miss Ann Edwards, some two miles up the Ceiriog Valley beyond the village of Glyn Ceiriog. When geologists confirmed that it was a type of granite particularly suited for making setts to pave the streets of towns and cities, a small group of businessmen hastily obtained a licence to quarry in the area and formed the Glyn Ceiriog Granite Company.

The production of granite setts started almost immediately but, as the quarry was at the bottom of a steep-sided valley, a way had to be found of getting the granite to the Glyn Ceiriog terminus of the recently opened Glyn Valley Tramway, which had interchanges with both the Shropshire Union Canal and the Great Western Railway.

A small network of internal tramways, laid on the quarry floor, was soon to be joined by the first of several inclines down from higher levels being developed to the south, but there was no route out, through the site of a recently established gunpowder works. The granite setts would have to be taken across the river to the Llanarmon–Glyn Ceiriog road, situated high up on the steep north-western side of the valley, then by horse and cart to the GVT terminus at Glyn Ceiriog.

To gain access to this road, a short narrow-gauge tramway was built across lands owned by Ann Edwards and Thomas Jones. The tramway ran westwards from the quarry entrance for a short distance before turning sharply to cross the river via an accommodation bridge, from which it gradually climbed for some 330yds, turning as it did so towards Glyn Ceiriog, before terminating on the steep escarpment below the Llanarmon road.[7] Here, a short 25yd-long incline, with a winding drum at its head, brought the tramway up to the level of the road, at a point about 500yds southwest of Pont-y-Meibion junction. The location of the incline, alongside the Llanarmon road, and other parts of the trackbed can still be witnessed. The cost to the Glyn Ceiriog Slate Company of moving a ton of granite the two miles from the quarry to the GVT terminus at Glyn Ceiriog was 2s., which was exceptionally high.[8]

[7] Details ex. GVT Plans & Sections 1877–1878 by Henry Dennis. Shropshire Record Office Ref. DP 483.

[8] Details from evidence given by Elias Griffith to the Parliamentary Committee examining the GVT Bill on 6th May 1885.

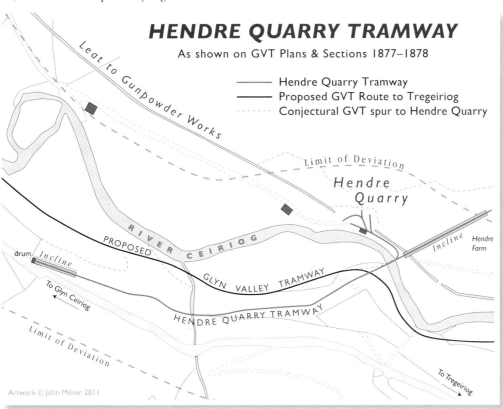

HENDRE QUARRY TRAMWAY
As shown on GVT Plans & Sections 1877–1878

——— Hendre Quarry Tramway
——— Proposed GVT Route to Tregeiriog
- - - - Conjectural GVT spur to Hendre Quarry

Leat to Gunpowder Works

Limit of Deviation

Hendre Quarry

drum Incline
PROPOSED
RIVER CEIRIOG
To Glyn Ceiriog
GLYN VALLEY TRAMWAY
HENDRE QUARRY TRAMWAY
Incline
Hendre Farm
Limit of Deviation
To Tregeiriog

Artwork © John Milner 2011

Extract redrawn from the 1877–1878 Plans & Sections of the Glyn Valley Tramway, which clearly shows the Hendre Quarry Tramway then in existence. The incline to the right of the quarry remained in use throughout the life of the quarry.

Left: *The course of the Hendre Tramway, still clearly visible today, looking from where it crossed the watercourse that runs down to the river towards Pont-y-Meibion.*

Right: *The base of the short incline at the end of the level in the left-hand photograph, which climbs up to the Llanarmon–Glyn Ceiriog road. At the top there was a 'winding drum', and transshipment wharf, located where today there is a lay-by in the road.*

© John Milner 2010

At this time, the estimated possible output of the quarry was 100,000 tons per annum, but the cost of transportation out of the valley was a serious obstacle in the way of its development. In order to compete on price with other granite companies, the company had to find a low cost means of getting the granite out of the Ceiriog valley and onto the main-line railway and canal networks. Transshipping the setts by hand, first into the carts on the Llanarmon Road, and then into GVT wagons at the terminus was very labour intensive, making the cost of moving them the two miles from the quarry, very high.

Although many proposals to improve the situation were made, the Hendre Quarry tramway remained in use until the late 1880s, when the GVT was eventually extended from Glyn Ceiriog to Hendre Quarry, as a result of the passing of the Glyn Valley Tramway Act 1885.

Postscript

With the exception of the Hendre Quarry Tramway, the other tramways and proposals described in this overview, although geographically peripheral to the Ceiriog Valley, have been included to help the reader appreciate the industrial context into which the Glyn Valley Tramway arrived in the early 1870s.

Other early horse-drawn tramways, such as the Deeside Tramway (1850s–post World War II) and Oernant Tramway (1856–1900s) were located in the neighbouring Dee Valley.

Many readers may consider that the Ceiriog Valley terminates where the aqueduct and viaduct straddle it at Chirk, but the GVT had no such boundary and throughout its early history, as a horse tramway, its interchanges with both the canal and railway networks were over the border in Shropshire, England, where many of the early proposals for a transport route up the valley had originated.

Chapter 3

The Tramway Pioneers

It had been recognised, when the Cambrian Slate Company (No.323) was formed in 1854 that, in order for it to succeed, it would need a more reliable means of transporting its finished slate down the valley, than by packhorse picking its way over the slow and arduous route to Aqueduct Wharf, Froncysllte, in the Dee Valley. This would be equally important to the future exploitation of the other mineral wealth locked in the geology of the Ceiriog Valley, principally granite, chinastone and silica, in order to market it at a competitive price. As related in chapter 1, the slate company began negotiating with the Wem & Bronygarth Turnpike Trust in 1857, to lay a tramway on the side of its new road, which was to be built up the valley, but without success. Many other schemes were proposed until eventually the Glyn Valley Tramway Act 1870 was passed, which paved the way forward for the construction of the tramway. However, it was to be many more years before an efficient and profitable route, with interchanges with both the canal and rail national networks, was available to the quarry proprietors and others, anxious to exploit the mineral resources of the valley.

There was no single man of passion to drive the tramway project forward and no generous benefactors to keep the company out of debt; only a few individuals with a simple desire to get the job done. Among these were the Glyn Valley Tramway Company's Engineer, Henry Dennis, the Parliamentary Agent, Theodore Martin, and the Engineer to the Shropshire Union Railways & Canal Company, George Robert Jebb.

Henry Dennis

A Cornish Captain of Welsh Industry

Henry Dennis was born at Bodmin, Cornwall, and was the fifth of eight children born to Mathias and Maria Dennis. Mathias was a successful dealer in textile fabrics and a clothier, but he died in 1831 at the early age of 46. Henry was educated at Bodmin Grammar School and started his career as an articled pupil under the Borough surveyor, Henry Coom. Upon completion of his training, he left to join the engineering staff of the Cornwall Railway Company. In the early 1850s, he was invited to North Wales by John Taylor & Sons, international mining engineers and agents with a base in Flintshire, to survey and supervise the construction of the 3ft-gauge Oernant Tramway, built to connect the Moel-y-Faen, Clogau and other slate quarries up the Horseshoe Pass to the Pentrefelin Slab & Slate Works, Llangollen, located alongside the Llangollen branch of the Ellesmere Canal. He then went out to Spain, where John Taylor and Sons was opening up the Pozo Ancho (Linares Lead Mining Co.), Fortuna and Alamillos lead mines in the Linares district of the Province of Jaén and it was here that he was to encounter the mining branch of his profession, which was

John Taylor 1779–1863

Mining entrepreneur and engineer of Flintshire, and founder of John Taylor & Son, international mining engineers. Although not connected with the GVT, it was he who invited Henry Dennis to join his company in North Wales.

Photo by Dr Ann Pulsford of Portrait in Tavistock Subscription Library.

Henry Dennis (19th March 1825–24th June 1906)

In 1857, when Henry Dennis entered into a partnership with Walter Henry Glennie, they became consultants to the Cambrian Slate Co. Ltd, which was embarking on major developments of the slate quarries in the Nant Lafar Valley, high above Glyn Ceiriog. The company was proposing to spend in excess of £20,000 on plant, tools, equipment, buildings, quarry tramways and inclines, to produce an annual output of 4,000 tons of finished slate. This was the beginning of the long association of Henry Dennis with the industries of the Ceiriog Valley. In the same year Henry Dennis and the Cambrian Slate Co. Ltd became involved in negotiations with the Wem & Bronygarth Turnpike Trust, to lay a private tramway on the side of its proposed road down the valley, to connect the Cambrian Quarries with the national rail and canal networks near Chirk. This appears to have been the very first scheme for 'Rails to Glyn Ceiriog'. It failed, but Henry Dennis became involved in several more schemes before the Glyn Valley Tramway was eventually built in the 1870s, with him as the GVT company's engineer.

Dennis Ruabon Ltd

to determine much of his future career. John Taylor and Sons was one of the most successful mining engineering companies of the Victorian era and by the 1900s, was managing seven Spanish mining companies and had mining interests all over the world, including the gold fields of India.

Henry Dennis returned to North Wales to become manager of a colliery owned by John Taylor & Sons, at Bryn-yr-Owen, near Rhosllanerchrugog, Ruabon. In 1857, he relinquished this post but maintained his connection with John Taylor & Sons, by continuing as the Colliery Agent until its closure, in order to enter into partnership,with his brother-in-law to be, Walter Henry Glennie, trading as Dennis & Glennie, Ruabon, surveyors and mining engineers. At this time, he was residing locally at *Hafod-y-bwch*, on the north side of Johnstown.

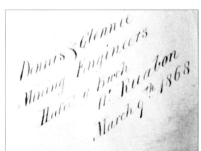

Collection: John Milner

In 1859, he had married Susan Hicks Stephens (Feb. 1831–April 1891), from Lostwithiel, Cornwall and they had six children, but three died in their infancy, leaving Susan Dewen (31st Jan. 1862–?), Henry Dyke (10th Nov. 1863–26th June 1944) and Walter Pen (26th Dec. 1864–16th Dec. 1928). A memorial to Susan Hicks Stephens, in the form of a stained glass window, is to be found in Ruabon parish church. In 1860, his then partner, Walter Glennie, married his wife's sister, Lucy. Both Henry Dyke and Walter Pen Dennis followed in their father's footsteps and became mining engineers, taking over the Dennis empire after their father's death in 1906.

In 1866, Messrs Dennis & Glennie saw an opportunity to make good use of the waste tips which surrounded the multitude of old coal pits and shafts on a 50-acre site near Rhosllanerchrugog, which, as well as containing coal waste, contained high proportions of brick clay. They became proprietors of the Ponkey Brick & Tile Works and built a modern well-laid-out works to extract clay from the waste tips to make bricks, tiles and other kiln goods. It was soon obvious that the clay from the coal waste tips was of an inferior quality and although the company struggled on for many years, the enterprise was not a success.

The Dennis & Glennie partnership ended in 1870, after which Henry Dennis traded alone and sank Legacy Colliery at Rhosllanerchrugog, which he worked for a few years. He became a formidable figure in local industries, investing in many, as well as taking up directorships, and was in the forefront in trying to obtain a better transport connection to the outside world for the Cambrian Slate Quarry and the other industries of the Ceiriog Valley.

He was managing director of the Wrexham & Acton Collieries Co., and the Ruabon Coal & Coke Co., which was styled as '*Coal Merchants to Her Majesty and the Royal Family*'; the engineer for, and a director of, both the Minera Lead Mining Co. and the Snailbeach Lead Mining Co.; becoming the manager of the latter in 1871 and surveying the line for the Snailbeach District Railways in 1872. He was the managing director of the Cefn Freestone Quarries, chairman of the Westminster Brymbo Coal & Coke Co., the United Westminster & Wrexham Collieries Ltd, the Wrexham Colliery Co. and many others.

While his main interest was in mining, he was also involved in the development of water and gas supplies and was chairman and director of the local Rhos Gas Co., the Ruabon Water Co., Ruabon Reservoir Company and, further away, the Barmouth Gas Co., Dolgelley Gas & Coal Co. and Dysynni Gas Co. (Towyn, Merionethshire, and home of the Talyllyn Railway). He also acted as engineer to the Wrexham District Tramway Co., for which he produced the Plans & Sections in 1872–73. Apart from his personal involvement in various companies, he advised and undertook survey work for numerous mineral workings on estates in the North and Mid Wales region. As well as his industrial activities, he also invested his wealth in property, mainly agricultural.

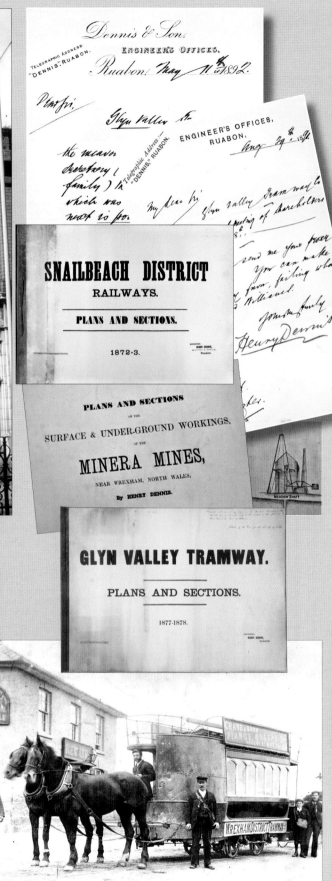

The imposing offices, in the High Street, Ruabon, of Dennis & Sons, once the hub of the Dennis empire, employing some 10,000 people in the locality, in a sad state prior to demolition. From 1891, the Glyn Valley Tramway was administered from these offices.

Courtesy: Venerable Bill Pritchard

Above right: *Sample Dennis letterheads of the 1890s period.* Middle right: *Some of the covers of many books of Plans & Sections for projects surveyed and drawn by Henry Dennis, including those for the Glyn Valley Tramway.*

Collection: John Milner,
Denbighshire Records Office
and Shropshire Archives

Henry Dennis acted as Engineer to the Wrexham District Tramway Co., for which he produced the Plans & Sections in 1872–73. The horse-drawn tram is photographed outside the New Inn, Johnstown, c1900.

Wrexham Archives Service

By 1880, Henry Dennis had acquired an interest in another brickworks, this time situated adjacent to the Ruabon New Colliery near his former home at *Hafod-y-bwch*. Both the brickworks and colliery were owned by the Ruabon Coal Company, which also owned the Brandie Coke Works to the west. Due to the trade recession, this company was in liquidation in June 1879, and the brickworks, colliery and coke works were purchased by the newly constituted Ruabon Coal & Coke Company, of which Henry Dennis was the managing director. The clay produced bricks of a distinctive red colour and this Hafod works became known as the 'Red Works'; it had 24 coal-fired 'beehive' kilns and eventually employed over 300 men. It produced the famous Dennis Ruabon Red Bricks and Tiles and continued to do so until recent times.

Henry Dennis established another new company, the Ruabon Glazed Brick & Fireclay Company, when he took over the Pant Brickworks, in Rhosllanerchrugog, in 1886, and extended it to produce a large range of glazed and enamelled kiln goods. In 1891, it was reported that the works, covering about 12 acres, had '*35 kilns of all kinds and varieties*' and 380 employees. The clay '*raised from the company's own pits*' burnt to a rich buff colour and the output included '*white and coloured glazed and enamelled bricks, buff facing bricks and terracotta, encaustic, tessellated and other fancy tiles*'.[1] A good proportion of the output was glazed white to satisfy the Victorian striving for hygienic surfaces, both in the home and public places, which led to this Dennis works being known locally as the 'White Works'.

Courtesy: Venerable Bill Pritchard

His various business concerns were all administered from his imposing and spacious offices in the High Street, Ruabon, with an equally enviable telephone number – 'Ruabon 1'. Naturally, the building was constructed in 'red' and 'white' Ruabon brick, incorporating decorative terracotta work for which both Hafod and Pant Brickworks were well known. Double mahogany doors opened into an entrance hall where an attractive mosaic floor, with the word 'DENNIS' boldly embedded in it, left visitors in no doubt as to where they were. A solid mahogany staircase led to the first floor and all the doors were in the same timber to match. Various sections of the ground floors were enriched with different tile patterns, demonstrating the variety available from the Dennis enterprises. The walls were decorated with panelling of glazed tiles, as were all the corridors in the building. On the first floor were several drawing offices, other administrative offices and a Board Room with a Spanish mahogany table.[2] This building served as the Head Office for all the Dennis companies and, post 1891, as that of the Glyn Valley Tramway Company, until the tramway closed in 1935. The building was demolished many years ago and all the paperwork destroyed.

[1] *Life in the Victorian Brickyards of Flintshire and Denbighshire* by Andrew Connolly published Gwasg Carreg Gwalch, Llanwrst, 2003.

[2] Account by Mrs Esther M. Jones, 1981, published in *Remembering Ruabon* by T.W. Pritchard. Bridge Books 2000.

Pant Brickworks 1906. Note the extent of this works, with the neat rows of 'beehive' kilns, the railway on the left of the illustration and the horse-drawn tramway on the right.

Courtesy: Ven. Bill Pritchard

At the zenith of his career, Henry Dennis had 27 various concerns under his wing, providing employment for over 10,000 people. For a period, he was chairman of the North Wales Coalowners' Association and their Mutual Indemnity Co., and represented the coalowners on the Coal Trade Conciliation Board. He was elected an Associate Member of the Institution of Civil Engineers on 31st May 1881 and in 1901 became President of the Mining Association of Great Britain. As recognition of '*his wonderful business aptitude and as a pioneer and captain of industry*', he was made one of the first Aldermen of Denbighshire County Council in 1888.

He served as a Justice of the Peace at Ruabon Magistrates' Court. He was very much Conservative in his political views but, placing his business interests to the forefront, he was never inclined towards standing as a candidate for Parliament.

From 1878, the family home was *New Hall Mansion* and farm, at Ruabon, which Henry purchased from Col. Cornwallis West. His hobby was breeding Shropshire sheep, for which he acquired a reputation, exhibiting at agricultural shows and even supplying them to Prince Bismarck, the eldest son of Otto von Bismarck, the German Chancellor! Local historian George Lerry relates that Henry was also a horse lover and once took two of his young children, who then had ponies, and rode with them all the way from Ruabon to Bodmin! He also recalls that Henry was full of energy and, over a cup of black coffee and a cigar, he would deal with all his correspondence and issue orders to his various works managers, who would be summoned to attend before 8.30 a.m., at which time precisely the whole of the Dennis family were expected to sit down for breakfast. According to George Lerry, Dennis appears to have had a particular fascination with the Emperor Napoleon, as *New Hall* contained several paintings of important events in the Emperor's life:

> '*On the walls of the rooms on the top landing of his home, where his sons slept, huge paintings of Napoleon crossing the Alps and of other outstanding events in the career of the French emperor were hung.*'

Dennis was taken ill after a motorcar journey, in his six-cylinder Napier, from *New Hall*, Ruabon, to his other residence, *Lanival*, at Bodmin, Cornwall, and died there on 24th June 1906. He was buried at Wrexham Cemetery (Grave No.02349) on 27th July and it was reported that 5,000 people attended, which says something about his popularity in the district. Shortly before his death, he had

Henry Dyke Dennis
10th November 1863
–26th June 1944

He was the elder son of Henry Dennis. After his father's death in 1906, he took over at the helm of the Dennis empire, which he ran until his own departure in 1944.

Dennis Ruabon Ltd

This mural on a wall of the Dennis Ruabon Hafod brickworks illustrates the extraordinary design and manufacturing expertise of Henry Dennis' workforce. The motto 'Industria Ditat' translates as 'Industry Enriches'. Close examination of this mural reveals the portrayal of various aspects of industry.

© John Milner 2010

been involved in finalising plans to sink shafts at Gresford Colliery, the sinking of which was undertaken by his United Westminster & Wrexham Colliery Company. After his passing, the Dennis business 'empire' was taken over by his elder son, Dyke Dennis, who was succeeded, on 26th June 1944, by Henry's grandson, Patrick Gill Dyke Dennis, who as 'captain' set about modernising the Hafod Brickworks, an action that probably secured its future. While many of Henry's business interests gradually succumbed to the changes in our industrial base, the Hafod Brickworks survived all the storms over the years. However, brick production had largely ended by the 1970s and thereafter the company concentrated on the manufacture of its red quarry tiles. In 2001, Dennis Ruabon Ltd became Dennis Ruabon Tiles Ltd and in 2003 it took over the Hawkins quarry tile business. Although production has since ceased new owners, Ruabon Sales Ltd, are still trading in tiles.

Some understanding of the impact that Henry Dennis made upon the industrial scene of the North East Wales area in particular came immediately after his burial, on 27th July 1906, when representatives of Hafod Colliery, Hafod Brickworks, Pant Brickworks, Snailbeach Lead Mining Co., Westminster Colliery, Wrexham and Acton Colliery and The United Minera Mining Co. called a meeting, at the Imperial Hotel, Wrexham, of all interested parties, 'to consider a proposal for perpetuating the memory of the late Mr Henry Dennis'. The response was overwhelming, not just from local companies, but from the workforce as well. Contributions of 100 guineas from each of Henry Dennis' sons brought the initial fund to about £1,000, and the Henry Dennis Memorial Fund was formed: 'To purchase Tickets of Admission for sick Workmen to the Men's Convalescent Home at Rhyl, or similar Institutions'. This was later extended to other venues further afield, such as Buxton and Harrogate. It had been suggested that a statue should be erected, but it was thought that the benevolent aspect of the fund was a much more appropriate way of remembering the pioneering spirit of Henry Dennis. The fund was still operational 63 years later.

The GVT Co. was not in the forefront of the move to honour this great industrialist, who had been both their engineer and a director for long periods during his career, although the company probably subscribed. The fund continued to operate until August 1970, after which it appears to have been terminated.

This concludes the background to the central figure, Henry Dennis, a truly remarkable man, who was to have enormous influence on the way that many industries in the Wrexham–Ruabon area were to develop over the years, including those in the Ceiriog Valley and, in particular, the first thirty years of the development of their only means of transport, the Glyn Valley Tramway, which was constructed to serve them.

Above: Henry Dennis and his wife, Susan Hicks, were buried in a family grave in Wrexham Cemetery. This neglected memorial is the sole reminder of a man who was once the Wrexham area's largest employer.

© John Milner 2010

The inaugural notice sent out by the committee that was formed, after Henry Dennis died, to establish a memorial fund to perpetuate his memory. Note that the Glyn Valley Tramway Co. was not at the forefront of this initiative.

Collection: John Milner

Sir Theodore Martin CB KCB KCVO

Personal Friend of Queen Victoria

Of all the landowners in the Ceiriog Valley, (Sir) Theodore Martin (1816–1909) was certainly the most outstanding as a man with personality and influence in high society. He was born in Edinburgh on 16th September 1816. His father, James Martin, was a solicitor and his mother, Mary, was the daughter of James Reid, a ship owner. It was only natural that he should follow in his father's footsteps and he practised as a solicitor in Edinburgh up to 1846, after which he moved to London where he specialised as a parliamentary solicitor, developing over the years an extensive and most profitable business, largely piloting private Bills through Parliament for many of the railway and industrial developments of the day. Through his great interest in drama, he became fascinated with the actress Helena Saville Faucit and eventually married her on 25th August 1851. In 1852 the newly-weds bought a house at 31 Onslow Square, London, where they cultivated a large social circle of friends, from the elite of Victorian society.

From his early days in Edinburgh, and then writing under the pseudonym *Bon Gaultier*, he had a very active literary interest, and undertook the translation of poetry of many well-known Continental poets. He was described as being one of the most accomplished as well as one of the most versatile men of letters of his times – essayist, poetic translator and parodist. His literary fame came when, on 14th November 1866, he was summoned to an audience with Queen Victoria, who commissioned him to write the biography of her late husband, the Prince Consort. *The Life of His Royal Highness the Prince Consort* was eventually published in five volumes in 1880, by which time Theodore Martin had become a personal friend and confidential servant of the Queen. He was rewarded for his services with a CB in 1878 and a KCB in 1880, followed by a KCVO in 1896. After Queen Victoria's death he published his personal recollections of her, entitled *Queen Victoria as I knew her*.

Sir Theodore Martin CB, KCB, KCVO 1816–1909

Sir Theodore Martin lived at 'Bryntysilio', Llangollen, and was Parliamentary solicitor for the GVT and other railway proposals in the Ceiriog Valley. He was very involved in local industrial development, a notable author, a personal friend of Queen Victoria and biographer of the Prince Consort.

The level of trust that the Queen Victoria placed in Sir Theodore is illustrated in a letter that she wrote to him on 29th May 1870, regarding her thoughts on Women's Rights:

'It is a subject which makes the Queen so furious that she cannot contain herself. God created men and women different – then let them remain each in their own position.'

He was also friendly with Sir Daniel Gooch (1816–1889), who was, in Theodore Martin's own words *'inseparably connected with the establishment and growth of railways and of ocean telegraphic communication'*. Daniel Gooch became locomotive superintendent of the Great Western Railway under Brunel and was responsible for the design of the locomotives that were so unmistakably GWR. In 1864 he became a Member of Parliament, which is when he probably had contact with Theodore Martin at Westminster. Daniel Gooch was also heavily involved in the laying of the first transatlantic telegraph line in 1866, using Brunel's famous ship, the *Great Eastern*, and became chairman of the Great Western Railway Company. Theodore Martin wrote an 'Introductory Note' for the publication of *The Diaries of Sir Daniel Gooch*, published in 1892.

Theodore Martin became involved in many of the industrial and railway proposals and developments in North East Wales, including those in the Ceiriog Valley, where, in 1854, he joined Alexander Reid, Robert Roy, and others in the newly established Cambrian Slate Company.

On 23rd August 1889, Queen Victoria embarked on a five-day visit to North Wales, accompanied by Prince and Princess Henry of Battenberg. She is here seen receiving an address from the Town Clerk of the Corporation of Wrexham. On 26th August she 'took tea' with her congenial acquaintances, Sir Theodore and Lady Martin, at their home, 'Bryntysilio', where she was entertained by the Llangollen Choral Society.

Collection: John Milner

On the morning of 26th August 1889, Prince and Princess (Beatrice) Henry of Battenberg, along with Princess Alice, and accompanied by Miss Phipps and Major Bigge, travelled by Royal Train from Llandderfel to Ruabon. At the Wynnstay Colliery the Princesses, dressed in white cloaks and wearing dust caps, descended the shaft and travelled to the coalface where Princess Beatrice, seen here, tried her hand at winning coal.

Collection: John Milner

A Royal Occasion and Tea with Sir Theodore

(Visited by the late Queen in 1889')

'Bryntysilio' was originally a small cottage named 'Braich y Gwynt', near Llangollen, and had been purchased by Sir Theodore and Lady Martin in 1865. By 1870 it had been greatly enlarged to become a stuccoed Italianate villa for their country retreat in the Dee Valley and is now a Grade II Listed Building used as an Outdoor Education Centre.

Collection: John Milner

In 1866, he acted as Parliamentary Agent for the promotion of 'The Glyn Valley Railway' and later 'The Glyn Valley Tramway'; he became much involved with the latter and later became chairman. He established firm roots as a landowner in the Cciriog Valley when, in 1869, he purchased the Glyn Estate from the trustees of Alexander Reid, who had died in 1866. This estate included the land occupied by the Cambrian Slate Quarry.

Sir Theodore's contribution to the development of the Ceiriog Valley slate industry was invaluable; he was a very experienced lawyer, a Parliamentary Agent, with access to members of the select committees of Westminster, and moved within a very influential circle of friends. Although he was resident over in the Dee Valley, he appears to have been very much part of the community in the Ceiriog Valley, and one can surmise that many events and developments appear to have come about as the result of someone, somewhere, being in the right place with the right contacts; this someone was more than likely Sir Theodore Martin.

In 1889, Sir Theodore Martin, despite being burdened with all the problems of the Glyn Valley Tramway Co., of which he was then chairman, had due reason to be jubilant; not from any act of goodwill by the GVT, but because of another event in his personal life. Back in 1861, he and his wife had spent the summer and autumn at a small cottage, *Braich y Gwynt*, later renamed *Bryntysilio* (The hill of St. Tysilio), in Llangollen. In 1865, they bought it and enlarged it to the point where one could describe it as being 'fit for a queen'. On 26th August 1889 it was indeed visited by one, Queen Victoria. While on her short tour of Wales, she travelled by train from Ruabon to Llangollen, and 'took tea' with her congenial acquaintances, the Martins, while being entertained by twenty members of the Llangollen Choral Society. It was reported afterwards that she was gratified by the loyalty shown by the Welsh people, and had thoroughly enjoyed the beauty of the scenery. What a pity that Sir Theodore, as GVT chairman, did not persuade her to visit the Ceiriog Valley and travel on the Glyn Valley Tramway – Royal patronage and perhaps even a 2' 4½"-gauge Royal Train!

In his 92nd year it was reported that:

> *'Sir Theodore Martin, the veteran poet and littérateur ... came to London this week from his Welsh residence. In an interview he said that the increasing years only added to his zest for the enjoyment of life, but he was saddened by the outlook from the present to the future.'*

He mourned the passing of the Victorian era and questioned what had happened to the giants of politics and literature. *'Men of today, are,'* he said, *'as* [Thomas] *Carlyle phrases it, intrinsically and extrinsically small men.'* What would he make of life today?

Sir Theodore's wife, Helena, died on the 31st October 1898 and he died on 31st August 1909; both are interred at Brompton Cemetery, London. As he had no children to inherit, his estate was broken up into individual lots and placed on the market.

Work is the true elixir of life. The busiest man is the happiest man.

Sir Theodore Martin

George Robert Jebb

Canal and Railway Engineer

George Robert Jebb was appointed Engineer to the Shropshire Union Railways & Canal Company in 1869, which position he retained until 1919. In 1871, as one of the conditions of the SUR&C Co. providing the additional capital that was required to construct the Glyn Valley Tramway, he was given direct control over its construction. It was, undoubtedly, his influence that moulded the tramway in all aspects, according to the established customs and practices of the canal company; from the architecture to the rolling stock and to the way that it was operated.

He was born at Baschurch, Shropshire, on the 30th November 1838 and was the son of John Jebb, a farmer who, by 1851, was the stationmaster at Baschurch. From 1854 to 1858 he served his pupilage under Alexander Mackintosh, M. Inst. C.E., (1820–1890), at that time the Engineer in charge of the 'Chester lines' of the Great Western Railway Company who, later, prepared the plans and estimates for the building of Wem & Bronygarth Road (1860) and the proposed Glyn Valley Railway (1866). In 1859, Jebb was appointed Resident Engineer on the construction of the Wrexham & Minera Railway and also the Bryn-yr-Owen Branch Railway, to the Bryn-yr-Owen Colliery in the Ruabon Coalfield, which was owned by John Taylor & Sons, and of which Henry Dennis had been manager. Between 1862 and 1869 he was engaged in a similar capacity on other railways in the area, including the Wrexham & Minera Extension Railway and, in nearby Flintshire, the Mold and Treuddyn Railway.

G. R. Jebb, Esq., 1842.

*George Robert Jebb
1838–1927*

As a much respected railway engineer, George Jebb was appointed Engineer to the Shropshire Union Railways & Canal Co. in 1869 and was responsible for overseeing the construction of the Glyn Valley Tramway in 1872.

© Institution of
Civil Engineers

For a time during 1863, he was in Galicia, where he was responsible for planning the course of the 20-mile Lemberg–Czernowitz Railway in part of the old Austrian Empire (now the Ukraine), which was built by Thomas Brassey, the celebrated railway contractor born in Chester.

In 1873, in order for the SUR&C Company to compete with the rapid expansion of railways, Jebb suggested that the length of canal from Llangollen to Weston, in rural Shropshire, should be converted to a 2ft 4in narrow-gauge railway and extended to Wem. This would have given the Ceiriog Valley industries a direct connection, via the GVT, into these areas, but nothing came of this suggestion.

Jebb had a long-standing friendship with Francis William Webb (1836–1906), engineering supremo of the London & North Western Railway, based at Crewe. On two occasions, in 1874 and 1879, he approached his friend to prepare a suitable design of locomotive for use on the GVT. Unfortunately, these proposals have not been located.

As well as his position with the SUR&C Co., on 1st March 1875, he accepted an appointment as Engineer to the Birmingham Canal Company at a salary of £250 per annum and, on his retirement from that company in 1912, became a member of its Management Committee. This canal company controlled a large network of canals (the Birmingham Canals Navigation) built at three different levels and connected in several places by a short series of locks, whose efficient working depended on an adequate supply of water on the top level being maintained by huge pumping engines, which lifted water back up from the lower levels. Jebb was responsible for replacing the original pumps, which had been supplied by Messrs. Boulton and Watt, in the latter part of the eighteenth and the early part of the nineteenth centuries, with 'modern' pumps.

At Ellesmere Port, where the Shropshire Union Canal connected directly into the river Mersey via locks, Jebb was responsible for the design and construction of deep-water quays, docks and warehouses and, in various parts of North Wales, the Potteries, and South Staffordshire, for numerous canal and railway improvements. He was appointed a member of the Upper Mersey Navigation Commission upon its formation in 1876, and was subsequently its chairman for 18 years. This was the period during which the Manchester Ship Canal was being promoted, designed and built, to give a direct route for sea-going vessels into the heart of Manchester, which was situated on the River Irwell, a tributary of the river Mersey.

In 1872 he was elected a member of The Institution of Civil Engineers, a Member of the Council in 1902, and vice-president in 1912, but resigned his membership of the Council in 1915, preferring not to be nominated for the office of president. He contributed to The Institution a Paper on '*A Plea for Better Country Roads*', which was read in 1906; perhaps inspired by the poor state of the roads in the Ceiriog Valley! He was admitted to the fellowship of the Royal Society of Arts in 1890 and, having a keen interest in Natural Science, particularly botany, he was an original member of the Chester Society of Nature Science. In 1912, he became president of the Smeatonian Society of Engineers, an elite Society for Civil Engineers constituted in 1771, not as a formal learned society, but as a dining club that would meet fortnightly during the London season, to provide: '*an opportunity for engineers to meet in a friendly atmosphere to discuss their work and all manner of topics*'. One of the founder members reported that: '*Conversation, argument and a social communication of ideas and knowledge ... were, at the same time, the amusement and the business of the meetings.*' [4]

[4] John Smeaton FRS, by Skempton, published TTL 1981

[5] Minutes of Proceedings Institution of Civil Engineers, Vol. clxv page 375, Obituary George Robert Jebb.

Jebb lived in Fairyfield House, Newtown Road, Great Barr (Birmingham) for more than 20 years, before retiring to Bucklebury Common, near Reading, where he died on 16th February 1927, after a brief illness.[5]

George Robert Jebb, the SUR&C Co. engineer, should not be confused with Richard George Jebb, The Lythe, Ellesmere, who was one of the first GVT Directors appointed in March 1873, nor with his son Arthur T. Jebb, who followed him onto the Board after his death in 1878.

A London & North Western Railway Claughton Class locomotive No. 37, built at Crewe Works in 1917, was named 'G.R. Jebb' after him. It is here seen in its London Midland & Scottish Railway livery, renumbered 5930. All three of the pioneers described in this chapter had locomotives named after them.

Collection: John Milner

Chapter 4

The Horse Tramway Era
1872–1876

With the SUR&C Co. Executive Committee meeting at Bala on 28th June 1871, having agreed to provide the GVT Co. with its £5,000 shortfall on capital, subject to its own engineer, George Robert Jebb, having full control of the construction of the new tramway and the SUR&C Co. having the sole right to operate it, the way was now clear to proceed with its construction. Although the SUR&C Co. had agreed to act as the sole operators of the tramway, the rates payable to them by the GVT Co. for so doing had not yet been agreed and in the October 1871 meeting Mr Cawkwell and Mr Robertson were empowered to decide upon an appropriate rate. At the same meeting, it was decided to invite tenders for the construction of the tramway. After some twelve years of proposals and failures, the Glyn Valley Tramway was at last close to becoming a reality, although precariously on the edge of failure through being starved of finance, restricted by being horse-drawn instead of by steam locomotive and having to work a very steep route up from Pontfaen towards the canal interchange at Gledrid. The latter route had been imposed upon the company by the stubbornness of Col. Robert Myddelton Biddulph, who had refused to allow the tramway to run through his Chirk Castle Estate to Chirk.

In March 1872, the first shareholders' meeting of the GVT Company was held and, with the election of Directors, the Company was constituted. Lord Trevor, Brynkinalt Estate (chairman), R. Myddelton Biddulph, Chirk Castle Estate, Richard Steele Perkins, Chirk, Richard George Jebb, Ellesmere, and one nominee from the SUR&C Co., Alfred Wragge, its company secretary, were appointed directors. The GVT company secretary was John Jones, a solicitor with Longueville, Jones & Co. of Oswestry, who was also clerk to the trustees of the Wem & Bronygarth Turnpike Road Trust, thus placing him in a precarious position with a potential conflict of interests. The address of Longueville, Jones & Co., Oswestry, became the registered office of the GVT Company.

Elias Griffith, local contractor and 'keeper' of the Hand Hotel, Chirk, having received the drawings and specifications for the tramway from Henry Dennis, wrote to the secretary of the GVT Co., on 23rd January 1872, confirming his Agreement, thus:

'I undertake to construct the Glyn Valley Tramway, including the purchase of Land, Works and Contingencies, and according to the plans and specifications submitted to me by Mr. Henry Dennis, the Company's Engineer, and subject to his Certificate for same, for the sum of £9,442 and to sign such formal contract as Mr. Jones, the Solicitor of the Company, may prepare.'

On 27th March 1872 the SUR&C Co. Executive authorized the first call of £2 per share on the 600 shares allotted to them, the shares being registered in the names of Lord Powis (183), Mr Moon

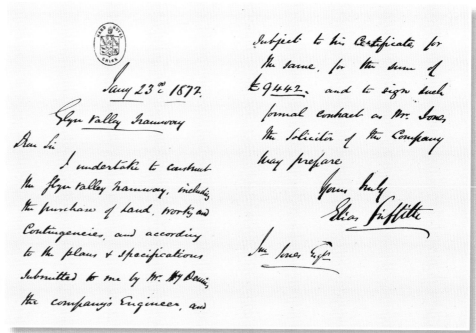

Right: The initial Letter of Intent from Elias Griffith, Hand Hotel, Chirk, undertaking to construct the Glyn Valley Tramway for £9,442, including the purchase of land. He was formally awarded the contract in May 1872 and it was signed on 10th July that year at an amended price of £9,552.

Shropshire Archives Ref. 800/41C/I

(183), Mr Stanton (184) and Alfred Wragge, company secretary (50). Even at this early stage, the GVT company was already experiencing financial problems, as it was reported at an Executive meeting of the SUR&C Co., on 24th April 1872, that it was considered desirable to proceed with the purchase of the land for the tramway, with the SUR&C Co. *'taking the risk as to the price of the rails'*, suggesting that difficulties were being experienced with sourcing rails for the track within the original contract estimate. Henry Dennis was acting as engineer and, on 25th May 1872, Elias Griffith was formally awarded the contract for building the tramway for an amended contract price of £9,552, which was now to cover the cost of labour and all materials, but excluded the purchase of the land as originally agreed. The contract was agreed following the assurance of Mr Roy, a director of the New Cambrian Slate Co., which was then promising the bulk of the traffic for the tramway with a resulting increase in trade for the canal, that the slate company would be duly registered, which it was on 8th June (No.6347).[1]

By this time, access to the land required had been agreed, and construction had been started, despite the contract not yet being formalised. The contract was eventually signed by Elias Griffith on 10th July 1872 and, on behalf of the GVT Co., by John Jones (Secretary), Henry Dennis (Engineer) and George R. Jebb (Engineer of the SUR&C Co.). Elias Griffith took on the entire construction from groundwork to laying the track at a price of £1,200/mile. Unfortunately, the drawings that accompanied the contract have not survived but, nevertheless, it provides a good insight into the way that the horse tramway was built:

[1] See *Slates from Glyn Ceiriog* by John Milner

[2] Penissa Glyn Lime Works refers to the limekilns above Herber Gate, the limestone being quarried near Penisa'r Glyn Farm and homestead, from whence it gets its name. The works was occupied by Richard Steele Perkins, one of the directors of the GVT Co., who died in 1876.

'The tramway be constructed from the canal at Gledrid to the Cambrian Slate Quarries ... with branches to the GWR at or near the Quinta Colliery Siding, also to the Bronygarth and to the Penissa Glyn Lime Works [2] ...The Contractor shall in a good and substantial manner and according to plans, sections and elevations, and a Specification already prepared by the Company's Engineer ... and in all respects to the satisfaction of the Engineer of the Company and the Engineer of the Shropshire Union Railways & Canal Company, to be certified under their respective hands, construct and make the several lines of tramway of a gauge of two feet four inches ... with all proper rails, plates, sleepers, pins, works, bridges, tunnels, drains, road and river diversions, fences, and accommodation works for land severed ... it being specially stipulated that the tramways and works are to be delivered by the Contractor in all respects complete and fit for traffic in slates, timber and general merchandize and produce, and that no claim for extra works or material

of any kind is to be made by the Contractor, unless in respect of Orders given under the hands of two directors of the Company. This Contract shall be fulfilled by the Contractor within 12 calendar months [amended from 18 months] *from the execution of this Contract'.*

The Specification allows some leeway in the latter requirement, by stating that the contract was to be completed within twelve calendar months of the contractor receiving notice in writing, from the engineer, to commence the work. In the event, as related above, Elias Griffith had started work the month before the contract was formally signed.

The detailed 19-page draft Specification for the contract, also signed by Elias Griffith on 10th July 1872, provides Henry Dennis with complete flexibility on design, while Elias was to undertake to do any alterations within the contract price. One example is that *'bridges throughout the line may be made either with arches or girders, as the Engineer may decide'*, regardless of any difference in cost. However, Elias was lucky in this respect as there was only one major bridge on the horse tramway, over the river at Pontfaen, and that was timber. However, the final contract did provide for the payment for any extra work requested by the GVT Company. All stone used for masonry had to be obtained from *'the quarries in the district and be of an efficient quality'*.

Fencing was specified as oak posts 7' 6" long x 4" x 4", fitted with iron hoops at the top to prevent splitting and *'well charred'* where buried in the ground, set 9' apart with four horizontal larch rails morticed and tenoned into the posts and an intermediate 4" x 1½" oak post. Field and level crossing gates were to be *'so hung that they shall shut and fasten themselves ... and to be painted three times in good oil colour, the last coat finished stone colour'*. Level crossing gates were to have the wording *'Shut the Gate'* painted on each side in 3" black lettering.

Quarter-mile posts were specified and were to be of oak, sawn square and charred below ground. They were to be fitted with a cast-iron number plate but, at the time the contract was signed, this had been amended to *'the mileage to be painted upon them in black figures'*, to reduce the cost.

The track was to be of a minimum weight of 21lb per yard in 21ft lengths, but was in practice 22lb per yard, with rail and ironwork quoted as being of the best Staffordshire or Shropshire boilerplate, *'free from blisters and scales and all other defects'*. Sleepers were to be of larch 4' 6" x 6" x 3" laid at 3ft intervals on a 9" bed of ballast of either stone or furnace cinders *'broken to a size so as to pass through a ring not exceeding 1½in diameter or gravel, sand, or ashes to be approved by the Engineer.*[3] Each rail on level crossings was to have oak guard timbers 10' x 7" x 6" fitted.

[3] The BoT records quote 4' 6" x 9" x 4½" as being the size of the sleepers, which is an acceptable dimension for light track.

The GVT Co., in the final version of the contract, became responsible for seeing that all land was acquired and handed over to the contractor, thus relieving Elias Griffith of that burden. However, the contract stated that should land not be made available in time then this *'... shall not constitute a valid excuse on the part of the Contractor unless so certified by the said Engineers'*. The Contract came with a few stings in its tail. Elias Griffith was to receive only £7,552 in cash with the balance of £2,000 in paid-up shares in the GVT Co. – a move, he stated in a letter to the GVT Co. in 1877, that he regretted as it was *'anything but a profitable one'*. Henry Dennis was to prepare a monthly statement of work completed and materials supplied by Elias Griffith, and to authorize part cash payment and part share issue, less 10% retained; records show that 20% of the payments was in fact retained. Three months after completion, Elias was to be paid half of the sum retained, with the balance paid at the end of twelve months – without any interest. Should the contract not be completed on time, there was a penalty clause of £50 per week for each week of overrun. Following completion of the tramway, Elias Griffith was to maintain it for a period of twelve months *'under the Rules and Regulations of the Company* [GVT]', for which he would be paid an additional £400 in cash.

Comparing the contract price of £9,552 for the tramway with the estimate of £39,987 for the construction of the earlier Glyn Valley Railway, which was to have been standard-gauge, one can see why it was so tempting to opt for a horse-drawn tramway on the route planned, although this was to prove to be a foolhardy and expensive decision in the haste to move things forward. In the first place, operation by horse-power only was totally inadequate for the volume of mineral traffic which materialised, secondly, the contract for construction did not cover many of the basic essentials required to make the line fully operational and, thirdly, the route from Pontfaen to Gledrid made for very uneconomical working due its steep gradients. The gradients from Pontfaen were 1 in 83/19/23/27/30 uphill, followed by a short level section (Upper Chirk Bank) and then 1 in 36/82/60 downhill to Gledrid Wharf.

The Track Gauge

The gauge for the track was stated as 2ft 4in in the Specification for the contract awarded to Elias Griffith, although when the tramway was built this officially became recorded as 2ft 4¼in. The gauge was written into the contract by hand after it had been drafted, suggesting that it was a last-minute decision by Henry Dennis. While it was exactly half the adopted standard-gauge for our national main lines, there is no evidence to suggest that this was Henry Dennis' reasoning for its selection. The Glyn Valley Tramway Act 1870 stated that the track was to be no wider than 4ft 8½in, nor narrower than 2ft, leaving the option wide open for the engineer to select either standard or narrow gauge.

Henry Dennis was later involved in promoting the Snailbeach District Railways, Shropshire, incorporated by Act of Parliament on 5th August 1873 and opened in 1877, and for which he also specified a gauge of 2ft 4in; that is how it was built and remained, although 2ft 3¾in was recorded in the W.G. Bagnall Ltd records, in connection with the Baldwin locomotives that the SDR Co. acquired after WW1. This was probably the 'fitted gauge'; the actual dimension over the wheel flanges rather than the actual track gauge. The SDR Co. was later to play an important role in the conversion of the GVT to steam power, thanks to it being of similar gauge. As related in chapter 2, closer to home was the Ifton-Rhyn Colliery tramway, which was purposely built to 2ft 4in gauge, as it was intended to connect it to the Glyn Valley Tramway in order to gain access for its coal output to national markets, utilising the GVT transshipment facilities onto the GWR at Preesgweene, as well as enabling a direct link to the Ceiriog Valley.

It is considered that the Quinta Tramway (pre-GVT) was also nominally 2ft 4in-gauge, as the Quinta and Trehowell collieries' company entered into an agreement with the GVT Co. to use the Trehowell–Gledrid Wharf section of its tramway, using the collieries' own wagons and horses. Had the Quinta Tramway been of a different gauge to that of the GVT, it seems very unlikely that the colliery company would have gone to considerable expense to re-gauge all the internal track and wagons at the colliery. Was this then perhaps the origin of the extra ¼in, making the adopted gauge 2ft 4¼in? However, one possibility is that the colliery wagons had loose wheels, enabling them to slide on the axles and adjust to a variation of gauge, as was the practice in several quarries. The first reference to the tramway having been built to a gauge of 2ft 4¼in appears in early Board of Trade documentation (as does 2ft 3in!) and was perpetuated throughout the horse tramway era. This then raises another question, as to where the additional ¼in came from when the line was converted to steam in 1887–88, making it 2ft 4½in-gauge. The answer in this instance is that, with the locomotives having thicker wheel flanges than the old wagons on the horse tramway, there was a need to retain the back-to-back dimension for check rails, thus dictating that the gauge be widened by ¼in. It is specified as such in the 1887 permanent way specifications, which further stated that the gauge on sharp curves was to be *laid a little slack as may be required*.[4] As a matter of interest, the Liverpool & Manchester railway was originally 4ft 8in, with the extra ½in appearing later, and a 2ft 4½in gauge tramway is recorded as having been in existence at Coalbrookdale, Shropshire.[5]

Today, the GVT's gauge of 2ft 4¼in is bandied about as being somewhat 'unique', but early industrial railways of 2ft 4in-gauge did appear countrywide and were catered for by manufacturers. Over recent years, there have been many theories promulgated to account for the use of the GVT

[4] See also chapter 7 page 189

[5] *Stone Blocks and Iron Rails* by Bertram Baxter, 1966.

2ft 4¹/₂in-gauge, but none has been adequately substantiated by confirmatory documentary evidence, so the search for the truth must continue.

The GVT Act of 1870 provided that the line to the canal could not be opened until an interchange had been made with the GWR mainline at Preesgweene. The only suitable access available to the GVT was across the Quinta/Trehowell collieries' land, on the Quinta Estate, which was owned by Thomas Barnes. He already had his tramway from the collieries and brickworks on the site, passing through a tunnel to a small interchange siding with the GWR on the Preesgweene side of Quinta Bridge, but following the failure of his Quinta Tramway down to the canal at Chirk Bank, his only solution for a connection with the national canal network was to use the new GVT metals between Trehowell Bridge and Gledrid Wharf, which were not sited on his land (see chapter 2). Barnes seized the opportunity to barter and refused the GVT Co. access to his Quinta Colliery site until a settlement was reached to allow him to use the GVT track to connect with the canal.

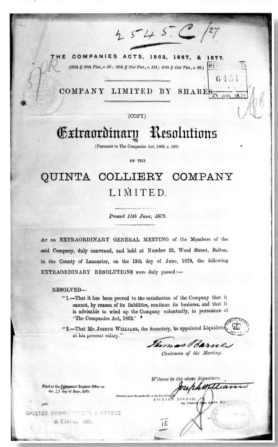

Notice of Extraordinary Resolutions passed at a meeting of the shareholders of the Quinta Colliery Co. Ltd, 13th June 1879, to wind up the company and appoint a liquidator, signed by Thomas Barnes, as Chairman of the meeting

National Archives

The result was an agreement that Barnes would have the use of the Trehowell Bridge–Gledrid Wharf section of the GVT, using his own horses, at a rate of 3d. per ton, thus giving him the connection that he wanted to the national canal network. In return the GVT Co. would have transshipment facilities onto the GWR at his new private standard-gauge sidings, which he was to build on his collieries' site to connect with the GWR mainline at Preesgweene, and for which he would be paid 3d. per ton transshipment cost. The GVT Co., perhaps, did not want to handle traffic on the short haul between Barnes' collieries and Gledrid Wharf, and Barnes, no doubt, had hoped that his traffic to the canal would equal that from the GVT to his exchange sidings, so that he would have his transport to the canal for nothing!

During the early 1850s, Thomas Barnes had bought the Quinta Estate from the family of the late Hon. Frederick West, who, in 1795, had married Maria Myddelton, one of the heiresses of the Chirk Castle Estate. West had sunk both the Quinta and Trehowell shafts, encouraged no doubt by the development of other mines in the area. In October 1865, the Quinta Colliery Co. Ltd, was registered with Thomas Barnes and his son, James Richardson Barnes, being amongst the major shareholders. A brick and tile works had also been developed on the site, and many properties stand in the area today built with the distinctive 'buff'-coloured brick from this works. On 15th November 1872 an Extraordinary General Meeting was called at which it was resolved to authorise the raising of additional capital and to incorporate the brick and tile works with the collieries. Two years later, the company was still trying to increase its capital, but it struggled on until 13th June 1879, when another Extraordinary General Meeting was called, at 25 Wood Street, Bolton, and the company placed into voluntary liquidation on account of it not being able to meet its liabilities. Thomas Barnes, as chairman of the meeting, signed the resolution. The Trehowell Colliery had been leased and worked by David Lomax since 1868 and it was from here that he also worked the Quinta Colliery thereafter. Trehowell Colliery was renamed the New Quinta Colliery, although it rarely appears to have been referred to as such. David Lomax, utilising the clay mined at the colliery, also operated the brickworks at Trehowell, making a range of kiln goods, which provided some important traffic up the valley for the GVT (see Chapter 6 pages 164, 166 and 167). [6]

[6] For further information on the Quinta and Trehowell Collieries see *A History of the Parishes of St. Martin's & Weston Rhyn* by C. Neville Hurdsman – Bridge Books 2003.

The GVT did not have proper transshipment arrangements with the GWR, as stipulated by its Act, until sometime in 1874, when standard-gauge sidings, described at the beginning of chapter 6, were installed at Trehowell Colliery, following an Agreement made between the GWR and the Quinta Colliery Co. in January that year. An array of sidings on the Quinta Colliery site, connected into the GWR main line underneath Quinta Bridge, and spread out to serve the collieries and brickworks on the Quinta site, as well as providing an interchange wharf for the GVT. Later, in 1888, at the time that the GVT Co. was about to abandon the Pontfaen–Gledrid line and a year before Trehowell Colliery was to close, a new Agreement was signed between the GWR and the Quinta Colliery (Trehowell) in respect of the sidings, which may have either been to extend the term of the Agreement or to procure their disconnection. The present whereabouts of these GWR Agreements has not been located, although they did exist in the Deed Office at Paddington in the 1960s, before dispersal.

The Cambrian Quarry Incline

The most expensive part of the Glyn Valley Tramway construction was to be a single-track incline up from the horse tramway terminus at Glyn Ceiriog to the Cambrian Slate Quarries, which was to be built on a strip of land, the upper part of which was covered in an agreement, dated 25th September 1872, to pay rent of £2 per annum to Theodore Martin of *Bryntisilio* and Edward Harper of Middle Temple, London, who were the owners of the Cambrian Quarries site. The cost of building the incline was originally estimated to be £2,237, which amounted to 18% of the total cost allocated for the entire tramway from the canal terminus at Gledrid to the Cambrian Slate Quarries. Why not double-track, as was the norm, so that it was self-acting, with the loaded wagons travelling down by gravity hauling the empty ones back up? As with all decisions on GVT expenditure, in these early years, it was a matter of keeping costs to a minimum. However, it would not have been economical to operate a single-track incline over such a long distance and common sense did prevail, because at a meeting of the SUR&C Co. Executive Committee, on 25th September 1872, Mr Jebb recommended that it was desirable that this incline had a double track and this was agreed, at an estimated additional cost of £280. A year later the incline had still not been built so, in order to complete this vital link, the New Cambrian Co. took up shares to the value of £280 in the SUR&C Co.! The directors no doubt felt that by taking up shares they could at least indirectly have some return via the SUR&C Co. on the traffic they were generating for the tramway and the canal. This extra work required on the incline proved to be far more expensive than first estimated. Elias Griffith was awarded a separate contract to double the incline for £400, but records suggest that additional costs brought the total to more than £550.

The Cambrian incline, when eventually completed, was 925yds long and rose some 300ft from its base. The gradients as stated in the 1870 Act were (ascending) 1 in 88, 13, 12, 5, 8, and 9.

Left: *Part of the lower section of the Cambrian Quarries incline, photographed in 1962, and looking up towards where the incline first crosses Nant Lafar.*

© David Ll. Davies

Right: *Facsimile created from a rubbing of an embossed tin plate on a cable drum, found near to the Cambrian Quarries winding house in the 1960s.*

Artwork © John Milner 2008

Right Bottom: *Plan showing the line of the Cambrian Quarries incline – from the 1936 Abstract of Title, when it was sold to Glyn Quarries Ltd after the closure of the tramway.*

Collection: John Milner

Loaded wagons were sent down daily in 'runs' of three wagons at a time, but the incline was so long that the men at the bottom could not easily visually communicate with the brakesman at the top. No operational details survive, but it is said that the man at the foot of the incline raised a white flag when the empties were ready, and that the brakesman at the top kept his eyes on him by means of a pair of binoculars. The incline to Rhosydd Quarry, Croesor, in Merionethshire, was worked in such a manner. What happened when the visibility was poor is not related, but presumably they would resort to an audio means of communication, such as a horn. Another solution may have been a 'mechanical device', with a wire running up the incline and connected to a bell or gong.

The other slate quarry above Glyn Ceiriog, the Wynne Quarry, was not connected to the GVT system until it was taken over by the Pant Glâs Slate & Slab Quarry Co. in 1886. This company built its own double incline, about 150 yards long with a gradient of 1 in 3, which connected the quarry with the GVT at the foot of the Cambrian incline.

It was not until 1899 that the top and bottom of the inclines at the Cambrian and Wynne Quarries were

The winding house at the head of the Cambrian Quarries incline about 1930, with Emlyn Davies and Harold Brown. The wire rope on the left is the 'under rope' going to the bottom of the drum and the one on the right the 'over rope' going to the top, so that loaded wagons going down draw the empties up.

Collection: Ceiriog Press

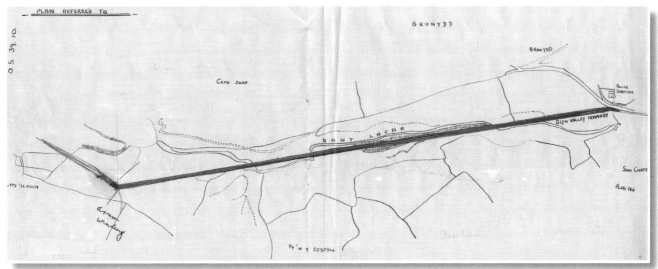

[7] For full details of the Cambrian and Wynne inclines see Volume 1 of this work *'Slates from Glyn Ceiriog'* by the author.

able to communicate by telephone, when both these quarries were in the ownership of the Glyn Slate Co., which installed an internal telephone system linking the quarries.[7] These were the first telephones in the valley.

By August 1872, the tramway company was struggling financially and had approached the SUR&C Co. seeking an advance payment on the share calls, to which the canal company responded that it had no objection providing that other contributors would do the same, and this they appear to have done. The SUR&C Co., having agreed back in March 1872, that it would assist the GVT Co. by paying calls on its shareholding in advance when requested to do so, was becoming concerned that the GVT Co. was not making any effort to pay off old creditors, in particular those who were the Shropshire Union's own Executive Committee members. In December that year, the Executive stipulated that the payment of calls then due should be appropriated by the GVT Co. to paying off the outstanding debts to Lord Powis (£549), Mr Moon (£549), Mr Stanton (£552) and Col. Bourne (£150). Effectively the SUR&C Co. was advancing payment to the GVT Co., not to assist with the construction of the tramway, but to ensure that the outstanding debts owed to its Executive Committee members were paid off!

The first GVT company return, up to 31st December 1872, shows that over half of the available finance had already been spent: £80 on purchasing land, £5,167 on construction and £531 on engineering and surveying. The only employee on the company's books was the secretary, who was being paid a salary of £50 per annum.

The first land to be paid for consisted of two short strips, with a total area of about a quarter of an acre, both of which were part of the site occupied by the former Upper Chirk Bank Colliery and, in 1872, were owned by Nathaniel Price of Gledrid. One of these strips crossed the former colliery yard and the other was a short embankment over which the 1820s waggonway had passed on its way to the canal wharf. An agreement to purchase both of these strips for the sum of £50 had been made on the 26th June 1872, and the GVT Co. was given access to them to begin construction work. Part of the agreement was that the tramway company would build and maintain a *'level crossing with gates'* and *'a good and sufficient watering place for cattle'* at points 'A' and 'B' on the plan included in the conveyance that was signed on 20th December 1872 (See opposite page). The route planned for the GVT continued along the trackbed of the former waggonway, crossing several more fields in order to reach the canal, all of which, by 1871, were in the ownership of Mrs Mary Vaughan Dymock of Penley Hall in the County of Flintshire. As well as the former trackbed the GVT Co. required a wide strip of canal-side land on which to develop a wharf. On 25th June 1875 these strips of land, amounting in area to nearly two acres, were conveyed from Mrs Dymock to the GVT Co. for a *'yearly rent of ten pounds by equal half-yearly portions'* payable on 25th March and 29th September. Mrs Dymock retained the right to use the wharf and *'to lay tramways'* from adjacent lands *'interfering as little as possible'* with the GVT operations there.

The main traffic down the tramway was expected to be slate from the Cambrian Quarries, high above Glyn Ceiriog, for which the incline was in the process of being built. At the end of January 1873, the SUR&C Co. received a letter from the secretary of the New Cambrian Slate Co. advising that good progress was being made with the new developments at the quarry and that he anticipated that *'a considerable amount of traffic would pass over the Glyn Valley Tramway'*. At the SUR&C Co. Executive meeting on 26th February, the Traffic Manager was instructed to consider the arrangements necessary to work the tramway and to communicate with *'the special sub-committee'*, set up to arrange its operation. Presumably this referred to what one would call 'final arrangements', as it was a bit late in the day to be thinking about how it was going to be operated! In fact, as events reveal, the facilities and staff required to operate the tramway appear not to have been considered in any detail.

The key to the development of the Cambrian Slate Quarry was not just the building of the incline, but the construction of the rest of Tramway No.3 from the head of the incline to Chwarel Uchaf

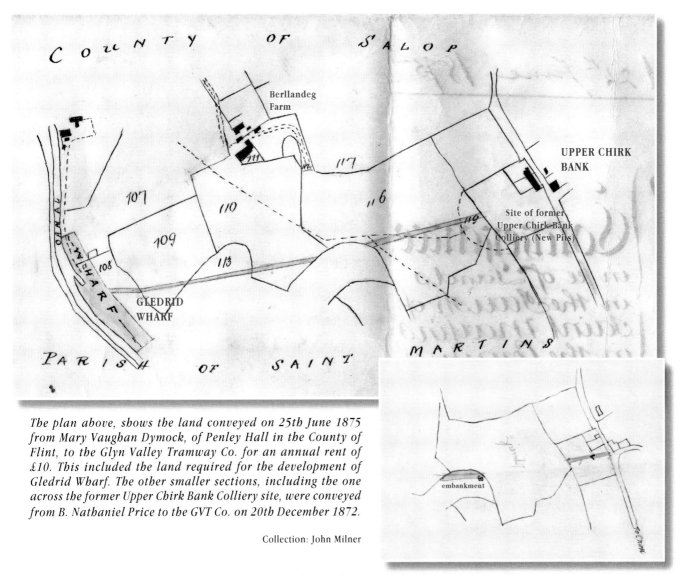

The plan above, shows the land conveyed on 25th June 1875 from Mary Vaughan Dymock, of Penley Hall in the County of Flint, to the Glyn Valley Tramway Co. for an annual rent of £10. This included the land required for the development of Gledrid Wharf. The other smaller sections, including the one across the former Upper Chirk Bank Colliery site, were conveyed from B. Nathaniel Price to the GVT Co. on 20th December 1872.

Collection: John Milner

Quarry (Martin's Quarry). Although the construction of the incline was in hand, it was not until 25th March 1873 that an Indenture was made between Theodore Martin and Edward Harper, who owned the land, and the GVT Co. for the rental of a strip of land measuring just over an acre at an annual rent of £10. This not only included the land required to complete Tramway No.3 to the quarry, but also some of the land required to complete the 1½-mile-long Tramway No.5 between Chwarel Uchaf Quarry and the Nantyr Slate Quarry, as authorized by the Glyn Valley Tramway Act 1870. This indicates that in 1873 the GVT Co. was considering the construction of the tramway to Nantyr.

The planned route of Tramway No.3 was on the south side of the Nant Lafar Valley, through the fields of Plâs Lleucu Farm to Chwarel Uchaf where it turned northwards into the quarry. Tramway No.5 was to make a junction with Tramway No.3, at the point where the latter turned into the quarry, and continue up the valley to follow the contours to Nantyr. In the event, Tramway No.3 was terminated on the lower stack yard of the Cambrian Slate Quarry and Tramway No.5 to Nantyr was never built, being abandoned by the Glyn Valley Tramway Act 1878 and superseded by a completely new route following the Teirw Valley up from Pandy.

Following its completion, on the 28th March 1873, the tramway was formally inspected by Mr William Jones and Mr Jebb, and the SUR&C Co. took possession, as operators, on 30th March. The SUR&C Co. was informed at its Executive meeting on 21st April 1873 that the GVT was now

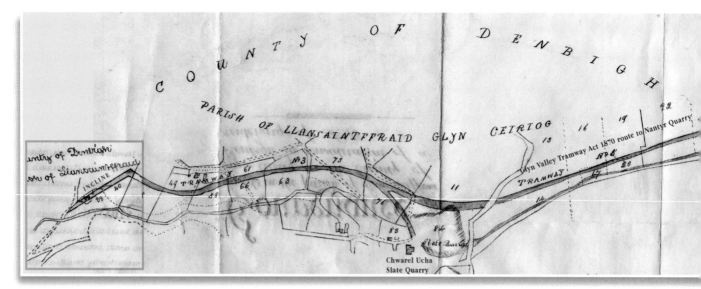

Plan from an Indenture made on 25th March 1873 between Theodore Martin and Edward Harper of the one part and the Glyn Valley Tramway Co. of the other part, for the rental of land at £10 per annum for the GVT line to Chwarel Ucha Quarry and part of the 1870 tramway route to Nantyr. The inset shows the land also agreed by Indenture on 5th September 1872 for the top part of the incline, at a rent of £2 per annum.

Whereas the incline was built by the GVT Company, the rest of the tramway to Chwarel Ucha was built by the quarry company and the extension to Nantyr never materialised.

being worked and that full Parliamentary Rates were being charged '*for the present*'. Future rates were to be discussed between Mr Jones, the GVT Co. secretary, and Mr Cawkwell of the SUR&C Co., as were the estimates '*of the accommodation required for the working of the traffic*'. Mr Jebb reported that in several respects the line was not yet complete, but that he understood that the contractor would supply deficiencies. However, as events unfolded, it was clear that the contractor was not going to supply deficiencies that were outside his contract without extra payment!

When the tramway opened on 30th March 1873, much work still remained to be done before it could be operated for profit. The main contract awarded to Elias Griffith had been to provide the materials and labour to lay a single track from the canal at Gledrid to the New Inn at Glyn Ceiriog, with short branches at Trehowell, Bronygarth, Herber and the Cambrian Quarries. However, the contract was limited to the earthworks for the track bed, the track itself and the crossings, fences and gates. The work necessary to create an interchange with the canal at Gledrid, or lay sidings there or at the other terminus at the New Inn, or, indeed, at other points along the route where they were likely to be required, was not included in the contract price. Elias Griffith had agreed to complete such 'extras' as required, at fixed unit prices recorded on a schedule, which was part of the contract.

As work progressed on the main contract, Henry Dennis signed monthly certificates, separately recording the value of work done by the contractor and the cost of materials used during the preceding month, to enable the contractor to receive regular stage payments from the GVT Company. These certificates show that between June 1872 and March 10th 1873, Elias Griffith was due £9,579, of which a total of £1,915 (20%) was to be retained by the company. Three months later, on July 19th, Henry Dennis wrote a further certificate for £1,500, which was the major part of the amount retained, but it was several years later before the GVT Co. was able to finally pay off all its dues to Elias Griffith.

By the official date of completion, 30th March 1873, the cost of building the tramway had risen from £9,552 to £11,751 but, even so, it soon became clear that, in an effort to minimise costs, the promoters had not included essential items of equipment, such as turntables, weighing machines, trucks and horses in its estimates. The tramway could not operate without them, but the GVT Co. could not pay for them. The company, already in financial difficulties, was now faced with the hopeless task of raising even more finance, which left the SUR&C Co., as the operator, no choice but to agree to pay for the essential 'extras', hoping to recoup this expenditure from the GVT Co. at some later date.

There is evidence in the records that the SUR&C Co. paid Elias Griffith directly for the 'extra works' completed outside his main contract with the GVT Co. and that the canal company provided the buildings, equipment, trucks and horses that were needed, from its own resources. These financial difficulties were compounded by the fact that a conveyance for the purchase of land, resulting from an agreement made before the contractor was allowed to start work, had been drawn up and the GVT Co. was due to pay the agreed amount.

The sum outstanding was for the purchase of the whole of a 14-acre field to the north side of Trehowell Bridge, through which the GVT was routed on its way to the Ceiriog Valley. On 25th March 1873, this land was formally conveyed, the GVT Co. paying £1,400 (£100/acre) to Edmund Burke Wood and his wife Elizabeth Sarah Burke Wood of Moreton Hall for this large field, over which the tramway had already been built, crossing one side diagonally to reach Trehowell Bridge, and requiring only a relatively short narrow strip of land measuring just over 1 acre.[8] The reason why the GVT Co. should have entered into an agreement to purchase this 14-acre field remains unexplained.

However, about 5 weeks later, on 1st May 1873, the bulk of this land, amounting to 12½ acres or thereabouts, was conveyed back to Edmund Burke Wood as *surplus to the requirements of the GVT Co.* for the sum of £1,200, leaving the GVT Co. as owner of the diagonal strip on which the tramway had been built, for which it had paid £200. A further transaction took place just ten days later, when these surrounding fields were conveyed from Edmund Burke Wood to Lord Arthur Hill Trevor, who was the Chairman of the GVT Board of Directors!

Other lands crossed by the tramway on its way through Pontfaen up to the Trehowell Bridge, which were part of the Quinta Estate, belonged to Thomas Barnes. No records of any of the agreements made with him have been found.

Elias Griffith was paid monthly for his work completed, this being evaluated by Henry Dennis, the GVT Company's Engineer. The amount paid was less a 20% retainer.

Shropshire Archives 800/44B

[8] See chapter 6 page 139

The two fields to the north of Trehowell Bridge, which were conveyed from Edmund and Sarah Burke Wood to the GVT Company on 25th March 1873, for reasons which are not clear. Five weeks later these were conveyed back, the GVT Co. just retaining the narrow strip required for the tramway.

Collection: John Milner

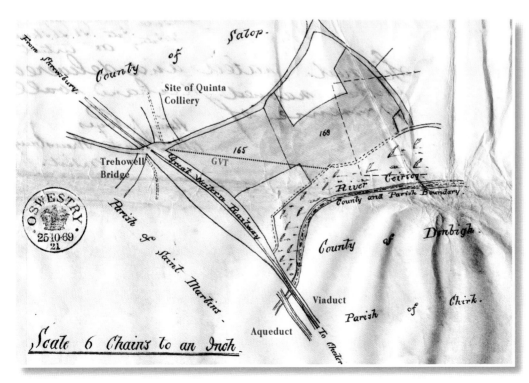

An immediate problem facing the SUR&C Co. as operator of the GVT was that it required several horses to work the steep grade up from Pontfaen, so on 28th May 1873 the Executive Committee approved the purchase of three more and Mr Jebb was instructed to have a stable for four horses erected at Pontfaen station. At the end of the following month, it was reported that *'the four horses engaged on the Glyn Valley Tramway are well employed'* and that another horse was required, which was duly authorised.

At the same meeting plans and an estimate for building a warehouse for the GVT at Gledrid Wharf were requested, and in August that year *'sufficient wagons not exceeding 100'* were authorised, the acquisition of which would naturally require more horses, thus creating a vicious circle of expense as traffic increased.[9]

At this time, horse-drawn tramways were common, but horses were costing 17s. 6d. each per week to keep; the SUR&C Co., although experienced in working horses on its canals, had to face up to the inefficiency of horse-power used on a tramway with steep gradients like those up from Pontfaen towards Gledrid, which was neither as cheap nor as easy as moving bulk loads on the canal.

By this time the SUR&C Co. had created a near monopoly of carrying on its own canals, and owned hundreds of narrowboats for which it supplied the horses. Each horse had *SUC* branded into one fore-hoof with its number into the other. The master-boatmen were issued with identity cards for their horses, which enabled them to be claimed at the stables. The company employed its own farriers, but stabling and veterinary services were bought in. There is no reason to think that the GVT, being operated by the SUR&C Co., would be much different, although horses would be supplied to the waggoners from the stables at Pontfaen or, at the Glyn Ceiriog end of the line, from the stables built for the GVT Co. on rented land to the rear of the New Inn (later the Glyn Valley Hotel), adjacent to the foot of the Cambrian Incline on Quarry Road.

The SUR&C Co. had very soon paid out in excess of £2,000 to complete essential works and provide essential extras.[10] This arrangement was in spite of an agreement made in June 1871, that the SUR &C Co. would provide no more than £5,000 capital towards the enterprise. At Gledrid, where a field alongside the canal had to be converted into a tramway/canal interchange, these

GLYN VALLEY TRAMWAY COMPANY.

REPORT of the DIRECTORS to the GENERAL MEETING of SHAREHOLDERS, to be held on the 31st MARCH, 1873.

Your Directors have the gratification of reporting the substantial completion of the main line of Tramway, which extends from the Shropshire Union Canal at the Gledrid to the New Inn at Llansaintffraid-Glyn-Ceiriog. The line of Tramway thence to the Cambrian Quarries is at the same time in a very forward state, and will shortly be ready for opening.

~~Upon its completion the entire staff and plant of the Contractor will be directed to~~ the Branch to the Great Western Railway, ~~for which all necessary preparations have been made.~~ *is complete*

The principal portion of the land for the entire line was acquired on terms satisfactory to the Directors, and they confidently expect to report to the next general meeting, not merely the completion of all the Tramways of the Company, but that they are in actual work by the Shropshire Union Railways and Canal Company.

The Directors who retire on the present occasion, according to the Company's Act, are Mr. JEBB and Mr. WRAGGE. One of the Auditors, Mr. J. EVANS, also retires, and all are eligible for re-election.

Annexed is a Statement of the Accounts to the present time.

A. E. HILL TREVOR, M.P., Chairman.

JOHN JONES, Secretary.

Company's Offices,
Upper Brook Street, Oswestry.

The Director's Annual Report presented to the shareholders on 31st March 1873, altered at the last minute to announce that the branch to the interchange with the GWR at Trebowell Sidings was 'complete'.

Collection: John Milner

REPORT OF THE DIRECTORS

OF THE

Glyn Valley Tramway Company,

TO THE SHAREHOLDERS AT THEIR ORDINARY YEARLY MEETING,

ON THE 24TH DAY OF MARCH, 1874.

Your Directors have the pleasure of reporting the construction and partial completion of the Main Line of Railway between the Shropshire Union Railway Canal at Gledrid and the Quarries of the Cambrian Slate Company at Llansantffraid. The Line to the Great Western Railway Company near Preesgwaen has also been constructed, although the Junction with that Company's Line has not been definitely agreed on.

By arrangement with the Shropshire Union Railway Company for working the Line, that Company took possession of the Line on the 30th March last, since which time they have been actively occupied in erecting the necessary Wharves, Offices, and conveniences, and making arrangements for working the Line. The gross returns of the traffic, up to the 31st December last (necessarily small in the imperfect condition of the Line) afford reason for believing that when the Line is wholly completed, and in full work, and the Slate and other traffic is developed, the returns will be satisfactory to the Proprietors.

The arrangements for working with the Shropshire Union Railways Company have hitherto been of a temporary character, but it is hoped that before another General Meeting definite terms will have been agreed upon satisfactory to both parties.

A Statement of Account, in the form prescribed by Parliament, will accompany this Report.

The Directors retiring on the present occasion are Colonel Bourne and Mr. Jebb, and the Auditor to retire is Mr. John Evans. All these gentlemen are eligible for re-election.

JAMES BOURNE, Col.,

Chairman.

Company's Offices, Oswestry,
24th March, 1874.

Contrary to the impression given by the 1873 report, opposite, this Director's Report for March 1874 shows that although the spur to the proposed interchange with the GWR, on the Quinta/Trebowell Colliery site had been completed, the details of the actual interchange facility with the GWR, which was a requirement of the GVT Act, still had not yet been agreed.

Collection: John Milner

extras included a network of sidings (£176), which had required the site to be levelled (£24), and a lift-up bridge across the canal, which provided the only road access to the site (£35). A warehouse for the storage of merchandise was erected (£166), and a dedicated slate wharf constructed to cater for traffic from the Cambrian Quarries (£18).

As it was intended to provide a passenger service up the valley from Pontfaen to Glyn Ceiriog, a passenger station, with an office, was built on the floor of the old quarry at Pontfaen (£176), and stables for four horses erected (£110). A weighing machine with its housing (£60), a turntable (£16) and two short lengths of sidings (£10) were also provided. Later a carriage shed with a workshop (cost unknown) was also built here and a short siding on the side of the Trust Road was extended as far as the road bridge at Pontfaen. The GVT track up the valley from Pontfaen to Glyn Ceiriog, had been built on the side of the Wem & Bronygarth Trust road and passed very close to the Toll House at Herber – so close that it was necessary to remove the bay window (£1)! Extra sidings were laid at the Gravel Pit at Herber (£25), Pontfadog (£24) and at Queen's Inn at Dolywern (£64). The terminus opposite the New Inn at Glyn Ceiriog, was built at the top of a steeply sloping field adjacent to the road, requiring a long retaining wall (£132) and, here, extra sidings (£164), a dedicated coal wharf (£181), stables for eight horses, at the rear of the New Inn and adjacent to Quarry Road (£219), a warehouse for storing merchandise (£165) and a ticket office (£7) were provided. The essential extra works had also included the doubling of the incline to the Cambrian Quarries, as already mentioned (£555).

In July 1873, the GVT Co. issued a call letter to the SUR&C Co. for the final balance of £600 on its share subscription. The SUR&C Co. thus became a fully paid-up shareholder, in what was a far from complete and operational tramway. Just to add to the problems, by October, the SUR&C Co. received a demand from Elias Griffith for *'extra works for traffic purposes'* to the tune of £300, and this was only the start. Although payment was authorised, the company became concerned

The New Inn terminus of the Glyn Valley Tramway photographed by Lettsome & Sons, photographers to the Queen, Llangollen. This is the only photograph so far found of the first 'open car' built by the Ashbury Railway Carriage & Iron Company. Note the warehouse, which is similar to the one at Gledrid, the crane and weighbridge (box structure by the roadside) adjacent to the wagons, and the diminutive booking office. Beyond the weighbridge is the coalyard with its small office. With a large contingent of village children, mostly dressed for the occasion, this appears to be a special event. The state of the warehouse doors suggest that this photograph was taken late in the life of the horse tramway.

Collection: John Milner

THE HORSE TRAMWAY ERA 1872–1876

89

Canal transshipment of goods to and from Chirk, was handled at the wharf at Chirk Bank, located between Gledrid and the Chirk Aqueduct, where there was a substantial warehouse.

Collection: John Milner

Herber Toll Gate, built by the Wem & Bronygarth Turnpike Road Trust, as it stands today. Contrary to accounts that have been related over the years, its bay window, traditional on tollhouses, was not demolished by a locomotive, but was removed in 1873 to provide clearance for the horse tramway, at a cost of £1, well before the steam era.

© John Milner 2009

with the frequency that it was paying out large sums on behalf of the GVT Co.; he was eventually paid for these extras by the SUR&C Co. on 25th March 1874.

In January 1874, the SUR&C Co. sought agreement that it would be paid interest on the sums it had paid out for extras, which the tramway company should have provided from its own capital, as there was no indication that the GVT Co. had the means of reimbursing the amount already owed. Agreement on the payment of interest was reached in March, but the SUR&C Co. had to continue to finance the tramway because the GVT had expended all its capital.

The contractor's obligation, under the terms of the original contract, to maintain or rectify defects was due to expire in March 1874, so, on the 3rd of that month, a sub-committee appointed by the SUR&C Co. comprising The Right Hon. The Earl of Powis, Col. Bourne MP, Mr G.R. Jebb and Mr Hope, accompanied by Henry Dennis, engineer of the GVT, John Jones, GVT Secretary and Elias Griffith, contractor, made an official inspection of the supposedly finished Glyn Valley Tramway. The resulting report provides an interesting insight into the tramway at its birth:

> 'The Committee proceeded from Chirk station across the aqueduct to the land at the south end, and inspected the proposed site of the cottages for the Company's servants engaged on the Glyn Valley Tramway. The Committee approved the site and directed that the cottages be put up in pairs instead of in four as proposed. At Chirk Bank the Engineer was instructed to have the trees on the slope felled and to arrange for planting larch next season. ... [They then] joined the Tramway at Gledrid Wharf. The Office, Warehouse and

An artist's impression of the warehouse at Gledrid Wharf. This warehouse, which was almost the same as the one installed at the New Inn terminus, was of timber construction with a slate roof. The stone wharf edge can still be witnessed today from the towpath opposite. See chapter 5 for full details of the warehouse.

Collection: John Milner
© Philip D. Hawkins

Crane, which had been erected here by the Company, were examined, also the wagons made for the Tramway in the Ellesmere Yard. The lift up Bridge to cross the canal was reported to be in progress.

The fencing of the Tramway at Gledrid Wharf and Pontfaen was pointed out as not being in accordance with the specification. Mr Jebb stated that he considered it strong enough for the purpose, and as the Contractor had made several additions to the Tramway, at the Engineer's suggestion, which were not in the specification, it was not considered necessary to make any representations on the subject. The attention of the Contractor was called to the state of the Woodguards at the crossing of the road at [Upper] Chirk Bank and other places, and he engaged to have them replaced with those of harder wood. [11]

The line on the elevated ground, near Pontfaen, was considered to be laid too near to the edge, and would be liable to be affected by heavy rains washing away the soil, it was stated that no alteration had appeared in the ground for years. The Committee considered that the Company should not be responsible for the restoration of the line in case of any slip occurring and that the Contractor should give an undertaking to the Company that if called upon at any time he will alter the course of the rails. The Committee recommended a channel to be made to conduct the water flowing down the cutting [running in front of Pontfaen Farm down to the station] to the other side of the Tramway. The Committee called attention to the absence of fencing, at the crossing of the road near Pontfaen, which was arranged to be put up.

Mr Barnes [Quinta], having applied for a siding to be put down to his Stone Quarry at Pontfaen at his own cost, it was recommended that this be done, also that one be put in at this place for empty wagons and a turntable for the accommodation of the General Traffic.

The Committee, having examined the New Stables and other works at Pontfaen, continued their inspection along the Tramway to the New Inn. Here a turntable was deemed to be much required, and it was recommended that one be put down. [12]

From the New Inn the Committee proceeded to the Granite Rock [Hendre Quarry], which has just been cut by the promoters of the Gunpowder Company, and inspected the 'setts' which were being squared and for which a large demand is [was] anticipated, they also inspected the arrangements for the manufacture of Blasting Powder at Pont y Meibion and the Chert Rock opened by Mr Lester of Stoke, for Grinding Stone and for Pottery purposes, and for the removal of which Mr Lester has constructed an inclined tramway from the top of the Rock to the Public Road. [13] *The Stone from the Rock is now being conveyed in considerable quantities by the Tramway.*

Returning to the New Inn, the Committee walked up the incline [Cambrian] and called attention to the masses of earth and rock, which appeared likely to fall upon the incline, and considered that the Glyn Valley Company should call upon their Engineer to undertake to be responsible during a period of 5 years for any damage, which may arise from them. It was noticed that at one point the stream is crossed by the incline and in lieu of a culvert being made to afford the proper passage for the water, slates have been tipped in the bed of the stream. It was considered that if at any time damage should arise to the Tramway in consequence thereof, the Glyn Valley Company should be responsible for its restoration.

The Committee examined the Quarries of the New Cambrian Slate Company. It was stated that the Tunnel to drain the Upper Quarry would be finished in three months time, when progress could be made with the manufacture of the better class slate. They were informed that the Slate Company had in hand orders, which they were unable to fulfil owing to the want of trucks, and the Committee ordered, that in view of the gradual increase of the Traffic on the line, 20 more of the trucks sanctioned by Minute 9720 be constructed. ...' [14]

[11] The timbers laid horizontally across the sleepers between and to the sides of the rails on a road level crossing.

[12] There does not appear to be any photographic evidence to suggest that a turntable was installed at the New Inn terminus.

[13] This incline was from Pen-y-graig (Pandy Rock) Quarry.

[14] Mr Jones (SUR&C Co.) had been authorised by the Executive Committee, on 27th August 1873, to order sufficient wagons 'not exceeding 100' needed to operate the tramway, but it would appear that only a part order had been placed, possibly to reduce capital expenditure. Whilst the wagons were required for the transportation of slate, they were probably, at this time, ordinary wagons as opposed to proper slate ones with the traditional lath sides.

The sub-committee drew Henry Dennis' attention to the insufficiency of the drains at various points along the tramway and the fact that many of the roller boxes on the Cambrian incline were broken. They considered that slate was not an ideal material for their construction and the GVT Co. should be held *'responsible for their restoration'*. Incline rollers (required to prevent the cables dragging on the ground) were traditionally made out of cast iron, running loose on an axle that was either anchored simply to cross-members of iron fixed to the sleepers, or mounted in a more sophisticated box unit, which appears to have been the case here. On the 27th April, the SUR&C Co. Executive minuted that they would undertake to replace them in wood, thus removing the liability from the GVT Company.

The SUR&C Co. Executive Committee had first considered the provision of cottages for GVT servants in December 1873 and, on 28th January 1874, it had been agreed to build four cottages and a house, the latter for the GVT's Agent or Manager, on SUR&C Co. land adjacent to the south end of Chirk Aqueduct. As revealed by the inspection report of the 3rd March 1874, the original

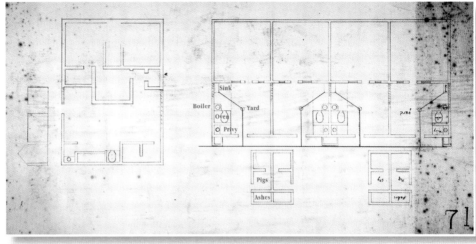

proposal had been for a terrace of four cottages and plans show that each was to have had its own privy, boiler, oven and sink in the yard outside, plus a pigsty and an ashpit in the garden. As a result of a recommendation made following that inspection, instead of the terrace of four as planned, two pairs of semi-detached cottages and a detached residence were built, at a cost of £835 3s. 7d.; the contract having being awarded to Elias Griffith.

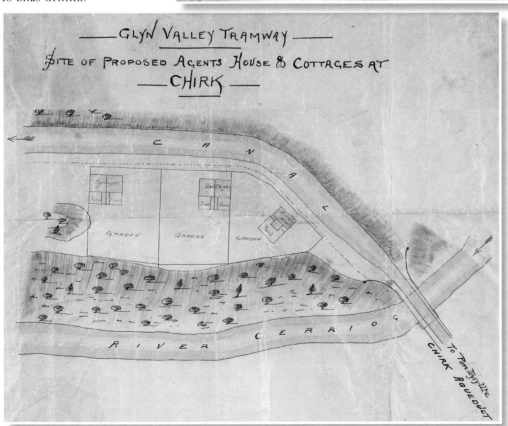

Above: *Unfinished SUR&C Co. drawings for the original 1874 proposal of a terrace of four cottages and a detached Agent's house, to be built on land at the southern end of the Chirk aqueduct to house GVT Co. employees.*

Shropshire Archives IMG16099

Left: *The revised SUR&C Co. plans for two pairs of semi-detached cottages, instead of a terrace of four. The Agent's house was given the prime position and all had gardens of generous proportions. These cottages became known as Aqueduct Cottages.*

The Waterways Archive
Gloucester
Licence Ref.: 0609 JM
Ref: BW152-20-4

Aqueduct Cottages

Aqueduct Cottages were built on land at the southern end of Chirk Aqueduct in 1874 by contractor Elias Griffith, of the Hand Hotel, Chirk, for the SUR&C Co. to house Glyn Valley Tramway employees, described as being employed at the 'tramway works'. . . . .

© John Milner 2009

. . . . . . The one above was a detached house built for the Agent and was known as Aqueduct House. In 1881, it was occupied by Thomas Greaves, who was then Clerk and Manager of the GVT.

The other four were occupied in 1881 by William Edwards, Joiner; Richard Parry, platelayer, and lodger William Taylor, Clerk; . . . .

© John Milner 2009

. . . . Richard Windson, carpenter, and his son Thomas, Clerk. The remaining cottage was occupied by two miners and a boot/shoemaker.

© John Milner 2009

The 1881 Census Return reveals that at that time, all but one of these canal-side cottages, known as Aqueduct Cottages, were occupied by GVT employees engaged '*at the tramway works*'. Aqueduct House (the Agent's house) was occupied by Thomas Greaves, aged 45, born Lancaster, who was clerk and manager of the tramway. In 1879, the rent payable for this house was £8/annum. The other cottages were inhabited by William Edwards, aged 30, born Chirk, a joiner; Richard Parry, aged 52, born Ellesmere, a platelayer, and his lodger William Taylor, aged 20, born Hoole, Chester, an office clerk; Richard Windson, aged 46, born Ellesmere, a carpenter, and his son Thomas, aged 16, an office clerk; and one was not housing GVT employees, but two miners and a boot/shoemaker.

As mentioned in the Committee's inspection report of the tramway in March 1874, another potential user of GVT lines had arrived in the valley, establishing a large works on what was later to become the site of the crushing plant for Hendre Quarry. This was the Patent Gunpowder Company, from Ewell in Surrey, which had been registered in 1872 after buying the rights of a patent granted to John Bell Muschamp for the invention of '*An Improved Explosive Substance and Process for Manufacturing the Same*'. This improved explosive substance was a nitrocellulose product and the process by means of which it was to be manufactured was a hazardous chemical reaction, in which the cellulose component in wood would be converted into nitrocellulose by treatment with a mixture of concentrated nitric and sulphuric acids. Nitrocellulose explosives had many times the explosive power of the traditional black gunpowder, but their manufacture was an industry still in its infancy and there was still much to be learnt about the hazards of their production, storage and transport.

The nominal capital of the Patent Gunpowder Company was £200,000 and by 1876 about half this sum had been raised.[15] It was a very ambitious company and set about advertising widely, as there were high hopes of worldwide markets for its explosives, for both weaponry and blasting purposes. As related later in this chapter, these expectations were to come to an abrupt end.

A rare example of the Patent Gunpowder Company's letterhead.

Collection: John Milner

[15] The Average Earnings Index shows that £200,000 in 1872 is equivalent to well over £10 million at the date of this publication.

One of the original buildings erected at Pont-y-Meibion, on part of Llechwedd Gwyn Farm, by the Patent Gunpowder Co. Ltd in 1874. Photographed in the 1960s it still retained most of its window frames. It is now a Grade II listed building.

© David Ll. Davies

The leat, built in 1874 to provide water for the Gunpowder Works, is still traceable along a large section of its length. Remarkably, although the leat has been disconnected from the river for many years, the sluice gate still survives.

© John Milner 2004

[16] For full details of the Hendre Quarry Tramway see chapter 2 page 61.

It was only after a number of failed attempts to obtain a licence to manufacture at sites elsewhere, that the company decided to locate in the Ceiriog Valley, but it was not an ideal site because it did not have an adequate transport system to connect with the national canal and rail networks at Chirk. The company's initial projection was that about 50 tons of hazardous chemicals (mainly concentrated nitric and sulphuric acids) would have to be brought up the valley every week, in order to reach the weekly target output of 10 tons of explosives. However, the total output from the works was expected to be greater, because the company intended to use the spent acids to make artificial fertilizer and was also considering the production of charcoal from trees grown adjacent to the site. With the GVT terminating at Glyn Ceiriog, almost two miles short of the works, the directors of the gunpowder company wanted something better and declared that they were: *'Desirous to see a railway running through the valley'*. However, they did not have their eyes set on a simple extension of the existing tramway – they wanted to see it converted to a standard-gauge railway!

In late 1873, during the construction of a leat from the River Ceiriog across Hendre Farm lands to the gunpowder works, the contractor Elias Griffith had noticed that the rock they were blasting was of a particular granulated form. Samples were shown to Walter Eddy, a mining engineer from Fron, Llangollen, and to Henry Dennis. The samples were checked by local geologists, who confirmed that it was particularly good-quality granite. A report following an investigation of the area described a granite face some 200ft high and 600ft wide – *'enough to find setts for paving all the heavy traffic streets in Europe for generations. ... The stone is a species of granite especially suitable for this purpose'*. A bold statement! Very soon afterwards, in January 1874, Elias Griffith, Henry Dennis and Richard Pritchard Williams of Llancadwaladr obtained a licence to search for rocks and minerals under the land of Hendre Farm and also under Nantswrn Farm, on the opposite side of the valley, where there was a similar outcrop of rock. The quarrying of granite for road setts at Hendre by the newly formed Glyn Ceiriog Granite Company (15296) began almost immediately, but the reserves at Nantswrn Farm were never exploited – it was to become a limited liability company (15820) in 1881.

The potential traffic in granite setts that could be generated for the GVT Co. was enormous, providing that the transport costs to its interchanges with the national canal and railway networks could be kept to a minimum. The quarry was situated at the bottom of the steep-sided valley, with no route out through the gunpowder works site and the nearest road, high up on the opposite side of the valley. The granite company built a tramway across the valley with a short incline up the escarpment to a roadside wharf, where the setts were transshipped into carts for the journey down to the GVT terminus in Glyn Ceiriog.[16]

The SUR&C Co., at its 25th March 1874 meeting, discussed the desirability of extending the GVT to Hendre in order to take full advantage of the increase in mineral traffic from the numerous quarries in the upper Ceiriog Valley and the promised output from the gunpowder works. Further action on this was deferred until such time as the GVT Co. made a formal approach, which it was unlikely to do at this time for any scheme requiring capital expenditure.

As well as the developments in the upper valley, the New Cambrian Slate Company, with slate quarries high up the Nant Lafar valley above Glyn Ceiriog, was also confident about the future, as accounts for 1874 reveal an entry for the *'making of a new wharf at Gledrid – £10 14s. 5d.'*. The following year, a figure given for *'the value of slates at Chirk'* confirmed that it had established its own facility at Gledrid and later accounts reveal that it had an office on the site.

At this time, an advert appeared in the *Oswestry Advertizer* giving prior notice that passenger services were about to be introduced on the GVT, although it conveniently glossed over the fact that the GVT station at Pontfaen, referred to as 'Chirk', was three-quarters of a mile from Chirk (GWR) station:

> *'On and after 1st April 1874, passenger cars will run daily (Sunday excepted) between Chirk and Llansaintffraid Glyn Ceiriog, calling at intermediate stations. The tramway runs through the pretty Vale of Ceiriog, which is celebrated for the beauty of its scenery and is much resorted to by anglers and tourists. The trains will run to and from Chirk in connection with GWR trains. Particulars as to fares etc. can be had on application to the local manager, Mr Charles Griffiths, Tramway Office, Chirk'.*

On the 22nd April 1874, it was reported that: *'at the request of the inhabitants at Glyn, a passenger car has commenced running between Pontfaen and the New Inn, and Mr Jones has ordered a suitable open car from Messrs Ashburys'.*[17] There was only one carriage available for use during the first few months of the service which, because no records have been found of its purchase or cost, may have been built locally in the GVT workshops at no cost to the operator of the line, the SUR&C Company. This carriage, of toastrack design, was completely open to the weather and therefore suitable for summer use only; it was still in use in 1891. In contrast, the *'suitable open car'* on order from Ashburys was a 4-wheel open carriage that, with its pew-like seats, somewhat resembled a *chapel on wheels*, and was fitted with a canopy and drop-down side curtains to keep the weather out – perhaps it was more akin to a Welsh version of a *Surrey with a fringe on top* from the musical *Oklahoma*! Neither of these two open carriages was suitable for all-weather use, but a further carriage ordered from Messrs Ashbury, and in service by December 1874, was a two-compartment closed coach with doors and, for the comfort of passengers in all weathers, was fully glazed.

The first mention of gravity working being used on the GVT appears in this contemporary account of a visit to Glyn Ceiriog via the tramway from the August 1874 issue of the Llangollen Advertiser. Having travelled from Pontfaen to Glyn Ceiriog by horse-drawn tram, the party was to find that the return journey in an open carriage was to send their adrenaline rushing:

> *'Our return was a novelty. We took our seats on the carriage with a man at the helm, we beg pardon, the brake, and without horse, engine, or any other aid, rattled down the valley at something like an average rate of eighteen miles an hour, arriving at Pontfaen in less that 20 minutes from the time we started. So pleasant a day deserved a pleasant wind up, and, when we reached the Hand (Hand Hotel, Chirk), a well laid table with covers for eight found eight ready candidates for its viands.'*

An anonymous description of the operation of the tramway, which appeared in a rare first-hand passenger account, published in the *Llangollen Advertiser* in September 1874, presents a rosy picture of the GVT in this period; a picture that appears to have been in the minds of passengers, right up to its closure:

> *'On Friday last, a small picnic party left Llangollen station en route for Chirk, and for the Glyn Valley by means of the new tramroad. The day was glorious, the sun shining brilliantly, with a gentle breeze from the west, which made the atmosphere extremely pleasant – in reality, it was a "fine morning" in the full sense of the term. After exchanging the usual salutations, and being asked by several friends to what part of the country we were bound, and having replied "To Glynceiriog", some of them were greatly amazed and puzzled as to how we would reach that pretty valley via Ruabon. "Dear me", exclaimed another, "what a roundabout way you take to Llansaintffraid Glynceiriog; the distance*

A SUR&C Co. letter from the General Manager's Office, Chester, which is from where the operational affairs of the Glyn Valley Tramway were being administered at that time.

Collection: John Milner

[17] The Ashbury Carriage and Iron Co. Ltd, founded by John Ashbury in 1837, was a manufacturer of railway rolling stock located at Knott Mill, Manchester. It moved to Openshaw in 1841 and in 1862 became The Ashbury Railway Carriage & Iron Co. Ltd. In 1902 the business was transferred to Saltley in Birmingham where it merged with other companies to become Ashbury, Brown & Marshalls. This was eventually absorbed into the Metropolitan Amalgamated Railway Carriage & Wagon Company Ltd, which later became the Metropolitan-Cammell Carriage & Wagon Co. Ltd.

Glyn Valley Tramway

Passenger Trains

List of Single Fares
From 1st April until further notice

Up		Down	
From Pontfaen		**From New Inn (Glyn)**	
To Castle Mill.	3ᵈ	To Queens Head Inn.	3ᵈ
„ Herber Toll Gate.	6ᵈ	„ Pontfadog.	6ᵈ
„ Pontfadog.	8ᵈ	„ Herber Toll Gate.	8ᵈ
„ Queens Head Inn.	10ᵈ	„ Castle Mill.	10ᵈ
„ New Inn	1/-	„ Pontfaen.	1/-

Pontfaen to New Inn and back or
vice versa One Shilling and nine pence

Intermediate Stations

From Castle Mill		From Herber Toll Gate		From Pontfadog		From Queens Head Inn	
To Herber Toll Gate	3ᵈ	To Castle Mill	3ᵈ	To Castle Mill	4ᵈ	To Castle Mill	10ᵈ
„ Pontfadog	4ᵈ	„ Pontfadog	3ᵈ	„ Herber Toll Gate	3ᵈ	„ Herber Toll Gate	8ᵈ
„ Queens Head Inn	8ᵈ	„ Queens Head Inn	6ᵈ	„ Queens Head Inn	3ᵈ	„ Pontfadog	6ᵈ
„ New Inn	10ᵈ	„ New Inn	9ᵈ	„ New Inn	6ᵈ	„ New Inn	3ᵈ

By Order
W Jones.
General Manager

Shropshire Union Offices
Chester April 1874

The first draft list of single fares produced in preparation for the introduction of a passenger service on the horse tramway on 1st April 1874.

Collection: John Milner

over Allt-y-Badi is only 2¹/₂ miles, while the distance by train and tram is 15 miles". We ejaculated, being bent on a day "out", the nearness of the place one way and the remoteness the other way was no object, but that we wished to reach there as easy and comfortable as possible.

We had seen much about the Glyn Tramway in the various papers, which aroused our curiosity to see and travel along it; and when we read, by Mr J. Hughes, in September's Greal ["Y Greal", a Welsh Baptist periodical, Llangollen], *our wish was intensified – in fact, we were determined, on the first opportunity, to see and judge for ourselves.*

We were at Llangollen station at 8.30 a.m., several minutes before the train was timed to arrive. About the time it should be at this station the signal was lowered to indicated that it had started from Glyndyfrdwy. When at Berwyn the bell was rung, which in former years used to indicate the arrival of the train at this (Llangollen) station; also, the signal used to be lowered when the train left Berwyn station. We wondered what could be the reason for these deviations; but, no doubt, the railway officials have some reasons of their own, although the public are not able to discern them. At last, we found ourselves comfortably seated on the train, and arrived at Ruabon at 9.15. Being, as usual, greeted there with "All change", we alighted, and after a few minutes waiting, the Chester train arrived and took us, in ten minutes, to the pretty station of Chirk.

From here we had to walk to the Pontfaen terminus of the Glyn Valley Tramway, the distance being about three quarters of a mile. By the way, there ought to be a car or bus running between Chirk station and Pontfaen, as it is very awkward for passengers who have heavy luggage to convey from one station to the other. After walking down the hill which skirts Chirk Castle Park, we crossed the bridge [Pontfaen bridge] under which the historical river Ceiriog delightfully flows, and separates the counties of Salop and Denbigh, and of course England and Wales as well. Roscoe sat upon this old bridge and surveyed the natural enchantments around him.[18] From here may be seen to advantage the beautiful viaduct that carries the railway, and the substantial aqueduct, which conveys the canal over the Ceiriog Vale and River, the one built by the late Mr Thomas Telford, and the other by Henry Robertson, Esq., M.P. Turning to the right, after crossing the bridge, we are immediately at the station-house – a snug little brick building, quite in keeping with the magnitude of the railway at the end of which it stands.[19] Having secured our tickets,

The Astbury-built open car (left) gave little protection from the weather, despite having side curtains that could be dropped down. A small, but more conventional, closed coach (above) was supplied later for winter use.

Collection: John Milner

[18] *'Wanderings and Excursions in North Wales'* by Thomas Roscoe, 1836.

[19] This is the only reference found so far that confirms that the station building at Pontfaen was built of brick.

which, we may state, were one shilling each to the New Inn, the other terminus of the line, we seated ourselves in a very comfortable open carriage capable of accommodating about fourteen persons, drawn by a spirited horse. Ten o'clock to the minute, the whistle is sounded, and off we go at a sharp trot. Soon after leaving the station, we cross a wooden bridge to the north side of the Ceiriog.

One carriage is generally sufficient to convey all the passengers at the end of the season. There is no guard, except a little white dog, which was continually on the look out to see that the line was clear. On two occasions, that morning, he jumped out and ran in advance of us to clear the road of a herd of calves and pigs, which were on our track. Our readers will bear in mind that the tramway runs alongside the new road constructed some years ago through the valley, without any sort of wall or fence between them: this road, by the way, is kept in a very sad condition, being in winter time a continuous "slough of despond" from one end to the other. It is greatly regretted that this thoroughfare, constructed at such an expense, is left from year to year without the least of repair.

The first mile we skirted the finely wooded park of Mr Biddulph, with the Ceiriog close to our left. Castle Mill station was reached in ten minutes, and in the same space of time we were at Herber Toll Gate station. Twelve minutes more took us to Pontfadog, while in another ten minutes we were at the Queen's Head, Dolywern, where two passengers came up. When another start was made, "Stop," exclaimed the good landlord of the inn, "there is a glass of ale for you". "Well, really," replied our jolly driver, "there must be some considerate Christian in the house". The glass being emptied, we were conveyed in seven minutes to New Inn station, Llansaintffraid [Glyn Ceiriog], the whole distance of six miles from Pontfaen being completed in forty-five minutes, amidst the most varied and beautiful scenery, autumn helping the display of its rich tints, so exquisite, and so indescribable, that, during the transit, we were rapt in speechless admiration.

A fine chapel is being built at Llansaintffraid by the Baptist connection, the contractors being Messrs. Ellis & Jones of Towyn. Being close to the New Inn, it will be much more convenient than the old chapel on the hill. There is also a large house and shop. Built by Messrs. Morris & Hughes of Llangollen, who intend carrying on business there. Further on, towards Tregeiriog, there is too a large powder mill [gunpowder] lately built. And between the extensive flannel factories and the quarries this pretty village seems to be in a flourishing condition. No doubt, with the facility of the tramroad, more quarries will be opened in the district, and we venture to predict that there is a glorious future in store for the charming valley of Glyn.

At six o'clock, we started over the mountain, towards home, which we reached at half-past seven, having spent one of the most enjoyable days of our lives.'

The journal of John Hughes (1802–1884) gives another contemporary first-hand account of travel on the horse tramway in 1874. On the 29th November that year Mr James Barnes of *Brookside* (son of Mr Thomas Barnes, Quinta) *'skilfully and carefully'* laid the foundation stone of the new Baptist Chapel in Glyn Ceiriog. A party from *'the Cefn houses and farms, Y Rhos, Penycae and Llangollen'* had travelled up via the main line to Chirk station and thence to Pontfaen to join the *tram*, which had conveyed them to Glyn Ceiriog for the ceremony:

'We had gone up by means of strong horses at a fast trot and greatly enjoyed the journey from y bont faen [Pontfaen] to the New Inn; we had two drivers/coachmen and two horses.'

The final part of the proceedings did not take place until 6.00 p.m., by which time daylight was fading and the last scheduled passenger tram down to Pontfaen had already left at 4 p.m. During the evening ceremonies the party had to depart early to catch its 'improvised' transport back to Pontfaen:

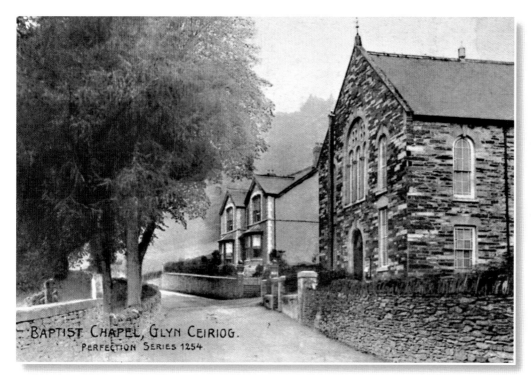

BAPTIST CHAPEL, GLYN CEIRIOG.
PERFECTION SERIES 1254

The Seion Chapel was built in 1874 from slate quarried from Hafod-y-Gynfor Quarry, Glyn Ceiriog. The foundation stone was laid by James Barnes, Brookside, on the 29th November that year. Thomas Barnes, his son James and guests travelled to and from the celebrations on the tramway.

Collection: John Milner

'The tram was waiting, that is, half a dozen or more slate wagons with boards across to sit on. There was neither horse nor steam and no engine, alive or dead, only a man at the brake. Mam and I were anxious and nervous to entrust ourselves to the mercy of a break-neck concern like this ... Mr Barnes in front and people from the bottom of the Glyn fearlessly enjoying the ride.[20] The wagon was released and, within three to four minutes we were at Pont Dolywern. Before we reached the bridge the speed was terrifying, but power was needed for the climb to the bridge. We stayed there for a long time while some passengers alighted; we did not stop again until we were by the Herber and again by Pont Melin y Castell [Castle Mill Bridge] where Mr Barnes and those who were with him got off. We were by the stone bridge itself [Pontfaen] half an hour and five minutes after leaving the New Inn.'

[20] They probably did it on a regular basis!

Returning to the trials and tribulations of the GVT, the SUR&C Co. Executive committee, at its meeting on 24th June 1874, was facing the reality of what it had taken on. Traffic on the GVT was on the increase; more horses were required to handle it, which were neither cheap nor efficient, and the reality was that this mode of power was an expensive way of running the tramway. It is hard to understand why they had turned a blind eye to this in the first place, or could it be that this was a backdoor ploy to achieve what they really wanted – steam power? Mr Jones was instructed to attend a meeting of the GVT Co. to be held the following day in London (somewhat short notice!) and to raise the question of the introduction of steam power. Also, Mr Jebb was asked to request a suitable design for a locomotive for the GVT from Francis William Webb, who was the locomotive supremo of the LNWR Co.; one wonders what kind of design this celebrated standard-gauge engineer came up with for the tramway? Jebb reported back in September that Webb had estimated that a suitable locomotive could be built for the sum of £250. Mr Jones was directed to approach the Wem & Bronygarth Turnpike Road Trustees and obtain their assent for the use of a steam locomotive on the tramway, without which neither the canal nor the tramway company could improve the prospects of the GVT.

As related in chapter 1, the SUR&C Co., in both 1846 and 1855, had seriously considered converting some of their canals into railways, no action being taken at either time, but in 1874 there was another proposal, which could have changed the fortunes of the GVT for the better by giving it a narrow-gauge connection into the heart of Shropshire.

Francis William Webb 1836–1906

Chief Mechanical Engineer of the London & North Western Railway and designer of the first steam locomotive proposal for the Glyn Valley Tramway.

Courtesy: SSPL

This scheme (See chapter 2 page 52) was mentioned by Randolph Mellor, a civil engineer, born c1832 in Bolton, in a report, dated 30th June 1874, to the shareholders of the nearby Ifton Rhyn Collieries, on his development proposals for that company.

Within his proposal he states that the gauge of his proposed tramway from Ifton-Rhyn Collieries to the canal be *'kept 2 feet 4 inches, the same as the Glyn Valley Tramway and the proposed conversion of the canal into a tramway'* and went on to say that: *'the proposal of the Shropshire Union Canal Company to convert their canal into a tramway should be kept in view. It appears that any attempt to do so must be strenuously opposed, unless more equal facilities for traffic be afforded'*.

From the 1870s onwards, the future of the Welsh section of the Shropshire Union Canal, including that to Weston, was in the balance. It is reported that Jebb had suggested, at the time of Mellor's report, that the canal from Llangollen to Weston be converted to a narrow-gauge railway and extended to Wem. Had this conversion been made it would have provided a rail transport link for coal, lime, slate and other minerals, as well as produce, from the Llangollen, Vron, Cefn Mawr, Chirk and Ceiriog Valley region southwards to the Midlands in direct competition with the GWR. At the same time, it would have fulfilled the original intentions of the Wem & Bronygarth Turnpike Trust, which failed in its mission to open up the area to trade. The SUR&C Co. appears to have rejected this proposal and the GVT did not get a narrow-gauge connection into rural Shropshire.

In December 1874, Thomas Edmunds, District Surveyor for the Llangollen Highway Board, wrote direct to the secretary of the Board of Trade drawing his attention to the state of the Turnpike road between Chirk and Glyn Ceiriog. Whilst the Wem & Bronygrath Turnpike Trust had built and fenced the new road, it had never been properly surfaced and was virtually impassable. Edmunds claimed that as some LHB roads crossed the Turnpike road this rendered these also impassable. To further exacerbate the situation the tramway had been built alongside the unfinished road and, contrary to The Glyn Valley Tramway Act 1870 (Section 46), which stipulated that *'The uppermost level of the rail shall be on a level with the surface of the road'* and that the public had the right *'to pass along or across any part of any road along or across which a tramway is laid, whether on or off the tramway, with carriages having ordinary wheels'*; the track had been laid anything from eighteen inches above the road to twelve inches below with, in some places, either a deep channel or large stones between the track and the road, thus further reducing the width available for traffic. The 1870 Act specified that there was to be 20ft of usable road for the use of ordinary traffic; one BoT report relates that it was only 7ft 6in wide in places from the edge of the tramway to the opposite hedge! The District Surveyor further complained that the tramway company was not operating the tramway in accordance with its Act, as that stipulated operation by animal power only, but was running trains down to Pontfaen by gravity, in charge of a brakesman *'to great nuisance and danger to the public'* – hardly, if the road was impassable in the first place!

The GVT was under an obligation to make good any part of the road that it broke up or disturbed in the process of building the tramway, but it was able to argue its way out of this, because the road trustees had not finished the road to an acceptable standard. The construction of the tramway not being executed flush with the road, as stipulated by the Act, highlighted another anomaly in its construction. The approved Plans & Sections, which accompanied the Act, showed sections of the tramway apparently rising above and falling below the road level, thus giving the Engineer for the tramway, Henry Dennis, a free hand to set the tramway levels as he desired, with full Parliamentary approval and irrespective of the stipulations in the Act. This had not been commented upon at the approval stage and the BoT appears to have endorsed the situation!

Under the Wem & Bronygarth Road Act 1862, the tramway company was supposed to pay the Trust £150/annum for the use of its land, subject to an increase in proportion to the tramway's earnings, which, Thomas Edmunds of the Llangollen Highway Board argued, should have been spent by the Trust on the road. He urged the Board of Trade to compel the Trust either to put the road in order or to hand it over to his Board.

Edmondson tickets of the horse tramway era, believed to be the original specimens from John B. Edmondson, Manchester.

The ticket 'New Inn to Herber Toll Gate' shown above has on the rear, in ink:
'April 1874 – H. Scholey – Colour Book P.111'

W.E. Hayward Collection (Railway Records) Ref. ZSPC 11/631 – Reproduced courtesy National Archives.

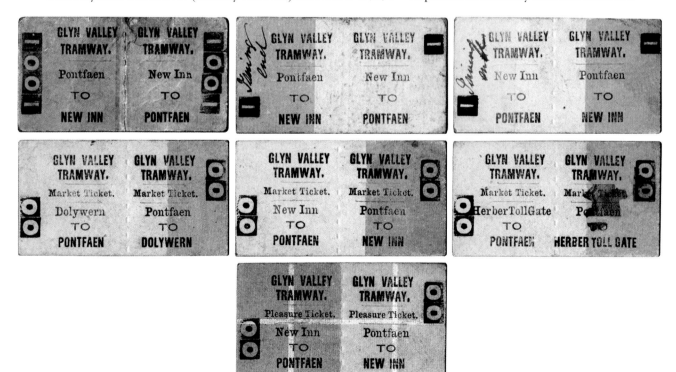

This early photograph of the horse tramway at Pontfadog illustrates how, in this location, the track was laid below the level of the road, which was the essence of complaints to the Board of Trade in 1874 and 1875.

Courtesy: Graham Greasley and Neville Hurdsman

The Llangollen Highway Board was not the only authority to complain to the BoT, as its complaint was followed by another, this time from the Oswestry Highway Board, which would have been responsible for the four short sections of the road in Shropshire that were traversed by the GVT: one at Pontfaen station near to the river (the county boundary), another opposite Pontfaen Farm, a third length past Yew Tree Cottages with two crossings and finally, the road from Trehowell Bridge to Upper Chirk Bank. It is not known what agreements had been made with the GVT Co. to build its tramway over Oswestry Highway Board roads.

By a strange oversight during the preparation of the 1870 Act, consultation with the Oswestry Highway Board was omitted and, when the tramway was completed, it was the Wem & Bronygarth Turnpike Trust's Surveyor who certified the tramway to be fit in accordance with the Act within the Oswestry Highway area, unbeknown to the authority responsible for those roads! The OHB complaint arose because a short length of tramway, on one of its roads above Pontfaen (which section is not recorded), had been built higher than the road. The GVT Co. had been requested by the OHB to bring the road up to the new level established by the tramway. This they had agreed to do, but *'the company executed the work so imperfectly that the road was almost impassable'*. The BoT craftily responded that it had no power to interfere with the condition of the roads, and its inspector, Lieut. Col. C.S. Hutchinson, in his report on the matter of the 10th April 1875, stated that the GVT Co. did not deny its obligation and he therefore suggested that *'they arrange with the Oswestry Highway Board a reasonable sum for putting the road in proper order and providing a sufficient drain, and handing this sum over to the Highway Board who would then complete the work.'* With regard to the complaint from the Llangollen Highway Board, Hutchinson reported that in all cases where its roads crossed the Wem and Bronygarth road the level of the tramway was properly arranged and did not interfere with its traffic, so there was no case against the GVT. Hutchinson further reported that:

> *'As the Wem and Bronygarth Road is (and was, I am informed before the construction of the tramway) in such a wretched state of repair as to be almost impassable, the fact of the level of the tramway being considerably above it is a matter of little present importance, as hardly any wheeled vehicles pass along it, and even if the road were in good order and much used the higher level of the tramway would not cause much inconvenience, as it is on one side of the road and the latter is in all parts amply wide enough for the passing of vehicles.'*

The BoT had also received a letter, as a result of a Glyn Ceiriog Parish Vestry meeting, held on the 18th March 1875 in the National School Room, saying that the residents of the area had been misled, as they were urged to support the building of the tramway and to buy shares in it, for which they would get a cheap service for merchandise and a good road down the valley.[21] They also emphasised that:

[21] Before the establishment of Parish Councils, the Parish Church was responsible for the conduct of all Parish business at its Vestry meetings.

> '... *the tramway is raised much above the level of the road – protected by a channel and stones, so as to prevent carriages of ordinary width going along the same and we have been led to understand that we should be prosecuted if we attempted to take our carts along the tramway. The mineral and luggage trains, and very often trucks with people in them, are sent down themselves* [by gravity] *with one or two brakesmen, and we think it a wonder that so few animals have been killed.*'

The last sentence seems to imply that animals had in fact been killed by virtue of the gravity working of trains on the tramway.

As if the GVT did not have enough problems, the unsatisfactory practice of sending trucks down by gravity had been highlighted by an accident that had occurred on 19th December 1874, when a gravity train carrying fare-paying passengers was derailed on the tramway bridge at Pontfaen, throwing its occupants and luggage into the icy cold waters of the River Ceiriog. This, of course, alerted everyone's attention, including that of the Board of Trade, which the GVT Co. was duty bound to inform. Mr Jaffray, whose party of friends it was that suffered injury, relates the story in his letter to the BoT dated the 4th March 1875:

> '... *The Tramway passes over the River Ceiriog, on a wooden bridge and by a curve* [Pontfaen], *which it is scarcely an exaggeration to say is about right angled ... while it is the practice to use a horse to draw the passenger carriage from Chirk, it was often the case that the down journey was accomplished by the momentum of the carriage or trucks, the speed being regulated by means of a brake ... returning from my Shooting Box beyond Glyn* [probably Nantyr] *no horse was attached, and a Brakesman in charge neglected to apply the brakes ... I am not sure that any serious accident to passengers has taken place previously, but trucks have several times shot over in the same place ... Apart from the consideration of cheapness, there is no reason why the river should be crossed at this dangerous angle.*'

Artwork © Philip D. Hawkins

Lieut. Col. C.S. Hutchinson from the BoT inspected the GVT, on 10th April 1875, to investigate the various complaints in respect of the road, and the accident of Mr Jaffray and his friends. His report stated:

'It seems to be a customary practice, both for passenger cars and goods trucks to be allowed to descend by gravity, from higher to the lower terminus, the speed being regulated by the brakesman. Mr Jaffray, two of his friends, and another person hired a special train to descend from the higher to the lower terminus on the day in question [19th December 1874]. There being no horse or car available, they were conveyed in a slate truck, their brakesman and baggage occupying a second one, and the descent being accomplished by gravity. During the journey the brakesman is said to have been frequently reminded as to the speed at which he was running, but without effect, and it is supposed that he was the worse for liquor, and on the train reaching the bridge over the River Ceiriog, where the tramway nears its lower terminus [Pontfaen] and takes two very sharp bends [one as it leaves the road to cross the bridge and the other as it leaves the bridge to run along the long embankment to the station], the trucks left the rails and the whole party was shot into the river, Mr Shakespeare and another, being severely injured ... This accident would not have occurred had the Company complied with the 59th Section of their Act, which provides that all carriages used on the tramway shall be moved by animal power only.'

Hutchinson went on to say that had the simple precaution been taken of setting the points for Pontfaen siding, which was a continuation of the roadside tramway, this accident would not have happened, and he suggested that these points should be so set in the future. On the question

The practice of carrying passengers in open slate wagons, as seen here on the Talyllyn Railway as late as the 1930s, was not confined to the GVT.

Courtesy: Talyllyn Railway
Archive/David Mitchell

No photographs of gravity run passenger or slate trains on the GVT have yet been found, but this 1920s photograph of a loaded slate train descending the Ffestiniog Railway by gravity and passing through Dduallt, gives a fair impression of what it would have been like, although a GVT slate train would not have been as long.

Collection: Peter Johnson

An artist's impression of a train load of granite setts crossing the tramway bridge over the river at Pontfaen, on its way to Gledrid Wharf. This is the bridge from which Mr Jaffray and his party were thrown into the icy waters of the River Ceiriog on 19th December 1874. Note the siding that continues alongside the road as far as the turning for Pontfaen road bridge.

Collection: John Milner
© Philip D. Hawkins

of the complaints from inhabitants about the speeds that the gravity trains were being run, his reply was '*They have the remedy, it appears to me, in their own hands if they choose to use the tramway by indicting the company for infringing the provisions of their own Act of Parliament* [Section 59].' In other words either refuse to use this means of propulsion or use the courts and not the BoT to rectify the problem!

As a result of this accident, Mr Jebb was instructed to ease the approach to the bridge across the river at an estimated cost of £200, and to extend what was then only a short siding on the north bank of the river as far as Pontfaen Bridge. Passengers were thus no longer carried across the river to the old terminus, but to a new one on the north bank by Pontfaen Bridge. There is no record of any building having been erected, the office staying at the old terminus on the other side of the river, as this was essential for controlling the mineral and goods traffic to and from Gledrid Wharf, but the new passenger terminus may well have had a tiny ticket office, such as the one provided at Glyn Ceiriog – best described as a slate-roofed privy with a serving hatch! Mr Jaffray had been quick to act on behalf of his friends, as a letter dated 22nd December 1874 was sent to the SUR&C Co. from his solicitors, Ward & Co., Birmingham, stating that the company would be held responsible '*for all damages arising from injuries there received*' as well as '*losses and injuries to baggage*'. One of the party, Mr Shakespeare, had a compound fracture of his leg and other injuries, while another, Mr William Hedges, suffered from severe internal damage. The other passenger, Mr Moses of Chirk, was also hurt. An examination of Mr Shakespeare, by Dr. McEwan of Chester, revealed that he would have a permanent shortening of his one leg. The SUR&C Co. committee, at its meeting on 28th July 1875, resolved to pay him compensation '*on the best possible terms*'. Later that year Mr Hedges filed a claim for £250, which the committee

An interesting view of Glyn Ceiriog c1880 with, in the foreground the new Baptist chapel built 1874/75, the New Inn next to the landmark tree (Pren Mawr), with the tramway terminus and GVT warehouse on the right. No building development has yet taken place on either New Road, the left-hand side of the High Street or Quarry Road. The Wynne Slate Quarry waste tip is only starting to creep towards the High Street. The timber building, lower left, nestling alongside the Cambrian Incline and Quarry Road, is the GVT stables, built on land rented from Thomas Allen Hughes.

Collection: John Milner

thought was far too high, so it was agreed to try and also settle amicably. It would appear that having seen that his fellow passengers had met with reasonable success in claiming compensation, the other injured passenger, Mr Moses, filed a claim for £200, which did not come before the SU committee until March 1877 – three years after the accident. The committee felt that he had no grounds for a claim, but by July that year the matter was settled with £100 being paid out.

A few weeks after Lieut. Col. C.S. Hutchinson's visit on 10th April 1875, the Llangollen Highway Board informed the BoT that since Col. Hutchinson's Report all carriages on the tramway had been moved by animal power, so technically gravity working would appear to have been short-lived. But, in reality, that was not the case, as there are references to gravity working right up to the conversion to steam in 1888.

Returning to the GVT Company's other problems, a joint meeting had been held at the SUR&C Co.'s Board Room, Chester, on 6th November 1874, attended by Colonel Bourne, Henry Dennis, Mr Jones, GVT Secretary, Mr Jebb, Mr Hope and Mr Potts, to discuss the position of the undertaking and its present unsatisfactory mode and cost of working. The question of whether the tramway should be extended further up the valley to Hendre Granite Quarry was also discussed. Such an extension would accommodate the expected increase in granite traffic and also serve the new Gunpowder Works and the Chinastone Quarries. It appeared evident that the time was favourable to obtain powers to enable this extension to be built and, at the same time, to obtain relief from the restrictions of horse power and to introduce locomotive power on the whole of the tramway. A provisional estimate for the extension was given as:

Say	Extensions, about 2 miles	£6,000
	Improvement of existing line	£2,000
	Procuring the Act &c	£1,000
	Engineering, land &c, &c	£1,000
		£10,000

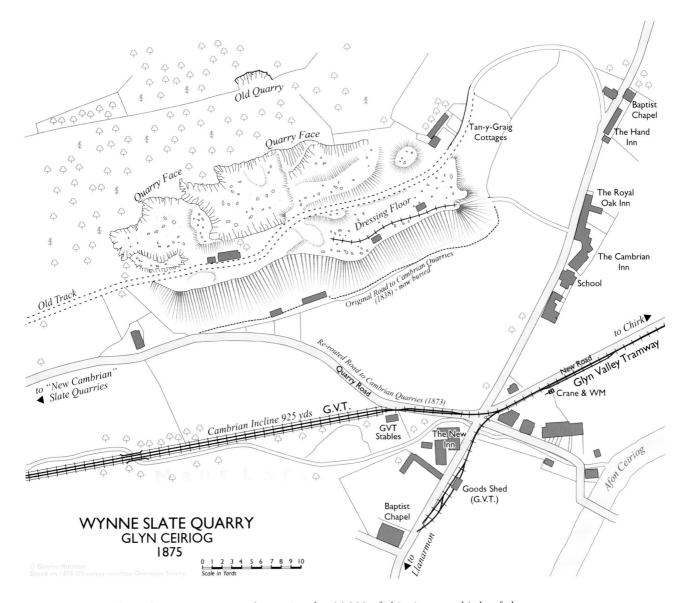

WYNNE SLATE QUARRY
GLYN CEIRIOG
1875

0 1 2 3 4 5 6 7 8 9 10
Scale in Yards

© Gordon Rushton
Based on 1875 OS survey courtesy Ordnance Survey

Henry Dennis undertook to guarantee a subscription for £4,000 of this: i.e. two-thirds of the construction cost of the extension, providing that the Shropshire Union Company would find subscribers for the balance of £6,000. However, the SUR&C Co. stated that any application to them on the subject must be accompanied by an ample guarantee of funding. Dennis responded that it might be assumed that the Granite Company, the Gunpowder Company, the New Cambrian Slate Company, the Lester Chinastone Quarry, Mr West's Quarries, and probably smaller slate companies would be willing to subscribe and, if desired to do so, he would undertake to see the parties concerned. As to the costs of the application, he also undertook to prepare the plans and to make no claim for payment until the SUR&C Co. sanctioned the project. This was a generous gesture, especially as the GVT Co. had no funds available, although he did have a vested interest in Hendre Quarry, as a promoter of The Glyn Ceiriog Granite Co.! The gunpowder company would have benefited but, unbeknown at the time, this company was to be a very short-lived venture.

The SUR&C Co. was keen to have traffic agreements with all the companies mentioned for the exclusive transport of their entire output via the canal, offering rates that were comparable with other carriers, in the expectation that the companies would be able to develop their major markets at destinations served by the canal. However, transport via the national canal network, although it was extensive in coverage, was unable to compete with the increasing attractions of rail transport.

The principal objectives, agreed at the meeting, were to proceed to extend the tramway to Hendre, to seek a repeal of the restriction on the use of horse power only, to improve the whole line for use by locomotives and to make improvements to the road, all subject to the approval of the SUR&C Co. The GVT company's solicitors, Longueville & Co., Oswestry, were instructed to proceed immediately to prepare notices of application to Parliament.

A statement made on 9th December 1874 showed that the GVT Co.'s finances were not in a healthy state, because there was a deficiency of £1,041 9s. 6d., accounted for by the following statement:

Old claims outstanding	£200 0s. 0d.
An advance made by Mr Jebb, but deducted from his subscription of £1,000	£100 0s. 0d.
Deficiency of subscriptions by about	£250 0s. 0d.
Doubling Incline (half the cost still outstanding)	£200 0s. 0d.
Other extras	£214 2s. 0d.
Irrespective of claims for interest paid by Lord Trevor and others, really as Guarantors for the Company	£341 2s. 0d.
Less Herber Branch which had not been built	-£263 14s. 6d.

An injection of additional capital was absolutely necessary, in order to reduce this deficiency, and also to fund the new venture that the company was about to embark on – the extension up from Glyn Ceiriog to the granite quarry at Hendre.

By the end of 1874, additional capital expenditure of £2,993 had been paid out by the SUR&C Co. to the contractor for additional work on the existing line. To further add to its despondency, the company revealed that during the past half-year of 1874, after taking into account interest and depreciation on the stock and buildings they had provided, the tramway had showed a loss of £98.

Everything appeared to be working against the GVT, including the weather, as George Jebb had reported at the 9th December 1874 Executive meeting of the SUR&C Co. that, as the result of a

A rare photograph of a horse tramway 'train', with a wagon and the van, ready to depart from outside the New Inn to Pontfaen and perhaps on to Gledrid Wharf.

Collection: John Milner

storm on 29th November, a flood had damaged the Cambrian Quarries incline. The incline was owned by the GVT, but the SUR&C Co. was obliged to repair it, as the GVT Co. had no capital. Jebb was seeking to build a culvert under the incline to alleviate flooding caused by Nant Lafar, which flows down to the Ceiriog from above the Cambrian Quarries and through the site.[22] Nant Lafar passed under the incline in three places and since its abandonment post 1936, further flooding has contributed to its virtual obliteration.

At its March 1875 meeting at Chester, the SUR&C Co. Executive Committee was beginning to become uneasy with regard to operating the GVT. The cost of working the tramway for the previous year had been £1,793, against receipts of £1,327 and discussions took place about extending the tramway, to attract more traffic, and the feasibility of converting it to steam power. Proposals included various extensions to the Cambrian Railways at Hindford, just to the east of Whittington, near Oswestry, and to Ifton-Rhyn Colliery, as well as the one to Hendre Quarry.

The matter of building an extension to Hendre was raised as a result of The Patent Gunpowder Co. pressing for this to be done. However, the directors of the Gunpowder Co. did not have their eyes set on an extension of the existing tramway; they wanted to see it converted to a standard-gauge railway! This was revealed in June 1875, when the company was conducting a series of experiments at Hendre Quarry to illustrate the qualities of its blasting powder. Apart from potential investors and customers, the chairman and deputy chairman of the London & North Western Railway Co. were present and the ensemble was informed by the Gunpowder Co. that:

> *'The tramway is on the narrow-gauge and is well laid, the permanent way being in excellent condition and there are no steep gradients [Not exactly true!]. The tramway is worked by horses, but the owners of property in the valley, and also higher up beyond Glyn, are naturally extremely desirous to see a line of railway running through the valley. They point to the fact that the present excellent tramway may, with little alteration, serve for the permanent way of the railway, and this in itself would save a very large expense; in addition to this, it is calculated that the present rails would fetch a price within 15 per cent of the cost of new rails.*

> *At the present time the works in the valley and neighbourhood, including the patent gunpowder works, the china clay works, and the slate and granite quarries, are of no inconsiderable importance, but those who know the district well are satisfied that there would be much larger development of mineral operations if better means of transit existed. Higher up the valley there are immense deposits of granite and slate, and no doubt the lord of the manor, Major West, would allow these to be worked at a modest royalty, and gentlemen who are competent to speak upon the point are convinced that, looking at the present and prosperous traffic, such a line as has been indicated would be a remunerative undertaking. Of course, if such a railway were made, the property of the Patent Gunpowder Company must be increased, and we believe that the directors and other influential gentlemen will not let the matter rest until the much to be desired line is constructed.'*

The envisaged railway was to be of standard-gauge, but the idea that a standard-gauge railway 'with little alteration' could replace the roadside tramway is, of course, total nonsense, and it shows a lack of understanding of the statutory differences. The point made was that money could be saved because the GVT already had a trackbed, which just needed widening, and the existing rails could be sold to offset some of the cost of new heavier ones. Realistically, they would have to opt for replacing the tramway with one of the earlier schemes to build a standard-gauge railway up the valley, such as The Glyn Valley Railway or The Ellesmere & Glyn Valley Railway, not just

[22] For further details on the Cambrian and Wynne Quarry inclines see Vol.1 of this series, *'Slates from Glyn Ceiriog'* by the author.

Cartridges from the Patent Gunpowder Co. would have been packed into wooden boxes, with leather hinges and straps, similar to this example found at the Wynne Slate Quarry.

Courtesy: Angela James
Photo: © Alistair Kerr Photography

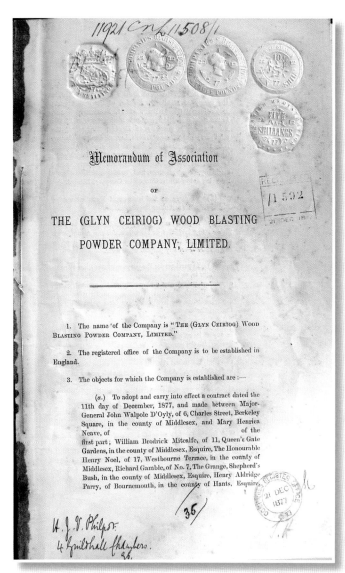

The title page of the 1877 Memorandum of Association of the The (Glyn Ceiriog) Wood Blasting Powder Co. Ltd, which only survived a short period, being placed into liquidation in 1879.

National Archives

a simple rebuild of the tramway. As related in chapter 1, the GVT directors and their predecessors had been down this route before with proposals to build standard-gauge railways up the valley, none of which came to fruition. No more was heard of this scheme.

The truth behind the need for a standard-gauge railway was that the Patent Gunpowder Co. would require large quantities of concentrated acids to be brought up the valley, and would be sending out hazardous explosive products in bulk. Utilising the narrow-gauge tramway would involve unnecessary transshipment requiring careful control, which would add to the costs, whereas a standard-gauge railway down the valley would make a direct connection with the national rail network. The high ambitions of this company were never fulfilled. The capital raised had enabled the company to build a fully equipped works and, in April 1875, start manufacturing nitrocellulose explosives. Unfortunately, the works was managed by an engineer, rather than a competent chemist, who did not realise that, during storage, the impurities in nitrocellulose powder gradually decompose into chemicals with low ignition temperatures, which could cause it 'spontaneously' to burst into flame and explode. There was no sampling and testing of the product, to determine its purity, at any stage during manufacture.

Small quantities were sold to quarries but, within weeks, the H M Explosive Inspectorate had tested samples taken at random during routine visits, and found them both impure and in a potentially dangerous state. The works was inspected, sampling and testing regimes installed, changes made to management and orders given to rework all the impure powder still on the premises. There were also a few orders from overseas, including one in January 1876, from Mr O'Conner, an agent in Australia. He ordered two tons of the powder made up into cartridges to a customer's specification. This was done and the cartridges put into store in the works magazine until 17th July 1876, when they were dispatched to the powder buoys off Gravesend, from where they were loaded into the hold of the *Great Queensland*, a large iron sailing ship, which set sail for Melbourne on August 6th. She was carrying about 2,500 tons of mixed cargo, which included 30 tons, or so, of common black gunpowder packed in kegs and barrels, as well as 183 wooden cases containing the two tons of patent gunpowder cartridges.

The *Great Queensland* was also carrying 33 passengers and a crew of 36, but she never arrived in Australia. An exhaustive enquiry into the loss, published its findings in July 1877, concluding that the ship had been completely destroyed by an explosion with the loss of 69 souls, soon after last being seen on August 12th, north of Cape Finisterre on the Spanish Peninsula, and '*in all probability, the cause was the spontaneous combustion of two tons of wood powder*' for which '*the Patent Gunpowder Company are alone to blame*'.

The company was disgraced and ceased trading. However, in December that year, the works was bought out by a much smaller company, The (Glyn Ceiriog) Wood Blasting Powder Co. Ltd, but this company also failed and was liquidated in September 1879. The Granite Company working the neighbouring Hendre Quarry, which was by this time a flourishing concern, took over the powder works lands in 1880 and good use was made of the site by building its stone-crushing plant there. The history of the Patent Gunpowder Works and the part it played in the tragic loss of so many lives on the *Great Queensland* appears to have been soon forgotten.[23]

In May 1875, the SUR&C Co. Executive Committee inspected the Cambrian Quarry and agreed to allocate a portion of its canal wharf at Calveley, near Tarporley (12 miles S.E. of Chester), for storage of the quarry's slates, along with interchange facilities with the London & North Western Railway. Although the company now had a more economical means of getting its slate away and out of the valley, there was still a trade depression and the demand for slates was low. Thus, while slates were being dispatched, via the GVT, from Glyn Ceiriog, they were ending up unsold at Calveley (and, no doubt, piling up at Gledrid as well), much to the concern of the SUR&C Co. which, by 1878, was demanding action over the excessive amount of slate being stored on its wharves.

In spite of the expenditure by the SUR&C Co. to make good the deficiencies in the system and provide all the facilities necessary to run an efficient tramway, the expected revenues from tramway traffic did not materialise. The New Cambrian Slate Company, registered in 1872, had been expected to be a major user of the GVT, but facing a fall in the national demand in slate, this company had been forced into liquidation in 1875 with insufficient funds to pay its debts. However, it had been immediately reconstituted under the same name on the 19th April (No.9417) and was struggling on with major developments at its quarries above Glyn Ceiriog, hoping that the demand for slates would soon return. At this time there was very little other traffic coming down the valley, as both Hendre Quarry and the Gunpowder Works were still in the early stages of development.

The GVT line to the GWR interchange at Preesgweene appears not to have been used to its full extent, which is substantiated by a letter from Mr Theodore Martin (he was not knighted until 1880), in which he stated that he had received a letter from the GWR Co. complaining that the LNWR Co. (in the interests of the SUR&C Co.) was putting difficulties in the way of the interchange traffic between the GVT and the GWR, a situation which had been mentioned previously in a GVT Directors' report of 1874.

In June 1876, the proposal to extend the tramway to Hindford, to connect with the Cambrian Railways, and also tap into the collieries at Moreton Hall, had been augmented by a further proposal to extend the tramway to Pandy (*The Glyn Valley Tramway (Pandy) Extension*) from

[23] The fully detailed history of The Patent Gunpowder Co. Ltd, The (Glyn Ceiriog) Wood Blasting Powder Co. Ltd, The Glyn Ceiriog Granite Co. and The Ceiriog Granite Co. is related by the authors in Volume 3 of the Industrial History of the Ceiriog Valley.

Glyn Ceiriog, Llansantffraid Bridge.

Although some ten years later, as it shows the incline from the Wynne Slate Quarry, this postcard of c1886 shows the terminus of the tramway with its goods shed and crane, the stable yard beyond it and the new Baptist chapel to the left.

Collection: Robert Jones

where a branch would connect with the Nantyr Slate Quarries (opened c1832), owned by Mr Richard Myddelton Biddulph, who had great expectations for their future. On 26th June, he had written to the SUR&C Co. stating that if the company would guarantee improvements to the GVT, then he would assist financially '*in the making of a junction from Pandy to Nantyr Slate Quarries*'. As already related, a route to the Nantyr Quarries via the Cambrian Quarries incline had been included in the Glyn Valley Tramway Act 1870, but despite the route having been planned and agreements reached in respect of the rental of land, it had not been built. To appease Mr Myddelton Biddulph, whose support the company needed to retain, a new tramway route was written into the Glyn Valley Tramway Act 1878, entitled the '*Glyn Valley Tramway (Nantyr) Extension*', consisting of two elements; a new road and a tramway running alongside it. Mr Myddelton Biddulph may have insisted on both in case the GVT Co. opted out of building the tramway. The Nantyr Quarry was never developed to any great extent, other than being worked for a short period in the 1870s and 1880s, employing about three men and neither the tramway nor the road from Pandy to Nantyr were built – they remained but an idle intent on a piece of paper. Because of the decline in traffic, the company had been keen to grab at any prospect of generating additional business and the earlier proposal to extend the GVT to connect with the Ifton-Rhyn Colliery tramway had been further considered on 7th December 1875, without any decision being arrived at.

By the end of 1876, the SUR&C Co. was concerned that only a third of the GVT traffic was passing through Gledrid Wharf, as the hoped-for monopoly of GVT traffic had not materialised. The tramway was entering a critical phase in its life. It was inefficient and the cost of operating it was escalating, effectively putting a stranglehold on the development of the quarries in the valley. However, there was hope for the future, with the potential for the development of interchange passenger services at Trehowell and the replacement of horse traction by steam power. It was to be several years before the GVT Co. was to regain control of its assets from the SUR&C Co., the Ceiriog Granite Co. was to take over as operator of the tramway and steam operation was eventually introduced.

Many local inhabitants supported the Glyn Valley Tramway and bought small quantities of shares in the GVT Co., in the belief that they would prosper from the new enterprise. The promises by the GVT Co. of a good return on their investment was sadly never to materialise. This share certificate, dated 11th May 1874 was issued to Mr John Evans of Talygarth, Glyn Ceiriog.

Collection: John Milner

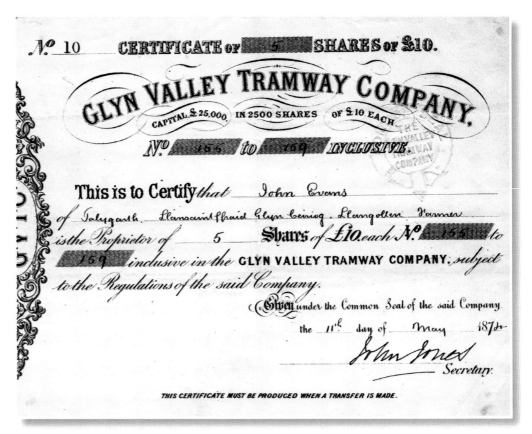

Chapter 5

The Horse Tramway Route

T he route built for the GVT horse tramway in the early 1870s, to connect the Ceiriog Valley with the national canal and rail networks via interchanges south of the river, at Gledrid and Trehowell, is better described separately from the route that the tramway took, following its conversion to steam operation in the late 1880s, when these interchanges were abandoned and new ones built in the Chirk area, on the north side of the valley.

The buildings and associated structures constructed for the horse tramway not only enabled slate, granite and other minerals to be brought down the valley and transshipped at the interchanges, but also provided a much needed passenger and goods service for the local communities. It is hoped that this chapter will give readers a better understanding of this first GVT tramway, the buildings that were constructed and what can be seen of it all today.

Pontfaen Station

Pontfaen was the centre of operations for the horse tramway and here was sited the passenger station alongside the Pontfaen–Bronygarth road, this being the limit of passenger working on the horse tramway at the Chirk end of the valley. It was also the point at which 'trains' were split into manageable loads for the steep climb to Trehowell. The station boasted a short 'platform' with stone walling dividing it from the road and set back to provide a 'pull-in' for carriages or carts, which is still clearly visible today. The actual track level, through the station, was a lot lower than the ground level there today, this having been raised as the result of the tipping of waste over the years. At the end of the platform was a brick-built office/waiting room. The stone-built retaining wall is still in place alongside the road where the station once stood.

The station area was situated within a large hollow that had been hewn out of the escarpment by earlier quarrying activities at Pontfaen Quarry, and which provided a level site suitable for the erection of facilities including a carriage shed, workshop and stables. The carriage shed was a timber-framed building, designed and erected by the SUR&C Co., with the overall dimensions 23' 6" x 36' 6", and a small smithy/workshop extension to one side. Two tracks entered the building, each through its own pair of double doors, and a short siding was located adjacent. Externally, it was clad with vertical boarding, the same as the warehouses at Gledrid and Glyn Ceiriog, and had a slate roof. The roof was topped with a louvered ventilator, in the traditional 'engine shed' style. This building was dismantled in 1888 and utilised in the construction of the new buildings at Chirk station. From dimensional checks and the door sizes, it appears to have been utilised for the new carpenters' shop. Local residents remember remnants of its footprint at Pontfaen, which was visible for many years, but the tipping on the site has now obliterated all.

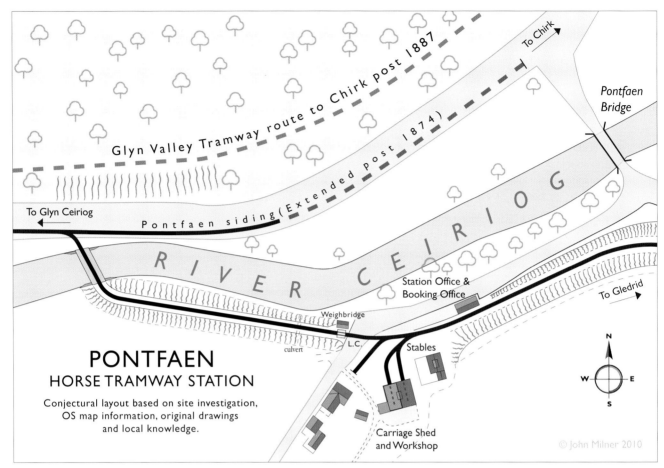

To Chirk

Pontfaen Bridge

Glyn Valley Tramway route to Chirk post 1887

Pontfaen siding (Extended post 1874)

To Glyn Ceiriog

R I V E R   C E I R I O G

Station Office & Booking Office

To Gledrid

Weighbridge

L.C.

culvert

Stables

PONTFAEN
HORSE TRAMWAY STATION

Conjectural layout based on site investigation,
OS map information, original drawings
and local knowledge.

Carriage Shed and Workshop

N
W   E
S

© John Milner 2010

The site of Pontfaen station c1950 looking towards the river and Chirk–Glyn Ceiriog road, in the trees at the bottom of the field. The tree to the right marks the start of the long embankment to the tramway bridge over the river. In the centre of the picture is a spoil heap, which may well have been from early working of Pontfaen Quarry.

Courtesy: Late James I.C. Boyd

The building was specifically designated as a '*carriage shed and repairing shop*'. As such, it was designed to house two passenger carriages and two or three wagons for repair, with a small area left as workshop space. Why, one would ask, did they need to have a carriage shed at Pontfaen when the first train of the day started from Glyn Ceiriog at 8.00 a.m., with the last train of the day terminating at Glyn Ceiriog at 8.15 p.m.?

Mr Bill Stokes, who was born and lived at No.17, Pontfaen, related in 1957 that the repair shops, stables, smithy and carpenters' shop were all located '*in the recess in the rock*' (meaning Pontfaen Quarry) just by his house, but that these had not been standing for many years. He had a sawmill housed in some old buildings next to No.17, which may well have been part of the tramway complex. The area of the quarry floor was limited by the close proximity of the quarry face, but the exact arrangement of the various buildings cramped into this small space has not been determined for certain. These included a four-horse stable, but it has been suggested that, at times when this was inadequate, neighbouring Pontfaen Farm was able to provide the extra stabling for the GVT horses. In recent years, cast off heavy-horse shoes have been dug up in the field below Yew Tree Cottages, which may indicate that GVT horses were turned out into this field.

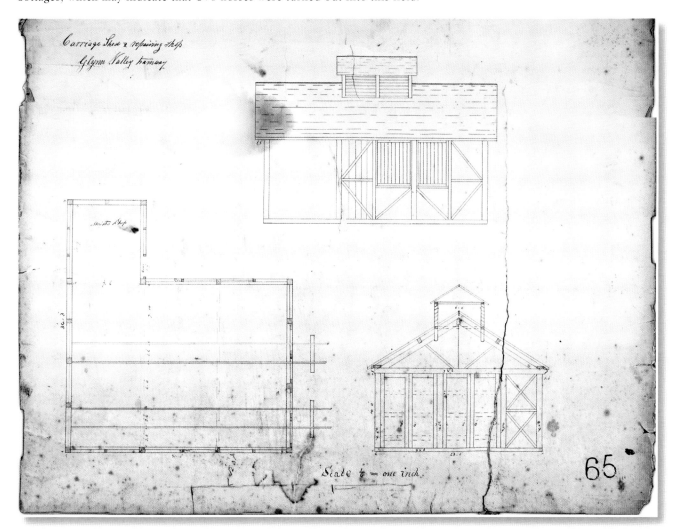

This original Shropshire Union Railway & Canal Co. drawing shows the design for the GVT 'Carriage Shed and Repairing Shop', which was built at Pontfaen station and generally referred to as the 'Works'. It was of typical all-timber structure, of similar design to the warehouses at Gledrid and Glyn Ceiriog. Its size was restricted by the area available in the old quarry at Pontfaen, where it was located. It was removed from Pontfaen in 1890 and appears to have been reused in the construction of the new carpenters' shop at the tramway's Chirk station.

Shropshire Archives Ref: 5465/51

Pontfaen to Trehowell Bridge

(Line of tramway shown in red)

From Pontfaen station, the tramway climbed up through a long cutting on the northern side of Pontfaen Farm. It emerged through the stone wall on the left, crossed the Pontfaen–Weston Rhyn road on the level, and continued on its own trackbed along the top edge of the field that slopes steeply towards the river, opposite Pontfaen Farm. . . . .

. . . . . The roadside wall, shown in (1), was not there in horse tramway days, and this top part of the field was then a wide grass verge. The tramway continued on this formation towards Yew Tree Cottages (2), before which it crossed to the other side of the Pontfaen–Trehowell road (3). From here it ran along the edge of the road until it reached Pen-y-Lan, where it left the road to make a short diversion on its own trackbed in order to avoid a steep 'dip' in the roadway. This can be seen on the map (page 120) and by site investigation. . . . . .

Photos © John Milner 2009

Pontfaen–Trehowell

From the station, the goods-only tramway headed eastwards on its own trackbed for 110yds, through a deep cutting to emerge to cross the Pontfaen–Weston Rhyn road on the level, almost at right angles because of the steep grade in the road. The point at which the tramway emerged can be identified by the difference in the stonework in the retaining wall in front of Pontfaen Farm, smaller random blocks having been used to make good the opening before the cutting was backfilled after the tramway was abandoned. The station site and the land through which the cutting ran were extensively disturbed in 2010–11, due to building development work.

On the opposite side of the road, the tramway ran along the top of the field that slopes steeply down to the river; the roadside wall that is there today is not shown on early maps. After only about 70yds, it left this field, just before Yew Tree Cottages, crossed the Pontfaen–Trehowell road, ran alongside the south side of it for 120yds and then, because of the severe undulation in the road at this point, took to its own trackbed, thus creating a steady gradient for a further 60yds before emerging to cross this road again on the level into The Wood. From here the tramway again ran on its own trackbed, now a public footpath that clings precariously to the steep wooded southerly side of the Ceiriog Valley for a distance of 150yds and from which there are superb views of the viaduct and aqueduct. It emerged to cross an open field diagonally to reach Trehowell Bridge,

. . . . . The tramway continued its climb, crossing the Pontfaen–Trehowell road a second time to enter The Wood, clinging precariously to the southern escarpment of the Ceiriog Valley and overlooking the Shrewsbury & Chester Railway's fine viaduct built to the design of Henry Robertson in 1848, before crossing the fields to reach Trehowell Bridge.

© John Milner 2009

which carries the Trehowell–Chirk Bank road (now named Trehowell Avenue) over the Great Western Railway main line.

Trehowell Bridge marked the peak of the Shropshire section of the tramway track at 375ft above sea level, having climbed about 75ft from Pontfaen, and provided the means for the GVT to cross the GWR main line, without the company having to build its own bridge, as originally planned. This bridge still carried the earlier Quinta Tramway, which ran from Quinta and Trehowell collieries and brickworks, down to the canal at Chirk Bank. Just before the GVT crossed the bridge at Trehowell, a branch crossed both the road and the Quinta Tramway, before entering the Quinta Collieries site to provide the interchange with the GWR, via the private standard-gauge Trehowell Colliery sidings. At the Chirk Bank end of the bridge, the Quinta Tramway was again crossed, this time by the mainline of the GVT, before the two tramways continued on their own independent routes to the canal.

The transshipment sidings layout between the GVT and the Trehowell Colliery sidings is shown on a surviving GWR plan (see pages 140–141). On the Chirk side of Quinta Bridge the GWR had built a long loop line adjacent to the 'Up' main line, with a head shunt at both ends and a slip line over to the Down line. A signal box on the Down side controlled the junction. Off this loop ran the private standard-gauge sidings, installed by Thomas Barnes, which climbed up the Quinta/Trehowell Colliery site, more or less parallel to the GWR, until it swung northwestwards, crossing the old Quinta drive, and terminating adjacent to Trehowell Lane. This siding, together with a short one off it, provided a wharf and interchange for the GVT, which entered the site at a somewhat higher level hugging the GWR boundary. There was a storage loop close to Trehowell Bridge. Other standard-gauge sidings served Trehowell Colliery and brickworks.

From Trehowell Bridge, the GVT continued on the virtually level road, now known as Trehowell Avenue, running along the left-hand side for 120yds, until it reached Upper Chirk Bank. Here it crossed the Chirk Bank–Preesgweene (Preesgwyn) road and entered the site of the former Upper

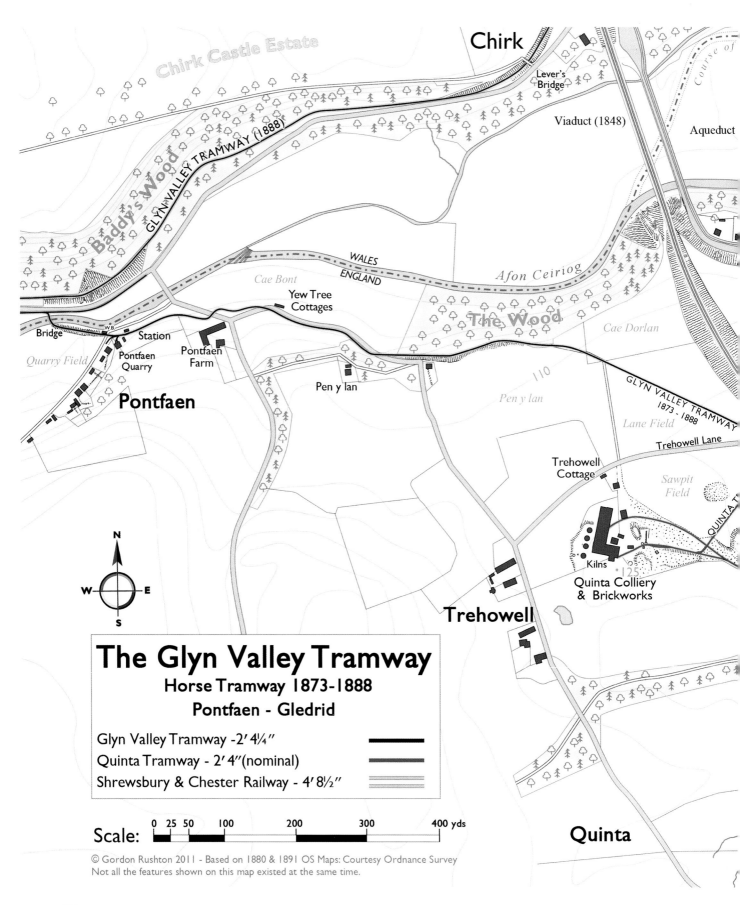

Chirk

Chirk Castle Estate

Baddy's Wood

GLYN VALLEY TRAMWAY (1888)

Lever's Bridge

Viaduct (1848)

Aqueduct

Course of

WALES
ENGLAND

Afon Ceiriog

Cae Bont

Yew Tree Cottages

The Wood

Cae Dorlan

Bridge

W.B.

Station

Quarry Field

Pontfaen Quarry

Pontfaen Farm

Pen y lan

Pen y lan

110

GLYN VALLEY TRAMWAY
1873 - 1888

Lane Field

Pontfaen

Trehowell Lane

Trehowell Cottage

Sawpit Field

QUINTA T

Trehowell

Quinta Colliery & Brickworks

Kilns

125

N
W E
S

Trehowell

The Glyn Valley Tramway
Horse Tramway 1873-1888
Pontfaen - Gledrid

Glyn Valley Tramway - 2′ 4¼″	
Quinta Tramway - 2′ 4″(nominal)	
Shrewsbury & Chester Railway - 4′ 8½″	

Scale: 0 25 50 100 200 300 400 yds

Quinta

© Gordon Rushton 2011 - Based on 1880 & 1891 OS Maps: Courtesy Ordnance Survey
Not all the features shown on this map existed at the same time.

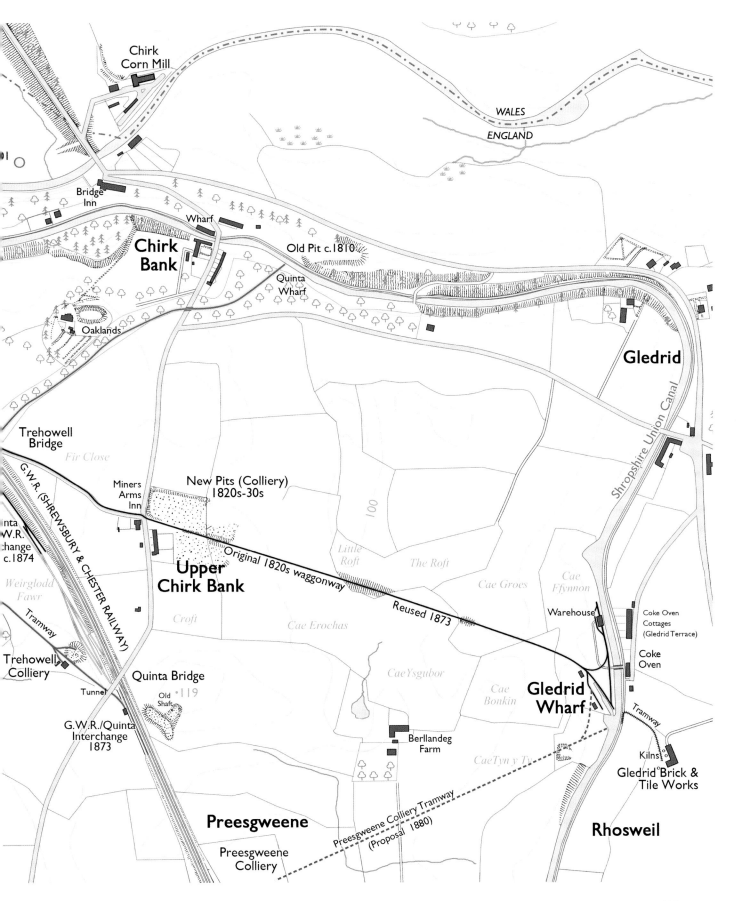

Chirk Corn Mill

WALES

ENGLAND

Bridge Inn

Wharf

Chirk Bank

Old Pit c.1810

Quinta Wharf

Oaklands

Gledrid

Trehowell Bridge

Fir Close

Shropshire Union Canal

Miners Arms Inn

New Pits (Colliery) 1820s-30s

nta W.R. change c.1874

Weirglodd Fawr

Little Roft

The Roft

Cae Groes

Cae Ffynnon

Warehouse

Coke Oven Cottages (Gledrid Terrace)

Tramway

Croft

Cae Erochas

Original 1820s waggonway

Reused 1873

Coke Oven

G.W.R. (SHREWSBURY & CHESTER RAILWAY)

Upper Chirk Bank

Trehowell Colliery

Quinta Bridge

Old Shaft

•119

CaeYsgubor

Cae Bonkin

Gledrid Wharf

Tramway

Tunnel

Kilns

G.W.R./Quinta Interchange 1873

Berllandeg Farm

CaeTyn y Ty

Gledrid Brick & Tile Works

Preesgweene

Preesgweene Colliery Tramway (Proposal 1880)

Rhosweil

Preesgweene Colliery

Trehowell Bridge
to
Gledrid

The view on the right *(4)*, shows the GVT route, crossing the GWR main line along the left-hand side of Trehowell Bridge before continuing to Upper Chirk Bank. It crossed the route of the earlier Quinta Tramway *(shown in yellow)*, which had passed over the bridge on the right-hand side, before crossing the lane to run between the two hedgerows seen on the left, on its way to the Quinta canal wharf at Chirk Bank. . . . . . .

. . . . . . At the end of Trehowell Lane, the tramway crossed the Chirk Bank– Preesgweene road *(5)* and entered what was the site of the former Upper Chirk Bank Colliery. From here, it used the trackbed of the 1820s colliery waggonway to Gledrid Wharf, passing through a corner of a field *(6)* and onto a substantial embankment, through what is now a wooded area *(7)*. In the photograph, this embankment can be seen to drop gently to field level on the right, but steeply on the left into a pit, thought to be either an early coal or clay working. From the end of this embankment, the tramway crossed more fields, before dropping steeply to Gledrid Wharf.

Photos © John Milner 2009

Chirk Bank Colliery, now hidden in a copse, from where it headed off down its own trackbed, along the route of the old 1820s colliery waggonway to the canal wharf at Gledrid, situated halfway between Gledrid and Rhôsweil canal bridges – a drop of some 60ft, gentle for most of the way, but less so closer to the wharf. This redundant former colliery wharf was developed into the GVT/ canal interchange.

From the colliery site at Upper Chirk Bank, the tramway proceeded in a straight line across the corner of an open field before passing onto an embankment that had been built by the colliery company along the edge of what is now a wooded area. It emerged to cross a number of other fields before swinging into Gledrid Wharf. Some of this section of the tramway route can be witnessed on the Google satellite image of the area.

Gledrid Wharf

The terminus of the GVT, Gledrid Wharf, was situated in a field alongside the canal and comprised two separate wharfs. The first of these was a long canal arm that had been constructed in the 1820s at an angle of about 45° in a northwesterly direction, and was accessed from the canal via a narrow entrance (about 9ft) from a turning basin. After the entrance, the arm opened out to accommodate two 70ft long narrowboats side-by-side, both with the maximum beam for boats on the Ellesmere Canal (6ft 10in). At the far end, there was a narrower extension that would take one additional narrowboat. The whole of the arm had been constructed in masonry and, although not visible from the towpath side of the canal, much of the stonework has survived and is, indeed, well preserved. However, one odd feature is that, in parts, there is an intermediate course of brickwork between the top and the lower courses of stone. Both sides of this dock were served by a GVT siding.

A second, newly walled wharf was created alongside the canal itself to accommodate a warehouse and a 2-ton crane for the GVT to deal with general merchandise. This was served by a siding that ran the length of the wharf, through the warehouse with a loop on the outside of it and was linked in two places to the siding alongside the dock, thus forming a triangle. A further section of walled wharf, beyond the Chirk side of the warehouse, was utilised for granite transshipment. These lengths of stone-walled wharf at the extreme edge of the canal bank are still visible from the towpath on the opposite side of the canal.

The drawing for the warehouse is labelled '*Proposed Warehouse at Rhôsweil*', but it is undoubtedly for Gledrid Wharf, as it shows the GVT track. It was a typical Shropshire Union Canal timber-built structure, 35ft long x 15ft wide and 11ft 8in to the eaves, built of spruce and with a slate roof, apparently identical in design to the warehouse later erected at Glyn Ceiriog. In May 1873, the SUR&C Co.'s Engineer's Office at Chester had produced the drawing and estimated the cost to be £378, which included sidings and the new wharf edge walling. The warehouse was beautifully constructed at the SUR&C Co.'s workshops (probably Ellesmere) and illustrates the true art of the joiner of the day. Each piece was numbered, so that it could be dismantled, transported to the site and re-erected – a flatpack well ahead of its time! Strangely, the drawings show that the bottom of the structure, instead of being raised off the ground on a stone or brick foundation, as was usually the practice, was to be buried in the ground. This is not good news for a timber building, and may account for the fact that after abandonment, due to rot, it was not salvaged as a complete building for use elsewhere, but was cannibalised with the good timbers from three of its walls being utilised on the buildings at Chirk station. Miraculously, the frame, roof trusses and some of the timber warehouse wall have survived the past 138 years, having been acquired to fulfil a totally different function elsewhere on private property, where it has been properly cared for.

A major problem with Gledrid Wharf was that it had no road access at all, which meant that it could not be used for purposes other than the interchange of tramway and canal traffic. To allow road traffic onto the site a lift bridge was installed, which gave access to the Holyhead Road, via the lane to Coke Oven Cottages.

The roof, corner posts and upper section of one wall of Gledrid Wharf Warehouse survive to this day, having been incorporated into a new building elsewhere some years ago. It is a shadow of its former glory, having lost its slate roof and the rest of its structure, but it is nevertheless one of the few surviving links with the horse tramway era.

© John Milner 2009

Built originally as a flatpack in sections, for ease of transportation from the SUR&C Co. workshops (probably Ellesmere) by canal to the site at Gledrid, this photograph shows the finer details of construction. This is typical of the craftsmanship of the Shropshire Union Co.'s joiners, who also made the early wagons for the tramway.

© John Milner 2009

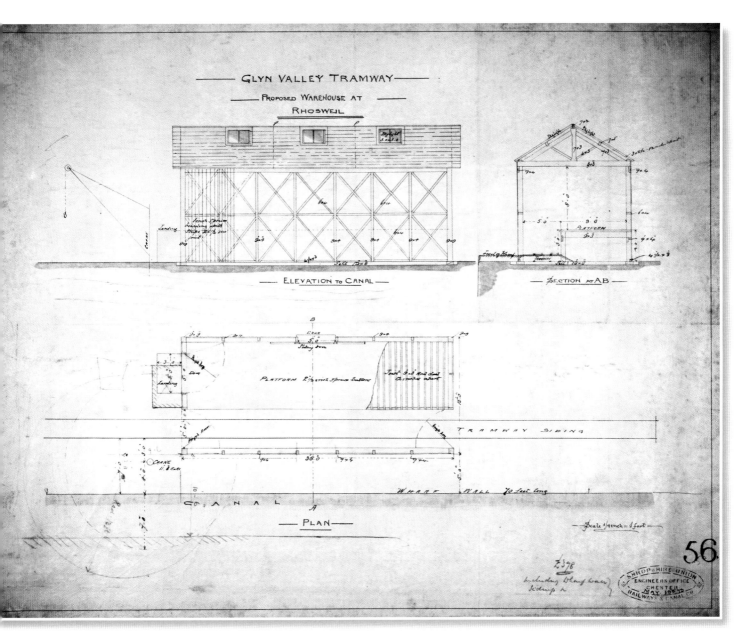

The original drawing for the GVT warehouse at Gledrid, drawn in the Engineers' Office of the SUR&C Co., Chester, dated May 1873. Note the price pencilled in of £378, which included 70ft of new wharf wall edging the canal and sidings. The cost of the wharf increased to £425 14s. 6d., which included £166 10s. 5d. for the warehouse and £35 3s. 9d. for the lift bridge (see Appendix 4). The warehouse at the New Inn terminus, at Glyn Ceiriog, was to the same design and survived intact into the 1950s.

Shropshire Archives Ref: SA-IMG15844

Gledrid Wharf

Left: Somewhat reminiscent of the days when the GVT wharf at Gledrid would have been bustling with activity, this beautifully restored narrowboat, PEARL BARLEY, chugs slowly past perhaps oblivious to the fact that this site was once the terminal of the Glyn Valley Tramway and the lifeline for the Ceiriog Valley.[1]

Much of the stone edging on this section of the wharf has collapsed, but the section out of view behind the cameraman is remarkably well preserved. Looking towards Rhosweil, the line of bushes at the top right-hand side mark the location of the dock.

© John Milner 2009

Left Bottom: A much earlier view of Gledrid Wharf(8) taken from the towpath side of the canal in 1956 and superimposed with the approximate layout of the GVT track. The trees and bushes behind the fence to the left and centre of the picture mark the long arm of the dock. The narrowboat, THE LORD NELSON, is an early wrought iron boat, over 100 years old at the time, and was then being used as a maintenance boat for dredging purposes. It could well have called at Gledrid Wharf during its commercial working days.

Courtesy: Edward A. Wilson

Below: Found on the wharf edge at Gledrid, a quantity of tramway stone sleeper blocks, used either in the original wharf edge walls or for later canal repair work. These may have originated from the Upper Chirk Bank Colliery's 1820s waggonway.

© John Milner 2009

[1] *'PEARL BARLEY'* is owned by Duncan and Dianne Davis, owners of the Black Bull Inn, Frosterley, Co. Durham. As well as being a canal enthusiast, Duncan was a top London photographer and is also interested in folk music and church bell ringing.

Above: *Gledrid Wharf looking towards the Poacher's Pocket (originally named the Navigation Inn and later the New Inn) and Chirk. Although now overgrown, the stone-built wharf edge is still intact alongside the canal. In the foreground is the location of the GVT warehouse, beyond which was the granite wharf and, in the background, the canal winding hole. Right: The remains of the stone wall edging of the Slate Wharf, on the south-west side of the dock, looking westwards. The cottage and the office have disappeared, although the site is scattered with a lot of dressed stones.*

© John Milner 2010

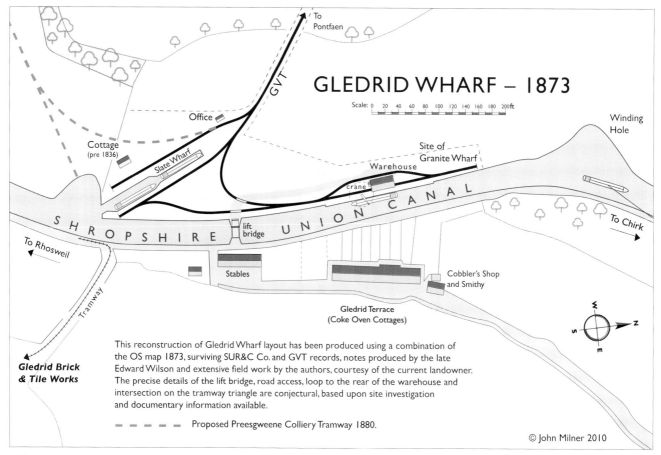

GLEDRID WHARF – 1873

This reconstruction of Gledrid Wharf layout has been produced using a combination of the OS map 1873, surviving SUR&C Co. and GVT records, notes produced by the late Edward Wilson and extensive field work by the authors, courtesy of the current landowner. The precise details of the lift bridge, road access, loop to the rear of the warehouse and intersection on the tramway triangle are conjectural, based upon site investigation and documentary information available.

- - - - - Proposed Preesgweene Colliery Tramway 1880.

© John Milner 2010

Looking towards the canal, the embanked approach to Gledrid Wharf can still be discerned. The position of the dock is marked by the middle line of trees with the trees on its right-hand side marking the outer boundary of the slate wharf, built for the Cambrian Quarries. The water-filled area to the left of the photograph is possibly the result of mine working subsidence.

The long arm of the dock, about 190 years after it was first built, is remarkably well preserved. Some of it has been filled in with rubble and roots of trees are damaging the walls in places. The photograph shows a section of the narrow end of the dock, which still retains its water level with the canal. A curious feature of some other sections of the dock walling is the presence of a single course of bricks below the top course of stone.

A well-preserved section of the slate wharf edging still remains, but the end of the dock has been filled in at some time. All traces of buildings have disappeared, although there are a lot of dressed stones scattered over the slate wharf area of the site.

Photographs: © John Milner 2009

Pontfaen–Glyn Ceiriog

In the other direction from the station at Pontfaen, the line to Glyn Ceiriog curved to the northwest and crossed the Pontfaen–Bronygarth road where there was a weighbridge. It passed onto an embankment, which ran in a westerly direction to the river. This embankment had been constructed using waste from the former quarry and earth excavated from the deep cutting below Pontfaen Farm. Upon reaching the river, the tramway took a sharp turn northwards to cross it on a timber-decked bridge supported on substantial stone abutments, the remains of which are still visible today in the form of large dressed-stone blocks scattered in the waters of the Ceiriog. The main line of the tramway left the bridge and immediately took another sharp turn (almost 90° according to BoT reports) westwards at a point some 180yds from the Pontfaen road bridge, from where it continued its journey to Glyn Ceiriog on the south side of the Wem & Bronygarth Turnpike Road. A short siding ran eastwards on the side of the road towards Chirk. This was extended to the road junction for Pontfaen, as a result of a serious accident at the bridge in 1874.

At Castle Mill, a siding ran over the river bridge and into the field, below the Bronygarth limekilns, which were high above the valley floor. Exactly how the lime was transported from the kilns to the tramway is not known; the only viable options would have been either an incline or an aerial ropeway. The limekilns are well preserved (See chapter 1 page 29). Beyond Castle Mill was Herber Toll Gate, and here another siding was sanctioned, intended to serve Penissa Glyn Limeworks, high above Herber on the Bronygarth road, which was occupied by Richard Steele Perkins (who died 1876). As stated in the '*deficiencies of subscriptions*' dated 9th December 1874, the siding was not built, resulting in a saving of £263 14s. 6d. out of the original estimate for the construction of the tramway (see chapter 4 page 110). The remains of the bank of three limekilns (see page 133) are still to be seen on the side of the road. However another siding, known as Herber Siding, was built on the roadside opposite a gravel pit, a short distance up the valley from Herber Tollgate.[1]

[1] This may have been a source of gravel for both the construction and repair of the Turnpike road, as well as the GVT.

The tramway left Pontfaen station, crossed the Pontfaen–Bronygarth road and ran along an embankment (on the left) to the river, which it crossed on a timber-decked bridge, before turning due west to continue on the side the Wem & Bronygarth Turnpike Trust road to Glyn Ceiriog. Insert: *a culvert through the embankment to the river.*

© John Milner 2010

The horse tramway bridge at Pontfaen has long since disappeared and the stone abutments washed away by successive angry waters of the River Ceiriog over the years. Some dressed stones still survive at the location of the bridge, including one block with its decking bolts still in situ.

© John Milner 2010

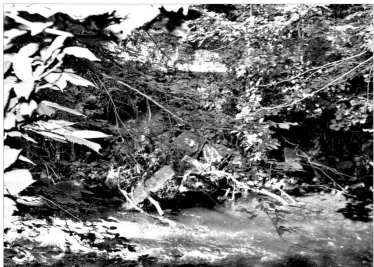

Left: *The level of the Chirk–Glyn Ceiriog road is visible. The line crossed the bridge and, with a very sharp curve, turned left to run on the side of the road to Glyn Ceiriog. Off this curve a siding continued on the side of the road to the right, as far as the Pontfaen turning. The tramway bridge was the scene of a serious accident on 19th December 1874 when passengers on a gravity-worked train were flung into the icy waters of the river* (see chapter 4 page 105).

© John Milner 2010

This photograph, taken post 1891, shows the Pontfaen siding on the north side of the river, which was extended up to the road junction at Pontfaen Bridge, as a result of the enquiry, by Lieut. Col. C.S. Hutchinson from the BoT, into the accident in December 1874 at the tramway bridge. Note the lonesome telegraph pole in the foreground, which carried a single cable from Chirk to the Telegraph Office in Glyn Ceiriog. Permission for the erection of poles along the highway was granted in 1891.

Courtesy: New Glyn Valley Tramway
& Industrial Heritage Trust.

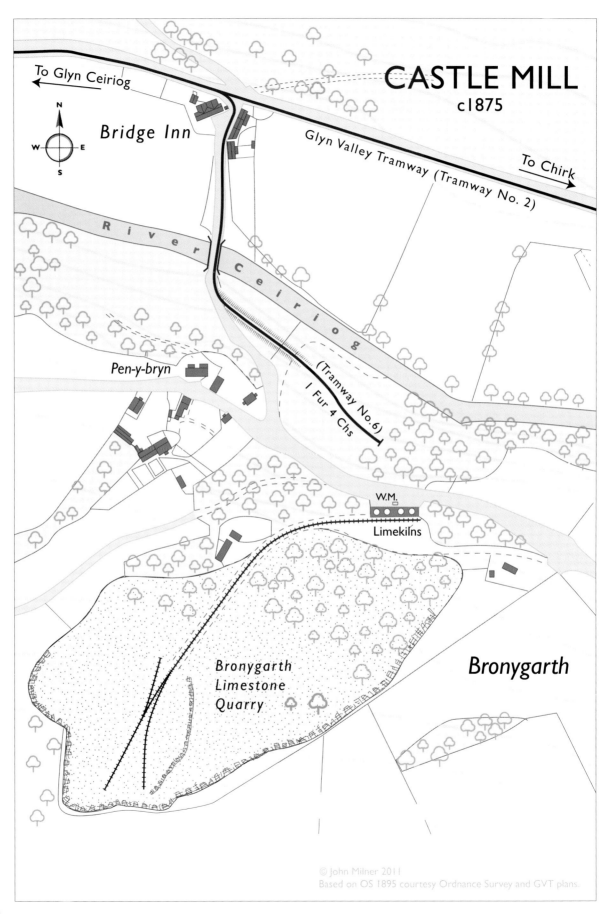

To Glyn Ceiriog

Bridge Inn

N
W E
S

Glyn Valley Tramway (Tramway No. 2)

To Chirk

CASTLE MILL
c1875

R i v e r   C e i r i o g

Pen-y-bryn

(Tramway No.6)
I Fur 4 Chs

W.M.

Limekilns

Bronygarth
Limestone
Quarry

Bronygarth

© John Milner 2011
Based on OS 1895 courtesy Ordnance Survey and GVT plans.

The picturesque hamlet of Castle Mill has, apart from property improvements, remained largely unaltered over the years, although it no longer has a mill and what was the Bridge Inn is now cottages. The siding to the Bronygarth limekilns ran up the right-hand side of the road and over the bridge behind the camera.

© John Milner 2007

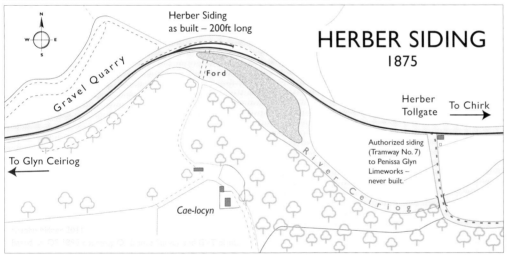

Herber Siding
as built – 200ft long

HERBER SIDING
1875

Gravel Quarry

Ford

Herber Tollgate

To Chirk →

← To Glyn Ceiriog

River Ceiriog

Authorized siding
(Tramway No. 7)
to Penissa Glyn
Limeworks –
never built.

Cae-locyn

Below: *The remains of the Penissa Glyn Limekilns, on the roadside above Herber Tollgate, to which a siding was authorized by the Glyn Valley Tramway Act 1870, but which was never built.*

© John Milner 2007

The GVT track ran so close to this gatehouse that it was necessary to remove its bay window, the defining feature of a toll house!

Further on up the valley was Pontfadog station, more aptly described as a 'stopping place' with nothing more than a siding by 1875 (later converted to a loop). At that time, there was no convenient waiting room in which passengers could shelter, other than the nearby Swan Inn, where the welcome included the temptation to partake of the refreshments on offer, with the concomitant risk of missing the train. Passengers had to wait until 1892, for the luxury of a GVT waiting room at Pontfadog.

The next stopping place was Dolywern where the tramway followed the road around a sharp, almost 90°, bend and crossed the river bridge on the left-hand side, running close alongside the Queen's Head Inn. A siding was built to serve the *Queen's* and the small community in the vicinity, which left the tramway before it turned sharply towards the bridge, crossed to the other side of the road and ran across the right-hand side of the bridge to terminate in front of the cottages that still exist today – there was no anticipation of heavy road traffic causing any problem at this time. Immediately after crossing the bridge, this siding had a kink in it to move it further to the side of the roadway; the stone walling bears witness to this today and also still retains one of the early milestones erected in 1894. The nearby chapel was not built until 1887, by which time the siding was defunct, as the line was in the process of being diverted for conversion to steam.

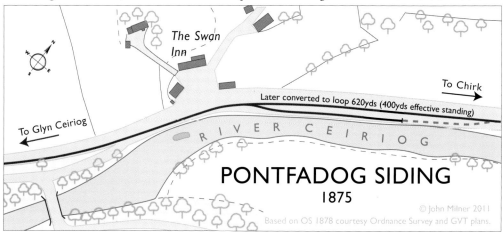

This post-horse tramway photograph of Pontfadog, dated 1892, shows the Swan Inn, said to date back to the 13th century. On the left is the newly built Baptist Chapel, Tabernacl y Bedyddwyr. The tramway ran along the nearside of the road, with the siding (later converted to a loop) off to the right of the picture. Note that the Waiting Room had not yet been built.

Collection: John Milner

Above: *Looking from Dolywern road bridge, showing the 'kink' in the walling, which was there to bring the GVT siding further to the side of the road.*

Top right: *To the right of the end of the wall in the photograph above is the Ainon Baptist Chapel, which was built in the same year that the GVT was converted to steam.*

Middle right: *On the road bridge at Dolywern, one of the nine surviving mileposts, installed on the old Turnpike by Denbighshire County Council in 1894.*

© John Milner 2010

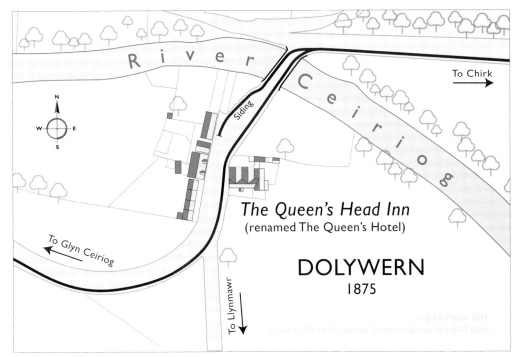

The Queen's Head Inn, Dolywern, by now renamed The Queen's Hotel, after the closure of the horse tramway. The old track and siding have been lifted, but the new Ainon Baptist Chapel has not yet been built. The licensee was William Roberts who, as portrayed by the sign, was licensed to sell ale, spirits and tobacco.

Collection: John Milner

This later photograph shows the Ainon Baptist Chapel, built in 1887, next to the river bridge. By this time, the GVT had been diverted to avoid having to use the road bridge and crossed the river on a new bridge at the back of the Queen's Hotel, where Sarah A. Lewis was the new licensee. Instead of boasting a horse tramway at its front door, the hotel was now able to advertise its own station on a narrow-gauge steam tramway at the bottom of its garden!

Collection: John Milner

[2] This field was owned by Thomas Allen Hughes and the site of the tramway terminus, about one-eighth of an acre in area, was never formally conveyed to the GVT Co. which continued to use it until its closure in 1935, without it ever having been acquired by the company by purchase or lease. See also chapter 9 pages 209–211.

The tramway continued uneventfully along the road to Glyn Ceiriog, crossing Pont Bell, and continuing along New Road to its terminus opposite the New Inn (now the Glyn Valley Country Inn). The land on which the horse tramway terminus was constructed had to be built up from the field level and be retained by a stone wall that still exists today.[2] The terminus consisted of a timber-built warehouse of typical SUR&C Co. design (with an internal crane), a 2-ton yard crane, weighbridge and small ticket office, the latter the size of a Tŷ Bach (privy). In 1874, it was recommended that a turntable be installed, the same as that at Pontfaen, but its location has not been identified. The warehouse survived long after the closure of the tramway. It was positioned on top of a length of the stone retaining wall and close examination of this today will reveal its exact position. At the end of the wharf was a walled and gated coal yard, some of the walls of which appear to have been demolished by the 1880s, leaving the double gates serving no security purpose at all.

From the top of New Road, a branch ran across the bottom of the High Street and up Quarry Road to connect with the bottom of the incline to the Cambrian Quarry, which ended just behind the GVT stables. Close to this point, the branch was also joined by the incline from Wynne Quarry, which was privately built in 1886. In New Road itself, adjacent to where the engine shed was later built, there was a loop for holding loaded or empty wagons, initially with a crane on the site.

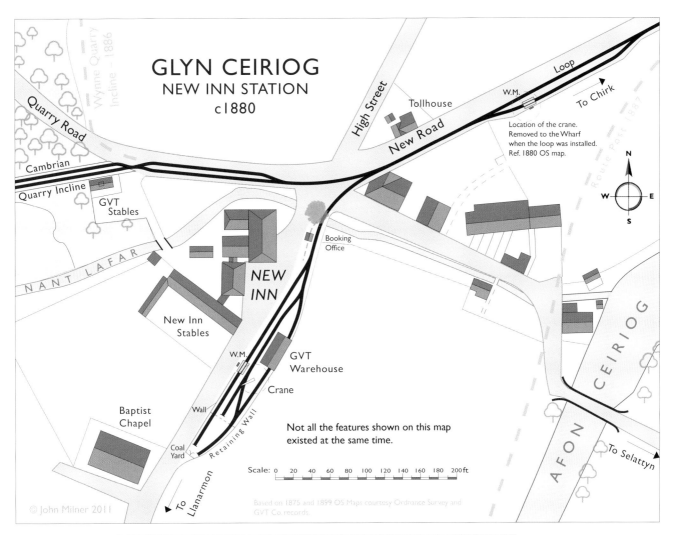

GLYN CEIRIOG
NEW INN STATION
c1880

Wynne Quarry Incline – 1886

Quarry Road

High Street

Tollhouse

New Road

Loop

W.M.

To Chirk

Location of the crane. Removed to the Wharf when the loop was installed. Ref. 1880 OS map.

Cambrian
Quarry Incline

GVT Stables

N

W E

S

NANT LAFAR

Booking Office

NEW INN

New Inn Stables

W.M.

GVT Warehouse

Crane

Wall

CEIRIOG

Baptist Chapel

Coal Yard

Retaining Wall

Not all the features shown on this map existed at the same time.

AFON

To Selattyn

To Llanarmon

Scale: 0 20 40 60 80 100 120 140 160 180 200 ft

Based on 1875 and 1899 OS Maps courtesy Ordnance Survey and GVT Co. records.

© John Milner 2011

The far end of the New Inn terminus of the tramway showing the booking office, crane, weighbridge, and coal yard with its office. When originally built the wall on the right, between the yard and the road, extended further towards the weighbridge but, by the time this photograph was taken, it had been reduced in length.

Collection: John Milner

The GVT warehouse at Glyn Ceiriog terminus of the horse tramway, in what looks to be fairly new condition. The witness of its location can still be seen in the wall. Posing alongside it is the Lavar Friendly Society (Clwb y Glyn), founded in 1843 to raise funds to support fellow members in need, and here accompanied by the Ceiriog Vale Brass Band.

Courtesy: Angela James

Another view of the horse tramway terminus at Glyn Ceiriog. Note the three skylights in the roof on the warehouse and the crane to the left. Also clearly visible is the stone wall (behind the crane), between the tramway and the road, forming the original enclosed coal yard. Underneath the crane jib and to the right of the warehouse are piles of granite setts waiting to be transported down the valley.

Courtesy: Heddwyn Edwards

Chapter 6

The Horse Tramway Era
1877–1883

By the end of 1876 the Glyn Valley Tramway was but three years old, during which time there had been additional construction costs, due to the initial contract having been cut to meet a budget. It had suffered expensive mistakes, particularly with the choice of the use of horse power and the arduous route to the canal at Gledrid, its failure to link directly with all the developing industries in the upper valley and a horrendous accident, which could have cost lives. Its viability was already being brought into question, but the solution to its problems was not to materialise for another twelve years!

An insight into the working arrangement between the GVT and one of its customers, David Lomax, who, since 1868, had been the lessee of the Trehowell Colliery and the Trehowell Brick & Clay Works on the Quinta site, is given in a report that was placed before a House of Commons Committee in 1885:

> '*The Glyn Valley Tramway takes the Quinta traffic at 10.00 a.m. and later I take it* [to Gledrid]. *I have carted more to the Canal than I have sent by the Tramway* [up the valley]. *... GWR traffic* [going to the GWR from the GVT] *is transshipped onto my standard-gauge branch line* [sidings] *and is transshipped out of the tram into GWR trucks. The GVT pays me 3d. per ton for transshipment.*'

The arrangement of the transshipment sidings at Trehowell is shown on surviving GWR plans.[1] The GVT branched at Trehowell Bridge, with the line to its interchange sidings entering the Quinta site at a higher level than the private standard-gauge sidings, enabling a wharf to be created; one of the GVT sidings butted up to the end of a standard-gauge one. What is intriguing is that a long artery ran from the Trehowell Colliery sidings at Quinta Bridge and abruptly terminated at Trehowell Lane. This was laid virtually on the footprint of the route originally proposed by the E&GVR in 1869. The fact that this standard-gauge siding was extended as far as Trehowell Lane, with a gated crossing across the old Quinta Drive, raises the question as to its purpose; was it perhaps the intention to develop the 14 acres of land on the north side of Trehowell Lane, originally purchased by the GVT Co. from Edmund Burke Wood in 1873, as an interchange wharf, thus relieving the GVT of having to rely on the goodwill of Thomas Barnes? Probably, we shall never know.

Throughout 1877, the GVT Co. continued to show a loss. This was due mainly to the difficulty of working with horses up the severe gradient from Pontfaen to Gledrid, but it was also a consequence of the line having been constructed 'on the cheap'. Derailments were common, and the operators were faced with claims for compensation. The only solution was to convert the line to steam power, but the company was tied by the Act of 1870 to use horse power only. The

[1] See the GWR Shrewsbury & Chester Railway plan of Trehowell sidings overleaf.

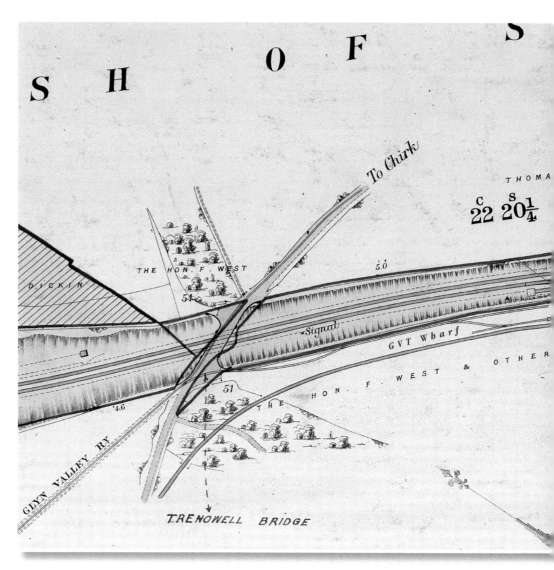

SUR&C Co. came under pressure from the New Cambrian Slate Co., and others, to improve the line and its operation. Richard Myddelton Biddulph, who had recently inherited the Chirk Castle estate from his father, Col. Robert Myddelton Biddulph, stated that he would assist in making a new line to his slate quarries at Nantyr: *'if the Glyn Valley Railway* [tramway] *would guarantee the improvements of the railway'.*

The question of the introduction of steam power on the GVT was again discussed by the SUR&C Co. Executive Committee in January 1877, but it was not to be as easy as the directors thought, and several years of discussion with the Board of Trade took place before this was to come about.

The financial problems of the GVT Co. were obvious from letters of the period. Not only did it owe employees' wages, it still had not finally settled the account of the contractor, Elias Griffith, for the construction work, who wrote to the company secretary, on 15th March 1877:

> *'I am really sorry to be so troublesome to you, but my balance on the above Contract, with interest up to June last, amounts to £740 and has been standing for nearly three years and a considerable part of this has been advanced by the bank at your suggestion ... for which I am charged interest ... the money has been fairly earned and you must not expect me to wait longer, as I cannot afford to do so. You are aware I had to take £2,000 in shares, which you also know is anything but profitable and, had it not been for your recommendation and Mr Dennis's, I would not have taken it.'*

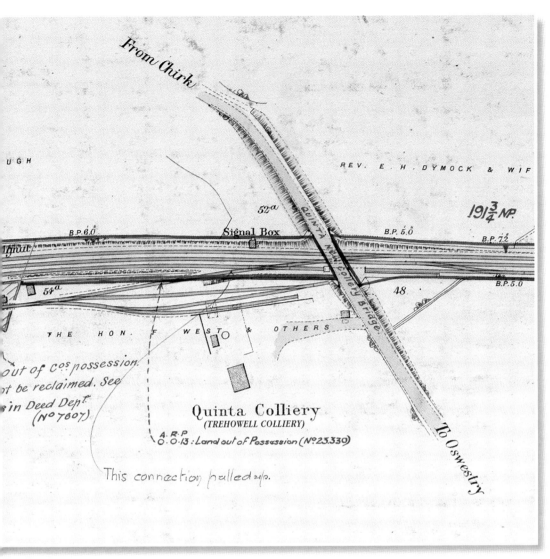

Section of the GWR plans of the Shrewsbury & Chester Railway showing the Trehowell Colliery sidings at Preesgweene and the Glyn Valley Tramway interchange sidings. Note the long standard-gauge siding on the left which curves towards Trehowell Lane and crosses the old Quinta Drive, virtually on the route of the proposed Ellesmere & Glyn Valley Railway of 1869.

On the Chirk side of Trehowell Bridge the earlier route of the Quinta Tramway is shown, heading northwards to the canal at Chirk Bank. On the right hand side of Quinta Bridge is the long siding from Preesgweene station, terminating at the former Trehowell Colliery tramway wharf.

Shropshire Archives
SA-IMG16825

Henry Dennis immediately reacted to this letter, by throwing the ball firmly in the court of John Jones, the Company Secretary:

'It really is too bad, keeping this man out of his money in this way. I find the tramway was taken over in March 1873, and the final certificate for the balance of contract £67 7s. 6d. was given in June 1874.'

Despite this intervention by Henry Dennis, Elias Griffith, along with other creditors, was still pressing for his money some two years later, with little sign of settlement.

In spite of all the difficulties, there was still some optimism that the tramway would become profitable in the long term and, in September 1877, the SUR&C Co. Executive Committee approved the erection of a 1-ton post crane inside the warehouse at Glyn Ceiriog, for unloading heavy goods that needed to be kept dry or secure. There was already a 2-ton crane on the yard, manufactured by R & J Ellis, Engineers, of Manchester, which survives to this day in the valley, with its maker's plate in situ. Originally, this crane had been installed in 1874, next to a track loop on New Road (shown on the 1875 OS map) partly on the site now occupied by the engine shed, but was moved to the wharf opposite the New Inn (Glyn Valley Hotel). It is not known what happened to the crane erected on the canal edge at Gledrid Wharf in March 1874, but it is reasonable to assume that it was similar, if not the same, to that at Glyn Ceiriog. It was transferred to the GVT station at Chirk, c1889. There is no evidence of a post crane ever having been installed inside

The GVT Yard Crane

The crane still has its original maker's plate attached – R & J Ellis, Engineers, Manchester.

One of the few artifacts still surviving from the horse tramway era – the yard crane from the Glyn Ceiriog terminus opposite the New Inn (Glyn Valley Hotel).

It was removed from the terminus in 1940 and moved to a new resting place in the Ceiriog Valley. Its date of removal is inscribed in the wall upon which it is mounted. At some time a new 'utility' jib has been fitted.

Photographs © John Milner
2003

the warehouse on Gledrid Wharf, but a post crane would have been needed here as well as at the terminus at Glyn Ceiriog.

A public meeting was held on 7th December 1877 to voice the reaction of the village towards proposals by the Glyn Valley Tramway Co. to provide a more efficient transport system for the valley, by changing the horse tramway to steam locomotion. John Morris, a quarryman, feared change and spoke with some cynicism when he recalled how, some 20 years earlier, the consideration of new proposals had resulted in, not a change for the better, but a far worse employment situation for the people. He was referring back to events in 1857, when the then Cambrian Slate Co. had offered the Wem & Bronygarth Turnpike Trust financial assistance, provided that a tramway for its exclusive use was built along the side of the new road up the valley, when he said:

> *'I have been living at the Glyn for 25 years and about 20 years ago I remember a similar meeting to the present one. ... This was successful in throwing out the Bill for making a tramway up the valley. What was the consequence? The slate quarries were closed for 5 years during which time the Glyn district was the poorest district in North Wales, and I was one of the sufferers, for want of employment.'*

On the 24th December, Thomas Barnes' son, James. R. Barnes, J.P., of Brookside, Bronygarth, wrote to John Jones, secretary of the GVT Co., commenting on these proposals to introduce steam power and saying:

> *'As regards the running of a Locomotive from Pontfaen to Rhosweil [Gledrid], I must say that I think this cannot be done with safety unless gates are placed across the road from The Lodge to Pontfaen and a proper man placed in charge of them. I shall be prepared to discuss terms for the erection of a house on the adjoining triangle of land, which belongs to my Father, if this is intended. One must have the High Road safe. Please let me know what you intend to do'.*

On the same date he also sent another letter to John Jones, but this time to him in his capacity as Clerk to the Wem & Bronygarth Turnpike Trust; the letter seems to somewhat contradict his helpful approach made directly to the GVT Co.:

> *'... my Father says, with respect to the running of a steam Locomotive on the W & B Road No. 2: "I think the Trustees of the Road should oppose in order to get something secured for making the turnpike road better, and if they present a petition against it they can probably get something done". ... I think the Tramway Co. ought to give an Undertaking to keep this road in repair, or else put it into such a condition that it can be handed over to the Highway Board. That Company should not have a monopoly'.*

The use of steam on the tramway was being discussed by the SUR&C Co. in broad terms only at this stage but, apart from the steam trials held in 1881, it was to be 1887 before the valley was to see steam operating on its tramway, by which time the SUR&C Co. was no longer involved and the line had been rerouted to Chirk. No action appears to have been taken in respect of James Barnes' letters.

The GVT was not only the lifeline for the Cambrian Quarries, but also for the Wynne Slate Quarry Co. Ltd, which was registered on the 1st May 1878: *'to purchase a freehold property known as "The Wynne Slate Quarry" ... and to connect the said Wynne Slate Quarry with the Glyn Valley Tramway by the construction of a branch line [incline] of railway or tramway'.* This is the earliest mention of making a connection from this quarry to the GVT found, but the incline was not built until 1886. The Wynne Slate Quarry nestled on the hillside directly above Glyn Ceiriog, the waste tips spilling over close to the gardens of the houses below, and had worked spasmodically since John Wynne had bought it on 9th September 1829.[2] The capital of the company was £25,000 divided into 5,000 shares of £5 each, but the company was unable to attract support and was dissolved on the 14th July 1879.[3]

[2] Lot 27 of the sale of Myddelton Biddulph estate land in Glyn Ceiriog on 1st August 1827.

[3] For the full story of the Wynne, Cambrian and other Ceiriog Valley slate quarries, see *Slates from Glyn Ceiriog* by John Milner.

At a meeting of the SUR&C Co. Executive Committee held in May 1878, Mr Moon reported that the Great Western Railway Co. had withdrawn its initial opposition to the suggestion of the erection of a platform (halt) on its railway for the interchange of passengers with the GVT and that he had agreed that the company would pay a moiety of the cost, not exceeding £100. The halt was to be built at Trehowell and a draft Agreement, issued by the GWR Co., also provided for the exclusive interchange of goods traffic, where the GWR Co. would have the opportunity to capture the canal traffic as well! Details of this proposed interchange have not been found, but no doubt lie hidden in the depths of the GWR archives somewhere, along with the missing GWR Agreements with the Quinta Colliery Company.[4]

[4] In 1935, the Great Western Railway had built a halt, appropriately named Trehowell Halt, next to Trehowell Bridge, with access steps down into the cutting on its south side from Trehowell Lane. It was built as part of its halt construction programme, which was aimed at countering emergent competition from bus services. It was closed in 1951.

By the end of June 1878, the draft Agreement had been amended to provide an interchange for passengers only and the contribution by the SUR&C Co. towards the cost reduced to a maximum of £50. Nothing further appears to have been done in respect of this Trehowell passenger interchange, but the GWR Co. was certainly not going to give up its quest for a fair share of the GVT traffic.

The tramway continued in operation, but not without incident, as on the 20th June 1878, there was an accident on the Cambrian incline, which could have resulted in a major tragedy. A number of wagons, some loaded with timber, were being run down the long incline when the hook retaining them fractured.

> *'They ran down the incline at a terrible rate but fortunately, when a hundred yards from the bottom some of the wheels being broken, they were thrown over the embankment, the result being that there was considerable damage and most of the trucks smashed. Although there were several platelayers* [these would have been GVT platelayers who maintained the incline] *working on the line at the time, they escaped without injury.'*[5]

[5] *Llangollen Advertiser* 28th June 1878.

Following this incident, workers who used to travel on the incline to and from work, although against regulations, were urged, for their own safety, to use the road in future. A breakaway rake of wagons full of workers would have spelt a significant tragedy for the community of Glyn Ceiriog.

A regular GVT horse-drawn passenger service between Pontfaen and Glyn Ceiriog had become well established. The arrival and departure times had first appeared in Bradshaw Railway Timetables in June 1877, which was followed by the first known timetable issued by the company for 1st May 1878, which shows three 'Up' Cars from Pontfaen to New Inn (Glyn Ceiriog) departing at 10.15 a.m., 1.30 p.m. and 7.15 p.m., stopping at Castle Mill, Herber Toll Gate, Pontfadog, *Queen's Head Inn* (Queen Hotel, Dolywern) and New Inn (Glyn Ceiriog), with 'Down' Cars departing at 8.00 a.m., 11.00 a.m. and 4.45 p.m. Cars did not run on a Sunday. On a Wednesday, which was traditionally Oswestry market day, the 'Up' 1.30 p.m. was cancelled and a *Market Car* was scheduled to run at 4.10 p.m. instead, with the 4.45 p.m. also being rescheduled to leave 15 minutes later at 5.00 p.m. Interestingly, the timetable states that the *'Tramway Trains run in connection with Trains on the Great Western Line'*, but it fails to spell out to the poor passengers that they were expected to walk all the way from Chirk station to the tramway terminus at Pontfaen, or vice versa, complete with all their luggage and regardless of the weather! Between July and December 1878, the departure time of the 'Up' Market Car was altered to 4.30 p.m. The 'Up' journey time allowed was 1 hour and the 'Down' somewhat less at ³/₄ hour.

Returning to the tale of woe, the Wem & Bronygarth Turnpike Trust, like the GVT Co., was experiencing serious financial problems and came to realise that its only salvation was to reach agreement with the GVT Co., paving the way for a new Act incorporating the use of steam power on the tramway. On 11th March 1878, an Agreement was made between the road trustees and the GVT Co. which, in the preamble, highlighted the root of the problems being faced:

> *'... the cost of working, maintaining and managing the tramway has proved to be greatly in excess of the receipts arising from traffic, and consequently no funds are available for payment to the Trustees of the annual rent of £150.'*

GLYN VALLEY TRAMWAY.
RUNNING OF PASSENGER TRAINS.
TIME TABLE
From 1st May, 1878, and until further notice.

UP.	DAILY. (Sundays excepted.)			DOWN.	DAILY. (Sundays excepted.)		
	a.m.	p.m.	p.m.		a.m.	a.m.	p.m.
Leave PONTFAEN (Chirk)...	10 15	1 30	7 15	Leave NEW INN (Glyn)......	8 0	11 0	4 45
Arrive CASTLE MILL.........	10 24	1 40	7 25	Arrive QUEEN'S HEAD INN	8 10	11 10	4 55
„ HERBER TOLL GATE	10 30	1 50	7 35	„ PONT FADOG.........	8 20	11 20	5 5
„ PONT FADOG.........	10 40	2 0	7 47	„ HERBER TOLL GATE	8 30	11 30	5 15
„ QUEEN'S HEAD INN	10 50	2 10	7 55	„ CASTLE MILL.........	8 36	11 36	5 21
„ NEW INN (Glyn) ...	11 0	2 30	8 15	„ PONTFAEN (Chirk)...	8 45	11 45	5 30

The Wednesday Market Car will leave New Inn every Wednesday at 11-0 a.m., returning from Pontfaen at 4-10 p.m. On Wednesdays the mid-day Car from Pontfaen will not run, and the Evening Car from New Inn will leave at 5-0 p.m. instead of 4-45 p.m.

Private Cars may be arranged for at Special Rates, on due notice being given.

The Tramway Trains run in connection with Trains on the Great Western Line to and from Liverpool, Chester, Oswestry, Shrewsbury, &c.

BY ORDER,

W. JONES,
GENERAL MANAGER.

Shropshire Union Offices,
Chester, April, 1878.

PHILLIPSON AND GOLDER, PRINTERS, CHESTER.

Probably the earliest surviving poster timetable, dated 1878, found in the Wrexham Peripatetic Club Minute Book. The timetable gives an overview of the passenger service being provided at that time. It however fails to advise passengers, who may be unaware, that they have a long walk between the GWR station and the tramway terminus or vice versa.

Denbighshire Record Office Ref.: DD/DM/734/1

The key elements of the agreement were that the Wem & Bronygarth Turnpike Trustees consented to the use of steam power on the tramway alongside their road and would forego the annual £150 rent payable to them by the GVT Co., in exchange for a one-off payment of £1,000, payable within six months of the passing of the Act. This payment would enable the Road Trustees '*to repair the road along one side of tramway, which road has from want of funds fallen into a state of great disrepair*'.

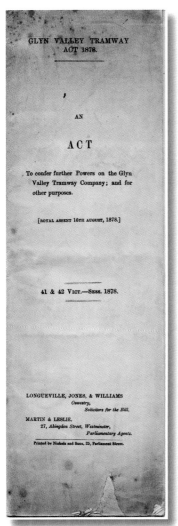

GLYN VALLEY TRAMWAY
ACT 1878.

AN

ACT

To confer further Powers on the Glyn
Valley Tramway Company; and for
other purposes.

[ROYAL ASSENT 16TH AUGUST, 1878.]

41 & 42 VICT.—SESS. 1878.

LONGUEVILLE, JONES, & WILLIAMS
Oswestry,
Solicitors for the Bill.

MARTIN & LESLIE,
27, *Abingdon Street, Westminster,*
Parliamentary Agents.

Printed by Nichols and Sons, 25, Parliament Street.

The Glyn Valley Tramway Act 1878 empowered the building of a 3¼-mile extension from Glyn Ceiriog to Tregeiriog, a line to Nantyr and a deviation at Dolywern.

Collection: John Milner

The GVT Co. was now able to proceed with a further Act, the Glyn Valley Tramway Act 1878, and this attained Royal Assent on 16th August 1878. This new Act provided for three new sections of tramway and a new section of road; Henry Dennis drew the Plans & Sections. The first section was a deviation of the line at Dolywern, to cut out the length of original tramway that ran over the road bridge that required negotiating two very sharp bends, one of them being far too tight for locomotive working; the second, a 3¼-mile extension, which was important to the future development of Hendre Quarry, from the New Inn at Glyn Ceiriog, passing the Gunpowder Works on the north side of the river to terminate in a field on the Llanarmon side of the crossroads at Tregeiriog; the third was a new road following the River Teirw from Pandy to Nantyr, and finally, the fourth, a tramway following this road, no doubt to satisfy Mr Myddelton Biddulph. The Nantyr Quarry was not developed to any great extent and neither the road nor the tramway to Nantyr was built.

Parliament approved the 1878 Act, but did not agree to the use of steam power, as it was not convinced, quite rightly, that locomotives could be used on the steep gradients between Pontfaen and Gledrid. The preparatory work undertaken to obtain this Act had been a futile exercise by the company, as it did not achieve what was intended – to introduce steam power – which reflected very badly on the judgement of its engineer, Henry Dennis.

By 26th March 1879, the continued failure of the GVT Co. to make a profit was causing great concern, and the attention of the GVT Directors was drawn to the cost of working the line. They were asked whether any reduction in maintenance costs could be made, and were warned that the canal company was considering relinquishing control of the operation of the tramway, with the question of withdrawal from the operation to be reconsidered in six months' time. In April, Mr Andrew, who was the GVT Co.'s Agent, was hauled before the SUR&C Co. Board where he was informed that the working of traffic on the tramway was not satisfactory. In June, the Board decided to discontinue issuing 'contract tickets' (what are today called 'season tickets') in order to claw back a little extra revenue and cut back on staffing costs when it reduced the total hours worked at the termini, by dispensing with the services of S. Davies, porter, at the same time as increasing the wages of GVT warehousemen W. Boate and C. Boate from 14/- to 16/- and 18/- to 20/- per week respectively.

When the SUR&C Co. entered into the arrangement to operate the tramway on behalf of the GVT Co. it was in the expectation that it would be able to attract the bulk of the traffic onto its canal, but it appears that it had resorted to 'placing difficulties' in the way of GVT traffic using the GWR interchange, in order to do so. In August that year, Theodore Martin (as GVT agent) forwarded yet another complaint that he had received from the GWR Co. stating that the SUR&C Co. were placing difficulties in the way of the interchange of traffic. The SUR&C Co.'s curt response was that the Glyn Valley Tramway Co. had done everything that the GWR had required it to do.

A little glimmer of hope had come in June 1879 in the form of the Board of Trade Provisional Order Confirmation Bill, which was to provide powers to operate steam on tramways for a period of twelve months, thus providing a trial period. As the GVT Act 1878 now allowed improvements and extensions to be made to the route, the SUR&C Co. realised that this would be an opportune time to take over full control of the tramway which would enable it to direct all the GVT traffic onto its canal. It was immediately arranged for Mr Jebb to report on the cost of adapting the line for a locomotive and to send another enquiry to Mr Webb, the Chief Engineer of the LNWR at Crewe about the supply of a suitable locomotive for the tramway.[6]

[6] A similar enquiry had been made in June 1874, as previously related in chapter 3 page 73 and chapter 4 page 101.

On 25th September 1879, a meeting of GVT Co. shareholders responded to the SUR&C Co.'s warning, made in March, that it would reconsider its position in respect of the operation of the tramway, by issuing an ultimatum in the form of a resolution that:

'... this meeting is of the opinion that the Directors should determine [end] the arrangements with the SU Co. unless that Co. is agreed to obtain powers to work the line by steam. If no satisfactory power is effected within 3 calendar months the Directors are authorised to determine the SU Co.'s possession, compulsory if necessary, to take steps to obtain powers for the use of steam or other loco power.'

To further fuel the anger of the GVT Co. shareholders, it appears that the SUR&C Co. had stopped paying some of the GVT ground rents, a situation that appears to have continued right up to 1881, when it was reported that Mr Barnes, Quinta Estate, was demanding payment from the SUR&C Co. of 10d. in respect of Tithe Rent owing!

At the SUR&C Co. Executive meeting on 29th October 1879, Mr Jebb produced details and estimates for a locomotive, and for the cost of alterations and relaying of the track in 56lb per yard rail:

Alteration of line between Pontfaen and New Inn, with diversion at Pont Dolywern and strengthening of present bridges.	£1,000
Alteration of tramway between Pontfaen and canal including new bridge over the river.	£ 600
Cost of locomotive as per Mr Webb's estimate.	£1,000
Cost of relaying the line with steel rails at 56 lbs per yd – allowing for the value of present rails	£4,000

The gradient from Pontfaen to the canal was spelling disaster for the tramway, and every possible option to improve the working at this end of the line was being explored. In November 1879, Mr Jebb submitted estimates for making a new line, about 1¼ miles in length along the northern side of the valley from Pontfaen to pass high up through the last arch of the Shrewsbury & Chester Railway viaduct and then, utilising the side of the aqueduct opposite the towpath, to cross over the valley to a new transshipping wharf at Chirk Bank. The estimated cost of such works was £2,700 and it was stated that it would ease the gradient, from Pontfaen to the canal, from 1 in 19 to 1 in 67. Nothing further was reported on this particular scheme, until it was discussed again, albeit briefly, in 1883, thereafter to be buried in perpetuity.

The overall cost of changing the GVT to steam locomotive working was carefully considered and, on 23rd December 1879, it was reported that this would be about £7,000, representing an annual charge of £690 against income, although this figure did not take into account repairs, maintenance and salaries.

The cost of transporting slate from the New Cambrian Slate Quarries down the valley on the GVT was high, which made the slates far more expensive than slates produced in other areas of North Wales. The slate industry country-wide was in decline and the Cambrian slates were being marketed at prices that were uncompetitive. If the GVT Co. was to take advantage of all the potential traffic on its doorstep then it had to make a positive move to create a more efficient operation, which would reduce the tolls charged. Carriage over the Glyn Valley Tramway was set at 6d. per ton per mile for slates, but this was only as far as the GWR at Trehowell sidings or the canal wharf at Gledrid. On top of this charge were forwarding transport costs via either the rail or the canal networks. A report had appeared in the 15th December 1877 issue of the *Mining Journal* condemning the high rates charged by the SUR&C Co. for the carriage of slates on the GVT. In June 1879, the New Cambrian Slate Co. disputed the SUR&C Co.'s method of charging for canal freight, but this fell on deaf ears. With the slate company working half time and the SUR&C Co. still storing a large quantity of unsold Cambrian slates on its interchange wharf with the LNWR at Calveley, near Crewe in Cheshire, the slate company was treading on dangerous ground. By October that

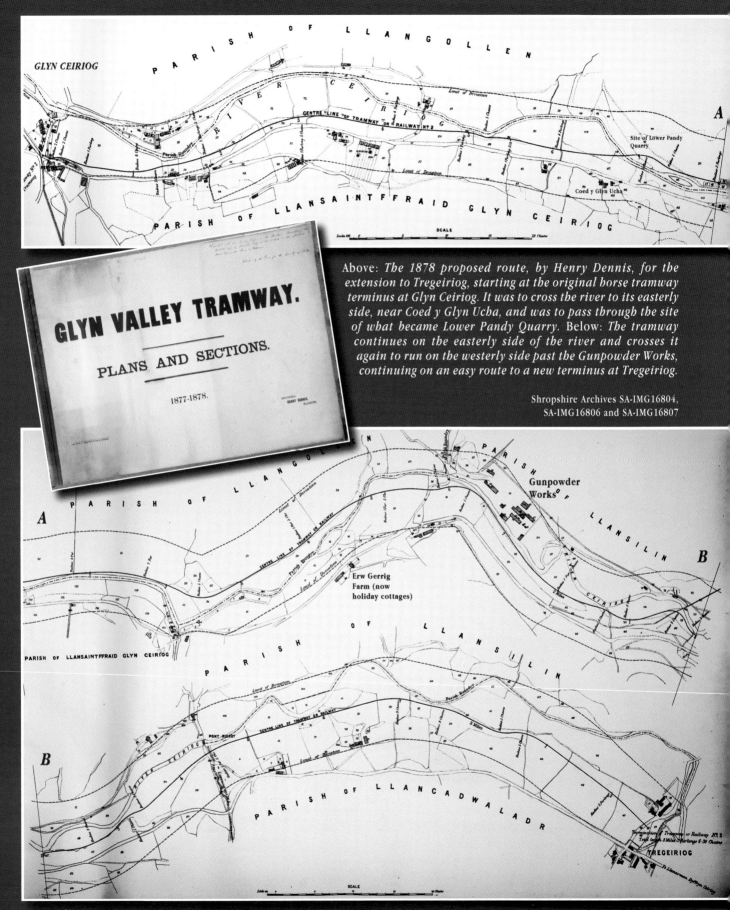

Above: *The 1878 proposed route, by Henry Dennis, for the extension to Tregeiriog, starting at the original horse tramway terminus at Glyn Ceiriog. It was to cross the river to its easterly side, near Coed y Glyn Ucha, and was to pass through the site of what became Lower Pandy Quarry. Below: The tramway continues on the easterly side of the river and crosses it again to run on the westerly side past the Gunpowder Works, continuing on an easy route to a new terminus at Tregeiriog.*

Shropshire Archives SA-IMG16804, SA-IMG16806 and SA-IMG16807

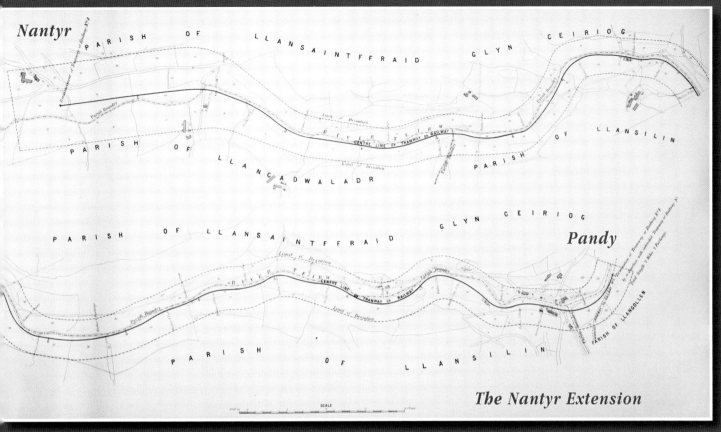

The Nantyr Extension

The proposed extension Nantyr started at a junction with the main extension to Tregeiriog at Pandy and followed the route of the River Teirw to a point below Ty'n-twmpath. No doubt, this was included to appease Mr Myddelton Biddulph, who wanted a connection to his Nantyr Slate Quarry, higher up the Nant Ty'n-twmpath valley. The quarry was never developed nor was the extension to Nantyr built. The extension to Nantyr would have been an extremely difficult line to build, because of the steepness and nature of this narrow valley, and consequently very expensive.

Shropshire Archives SA-IMG16809

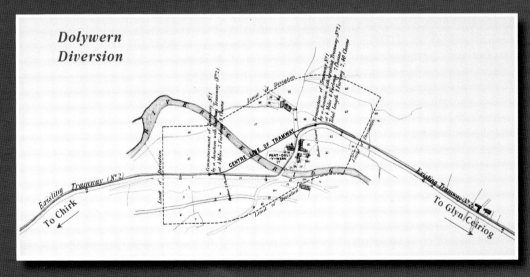

Dolywern Diversion

The deviation at Dolywern was essential to locomotive working, in order to eliminate the sharp radii on the old horse tramway, particularly on the approach to the road bridge, which itself was deemed to be too weak for use by locomotives.

Shropshire Archives SA-IMG16805

This interesting view of Hendre Quarry, in its early stage of development, shows the overburden being removed from the top surface of the granite and the second gallery starting to be developed from both sides. Note the first and second inclines on the extreme right, the abandoned incline towards the centre and, upper left, a small waterwheel, the purpose of which is unclear.

Collection: Robert Jones

year, the canal company was considering returning all the slates to the slate company! In March the following year, the dispute had not been resolved and the New Cambrian Co. was seeking to discontinue having to pay rent for its office on the canal wharf at Gledrid.

The SUR&C Co., having digested the resolution made by shareholders of the GVT Co. in September 1879, to terminate the arrangement under which it operated the tramway, unless it had taken steps to convert it to steam power and having investigated the costs involved, the directors decided, on 4th February 1880, that enough was enough and that they would dispose of their interest in the concern in favour of the shareholders of the GVT Company. Negotiations started immediately but, as with most things regarding the GVT, all was not to work out as expected.

By this time, the Hendre Granite Quarry was showing signs of developing into a successful business, and the SUR&C Co. soon started to become uneasy with its decision to dispose of its interest in the GVT, as it could see that it was about to forfeit a huge amount of potential traffic for the canal – traffic that was desperately needed.

In spite of the motion, for the GVT Co. to obtain possession of the tramway from the SUR&C Co. being carried, nothing more was done and the canal company continued to operate the tramway. The SUR&C Co. appears to have had a complete change of mind about its involvement because, at the Executive Committee meeting on 30th June 1880, it was proposed that the company should become the purchaser of the GVT and a complete inventory of SU property on the line was ordered. In October 1880, it was reported that no arrangements had yet been made with the GVT Co., so the SUR&C Co. looked for a legal way to obtain complete control but, in November 1880, its solicitor advised that it would not be possible to include powers to take over the GVT in a current LNWR Bill. Despite this setback, the question of relaying the track with new rails of heavier section was discussed by the SUR&C Co., but no further action was taken.

A meeting of the GVT Co. was convened in Oswestry for the 5th February 1881 to take into consideration the desirability of taking legal steps towards obtaining possession of the tramway plant and buildings still in the hands of the SUR&C Co. The SUR&C Co. asked Mr Stanton and

Col. James Bourne, accompanied by Mr Thomas Roberts, being GVT shareholders, to attend the meeting on its behalf and to vote against the proposed objective. Despite their objections the motion to take legal means to regain possession of the tramway was carried. This meeting also decided to appeal again to the Board of Trade for permission to use a locomotive on the line.

At this time, most of the tramway's income was being generated by Hendre Granite Quarry. The operator of the quarry, the Glyn Ceiriog Granite Co., realising that failure to secure the tramway's future could seriously damage its ambitious development plans, approached the SUR&C Co., on 25th May 1881, and made an offer of £1,500 for the purchase of the tramway plant and buildings, but the canal company turned it down. The following month, Mr Roberts and Mr Jebb, acting on behalf of the SUR&C Co., were authorised to negotiate with the GVT Co. and the GCG Co., to reach a settlement on the best terms. Having had its direct offer to the SUR&C Co. rejected, the granite company appears to have entered into discussion with the GVT Co. with a view to taking over the operation of the tramway. The canal company was duly advised, on 27th July, that the GVT Co. (acting in association with the GCG Co.) was prepared to offer £1,800 for the plant and buildings, which would be paid by 31st August 1881, leaving the canal company with its horses, harness and share capital.

The GVT Co. appears to have had no intention of becoming the operator of its own tramway, and was facilitating the purchase of the buildings and equipment by the granite company, because the GCG Co.'s Memorandum of Association did not permit the company to become a 'public' tramway operator. On 23rd August 1881, this was rectified by restructuring the company, which became the Ceiriog Granite Co. Ltd (15895), although it was not registered until 20th September. Its Memorandum of Association this time was very much broader in its permitted scope of activities, allowing the company to operate a 'public' tramway. The principal directors of the new company were Richard Myddelton Biddulph, J.C. Edwards, Walter Eddy, John Daniel Lloyd, John Morris, John Parsons Smith and Ellis Lever.

At the SUR&C Co. Executive Committee meeting on 28th September, it was reported that payment had been received from the GVT and that, in addition, it had purchased five of the canal company's horses complete with their harness' for an additional £181, making the total £1,981. In order to give the CGC Co. time to put its affairs into order, the GVT Co. had effectively acted as intermediary by purchasing all the tramway equipment from the SUR&C Co., which it then sold on to the newly formed Ceiriog Granite Company.

The SUR&C Co. ceased to run the tramway on 31st August 1881 and its operation was taken over the following day by the Ceiriog Granite Co., initially for a period of twelve months, at the end of which a long-term arrangement was to be discussed, based upon the results of the first year of operation.

The canal at Chirk Bank, looking towards Gledrid, with the warehouse and its crane. Moored alongside on a still early-autumn day is a Shropshire Union maintenance boat.

Collection: John Milner

Thus the SUR&C Co. was relieved of its operational involvement in the GVT, although not entirely of its interest, as it still held 50 per cent of the shares and was entitled to appoint a director to the GVT Board. The table below shows it had made a loss of more than £7,000 on working the tramway from 1873 to 1881. Its net loss on the tramway, over the nine years, as reported to the SUR&C Co. Executive Committee in October, taking into account depreciation and the sale of the tramway, was £3,179, which it resolved to clear from its accounts by charging £1,000 against revenue each half-year.

Loss on working				7,061	19	0
Cost of plant				2,333	13	10
Cost of works				2,297	0	3
Cost of horses				862	0	0
				£12,554	**13**	**1**
Less:						
Reserved for depreciation in buildings	1,235	2	4			
Reserved for depreciation in horses	205	3	10			
Interest in suspense	2,792	17	7			
Amount written off	2,800	0	0			
	£7,033	**3**	**9**			
Loss up to 30th June				**£5,521**	9	4
Less Sale of Tramway:						
Received from Glyn Valley Co.	1,981	12	7			
Value of horses retained [1]	360	0	0			
Net loss				**£3,179**	16	9

[1] Taking into account that the GVT had paid £181 for 5 horses, this suggests that the SUR&C Co. may have been using as many as 15 horses to operate the tramway.

The First Steam Trials

The year 1881 was the turning point in the GVT history and, from this time on, the finances of the tramway became dependent on the success of the Ceiriog Granite Co. but, before that company could develop further, it had to be served by an efficient means of transport. It was totally impracticable to continue to operate the tramway economically with horse power, so the GVT Co. once again turned its thoughts to steam locomotives as being the only logical solution to the problem – which it was.

On 9th August 1881, the GVT Co. had applied to the Board of Trade for an Experimental Licence to use steam power. However, at the very time that the application was being drafted for presentation to the Board of Trade, the company was taking the law into its own hands. It was trying out a steam locomotive on the tramway regardless of not having any licence to do so!

Two weeks earlier, at the SUR&C Co. Executive Committee meeting on 27th July, it was reported that the GTV Co. had requested permission to take an engine over the line. The canal company had not been willing to consent to this, because the GVT Co. did not have a BoT licence to do so, although trials were in progress. As several of the SUR&C Co.'s trucks were being used, it was resolved that their hire should be taken into account upon the final settlement of the sale of the tramway equipment to the GVT company.

The trials were conducted over a period of about five days, with the staging of an event for the public two days earlier on the 25th July 1881, when the directors and prominent local people were invited to take a trip on the tramway, hauled by a diminutive steam engine reported as being named *'The Times'*.

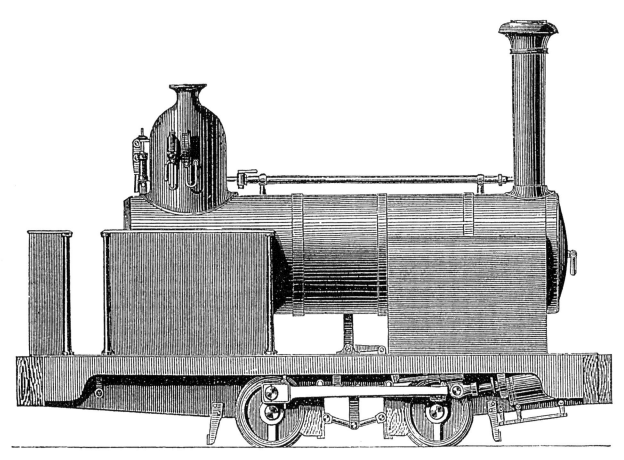

A description of this occasion, which appeared in the *Oswestry Advertizer* on 27th July 1881, gives some insight into this historic event in the Ceiriog Valley:

'... *Great excitement was occasioned all along the valley and at various points numbers of persons had assembled to witness the experiment. The run was made between Pontfaen up to the New Inn with no mishap. ... At the first trial trip Mr E. Griffith, Chirk and Mr H. Dennis, Ruabon were present. On Monday, gentlemen travelled along the line drawn by "The Times". Amongst these were Sir Theodore Martin, Mr Jebb, The Lyth, [Ellesmere], Capt. Gill, Trewern, Mr John Morris, Mr J.C. Edwards, Trevor Hall, Dr. Lloyd, Chirk, Mr Griffith, Mr Dennis, Mr Robert Hughes, Oswestry and Mr W. Griffith, Chirk. The journey was successful in every way and all were pleased with the trip.*'

On the 30th July the *North Wales Guardian* similarly reported, adding:

'... *Among the company present (on the 2nd trial run on Monday 25th July) was Sir Theodore Martin, who has always taken a great interest in the Company. At the end of the outward journey, the passengers found a band and a large crowd awaiting their arrival, who gave them a hearty reception.*'

The *Mining Journal*, on the same day, reported that:

'*The little valley of Glyn Ceiriog was placed in a state of unusual excitement on Saturday last* [23rd July], *as on that occasion its solitudes were first invaded by the "iron horse", in the shape of a small locomotive of some 8-horse power, which ran on an experimental trip along the line of tramway laid down a few years ago from Pontfaen to Glyn. The engine, "The Times", has just gained a prize at the Derby Agricultural Show. It is, of course,*

This illustration of TUNIS from 'Engineering', dated 15th July 1881, is described as a 'Tank Locomotive (28in gauge), by Mr. W.G. Bagnall, Engineer, Stafford.' It was exhibited at the Royal Agricultural Society of England show at Derby that month, after which it visited the Ceiriog Valley for some unofficial steam trials on the GVT.

'Engineering'

necessarily small, but the experiment was regarded in every way as being successful. We may add that hitherto the tramway has been worked by horse-power for the up journey and by gravitation for the down journey, during which the horses were conveyed back to Pontfaen in suitable horse boxes.' [7]

'The Times' was tiny and hardly suitable for the kind of traffic envisaged on the GVT, but at the time it must have sounded an attractive proposition. It was 2' 4" gauge and lightweight, therefore being suitable for the horse tramway track and, certainly, would have been more efficient than horses.

It was originally considered by early GVT historians (the author included!) that the most likely possibility was that a locomotive had been borrowed from the Snailbeach District Railways in Shropshire, built to serve the Snailbeach Mine Company. Henry Dennis was the engineer of the SDR and a director of the mine company. This can now be dismissed once and for all, not only by virtue of this account, but also by the lack of any such evidence from the Snailbeach District Railway records.

The locomotive in question (Works No.358) was a small 0-4-0 of 2ft 4in gauge with an inverted saddle tank and had been built by W.G. Bagnall, of the Castle Engine Works, Stafford. According to Bagnall historian, Allan Baker, it was thought to be the first locomotive built by them with outside cylinders. He also states that the construction of No. 358 was started in February 1881 and that it appears to have been built for stock, there being no customer for it at the time. It is strange that a gauge of 2ft 4in should be selected for a stock item and this remains a mystery. It had inside frames, a wheelbase of only 2' 9", the wheel diameters being 1' 3", and inclined cylinders which

[7] This is the earliest confirmation of horses travelling down the valley in a specially built wooden wagon, known as a 'Dandy' wagon, attached to the rear of gravity trains. This was not an iron-clad Ffestiniog Railway style 'Dandy' wagon, as assumed by Dr Bernard Rocket in his book of GVT goods wagon drawings, but a wooden open-top 'horse box'. Vincent Hughes, of the Garage, Chirk Bank, related in 1957 that the horse 'Dandy' had been converted to a van and Henry Lloyd, the GVT's carpenter, also related that after the conversion of the tramway to steam, the 'Dandy' wagon stood beside the loop at Pontfadog for many years. (see photograph page 159).

were $4^1/_2$" bore x $7^1/_2$" stroke. The engine had a copper firebox and 26 brass tubes $1^3/_4$" dia., a working pressure of 140psi and its weight in working order was only $3^1/_4$ tons.[8] The firebox was designed to burn either wood or dried sugarcane, thus suggesting that it was originally destined for export. The firebox was tiny, with a fire grate area of only $2^1/_4$ sq ft. On top of the boiler was a handrail, which doubled as the blower pipe, so it was woe betide any poor soul that grabbed it while the blower was on! The inverted saddle tank, running under the smokebox end of the locomotive, held 70 gallons of water and acted as a counterbalance for the firebox to ensure even distribution of weight (at least while it was full of water!). One injector and one pump fed the boiler with water.

[8] Working pressure quoted as 110psi in the *Engineering* journal 15th July 1881.

The week before its appearance in the Ceiriog Valley, the Bagnall locomotive had been exhibited at the Royal Agricultural Society of England Show, held at Osmaston Park, Derby, and was entered under the name '*Tunis*'. The *Staffordshire Advertiser*, dated 18th July 1881, reported that it was '*in steam but stationary*' (presumably jacked up on blocks to allow the wheels to turn) and that: '*It should be capable of taking a load of 40 tons on the level at the speed of eight miles per hour, indicating about 12-horsepower.*' The manufacturing cost was £261 5s. 0d. and the selling price £315 0s. 0d.

The name '*Tunis*' would certainly have been topical, as in 1881 Tunis itself was invaded and forced to become a French Protectorate, after years of rivalry between France and Italy.[9] It is the opinion of Bagnall historian, Allan Baker, that it would be typical of Gordon Bagnall to pick upon a topical subject and to name an unsold engine accordingly, as a way of drawing attention to his exhibit. How it came to be that reports in three separate publications quoted the name, during its sojourn in the Ceiriog Valley, as '*The Times*' is a mystery, but the word '*Tunis*' could quite easily be misread as '*Times*' by a journalist who, perhaps, passed this incorrect detail on to others. It is known that Bagnall did juggle the names about on locomotives while exhibiting at other shows and there is a loose connection between Bagnall and the Walter family who were involved with *The Times* newspaper, in that Gordon Bagnall's business partner, Thomas Walter, was the great grandson of John Walter who founded the newspaper.[10] One other possible explanation could be that Bagnall named it '*Tunis*' at the Derby Show as a publicity stunt. However, the name '*Tunis*' is confirmed in the Bagnall records, although there is no mention made of the GVT trials. The *Staffordshire Advertiser* reported that it was part of a larger exhibit of the wares of W.G. Bagnall and that it '*attracted much attention, being the only locomotive on the Ground*'.

[9] Worthy of mention is that the Derbyshire Yeoman public house in Derby is named after the Derbyshire Yeomanry Regiment. One of the battles that they fought was the Battle of Tunis and the pub has a 'Tunis Room' to this day.

[10] See *Bagnalls of Stafford* by Allan C. Baker & T.D. Allen Civil.

Soon after the RASE Show at Derby, '*Tunis*' was transferred to the Ceiriog Valley for the trials on the GVT. So how did it come to be on trial on the tramway and what is the connection with Bagnall? The connection may have been via one of two prominent supporters of the GVT; either Mr. Richard Myddelton Biddulph, GVT director, or Sir Theodore Martin, who was present at the trials.

The first possibility is the connection between W.G. Bagnall and the Myddelton family. Gordon Bagnall's daughter related that her father was an accomplished marksman, had won several prizes at Bisley and that his sporting companions had included the Myddelton family of Chirk Castle.[11]

[11] Interviewed by Allan Baker in the 1970s.

Opposite: The only known photograph of TUNIS (W.G. Bagnall No.358), which was used for steam trials on the Glyn Valley Tramway in July 1881, seen here working on sewerage works for the District Council of Vlissingen (now Flushing) in the main street of Walstraat, Holland. Since its appearance in the Ceiriog Valley, it had been sold to Figee Bros. in February 1882 and had acquired a small tender, cab and, if compared with the sketch, it appears to have lost its 'Bagnall' chimney cap. Note that TUNIS is somewhat crudely painted on the side tank.

Collection: S. de Lange
Courtesy: Hans de Herder

Bagnall would have probably been aware of the GVT and what better than a personal connection, although in the end he was not favoured with orders for new locomotives for the tramway.

The second possibility is a connection through Sir Arthur Percival Heywood (1849–1916), whose home was at Duffield Bank, Derbyshire, and who was a great advocate of 'small'-gauge railways. Heywood's only real success in this field was the demonstration railway that he built on his own estate and the 15"-gauge Eaton Railway that he also built for the Duke of Westminster at Chester, in 1895.[12] It is known that he was 'friendly' with Gordon Bagnall and that interested parties at the Royal Agricultural Show at Derby, in 1881, were invited to attend Heywood's nearby Duffield Bank Railway, where special events were laid on for them, to demonstrate his philosophy on 'the minimum gauge'.

Although there is a lack of any tangible evidence, it seems reasonable to consider that Sir Arthur Heywood and Sir Theodore Martin knew each other through their London activities, and that the latter may have been advised of the Bagnall locomotive *'Tunis'* at the Derby show being available. All this is pure conjecture, but nevertheless worthy of mention, if only to fuel debate or inspire further research.

Six weeks later, on the 14th & 15th September 1881, W.G. Bagnall exhibited *'his dwarf tank locomotive and portable railway'* at the Staffordshire Agricultural Show. Prior to the Show, a Bagnall advert in the *Staffordshire Advertiser* for 10th September announced that a *'LOCOMOTIVE will be shown RUNNING on PORTABLE RAILWAY with small carriages'* (sic). Although not named, those who have studied the Bagnall records have, by a process of elimination, established that this locomotive has to be *'Tunis'*. Its removal from the GVT to Stafford ties in with a comment by Major-General Hutchinson, Board of Trade, in his report of 19th September, stating that: *'The engine alluded to in the application had been removed from the line, and I had no opportunity of inspecting it'.*

By the 30th September 1881, this locomotive was being offered for sale in the *Engineer* and the *Colliery Guardian*. It was last advertised in the latter in March 1882, but had actually been sold the month before to Bagnall's Dutch agents Figee Brothers, Haarlem Engine Works, Haarlem, near Amsterdam, for £315. Initially, it was used by a Dutch contractor, C. Langeveld, at Nieuwer Amstel, near Amsterdam, who had it about June 1882, and it was with J.A. van der Straaten, Bergambacht, by 27th May 1884. At the end of 1893, it appears to have been out of use after which it passed to Terwinot & Veenkamp at Heukelom, near Utrecht where, on 18th June 1895, the boiler failed inspection. Having been repaired it was again declared fit for use in the November of that year. About 1901, it passed to J. Blok at Gravendeel, near Dordrecht, and six years later was put into use by the District Council of Vlissengen (Flushing) where it was photographed while working on sewerage works in the main street of Walstraat. Throughout, it had maintained its name *'Tunis'*. Finally, in 1916, its boiler certificate was withdrawn and it was sold, presumably for scrap. The only surviving Bagnall record is an order for spares, dated 14th August 1896, from Luis Smulders & Company, General Engineers, based in Hertogenbosch, Holland. The order quotes the engine name as being *'Tunes'*, but the photograph reproduced on page 154 confirms that it was still *'Tunis'*.[13]

With the GVT Co. not having an Experimental Licence from the Board of Trade, it was treading on very thin ice by carrying out such trials. They had attracted a lot of attention in the press and

[12] See *Sir Arthur Heywood and the Fifteen Inch Gauge Railways* by Mark Smithers (Plateway Press).

[13] Further information on *'Tunis'* in Holland is given in *'Nederlandse Industriel Locomotieven'* by Hans de Herber (ISBN 90-71513-41-6). The above information courtesy Allan Baker/Hans de Herber.

Opposite: *Although much later than the period being described, this 1927/28 photograph of the horse-drawn maintenance boat STARLING on Chirk aqueduct provides a good impression of the early working boats on the canal. The boat is thought to be carrying clay to Trevor for repairs to the canal. The skipper is Jack Evans, his mate Tom Price, the dog 'Jip' and the horse 'Big John'.*

Courtesy: Harry Arnold
© Waterways Images Ltd

undoubtedly it was this exposure, judging by comments in the subsequent report, that alerted the BoT to this unofficial steam operation.

It was not until after the July 1881 trials, that the Company's solicitors, Messrs Longueville, Jones & Williams of Oswestry, applied to the BoT for permission, under 'Section 3' of the Tramways Orders Confirmation Act 1879, for the experimental use of steam power on the tramway for one year. They received a prompt and curt reply on the 9th August, advising that their application had to be made in the *'prescribed'* manner and conditions met. It was not going to be as easy as they thought to cover their tracks, so to speak! The conditions included agreement, by all the road authorities involved, on the use of steam power. Thus, before an application could be made to the Board of Trade, the GVT Co. had to obtain the blessing of the Trustees of the Wem & Bronygarth Turnpike Trust. The Trust, having given consideration to the plight of the GVT Co., resolved, at a meeting held at Longueville & Co., Oswestry, on 17th August 1881, that they would:

> *'... consent to an application being made ... for a licence to use steam or any mechanical power in addition to or in substitution for the animal power authorised by the Glyn Valley Tramway Acts 1870 and 1878, or one of them, for moving carriages on any of the tramways ...'*

The Llangollen Highway Board went one better and, on 24th August gave its 'instant' consent. The GVT Co. wasted no time and the following day a revised application was lodged with the BoT for a licence to use steam power on the Pontfaen–Glyn Ceiriog section of the tramway for a period of one year (licences at that time needed to be renewed annually).

The revised application to the BoT this time included a deviation at Dolywern, the latter authorised by the GVT Act 1878, and was supported by the written consents related to above. Signed by John Jones, Secretary to the GVT Co., the statement was made in the application that *'The name of the maker of the proposed Engine is Mr W.G. Bagnall of Stafford.'* This seems to suggest that at that time the company deemed the unofficial trials to be a success and that they intended to purchase either *'Tunis'* or another engine from Bagnall.

On the 26th August, the Board of Trade swiftly minuted a request for Major-General Hutchinson, to inspect the line and report back, although the GVT Co. was not notified of this until 6th September. The tramway was duly inspected shortly afterwards by Hutchinson, on behalf of the Railway Department, BoT., his report being dated the 19th September 1881.

The report was not favourable, on account of the fact that the tramway did not comply with Section 46 of the 1870 Act, which stated that the track had to be laid as a 'tramway' in the true sense, with the rails flush with the roadway. From the outset, as previously related, the tramway had never been laid flush with the road surface, except where there were crossings, and yet this situation had been accepted throughout by the Board of Trade without comment – until now! It stated that in some areas, the tramway had taken up as much as 10ft of the roadway, making the latter impassable and that it crossed two County bridges, at Dolywern and Glyn Ceiriog, which were by no means in a satisfactory condition. These were described as being *'constructed with elliptic brick arches of about 40ft span, and the arches have very much lost their shapes.'* It was recommended that: *'A special construction should be adopted in coping with the two County bridges, so as to distribute the load; the line should be carried less close to the parapets ...'*

There was also some concern within the local authority that the use of steam locomotives could have a detrimental effect on the structure of the two County bridges and their speed could be a hazard. On the 7th November, the County Surveyor for Denbighshire, at the request of the Clerk of the Peace, wrote to the BoT trusting that Major-General Hutchinson *'will require some special safety arrangements as to construction, and make regulations as to speed, in approaching and passing over the bridges ... particularly the one at Dolywern where you reach the bridge by a very awkward curve from the Chirk end'.*

Despite the concerns at that time, these bridges are still standing and, 130 years later, now carry the heavy traffic of today.

Also mentioned was that there was: *'a short piece of line (about ¹/₄ of a mile long) joining No.2* [tramway No.2] *at the before mentioned point, 35 chains* [770yds or just under half a mile] *from its commencement* [at Glyn Ceiriog], *and not authorised either by the Act of 1870 or the subsequent Act of 1878'.* Although nowhere near a quarter of a mile long as stated, this could only be the siding at Dolywern, which left the main line from Chirk, just before it swept sharp left onto the road bridge. At this point, it crossed the roadway to the right hand side before crossing the bridge (the main line continued across the bridge on the left-hand side), and carried on up the right-hand side of the road to terminate at a buffer stop opposite the cottages next to the site of the later-built (1887) Baptist chapel. One has to presume that the length quoted is a clerical error. This siding would not have needed to be authorised by the Acts.

The report further commented that:

'The state of the road (at the present in the hands of the Wem and Bronygarth Road Trustees, who did not put in an appearance at the inspection) is very bad, in fact it is impassable. In November next it passes into the hands of the Llangollen Highway Board, whose chairman and surveyor were present at the inspection.'

The roads in the Ceiriog Valley, owned by the Wem & Bronygarth Turnpike Trust, became *main roads* under the Highways and Locomotives (Amendment) Act 1878 and legal control duly passed to the Llangollen Highway Board in November 1881.

Major-General Hutchinson commented in his report that: *'It was a mistake to include any portion of the tramways authorised by the Act of 1878 in the application, none of these having been yet constructed.'*[14]

Dolywern showing the main line of the horse tramway across Pont Dolywern, the rear of the Queen's Hotel and the tramway siding on the nearside of the bridge and road. Standing on the bridge is the open carriage, with lettering just about visible on its centre panel, two pairs of bolster wagons, one pair loaded with cut timber, and up against the buffer stop is the horse 'Dandy', with end loading, converted to a van.

Collection: Late Dewi Jones
Courtesy Anne Jones

[14] The tramways authorised in the Act included the deviation at Dolywern, the *'Glyn Valley Tramway (Pandy) Extension'* and the *'Glyn Valley Tramway (Nantyr) Extension'.*

The New Inn, Glyn Ceiriog, photographed in the 1890s with the village youth again in attendance. In the background at the tramway station can be seen the crane, a horse and cart backed up to the loading doors in the warehouse and piles of what look like granite setts. Note the point lever, in front of the tree, for the short siding that disappears under the booking office.

© Gwilym Hughes

He also stated that the track was 2ft 4in gauge with 22lbs/yd flat-bottomed rails secured to 4½" x 9" x 4½" sleepers with dog bolts. At crossings the levels were uniform with the roadway and checkrails were fitted with crossing timbers. The steepest gradient was 1 in 36, with an average of 1 in 100, and the sharpest curve having a radius of 2 chains (44yds). As related previously, some sections of the tramway were either laid on a small 'embankment' or in a 'cutting' relative to the road level, thus reducing the width of the road available for public traffic.

On the 7th November 1881, Messrs Longueville, Jones & Williams, the GVT Company's solicitors, wrote to the BoT in response to Major-General Hutchinson's comments in his report of 19th September, 1881, regarding the levels of the tramway relative to the road, which was that month in the process of being taken over by the Llangollen Highway Board. They pointed out that following his report dated 10th April 1875 it was accepted that the levels of the tramway (shown on the deposited Plans & Sections, as being above and below the road level) had received Parliamentary approval when the Glyn Valley Tramway Act 1870 was passed. The only other legal voice in the matter, the Wem & Bronygarth Turnpike Road Trust, had also given its approval at the time. Longuevilles also pointed out that as the road was useless and incomplete when the tramway was built, and that it still remained so, then the GVT Co. could not be expected to apply funds, even if it had them, to rendering the road usable by the public. The GVT Co. did however agree to rectify any sections where the tramway had reduced the roadway width to less than 18ft. Longueville's letter concluded: '*We are in a position to assure you that it will be a matter of considerable moment to the locality and general public, that locomotive power on the Glyn Valley Tramway should, at once, be legally authorised, and we would submit our hope that you will not see fit to withhold the preliminary certificate ...*'

This was not enough to satisfy the BoT, which informed the two highway authorities and others of the decision not to grant a licence and the reasons why, inviting them to submit their comments. However, it was not until 14th December 1881 that the GVT Company received a formal letter, stating that a licence for the use of steam power would not be granted until:

'... the Board of Trade are satisfied that the bridges have been put into a satisfactory condition, and that the construction of the tramway on those bridges has been altered so as to properly distribute the load, as recommended by Major-General Hutchinson.'

Again, the GVT Co. had been thwarted in its attempt to convert the tramway to steam!

Meanwhile, the Oswestry Highway Board had become aware that both the Llangollen Highway Board and the Wem & Bronygarth Trust had been consulted and requested to give their approval for the use of steam power on the GVT, whereas it had not. No doubt, the Oswestry Board was, under the impression that steam locomotives were going to be run on the Pontfaen–Gledrid section of the tramway in its area, the GVT Co. having not informed it otherwise. There was, of course, no intention to do so. However, the issue was raised with the BoT which, probably thinking that there should have been a letter of approval from the OHB, wrote to the Clerk of the Peace for Salop, who on 28th October, responded advising them that: *'it is not intended to use steam power on any portion of the Glyn Valley Tramway in the County of Salop'.*

As a result of the newly registered Ceiriog Granite Co. Ltd having taken over the operation of the tramway from the SUR&C Co. on 1st September 1881, the administrative and operational structure of the GVT became unwieldy and decision making more difficult, as the two principal shareholders, viz. the directors of the GVT Co. and the SUR&C Co., had their own conflicting interests and a third party, the Ceiriog Granite Co., was now the owner of all the rolling stock and was operating the tramway on behalf of the GVT Company. The SUR&C Co. still owned 50% of the GVT Co. shares and, although it was anxious to relieve itself of any financial involvement in the operation of the tramway, it still wanted to retain the opportunity for its canals to benefit from the future traffic that would be generated by the tramway, especially that from the Ceiriog Granite Co.'s increasingly successful quarry at Hendre. However, the objective of the directors of the GVT Co. was not to help the SUR&C Co. gain a significant share of this traffic, but to break the link with this company by purchasing its GVT shareholding, which would then give them the freedom to transfer the bulk of their tramway traffic onto the GWR network. To the annoyance of the SUR&C Co., it was revealed in March 1882 that the Great Western Railway Co. was actively attracting GVT traffic onto its lines by giving GVT workers a financial incentive to direct traffic to the railway rather than to the canal!

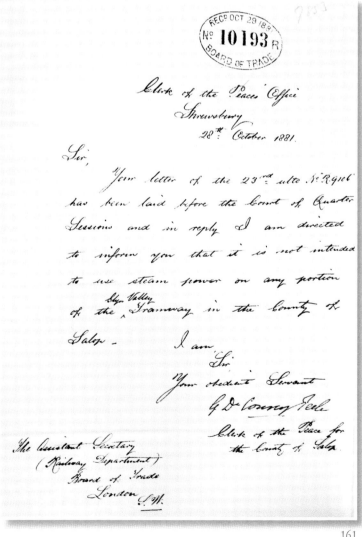

The letter from the Clerk of the Peace's Office, Shrewsbury, to the Board of Trade, advising them that the GVT Co. was not intending to use steam power on the Pontfaen–Gledrid section of the tramway, which was in Shropshire.

Courtesy: National Archives

Following the failure of The (Glyn Ceiriog) Wood Blasting Powder Co. Ltd, liquidated in 1879, the Ceiriog Granite Company took over the site of the former gunpowder works in 1880, which was soon developed, utilising the existing buildings, for the manufacture of granite setts. Note the short incline from the lower to the upper level of the site. The two-story building on the right still survives and is today a listed building.

Collection: John Milner

Records for 1881 confirm that from the first week of September, that year, the Ceiriog Granite Co. Ltd was indeed operating the tramway on behalf of the GVT Co. and for working expenses for the first four months up to 31st December 1881, it charged the GVT Co. £791 7s. 0d.

During the first month or so of its operation, the granite company continued to use SUR&C Co. weighbills with the canal company's name manually crossed out and overwritten to read '*Glyn Valley Tramway Co.*' after which it used printed GVT weighbills. It is interesting to note that on these, for the first time, truck numbers were recorded and an analysis of those surviving, from 1881 to 1883, reveals that there were 105 wagons in service numbered, curiously, from '0' to '104'. The GVT must have been the only railway with a wagon numbered '0'! Three trucks numbered 29, 59 and 64, do not appear at all. These may well have been either out of use at that time or converted for other purposes. From photographic evidence of the period it is known that at least six bolster wagons were in use for the carriage of timber. There is no mention on the weighbills during this period of the horse tramway van, which is known to have existed, but it is assumed that it had no number and was used to carry fragile and perishable goods, which, according to surviving weighbills, were not allocated truck numbers.

The principal waggoner recorded on the weighbills was John Brown, although the names of others, including that of John Roberts and G. Hughes, did occasionally appear. During this earlier period,

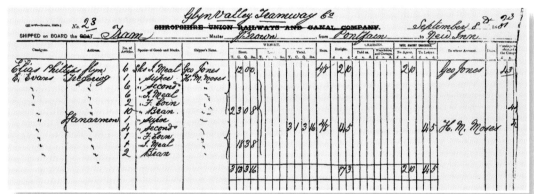

One of the first weighbills, No.23, issued after the Ceiriog Granite Co. had taken over the operation of the tramway. The company continued to use weighbills printed with the canal company name amended to read GVT Company.

Collection: Ceiriog Memorial Institute

when the SUR&C Co. was operating the tramway, the waggoners were listed as '*Masters*', in true canal fashion. Each of the masters would have been responsible for engaging his own assistant waggoners when required and they would operate as a team. Additional waggoners would specifically be required for the Pontfaen–Gledrid section, as trains had to be split because of the gradients.

In 1881, John Brown was living in the tollhouse at Glyn Ceiriog which, in later years, was purchased by the GVT Co. He had married Sarah (née Mathews) in 1867 and they had ten children. John Roberts was described as *tramway car driver* in the 1881 Census, which suggests that he was a regular driver of the passenger tram.

At the time that the operation of the tramway was taken over by the Ceiriog Granite Co. Ltd in 1881, the traffic prospects looked very favourable indeed. Granite traffic was on the increase. Some 10,000 tons were carried in 1882, turning a previous operating loss into a modest profit of £15 for the year. The boom in building street tramways had created a big demand for granite setts, and these were being supplied to Wolverhampton, Birmingham and Wigan for paving their tram-lined streets. In spite of this expanding market, the inefficiency and consequential heavy cost of using the horse-drawn tramway made the Ceiriog Granite Company's setts more expensive than those from other quarries and this led to a decline in granite traffic on the GVT, which, compounded with the absence of slate traffic, did not augur well for its future. However, it was not long before the company realised that the conditions set out in the Agreement that it had made to operate the tramway would hamper its long term development and that its involvement was not going to be financially viable. In fact, the granite company repeatedly gave notice to the GVT Board that it would continue to operate the tramway only for a further month.

An example of typical granite setts, as would have been supplied and carried in large numbers on the GVT.

Since 1875, the SUR&C Co. had been concerned about the excessive quantity of Cambrian Co. slates remaining unsold on its interchange wharf with the LNWR at Calveley, Cheshire; it had been struggling for years to obtain the payment due for their carriage from the Cambrian Quarries. In March 1882, the canal company seized the stock of slates and on the 29th March 1882 the New Cambrian Slate Co. went into liquidation, owing the canal company £74.

A cross-section of the track on the Walsall Corporation Tramways, which used Ceiriog Granite Co. setts in large numbers, showing how they were used to finish the road surface level with the track.

Tramway Journal
Collection: John Milner

Although the GVT had been built primarily to enable the Cambrian Quarry to transport its slate out of the valley, by the 1880s granite from Hendre Quarry was providing the bulk of the traffic. There also was considerable 'Up' traffic, as well as the passenger service, contributing to the revenue.

The 'Up' traffic to Glyn Ceiriog remained fairly steady and can be categorised as general supplies, coal and building materials. To take September 1881 as an example, 78 tons 19 cwt of general goods were transported up the valley plus 56 tons 2 cwt of coal. Weighbills at that time show that apart from animal feed supplies, the general goods included such items as mineral water for the Royal Oak at Glyn Ceiriog; 2 boxes of tea; 20 sacks of corn for the Glyn Mill; 1 case of currants; 1 bag of tobacco; a casket of oil; and lime from Bronygarth Lime Works. Examples from the following year include: '*1 box of hammers for the Granite Co.*', followed by '*a quantity of luggage for Hughes, School Master, Glyn*' and '*28 steam pipes*' to George Morris. George Morris was a master flannel manufacturer who had recently built the new single-story flannel mill, at Felin Newydd (New Mill), which he referred to as *New Factory*, just over ¼ mile to the east of Pont Bell, where he employed 12 men and 18 children.

During 1882, the tramway carried 814 tons of coal from David Lomax, lessee of Trehowell Colliery. On the 11th May, 31 wagons of coal were shipped out from Trehowell for various destinations up the Ceiriog Valley – this would have meant a number of individual trips with trains of up to six wagons each. The weighbills show that when an order exceeded 10 cwt (½ ton) the customer could have it delivered direct to 'New Inn' (the coal wharf at the Glyn Ceiriog terminus of the tramway) or 'Queen' (the 'Queen's Hotel' at Dolywern), from where it could be collected; smaller quantities had to be purchased from the local coal merchant. The local blacksmith at Glyn Ceiriog, J. Oliver, would order his coal (and possibly coke as well) 4 tons at a time.

[15] Brynkinalt Colliery was sunk about 1870 by a Mr Blakewell, but Black Park had been worked as early as the 1600s by the Myddelton family of Chirk Castle.

After 1883, orders from up the valley for coal direct from Trehowell began to fall, as the quality quickly deteriorated once the good seams became worked out, the colliery finally closing in April 1889. Better-quality coal was available from Black Park and Brynkinalt Collieries at Chirk.[15] However, the cost of coal at the pithead was 8s. 6d. per ton but, with the GVT Co. charging double the authorised Parliamentary toll of 3d. per ton per mile, it had increased to 11s. 6d. per ton by the time it had reached Glyn Ceiriog! Coal from Black Park and Brynkinalt Collieries, was brought by horse and cart to Pontfaen and then manually transshipped into GVT wagons. A merchant or agent, J. Roberts, was listed as the consignor of coal ex Brynkinalt from the loading point at Pontfaen. This coal trade steadily contributed to an increase in traffic up the valley. But this traffic, too, soon began to decline, as it was cheaper to transport it direct by horse and cart all the way up the valley, than to transship at Pontfaen and incur the extra cost.

The GVT also carried coke up the valley from the Chirk Gas Company, mainly to the Glyn Ceiriog Baptist Chapel, within which a 'modern' coke stove had been installed as, at that time, coke was proving to be a cleaner, more easily handled and efficient fuel than coal for heating large buildings. Bricks, ridge tiles and earthenware drainage pipes were supplied in abundance from the Trehowell Brickworks and smaller consignments from the Gledrid Brick & Tile Works. On the 10th and 11th October, 1881, bricks were despatched from Trehowell to '*Glyn Mill Siding*', Pontfadog, for the attention of Robert Davies, mason of Glyn. Glyn Mill, or Felin Lyn, to give it

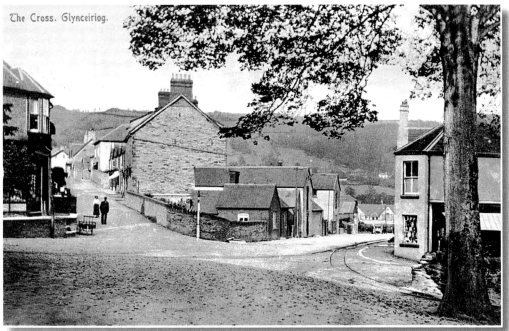

The Cross. Glynceiriog.

John Brown, in his distinctive jacket and cap, at the New Inn terminus. He lived with his wife Sarah and their ten children in the tollhouse at Glyn Ceiriog, the small red house in the centre of the picture opposite. The GVT Co. purchased this after it ceased to be a tollhouse. Note the tramway coming up from New Road into the New Inn terminus on the right and the branch on the left to the Cambrian Quarries incline.

Collection: John Milner

SUMMARY OF ALL JOURNEYS MADE UP THE VALLEY RECORDED BETWEEN SATURDAY 10TH SEPTEMBER 1881 AND THURSDAY 15TH SEPTEMBER 1881.

Day	Date	No.	From	To	Consignee Address	Truck Number	Goods	Shipper	T	Cwt	Q	Lbs	Rate	£	s	d
Sat	10th	31	CANAL	New Inn	R Jones, Glyn		1 case C. sugar and 1 box goods	D. Jones & Co.		1	3	10	each		1	0
					Elias Phillips, Glyn		5 packages goods	D. Jones & Co.		7	2	24	7/2		2	9
					John Hughes, Glyn		12 packages goods	D. Jones & Co.		13	2	10	7/2		4	11
					E. Evans, Tregeiriog		10 packages goods	D. Jones & Co.		7	3	23	7/2		2	10
		32	CANAL	Queen	J. Jones, Llwynmawr		7 packages goods	D. Jones & Co.		9	1	12	6/3		2	11
		33	Pontfaen	New Inn	E. Phillips, Glyn		1 sack sharps and 5 sacks bran	George Jones		6	0	0	4/8		1	5
		34	Trehowell	New Inn	Hugh Hughes, Penrhiewl, Tregeiriog	25, 30, 33, 41	1,000 pipes	Lomax	2	8	0	0	4/3		10	2
					E. Phillips , Glyn	0, 26	coal	Lomax	1	0	0	0	3/-		3	0
					John Lewis , Cefnybuinch, Glyn	39, 63, 85	coal	Lomax	2	10	0	0	3/-		7	6
		35	Pontfaen	New Inn	J. Hughes, Glyn		1 case matches	ex-GWR Co		1	3	4	each		1	0
					Rd Edwards, Glyn		14 bales, bedstead and 1 parcel	ex-GWR Co		6	3	0	6/4		2	2
					J. Hughes, B. House, Glyn		1 truss	ex-GWR Co.		1	1	0	each		1	0
					R. Edwards, Glyn		1 truss	ex-GWR Co.		2	0	20	each		1	0
		36	Pontfaen	New Inn	J. Davies, Garth		9 boxes tea	ex-GWR Co.		1	0	0	each		1	0
					Granite Co. Glyn		2 barrels powder	J. Thomas		2	0	0	each		1	0
Mon	12th	37	Trehowell	New Inn	John Davies, New Mill	56, 68, 73, 87	coal	Lomax	5	7	0	0	3/-		16	1
		38	CANAL	New Inn	Roberts & Edwards, Glyn		1 bundle empty wraps (RETURN)	R& S Ltd, Manchester			1	0	each			3
		39	CANAL	New Inn	R. Edwards, Glyn		10 packages goods	Williams		11	1	14	7/2		4	1
					Thos. Hughes, Glyn		2 boxes cheese and 3 loaves sugar	Williams		1	3	6	each		1	0
					Elias Phillips, Glyn		1 bag sugar, 1 case beef, ½ box soap	Jones		4	0	10	7/2		1	6
					J. Hughes, Glyn		1 barrel P. oil	D. Jones & Co.		3	1	20	7/2		1	3
		40	CANAL	Queen	John Jones, Llwynmawr		7 packages goods	Williams		8	2	8	6/3		2	8
Tues	13th	41	Pontfaen	New Inn	J. Hughes, B. House . Glyn		1 parcel	ex-GWR Co				10	each		1	0
Wed	14th	42	Pontfaen	New Inn	Thomas Edwards, Post Office, Llanarmon		3 sacks flour, 4 sacks Indian meal, 3 sacks bran, 1 sack Ind:an corn and 3 sacks gurgeons	H M Moses	1	5	2	17	4/8		6	0
					R. Edwards, Glyn		6 boxes S. ash and 1 box boots	ex-GWR Co.		4	3	5	each		2	0
		43	Pontfaen	Queen	J. Foulkes, Queens Head		1 jar spirits and 1 case spirits	ex-GWR Co		1	0	3	each		1	0
					Hughes, Llwynmawr		1 cask wine	ex-GWR Co		1	0	13	each		1	0
		44	Trehowell	Queen	Thos Davies. Queen	50	coal	D. Lomax		10	0	0	3/1		1	7
		45	Trehowell	Herber	Daniel Morris, Herber	96	coal	D. Lomax		10	0	0	2/10		1	5
		46	Trehowell	New Mill	John Davies, New Mill	21, 70	coal	D. Lomax	3	11	2	0	3/-		10	8
Thurs	15th	47	Pontfaen	Queen	Roberts, Dolywern		3 sacks super, 3 sacks seconds, 3 sacks Indian meal and 1 sack gurgeons	H. M. Moses	1	3	0	77	4/-		4	7
		48	Pontfaen	Pontfadog	Elizabeth Price, Pontfadog		3 sacks seconds, 3 sacks gurgeons and 1 bran	H. M. Moses		10	0	1	3/8		1	10
		49	Pontfaen	New Inn	E. Phillips, Glyn		1 box stationery	Parry & Son			1	0	each			6
					E. Evans, Tregeiriog		4 sacks seconds, 1 sack Indian meal and 1 sack gurgeons	H. M. Moses	1	2	1	11	4/8		5	3
		50	CANAL	New Inn	George Morris Factory, Glyn		4 P. pine plank, 6 white deal plank, 11 oak stanks and 89 E. spruce boards	Griffiths	1	10	3	0	3/8		5	7

NOTE: For all journeys listed, except Nos. 38 and 41, the waggoner was John Brown. On journeys 38 and 41, it was J. Roberts who, in both these cases carried just one small item. Goods not allocated a truck number were carried in the van or, in the case of timber, on bolster wagons.

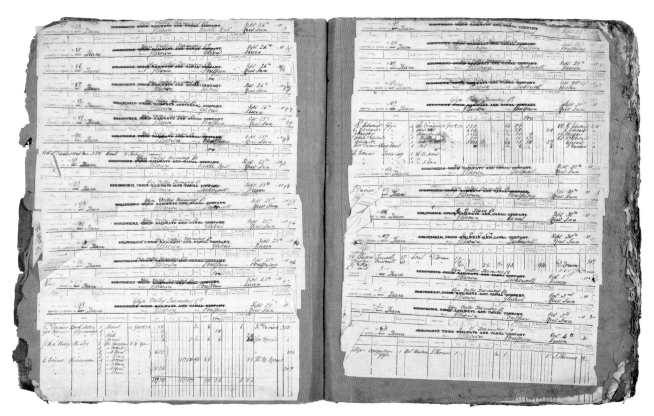

A surviving GVT weighbill book, covering the period 1881–1883. The new GVT weighbills, which replaced those used by the SUR&C Co, included columns for recording wagon owners and numbers. This one is for a consignment of two wagon loads of bricks from Trehowell brickworks to Glyn Ceiriog.

Collection: John Milner
Book image: © Alistair Kerr

its Welsh name, is located between Pontfadog and Llwynmawr, and was an important grain mill for the local community. The mention of a siding at this location is a complete mystery, as no record has been found of its existence. However, David Ll. Davies has related to the author that deliveries of grain for the mill in horse-tramway days were 'dropped off' at Pandy Bach Farm, on the main road and opposite the tramway, just a few yards from the lane leading to Felin Lyn.[16]

Barrels of gunpowder were transported on a regular basis. No special vehicle was provided by the GVT, unlike the other narrow-gauge quarry lines in Wales, which had purpose-built iron-clad covered wagons; this was the Glyn Valley Tramway and gunpowder and other hazardous products were carried by the tramway as if they were ordinary items of freight. In one instance a weighbill includes two barrels of gunpowder for the Granite Co., with another one for a case of matches, both despatched from Pontfaen, presumably in the van to keep them dry! Gunpowder is recorded as having been despatched to Phillips at Craig-yr-Bryn Quarry and '*28 rails via GWR*' to the Craig-yr-Oryn Slate Co.; both small slate quarries high above Llwynmawr.

On 25th January 1883, a consignment of ten iron wagons was despatched by David Lomax, Trehowell Colliery, to *The Queen* (Dolywern) for the Craig-yr-Oryn Slate Company. The weight of the consignment was only 4 tons, which suggests that these were probably surplus mine tubs from either Trehowell or Quinta Colliery and were acquired by the slate company in anticipation of underground working, but this did not start until two years later. One such wagon survived until fairly recently but, sadly, it was buried before it could be rescued. A further consignment on 31st

[16] *Watermill – Life Story of a Welsh Cornmill* by David Llewelyn Davies. Ceiriog Press 1997, and discussion with the author.

Although on a relatively small scale, in comparison with other areas, the local flannel industry was an important element in the economy of the Ceiriog Valley. It was never to provide any great volume of traffic for the GVT and the output of the mills began to decline after World War I. The photograph shows Upper Mill, built in 1818, which finally closed in 1951.

Collection: John Milner

January for the Craig-yr-Oryn Slate Co. was another batch of rails, 52 in number, delivered again via the GWR.

Apart from the usual traffic, several shipments from a Mr Rowlands of Llangollen stand out as being somewhat unusual – manure! However, this is unlikely to have been 'manure' in the usual sense of the word, but artificial fertilizer in some form of agricultural lime. On the 28th April 1883, some 19 tons were despatched to Glyn, which would have been 10 wagon-loads. Lime from the Bronygarth Lime Works was despatched from Castle Mill virtually on a monthly basis. This may have been quicklime from the kilns for building purposes. Contrary to common belief, this lime was shipped out in bags that, from details on the weighbills, would appear to have weighed 1½ cwt each. Another unexpected 'import' was a consignment of 1 ton 3 cwt of granite screenings from Gledrid to Mrs Eliza Green in Glyn Ceiriog; somewhat like 'sending coals to Newcastle'.

As related in chapter 1, between October 1882 and January 1883, 18,000 bricks were transported from the Gledrid Brick & Tile Works, via Gledrid, to John G. Briscoe of the *Laurels* (later renamed *Plâs Garth*), Garth, Glyn Ceiriog. Briscoe was 32 years of age and was recorded in the 1881 Census as being a *gunpowder manufacturer* living in Glyn Ceiriog. His family had been connected with the Liverpool gunpowder trade since the 1700s and had made a fortune out of the slave trade, but there is no evidence that he was connected with the Gunpowder Works at Pont y Meibion.

During the period 1881–1883, the volume of goods coming into the valley, via the canal wharf at Gledrid, was disappointingly low, but although the quantities were not high, the range of merchandise regularly transshipped there was quite extensive. This included: timber, paraffin oil, salt, ale for the local pubs, cheese, bacon, coffee, flour, sugar, rum, treacle, herrings and other food products, soap and books for W. Davies, the bookseller. Single consignments were also recorded of '1 couch, bedsteads and bedding' for Mrs A. Jones, Dolywern, tobacco for J. Parry, Pandy, a case of salmon and '2 Powers looms' for Edward Edward[s] of Glyn.[17] However, the volume of general merchandise traffic generated via Pontfaen (mainly from the GWR at Chirk) going up the valley far outweighed that from Gledrid.

[17] Ale started to be transshipped at Pontfaen from April 1883, probably arriving from breweries either in Oswestry or Wrexham.

Throughout this early period, there was little growth in passenger traffic and the timetables had hardly changed. Carriage accommodation was limited and, on special occasions, passengers were carried in open trucks. Between January and September 1881 there were three 'Up' Cars per day, leaving Pontfaen at 10.15 a.m., 1.30 p.m. and 7.15 p.m. On Oswestry market day, a Wednesday, the 1.30 p.m. was replaced with one at 3.45 p.m. and an additional service at 6.25 p.m. 'Down' cars remained at 8.00 a.m., 11.00 a.m. and 4.45 p.m. departure from Glyn Ceiriog. By this time, Herber Toll Gate had ceased to be a stopping place. The timetable was cut in October to two 'Up' cars per day, leaving Pontfaen at 10.15 a.m. and 6.25 p.m. with, in addition, a Market Car at 3.45 p.m. on a Wednesday, and two 'Down' from Glyn Ceiriog at 8.00 a.m. and 4.45 p.m. The timetable remained so until January 1886, when a 'Down' Market Car was added, leaving Glyn Ceiriog at 11.00 a.m. The return fare from Pontfaen to New Inn was 1s. 9d., with single tickets costing 1s. each. At this time, Griffith Roberts of Chirk was the General Manager. No further GVT timetables appeared in Bradshaw until 1900.

By 1883, the tramway was in a serious state of decline and decay. Other railways, built in North and Mid-Wales during the same period, to serve similar situations to that of the Ceiriog Valley, had all met with reasonable success, and some long outlasted the GVT. From the start, the GVT Co. had been forced into accepting a route from Pontfaen to the canal at Gledrid, instead of an easier one on the north side of the valley to Chirk, to connect with the canal and the GWR. The gradients, as previously related, between Pontfaen and Upper Chirk Bank, were 1 in 83/19/23/27/30 uphill, making it almost impossible to work economically, especially by horse power.

At the beginning in 1871, the SUR&C Co. had operated the tramway under an agreement with the GVT Co. It was only natural that as, a canal company, it concentrated on generating traffic for its canal. In the process of so doing, it failed to recognise the national move from canals to railways as a means of transport; a move that was to become vital to the GVT's survival. When the Ceiriog Granite Co. Ltd took over the operation of the tramway on behalf of the GVT Co., in 1881, the emphasis moved to transporting its granite down the valley from Hendre Quarry. The GVT Co. had, in effect, mismanaged the tramway from the beginning as, due to the shortage of capital and without the will to operate it, it had opted for the easy solution of letting other companies operate it for them: companies that had their own interests at heart and not those of the GVT shareholders.

The situation had become so dire that the GVT Co. shareholders passed a resolution, on 27th March 1883, authorising an application for an Act of Parliament to enable the GVT Co. to lease or otherwise dispose of the line, and to obtain further powers to wind up the company. The SUR&C Co., at its April meeting, expressed its concern and that of its masters, the LNWR Co., about the situation. The following month, the SUR&C Co. agreed to sell its shares in the GVT Co. at 60% discount, but also made an alternative proposal. The proposal was that if the GVT Co., or another interested party, were to put the line in order, and build the necessary deviations, then the SUR&C Co. would undertake to work the line with steam locomotives, on agreed terms. It also offered to build Jebb's 1879 proposed route from Pontfaen to the canal, which was to run under the railway viaduct arch at its northern end and over the aqueduct to a new wharf at Chirk Bank.

At a meeting of the SUR&C Co. Executive Committee on 21st December 1883 a letter from Mr Hales to Mr Moon, dated 16th December, was read, reporting that he had ascertained that the Great Western Company was contemplating taking over the Glyn Valley Tramway. It was further reported that as the Parliamentary powers for the extension of the line had by then expired, it was probable that no steps would be taken in the matter at present. The subject was left for further discussion at the next meeting. Unbeknown to them, on that very same day, Henry Dennis was with GWR Co. officials meeting Major-General Hutchinson, at the Board of Trade, to discuss the operation of the tramway by steam power. Hutchinson stated that there was no objection to working it by a *'tramway locomotive'*, providing that the speed was restricted to 8 m.p.h. and that an automatic arrangement was fitted to prevent the locomotive exceeding 10 m.p.h. This was a turning point for the tramway, although there were many problems still facing the GVT Co. before steam power could be introduced.

However, by early 1884, there was already a steam locomotive at work in the valley at Trehowell Colliery. This was a standard-gauge locomotive designed and built by Isaac Watt Boulton in the early 1860s. He was born in Stockport in 1823 and founded an engineering business in Ashton-under-Lyne, dealing mainly in the hiring and selling of second-hand locomotives. As his name suggests, he had family connections with the world-renowned company Boulton & Watt, founded in 1775 to exploit Watt's patent for a steam engine with a separate condenser. Herein lies a local connection in that, in 1763, John Wilkinson, the 18th century ironmaster, had taken over from his father, Isaac Wilkinson, as manager of the Bersham Ironworks, near Wrexham, which incorporated

'Rattlesnake'
Trehowell Colliery

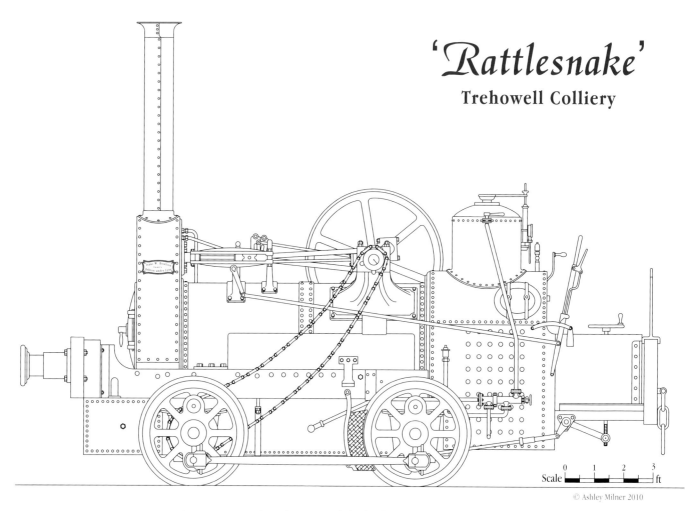

Scale 0 1 2 3 ft

© Ashley Milner 2010

an important gun foundry. In 1774, he built the first boring engine that was capable of boring cast cannon barrels to the high degree of accuracy required for efficient firing. Having met Watt in 1773, through his partner, Mathew Boulton, Wilkinson used this engine to bore steam engine cylinders for Boulton & Watt, to whom he became a main supplier; the first cylinders were delivered in 1775.

The Trehowell locomotive was, in effect, a cross between a traction engine and a railway locomotive. It comprised a single cylinder, peculiarly mounted within the upper part of the smokebox, driving a crankshaft and flywheel, with chain drive to the front axle, being mounted on 3ft diameter wheels similar to those produced by Aveling & Porter. It had worked for about twenty years as a contractor's locomotive, and was acquired by Lomax, lessee of Trehowell Colliery, in January 1884 for the sum of £100. Whether or not it was intended for use on the Trehowell Colliery private sidings is not known, but it appears to have ended its days as a stationary engine at the colliery. Its name was *Rattlesnake*, which is thought to originate from the rattle that its long chain drive made when it was running, and which, if the chain was slack, probably assumed a snake-like movement. Prior to it being acquired by Trehowell Colliery, it had seen service in many parts of the country on various railway construction contracts, including grinding the mortar to build the L&NWR station at Stockport c1864 and work on the Runcorn railway bridge 1866–1869.

Chapter 7

Horse to Steam Power
1884–1887

By March 1884, Elias Griffith of Chirk, then manager of Hendre Granite Quarry, was also managing the tramway, but there was some unease among the employees, who would have been happy for the SUR&C Co. to take it over again. This was not to be so, as the SUR&C Co. rejected the suggestion, having already had its fingers burnt once.

As well as the problems faced by the granite company as operator, the GVT Co. itself was in severe financial difficulties and had large debts that had been outstanding for a long time. On 5th July 1884, Henry Dennis had to resort to issuing a Writ for the £1,200 due to him for work that he had done in preparation for the 1878 Act and, likewise, on the same date Messrs Longuevilles did so for £739 16s. 10d. of unpaid fees. Although these particular accounts were settled on 5th August, the prospect of the tramway obtaining the large injection of capital that it needed to improve the line and enable it to survive, appeared increasingly unlikely. By October, the situation had not improved and the GVT shareholders decided to try to form an independent company to purchase

An artist's impression of Gledrid Wharf, which was destined to become redundant with the conversion of the tramway to steam power. On the right of the warehouse is the wharf for the transshipment of granite and, to the left, the lift bridge installed to give access to the wharf from the towpath side of the canal.

the tramway, the promoters being Richard Myddelton Biddulph, Henry Dennis and Elias Griffith. However, nothing came of this either and there were no further developments until the following January, when the GVT shareholders met to discuss the presentation of a new Bill to Parliament, which would ultimately change the fortunes of the GVT.

With Major-General Hutchinson, of the BoT, having stated in December 1883 that there was no objection to the use of steam power, subject to conditions including the restriction of speed, the directors of the Glyn Valley Tramway Co. had at last been prompted to take action.

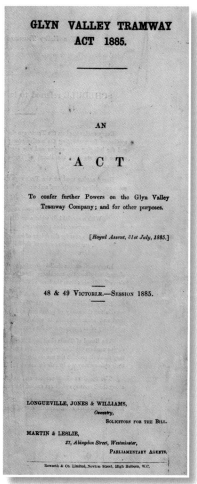

GLYN VALLEY TRAMWAY ACT 1885.

AN

'A C T

To confer further Powers on the Glyn Valley Tramway Company; and for other purposes.

[*Royal Assent, 31st July, 1885.*]

48 & 49 VICTORIÆ.—SESSION 1885.

LONGUEVILLE, JONES & WILLIAMS,
Oswestry,
SOLICITORS FOR THE BILL.

MARTIN & LESLIE,
27, Abingdon Street, Westminster,
PARLIAMENTARY AGENTS.

Roworth & Co. Limited, Newton Street, High Holborn, W.C.

The Glyn Valley Tramway Act 1885 gained Royal assent on 31st July 1885, and was the turning point in the GVT Co's. history, giving it the right, at long last, to use steam power on its tracks, subject to BoT conditions.

Collection: John Milner

Before the Bill could be presented, one matter arose that had to be resolved. The SUR&C Co. was agitated because it feared that it might not get the same facilities for interchange traffic as those to be afforded to the GWR. It was finally agreed to provide for a canal interchange at Black Park Basin, and to offer the SUR&C Co. the same deal as that offered to the GWR, with the condition that both interchanges would open at the same time. However, the GVT Co. agreed to extend the tramway only as far as the entrance to Black Park basin, leaving the canal company to build the interchange facilities at the basin. This effectively relieved the GVT Co. of the commitment to open both at the same time, should the SUR&C Co. not have its new wharf ready!

In anticipation of a successful passage of the Bill through Parliament, an agreement, dated 23rd February 1885, was made to purchase the £6,000 GVT shareholding still in the hands of the SUR&C Co., for the sum of £2,400, which it said was to '*be paid on or before the Works authorised by the Bill are commenced but, in the event of the promoters being unable to raise the necessary capital, this undertaking becomes null and void*'. It was signed by the promoters of the Bill: R. Myddelton Biddulph, Elias Griffith, James Coster Edwards, John Daniel Lloyd, Henry Dennis and Robert Henry Frederick Stuart, a civil engineer from London.

A Bill was presented to Parliament: '*To confer further powers on the Glyn Valley Tramway Company; and for other purposes*'; it was the '*other purposes*' element of the Bill that would provide the real turning point for the tramway's fortunes. These being for the use of '*steam power or any mechanical power, but not including electricity*' and the abandonment of the Pontfaen–Gledrid section in favour of a new Pontfaen–Chirk section.

However, before the Bill could be progressed in Parliament, David Lomax, lessor of the Trehowell Colliery, raised an objection and, on 6th May 1885, a House of Commons Committee sat to hear his concerns. Evidence in favour of the GVT Co. was given by its engineer, Henry Dennis, and by Elias Griffith; also present was the SUR&C Co. Engineer, George Robert Jebb.

Lomax stated that the greater part of his output was dispatched via the GVT and, if the company was empowered to abandon the Pontfaen to Gledrid section, then his colliery would be completely cut off, but what he failed to say was that it would only be cut off from the valley and Gledrid Wharf. He still had his outlet via his own private sidings with the GWR at Trehowell. In 1884, his traffic to the canal at Gledrid Wharf had been 43 tons and up the valley, via the GVT, 498 tons. Despite arguments put forward by Henry Dennis, the House of Commons Committee decided to find in favour of David Lomax. The tramway from Pontfaen to Trehowell could be abandoned by the GVT Co., as a public tramway, but the track was to be left in situ, and remain connected to the existing tramway system at Pontfaen, for the exclusive use of Lt.-Col. James R. Barnes (son of Thomas Barnes) of the Quinta Estate. Furthermore, the GVT Co. was to supply the Quinta Estate with wagons, and convey them from Pontfaen to the canal at Chirk (Black Park Basin) for the sum of 3d. per ton for the entire distance, or to Glyn Ceiriog for the rate of 3d. per ton less than the rate charged to other parties. His need to transport his coal and kiln goods to the canal at Black Park seems to indicate that he was not intending to utilise the canal wharf at Gledrid and that this was being abandoned. It was fortunate that the traffic from the Quinta Estate was, at this time, already in decline, so this clause in the Act did not present any long-term problems to the GVT Co., as both the colliery and brickworks were closed 5 years later.

With Lomax and Lt.-Col. James Barnes satisfied, the Bill passed through Parliament and the Glyn Valley Tramway Act 1885 gained Royal Assent on 31st July. At long last, the Act contained all the necessary provisions to convert the tramway to steam power, as well as authorizing two deviations, which avoided the weak road bridges, and two new tramways:

1. A deviation at Dolywern, with a new bridge across the river to eliminate the loading and the sharp bend on the road bridge.

2. A deviation at Glyn Ceiriog, with a new bridge across the river (alongside the Pont Bell road bridge) to similarly eliminate the loading on the road bridge at the Chirk end of the village.[1]

3. A new tramway from Glyn Ceiriog to the Hendre granite quarries and beyond, starting at the horse tramway terminus opposite the New Inn and terminating close to the crossroads in Tregeiriog. The tramway was to run through the former Gunpowder Works site on the south side of the river, whereas the proposed 1878 route had run on the north side.

4. A new tramway from Pontfaen to Chirk, to form interchanges with both the Great Western Railway and the Shropshire Union Canal.

One of the most important clauses of the 1885 Act empowered the Board of Trade to make by-laws governing the use of mechanical power, and a schedule, relating to same, was attached to the Act:

'Every engine used on the Tramways shall be fitted with such mechanical appliances for preventing the motive power of such engine from operating, and for bringing such engine and any carriage drawn or propelled by such engine to a stand, as the Board of Trade may from time to time think sufficient.

Every engine used on the Tramways shall have its number shown on some conspicuous part thereof and shall be fitted:

With an indicator by means of which the speed shall be shown.

With a suitable fender to push aside obstructions.

With a special bell, whistle or other apparatus to be sounded as a warning when necessary.

With a seat for the driver of such engine so placed in front of such engine as to command the fullest possible view of the road before him. [Hence the reason why the tram engines usually ran cab first]

Every such engine shall be free from noise produced by blast or clatter of machinery and the machinery shall be concealed from view at all points above four inches from the level of the rails, and all fire used on such engines shall be concealed from view.

Every carriage used on the Tramway shall be so constructed as to provide for the safety of passengers and for their safe entrance to and exit from, and accommodation in such carriage and other protection from the machinery of any engine used for drawing or propelling such carriage.

The Board of Trade shall be at liberty from time to time to inspect any engine used on the Tramways and the machinery therein, and may whenever they think fit prohibit the

[1] Pont Bell road bridge had been built at a cost of £260 and named after its constructor, George Bell, who was also responsible for building a bridge over the River Tanat, near Llanyblodwell. At the time of the opening of the New Road on 25th June 1860, its timber supports were still in place. Pont Bell bridge was demolished and rebuilt in 1985.

use on the Tramways of any such engine, which in their opinion may not be safe for use on the Tramways.

The speed at which engines and carriages may be driven or propelled along the Tramways shall not exceed the rate of eight miles an hour.

The speed at which engines and carriages may pass through moveable facing points shall not exceed the rate of four miles an hour.'

This schedule of compliances was not specific to the GVT, but was based on those drawn up for the use of steam locomotives running on rails on a public road under the Use of Mechanical Power on Tramways Act of 1879, which applied mainly to such use on town tram systems. The first steam tram locomotives had been operated in Leicester in 1876 and, on a larger scale, in Leeds in 1878. These 4-wheel tram locomotives, built by Kitson & Co., Leeds, were totally enclosed, had condensing gear and could be driven from either end. Beyer, Peacock & Co. Ltd of Manchester, the company that was selected to build the new locomotives for the GVT, was well experienced in this field, having built, between 1881 and 1886, 71 vertical-boiler tram locomotives to a patented design and another 16 to its own design, with horizontal boilers. Other roadside narrow-gauge lines, operating as 'railways' and with more in common with the GVT, were built in Ireland.

A later example (1910) of the 3'6" gauge 0-4-0 steam trams built by Beyer, Peacock & Co. Ltd in the 1890s for the East Java Tramways. Some 200, of varying designs, were built to replace horses on our urban tramways and for use on overseas tram systems. The design principles were incorporated into the more conventional GVT locomotives in order to comply with the Board of Trade specifications.

Collection: John Milner

The 1885 Act reiterated the requirements in the previous Acts for the rails of the tramway to be level with the road. Provision was also made within the Act for the outright purchase of the SUR&C Co. shareholding and, for the first time as far as the GVT was concerned, for the carriage of Her Majesty's Mails for a fixed annual fee.

The GVT Co. directors now faced new challenges, as they contemplated the complete rebuilding and extension of the line. They had been somewhat slow to accept that the conversion of the line to steam power would be the answer to the GVT's traffic problems, although the previous operators, the SUR&C Co., had begun discussing the use of steam locomotives as early as 1875, perhaps encouraged by the successful operation of steam on the quarry tramways/railways of the North Wales slate industry. Only a few of the major North Wales slate tramways of the era remained horse-operated, such as the Croesor Tramway, which ran down the Croesor Valley to Porthmadog, and the Ratgoed Tramway at Corris, to name but two.

One of the first challenges was the raising of the capital required for the conversion. The owners of the existing shares in the GVT Co., representing a paid-up capital of £17,610, were persuaded to accept a new share issue amounting to £8,205. Creditors agreed to accept £2,000 in full payment of their claims, and the company agreed to purchase back the rolling stock from the Ceiriog Granite Co. for the sum of £641. The purchase of the SUR&C Co. shareholding, although agreed, was left in abeyance for the time being. Preference stock to the value of £15,000 was issued, the prospectus promising a 10 per cent return, based upon an estimated traffic of 85,000 tons per annum.

This prospectus for 1885 goes out of its way to point out that the main objector to the original tramway making interchanges at Chirk and Black Park, had been the then owner of the Chirk

Castle Estate, Col. Robert Myddelton Biddulph. Had his consent been given before the 1870 Act, the story of the Glyn Valley Tramway, up to this point in its history, would have been very different and probably been hailed as a success story, rather than a failure. However, his son, Richard Myddelton Biddulph, who had inherited the estate about the time that the horse tramway had opened and was one of the promoters of the 1885 Bill and on the Board of Directors, had given his consent for the GVT Co.: '*to construct the line through his land, upon most favourable terms, so as to make the desired connection* [with the GWR and the canal at Chirk], *and in this way to assure the success of the undertaking*'.

The engineer for the project was one of the promoters of the Glyn Valley Tramway Bill 1885, Robert H.F. Stuart, a civil engineer of 6 Westminster Chambers, Westminster. He was born in France about 1855 but, by the time he was 16 years old, the family had returned to live in London and he trained to be a civil engineer. At the time that he became involved with the GVT, he was 29 years old, lived in Richmond and was working as an engineer on public works.

His '*Estimate of Cost of Construction and Equipment of Line from Black Park Wharf, Chirk, to the Granite Co's Works at Glyn Ceiriog*', dated 3rd September 1886, was £12,687 12s. 7d. He estimated that about 9 acres (exclusive of Chirk Castle Estate land), would have to be purchased costing about £50 per acre (£450), 10¼ miles of permanent way, including sidings, laid at an average of £479 9s. 6d. per mile (£4,914 12s. 6d.), earthworks would cost £908 9s. 2d. and retaining walls £486. Three public road bridges (£700) and three river bridges (£750) were required, fencing would cost £748 and two passenger stations £100.

The estimates for rolling stock included two locomotives at £700 each, but only one passenger coach at £200, which suggests that Stuart had been instructed to keep initial costs to a minimum, as had been the case with the original horse tramway. However, there was concern among some directors that locomotives costing £700 would not be adequate to operate the line; their precise concern is not stated. The tramway company may not have been expecting much passenger traffic to be generated from a direct interchange with the GWR at Chirk station, but to provide only one coach appears to be a gross underestimate of its likely use, considering the success of the former horse-drawn service and the clamour for the reintroduction of passenger coaches on the line.

An extract from the estimates compiled by Robert Stuart and dated 3rd September 1886. The estimated total, after deduction of the value of the old tramway rails, was £12,687 12s. 7d.

Issue of 1,500 Preference Shares of £10 each, bearing interest at the rate of 5 per cent., with right to participate in profits when 5 per cent. is paid on the other Capital of the Company.

THE GLYN VALLEY RAILWAY.

INCORPORATED UNDER SPECIAL ACT OF PARLIAMENT.

Authorised Capital, £38,020, in 3,802 Shares of £10 each.

ISSUE OF 1,500 5 PER CENT. PREFERENCE SHARES.

Payable £1 per Share on Application.
£2 per Share on Allotment.

DIRECTORS.

LORD TREVOR, Chairman, Brynkinalt, Chirk.
SIR THEODORE MARTIN, K.C.B., Bryntysilio, Llangollen.
R. MYDDELTON BIDDULPH, Esq., Chirk Castle, Chirk.
J. C. EDWARDS, Esq., Trevor Hall, Chirk.
H. DENNIS, Esq., New Hall, Ruabon.

BANKERS.

LONDON & WESTMINSTER BANK, Lothbury, London.
Messrs. CROXON & Co., The Old Bank, Oswestry.

SOLICITORS.

Messrs. LONGUEVILLE & Co., Oswestry.

ENGINEER.

ROBERT H. F. STUART, Esq., A.M. Ins. C.E., 6, Westminster Chambers, Westminster.

Applications are invited for 1,500 Preference Shares of £10 each, bearing interest at the rate of 5 per cent. per annum, with participation of profits when 5 per cent. is paid on the other capital of the Company.

THE GLYN VALLEY RAILWAY, originally authorised in 1870 as a Tramway, extended from the Shropshire Union Canal at Gledrid, to the Village of Llansaintffraid, Glyn Ceiriog, North Wales, and was to be worked by horse power.

An estimate of the traffic and profit is appended.

£10,000 of the £15,000 Preference Shares have already been subscribed for.

Subscribers for the Preference Shares will, besides receiving the dividend of 5 per cent. per annum, be also entitled to participate pro rata in all additional profits after payment of 5 per cent. per annum on the other Shares of the Company.

Prospectuses and Forms of Application for Shares may be obtained of the Bankers, Solicitors, and Secretary.

By Order of the Board,
EDW. WILLIAMS,
Secretary.

From information direct from the Collieries, Slate and Stone Quarries, and other works on the course of the line, the following is the

ESTIMATE OF TRAFFIC PER ANNUM.

OUTWARD TRAFFIC.

	Tons.		
Granite Setts and Macadam	60,000		
Slates	3,000		
China and Fluxing Stones	5,000	Tons—75,000 at an average rate of 2/-	£7,500
Timber			
Flannel	5,000		
Agricultural Produce, &c.			

INWARD TRAFFIC.

Coal		
Agricultural Lime		
Building Materials	Tons—10,000 at an average rate of 2/6	£1,250
Merchandise, &c.		
Passengers and Parcels		500
Gross Receipts		£9,250

ESTIMATED PROFIT.

Receipts, as per Estimated Traffic, £9,250	Estimated Working Expenses and Depreciations, say 60 % of Gross Receipts £5,530
	Balance Profit ... £3,720
	£9,250

Thus shewing a Dividend of 10 % upon the whole Capital of £38,020.

Two pages of the privately circulated Prospectus of 1886 for the issue of 1,500 5% Preference Shares, which includes Henry Dennis' name as a director, although he had not consented. The page on the right gives an indication of the volume of traffic and profit that the GVT Co. expected.

Collection: John Milner

[2] James Coster Edwards (1828–1896) was the first to exploit the use of the red Ruabon clay for the manufacture of the familiar bright red architectural terracotta ware and bricks, much loved by Victorian architects.

[3] *Wrexham Advertizer* 30th June 1888.

It appears from comments made by Henry Dennis, in a shareholders' meeting in 1888, that the 1885 Prospectus had been compiled by three of the promoters, Richard Myddelton Biddulph, Elias Griffith and Robert Stuart, with no input at all from Henry Dennis himself, who had been the company's engineer. He was becoming wary of the developing situation and was anxious to extricate himself from it. At this time, the Board of Directors comprised Lord Trevor (chairman), Sir Theodore Martin, Richard Myddelton Biddulph and James Coster Edwards, of Trevor Hall.[2] On the first version of the 1885 prospectus, Henry Dennis had been named as the fifth director and Robert H.F. Stuart as both engineer and secretary. When Henry Dennis, found that he had been listed without his consent, he immediately instructed Edward Williams, the newly appointed company secretary, to remove his name. As a consequence, Elias Griffith (one of the promoters of the Bill) had written to him asking if he would reconsider his action and consent to being a director; one of the letters had the following postscript:

> *'I have told Mr Williams to reinstate your name in the Glyn Valley* [Tramway Co.] *Directory. You must not say nay, otherwise the devil will again be let loose, and over the precipice we go.'*[3]

However, Dennis made it clear to Mr Williams that, as he had '*nothing to do with the Prospectus*', he '*would not be on the Board*'.

In spite of the optimism, in some quarters, following the passing of the new Act, the preference stock issue of 1885 was not a complete success and it was reported to the SUR&C Co. Executive Committee on 24th March 1886 that the GVT Co. found itself unable to raise the necessary capital for the restructuring of the company and consequently had decided to close the tramway. It appeared that the project had failed and Robert Stuart moved on, to become the general manager and resident engineer for the North West Argentine Railway, a 60-mile-long metre-gauge railway, running parallel to the Aconquija range of mountains in the province of Tucuman.

Passenger traffic on the GVT officially ceased on 31st March. The directors of the company requested a meeting with the SUR&C Co., but the latter decided not to entertain any proposals from the tramway company on the subject. It appeared that there was no way forward.

The prospect of permanent closure of the tramway would have been a devastating blow to the people of the valley, as not only would they lose their passenger service, but those working in the quarries were likely to lose their livelihoods as well. The granite reserves being worked by the Ceiriog Granite Co. at Hendre Quarry appeared to be inexhaustible and, if the cost of transport out of the valley were to be reduced, the quarry would find ready markets for granite setts throughout the Midlands and Lancashire, as well as for good-quality roadstone. The prospects of the slate quarries, which had been worked only spasmodically over recent years, had recently improved in 1883, when the Pant Glâs Slate & Slab Co., under the chairmanship of George Rooper, a London solicitor, took over the lease of the Wynne Slate Quarry for which he had plans for major developments, including opening up some of the Cambrian Quarry slate beds. By April 1885, the Wynne Quarry was at work again and a start had been made to build its own incline to connect with the GVT at the bottom of the Cambrian incline. The Wynne incline was opened in 1886 but, unlike the Cambrian incline, which was the property of, and maintained by, the GVT Co., this was owned, maintained and operated by the quarry company.

George Rooper (in the doorway) with his wife to the left, on 8th July 1898 at the homecoming of his son Francis after his marriage to Florence Trelawney. The newly wed couple stand to the right of the doorway. This photograph was taken outside Bronydd, the Roopers' residence at the Wynne Slate Quarry, by Lettsome & Sons, of Llangollen, 'photographers to the Queen' [Victoria], with the Ceiriog Vale Brass Band in attendance.

Courtesy: Angela James

This threat of closure did not last long. By May 1886, sufficient capital to continue with the conversion of the tramway to steam operation had been found and the crisis was over – the age-old principle of creating a crisis to solve one! The directors themselves had purchased most of the preference shares; a decision they made in haste that, later, most of them regretted.

Henry Dennis by this time had become a GVT Co. director and was acting as the company engineer. On 14th September 1886 he presented detailed plans for a new line from an interchange with the GWR at Chirk station, to connect to the existing tramway near Pontfaen, an extension from Glyn Ceiriog to the granite quarry at Hendre, and the conversion of the horse-drawn line between Pontfaen and Glyn Ceiriog, all to be worked by steam power. His estimated total cost for the conversion was £15,000, which included the purchase of land, earthworks and track and the discounted sum of £2,400 due to be paid to the SUR&C Co. for its £6,000 shareholding. The sum of £15,000 did not include the cost of constructing sidings at Chirk station, nor an extension to Black Park canal basin nor a spur from the Hendre extension to Pandy.

Before the GVT Co. could start on the construction of the extensions and deviations, it had to obtain legal possession of the extra land it required. Once the Glyn Valley Tramway Act 1885 was passed, the present owners were compelled to release to the GVT Co. any land required within the limits of deviation shown on the plans and sections that had accompanied the Bill. If a fair price could not be agreed by negotiation, then the two parties could call on the service of arbitrators, whose decision was final, to determine its value. Some lengths of the 1885 proposed route followed, exactly, the line drawn by Henry Dennis in the plans and sections that he had

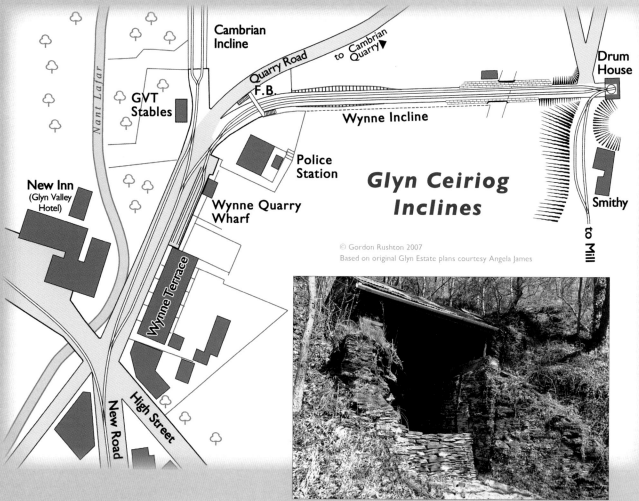

Cambrian
Incline

Quarry Road

to Cambrian
Quarry ▶

Drum
House

GVT
Stables

F.B.

Wynne Incline

Smithy

New Inn
(Glyn Valley
Hotel)

Police
Station

Glyn Ceiriog
Inclines

Wynne Quarry
Wharf

Nant Lafar

Wynne Terrace

to Mill

© Gordon Rushton 2007

Based on original Glyn Estate plans courtesy Angela James

New Road

High Street

The Wynne Slate Quarry, Glyn Ceiriog, had its own incline in 1886, to connect with the GVT in Quarry Road, near to the foot of the Cambrian Quarries incline.

Above right: *The Wynne incline winding house in 2004 and, far right, looking down the incline towards Quarry Road.*

© John Milner 2004

Right: *A very rare photograph showing the incline in situ, taken from the footbridge at the bottom.*

Collection: John Milner

Mʳ David Roberts

1887.

THE GLYN VALLEY
TRAMWAY ACT, 1885.

NOTICE

*To Landowners of intention to
take Lands.*

Longueville & Co.,
OSWESTRY.

THE GLYN VALLEY TRAMWAY ACT,
1885.

NOTICE OF INTENTION TO TAKE LAND.

In pursuance of the Glyn Valley Tramway Act, 1885, (herein called "The Special Act,") and the several Acts and portions of Acts of Parliament therein incorporated or referred to, I, the Secretary of and for and on behalf of The Glyn Valley Tramway Company, constituted under the provision of the Glyn Valley Tramway Act, 1870, give you notice that the said Company require to purchase and take for the purposes and under the provisions of the Special Act, the lands and hereditaments mentioned and described in the Schedule hereunder written, and which belong or are reputed to belong to you or some or one of you, or in which you or some or one of you have or are reputed to have or claim some estate or interest. And the said Company are ready and willing to treat for the purchase of the said lands and hereditaments, and as to the compensation to be made to all parties for all damage that may be sustained by reason of the execution of the works authorised by the Special Act. And I hereby further demand from you particulars of your estate and interest in and of the claims intended to be made by you in respect of such lands and hereditaments or otherwise by reason of the execution of the works authorised by the Special Act. And if for the space of 21 days after the service of this Notice you shall fail to state such particulars and claims, or to treat with the said Company in respect thereof, or if you and the said Company shall not agree as to the amount of compensation to be paid to you, the amount thereof will be settled as by the said Acts provided for settling cases of disputed compensation.

Dated this   20ᵗʰ   day of   June   1887.

To Mʳ David Roberts

and all and every other persons or person having or claiming any estate or interest in the lands and hereditaments described in the Schedule hereto, or enabled by the said Acts to sell and convey the same or any part thereof.

Edw. Williams

SECRETARY
TO THE SAID COMPANY.

THE SCHEDULE ABOVE REFERRED TO.

All those several pieces of land situate and being in the parish of Llangollen — - in the county of Denbigh, and containing altogether by admeasurement - - - - - ~~acres~~ - - - - ~~roods, and~~ thirty nine perches, statute measure or thereabouts be the same more or less, which are coloured pink on the map or plan thereof hereunto annexed, and respectively numbered 5 - - - - - - - - - - in the parish of Llangollen - - . - — — — — — on certain plans of The Glyn Valley Tramway, and in the Books of Reference thereto respectively deposited with the Clerk of the Peace for the county of Denbigh.

The granting of an Act of Parliament entitles a company constituted under that Act to take land for the purpose of executing the works that are authorised in the Act. This example of such a notice was issued to Mr David Roberts for land at Dolywern, under the statutory powers of the Glyn Valley Tramway Act 1885 and was dated June 1887. Landowners had 21 days to lodge the details of their land and state the compensation they expected, which would be settled either by negotiation or arbitration.

Collection: John Milner

prepared for the GVT Act 1878, and existing documents show that some negotiations for the purchase of land had started at that time.

The extension from Pontfaen to Chirk, where the interchanges with the standard-gauge GWR and the Shropshire Union Canal were to be built, was to climb out of the valley up through the wooded slopes of Baddy's Wood on the Chirk Castle Estate. A small stretch of estate land was also required to accommodate a siding at the side of the road opposite a small gravel quarry, further up the valley, near to Herber. The GVT Co. was able to make an agreement to lease 11 acres or so of the land required, at £10 per acre per annum, amounting to an annual charge of £144 11s. 3d., which considerably reduced the capital outlay at a time when the company was financially stretched. The lease was redeemable in the future for the sum of £2,291 5s 0d. Various buildings standing on the land were valued at £31. In the early 1890s, the GVT Co. purchased additional land from the estate at Chirk station, paying £957 for the 5-acre field between its sidings and the canal. Work was to start by constructing the extension down from the GWR station at Chirk to Pontfaen and, at the same time, relaying the track from Pontfaen to the New Inn, Glyn Ceiriog. In order that the two new bridges could be built over the River Ceiriog, the line was to make two short diversions, one at Dolywern and the other at Pont Bell. Formal 'Notices of Intention to take Land' for these diversions were issued by GVT Co. on 20th June 1887 and negotiations began. Legal agreements to purchase were made incorporating arrangements to allow the GVT Co. access to the land to begin work, before the final conveyances were ready to be signed.

Following the GVT Act 1878, this drawing, prepared by Henry Dennis in August 1881, shows the then proposed 'straight' alignment of the deviation at Dolywern. It accompanied the first 'Notice of Intention to take Land' issued to David Roberts, shopkeeper of Dolywern. The conveyance of this land shown in red was not completed until 7 years later.

Collection: John Milner

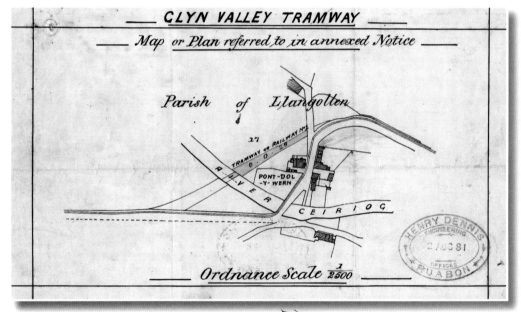

Right: This sketch, redrawn from the original conveyances, shows the revised 1887/1888 alignment of the deviation at Dolywern, now on a reverse curve rather than being straight, as drawn in the illustration above. C–D on the blue section is the location of a gated accommodation crossing. Land was purchased from John Jones of Woking (red), David Roberts, Dolywern (blue) and Samuel Hughes, Dolywern (green).

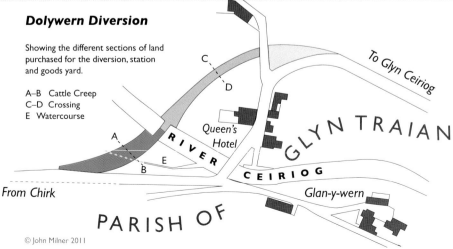

Dolywern Diversion

Showing the different sections of land purchased for the diversion, station and goods yard.

A–B   Cattle Creep
C–D   Crossing
E   Watercourse

© John Milner 2011

The 1887 deviation at Dolywern, looking from the Chirk end, photographed not long after the track was lifted in 1937. Note the cattle grid next to the 'Dolywern' sign, the wrought iron hurdle fencing and the plate-girder bridge over the river. On the left-hand side of the embankment, the entrance to the cattle creep through it can just be seen. The embankment, cattle creep, bridge and hurdles are still in situ today.

Collection: John Milner

The Dolywern diversion, just over 275yds long and incorporating the new bridge, required embankments to be built on both sides of the river. The land to the north, amounting to 36 perches, was purchased for £175, from John Jones of Manor House, Send Green, Woking, who insisted that due provision was made for:

> *'the preservation of the two existing watercourses ... to allow the same to flow through and under the embankment'* and that *'the company shall also construct a cattle arch* [creep] *... not less than six feet wide and having a square girder top to enable cattle to pass and repass to and from lands of the Vendor, which will be severed by the proposed railway'.*

South of the river, 39 perches of land were purchased from David Roberts, shopkeeper of Dolywern, for the sum of £120, which was the valuation agreed by two arbitrators, Thomas Whitfield and William Williams, both surveyors of Oswestry, on condition that the company would build water channels to maintain the irrigation system and construct a floodgate where required. The land taken was to be fenced *'with iron hurdles only (not with quickthorn)',* which would incorporate field gates giving access to *'a level crossing'* to connect the two sides of the severed land. A third plot adjacent to the road, of 29 perches and triangular in shape, on which the company planned to build a small goods yard, was purchased from Samuel Hughes, maltster of Glan-y-wern, Dolywern, for £55.

For the short diversion required to incorporate the new bridge close to and parallel to Pont Bell at Glyn Ceiriog, small plots of land had to be purchased from three different owners. Eliza Green, the owner of adjacent Old Pandy flannel mill and the widowed daughter of the late John Mason, who had built and operated the nearby 3-storey flannel factory at Lower Mill, until his death in 1862, agreed a price of 5s., on condition that the GVT Co. *'provide a clean and suitable covered wagon for the conveyance ... of goods manufactured by them* [the mill]'.

David Jones, a retired farmer, formerly of *'Hafod-y-gynfor',* Glyn Ceiriog, was paid £15 for a strip on the other side of the river, and Susannah Wynne, £5 for a triangular patch next to the road. Susannah Wynne, widow of Edward Wynne of New Hall (Plas Wynne), who had died childless in 1884 was the last surviving member of the Wynne family, who had been the owners of the Wynne Slate Quarry.

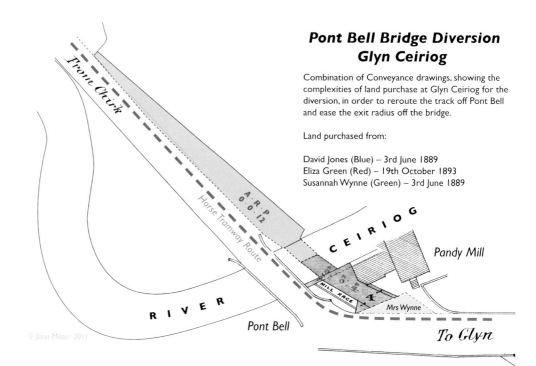

**Pont Bell Bridge Diversion
Glyn Ceiriog**

Combination of Conveyance drawings, showing the complexities of land purchase at Glyn Ceiriog for the diversion, in order to reroute the track off Pont Bell and ease the exit radius off the bridge.

Land purchased from:

David Jones (Blue) – 3rd June 1889
Eliza Green (Red) – 19th October 1893
Susannah Wynne (Green) – 3rd June 1889

The 1887 diversion of the tramway at Glyn Ceiriog, photographed after the tramway was lifted in 1936, with the original Pont Bell road bridge on the left (rebuilt 1985), the plate-girder bridge for the tramway in the centre and Old Pandy (Fulling Mill) on the right. The bridge abutments can still be witnessed today, although the mill has undergone changes in more recent years.

Collection: John Milner

The extension, nearly two miles in length, from Glyn Ceiriog to Hendre Quarry, was to be laid over private land. The issue of the 'Notices of Intention to take Land' to the eleven landowners on the route was delayed until October 1887. At a meeting of shareholders in January 1888, when the Secretary was asked why the company *'could not have treated for the land about twelve months ago'*, he replied that when the company negotiated for the purchase of land, it was expected to pay for it, and the company was *'not in a position to pay for it twelve months ago'*. From the ensuing discussion, it became apparent that even six months earlier, the company did not have the finance available to enter into contracts to purchase the land for the extension.

The total length of track, from Chirk to Hendre Quarry, was about nine miles and Henry Dennis divided the schedule of work into four different sections, for each of which contracts were drawn up for placing out to tender:

Section No.1

At a total estimated cost of £3,743, Section No.1 was a new line, 1 mile 1 chain in length, to climb steeply up from the road in the valley near Pontfaen to form an interchange with the GWR at Chirk station. It did not include any work on the extension to Black Park Colliery Basin, where an interchange with the canal was to be built. The construction work was divided into two contracts:

Contract No.1, for the substantial earthworks required, was awarded on 23rd March 1887 to a local contractor, Griffith Griffiths of Chirk (not to be confused with Elias Griffith), at a contract price of £2,607. The route included a cutting, which severed one of the access roads to Chirk Castle, necessitating the building of a bridge, which became the subject of a separate Agreement dated 20th June 1887.

Contract No.2, for the laying of the track on this section, was awarded to a another local contracting firm, H. Croom Johnson of Holly Bank and King Street, Wrexham (not to be confused with Cudworth & Johnson Ltd, locomotive dealers and founders, also of Wrexham).[4] His tender, dated 29th July 1887, quoting a rate of 15s. 6d. per chain (22yds), was accepted. All the track materials were to be provided by the GVT Company.

Harry Croom Johnson J.P., of Wrexham, ran a company that was mainly involved in road construction and quarrying activities. In 1891, he is recorded as being a promoter of the Teirw Hill Roadstone Co. Ltd, Pandy, and in April 1904 as managing director of the Arenig Granite Co. Ltd (No.78710), whose quarry was located near Bala and registered office at 10 Egerton Street, Wrexham. About the same time as the rebuilding of the GVT, he also had a contract to build the Kerry Tramway, which ran from Kerry station on the Cambrian Railways, near Newtown, to the Bryn-Llywarch Estate (owned by Christopher Naylor, whose family also owned the Leighton Estate, Welshpool), and some of the old rail lifted by him from the GVT was utilised in its construction. On the closure of the Kerry Tramway, in 1895, this rail was sold to Messrs Thomas Beatson, Derby, railway equipment dealers.

Section No.2

At an estimated cost of £3,996, Section No.2 was for the relaying of the horse tramway on the side of the public road, between Pontfaen and Glyn Ceiriog, for which there was one contract:

Contract No.3, for taking up the old light-weight tramway track between Pontfaen and Glyn Ceiriog and relaying with track more suited for steam operation, including the ballasting, was also awarded to H. Croom Johnson. The specification for this section, a distance of 5 miles, 3 furlongs and 3 chains, included *'the laying of loop lines for passing places at the several points selected by the Engineer'*. The tender accepted from Croom Johnson was dated 23rd August 1887, and quoted a rate of £2 1s. 3d. per chain (22yds). Again, all the track material was to be provided by the GVT Company.

Col. Robert Myddelton Biddulph (1805–1872), owner of the Chirk Castle Estate, Manor and Lordship of Chirk, whose early opposition to building a tramway through his land to Chirk seriously hampered the prospects for the GVT and delayed industrial development in the Ceiriog Valley. It was not until his son, Richard Myddelton Biddulph, took over the estate after his death, that the GVT Co. was to encounter a more cooperative relationship, enabling it eventually to re-route the tramway to Chirk.

© Christies Images Ltd

[4] Cudworth & Johnson Ltd was originally Arthur Cudworth, St. Marks Engineering Works, Wrexham.

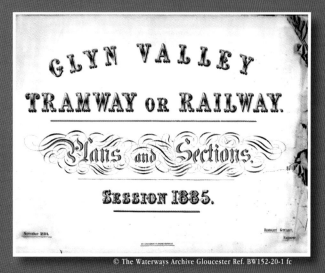

Below: The 1885 Robert Stuart drawings for the deviation of the GVT from Pontfaen, through Baddy's Wood to Chirk and the proposed new wharf on the canal, near to the entrance to Black Park Wharf. Note that on the bottom drawing interchange sidings have been pencilled in at Chirk station.

Opposite: The three Robert Stuart drawings of 1885 show the proposed route of the extension from Glyn Ceiriog to Tregeiriog, which was to start at a junction with the existing tramway outside the New Inn. It was to cross to the east side of the river at Coed-y-Glyn and run through Lower Pandy Chinastone Quarry. At Pont-y-Meibion it was to pass through the gunpowder works site and the edge of Hendre Quarry, cross the river to the west side just before Hendre Farm and to finally terminate in the centre of Tregeiriog. The section from the gunpowder works to Tregeiriog was destined never to be built, despite fierce lobbying by the residents of the upper valley.

Courtesy: The Waterways Archive Gloucester
Licence Ref: 0609 JM
National Waterways Museum

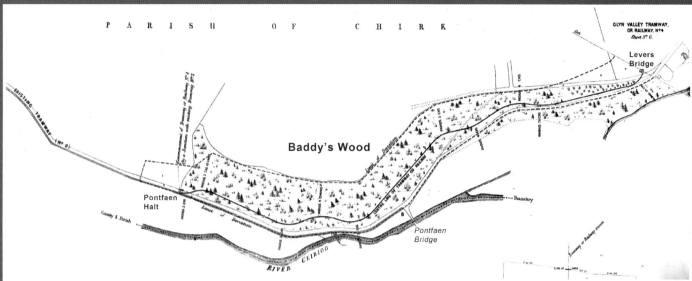

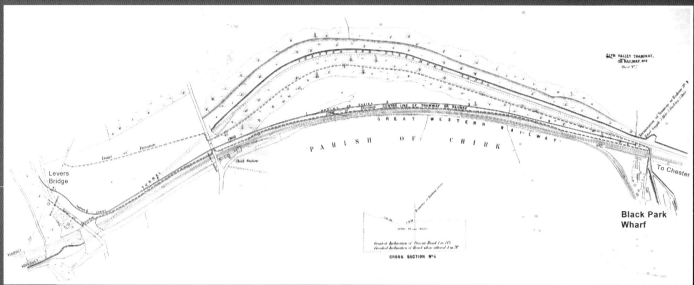

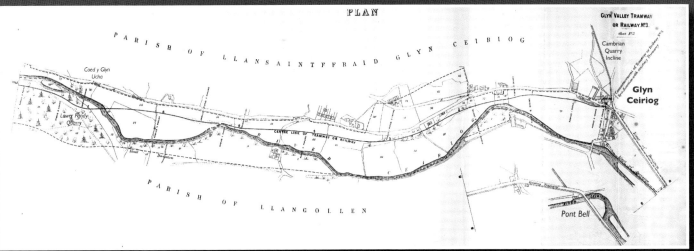

PLAN

GLYN VALLEY TRAMWAY
OR RAILWAY No 3.
Sheet No 2

PARISH OF LLANSAINTFFRAID GLYN CEIRIOG

Cambrian
Quarry
Incline

Coed y Glyn
Ucha

**Glyn
Ceiriog**

Lower Pandy
Quarry

CENTRE LINE OF TRAMWAY OR RAILWAY

PARISH OF
LLANGOLLEN

Pont Bell

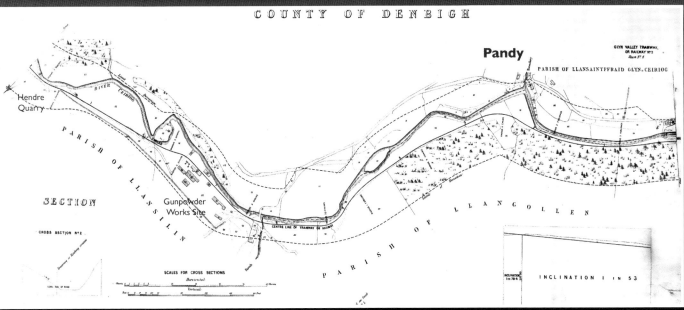

COUNTY OF DENBIGH

Pandy

GLYN VALLEY TRAMWAY,
OR RAILWAY No 3
Sheet No 4

PARISH OF LLANSAINTFFRAID GLYN = CEIRIOG

RIVER CEIRIOG

Hendre
Quarry

PARISH OF LLANSILIN

SECTION

Gunpowder
Works Site

CENTRE LINE OF TRAMWAY OR RAILWAY

PARISH OF LLANGOLLEN

CROSS SECTION No 2

SCALES FOR CROSS SECTIONS
Horizontal
Vertical

INCLINATION 1 IN 53

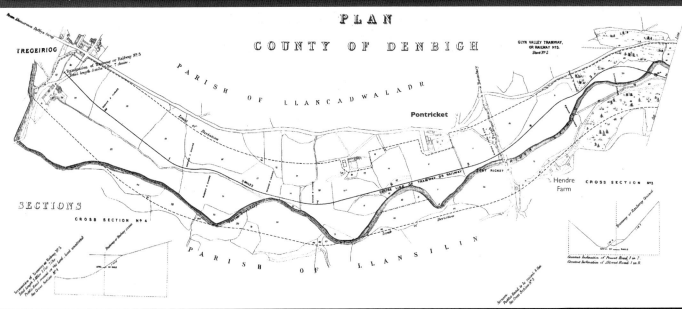

PLAN

COUNTY OF DENBIGH

GLYN VALLEY TRAMWAY,
OR RAILWAY No 3.
Sheet No 5

TREGEIRIOG

PARISH OF LLANCADWALADR

Pontricket

CENTRE LINE OF TRAMWAY OR RAILWAY

Hendre
Farm

CROSS SECTION No 3

SECTIONS

CROSS SECTION No 4

PARISH OF LLANSILIN

Section No.3

At a total estimated cost of £1,611, Section No.3 was for the two short diversions, with a total length of 340yds, each of which included a plate girder bridge with a span of 40ft across the River Ceiriog. The estimate for the bridge alongside Pont Bell, at Old Pandy (fulling mill), Glyn Ceiriog, was £543, whereas that for the bridge at Dolywern, which required more land and the building of embankments incorporating a cattle creep, was £1,068.

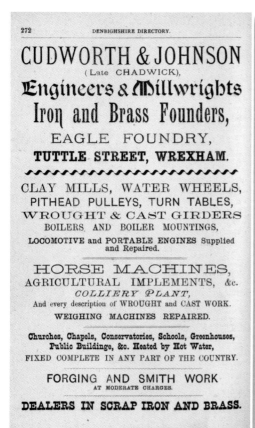

An advert for local engineering firm Cudworth & Johnson, of Wrexham, not to be confused with the GVT contractor H. Croom Johnson, also of Wrexham, although the company did, in later years, undertake locomotive repair work for the GVT.

Flintshire Record Office
BP 8835 p.272

Contract No.4 for the building of the bridge abutments and embankments was awarded, on 14th September 1887, to Griffith Griffiths of Chirk, the contractor who was already at work on the earthworks from Pontfaen up to Chirk, at a contract price of £270. In his tender, submitted on August 29th, he agreed to '*build four free stone abutments for two bridges over the River Ceiriog ... with all cuttings, embankments, a cattle roadway, drains and the ballasting of 15 chains in length ... for the sum of £270*'. The tramway company was to provide all the soil to finish the embankments, and was to '*do all the cartage of stones etc. from Pontfaen*' to the two bridges. A rival tender for this contract for the sum of £323, had been submitted by a David Davies.

Section No.4

At an estimated cost of £4,860, Section No.4 was a new line (extension), 1 mile 7 furlongs in length, from Glyn Ceiriog to the Ceiriog Granite Company's quarry at Hendre, including another 40ft plate girder bridge over the river at Pandy, for which there were two major contracts:

Contract No.5, for '*the earthwork and the completing of the road preparatory to taking the permanent way*', was awarded to John Jevons & Son, of Grange Road, Dudley. Their tender, with a contract price of £1,700, was informally accepted at a GVT Co. meeting in London on 1st November 1887, the formal contract being signed on 10th January 1888 with Mr Thomas Rollinson of Wordsley, Stourbridge and Mr John Tennant of Gornal Wood, Dudley, acting as sureties for Jevons & Son.

A separate contract for the laying of the track was awarded to H. Croom Johnson, who had undertaken all the other track work. The cost of the track for the extension, inclusive of all materials and the laying, was £2,696.

These estimates for the construction of the extension did not include either the short spur that was later built at Pandy or the continuation of the line from Hendre to Tregeiriog. The latter, although authorised, was not even considered, much to the annoyance of the residents of Tregeiriog and Llanarmon D.C., who were later to take their grievance to the Board of Trade.

The specifications for the major contracts give a very good insight into the way that they were executed, and the construction details for the new earthworks and track. Unfortunately, the drawings that were associated with these specifications have not been found.

The tender for Contract No.1 was signed by Griffith Griffiths, contractor of Chirk, on 14th March 1887, and was accepted on 23rd March 1887. According to the specification, the works were to be started within 14 days of acceptance and carried out with all due speed, without intermission, with the whole delivered up to the GVT Co. in working order within 5 calendar months. The penalty for a delay was £5 per working day. After the works had been properly completed and handed over to the GVT Co., the contractor was to repair and maintain them, including the packing of ballast as required on the permanent way, for a period of 12 calendar months. Griffith Griffiths also submitted a Schedule of Prices, which he would charge for any 'extra works' requested by the GVT Co.'s engineer. Included in the contract were widening and embanking works on the Chirk–Pontfaen road.

The 20-page comprehensive Specification for Contract No.1 stated that work included '*the supply of all materials, labour, horsework and plant required for, and the construction complete in every respect ready for the laying of the permanent way (but exclusive of the rails, sleepers and fasteners and the laying of the same) to the entire satisfaction of the engineer*'. Apart from the usual detailed specifications for groundwork, settling, topsoil and planting, it gives us an insight into the building of some of the structures of the tramway:

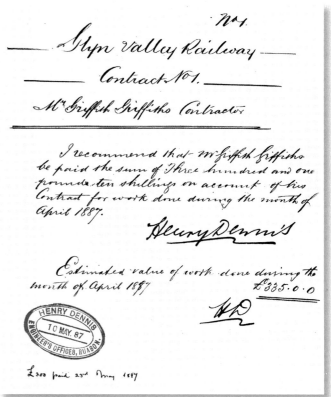

> '*All stone used for masonry is to be obtained from the Cefn Freestone Quarries Co. ... Mortar to be composed of one part freshly burnt hydraulic lime and one to one and a half parts clean sharp sand or well burnt furnace ashes – thoroughly mixed with sufficient water. ... Masonry of bridges to be coarse rubble, all stones in face work to be properly bedded and headers extending through or at least two feet into the wall ... Masonry in retaining walls, fence walls and culvert faces to be in random rubble, the face stones to be properly bedded. ... The tops of retaining walls and fence walls to be finished with a course of stones set on edge ... The stone for dry packed slopes is to be Cefn Quarry Burrs to be neatly fitted and interstices filled in with spawls [slivers of stone]. ... Fencing to consist of split oak or sawn larch posts – morticed to receive the ends of rails, 4 in number, to be carefully fitted into the mortice without any wedging. ... Rails [fence] to be supported in the middle by an intermediate post. ... pipes for culverts to be obtained from the Ruabon Glazed Brick & Fire Clay Co. Ltd – to be jointed in Portland cement.*'

The Griffith Griffiths contracts stipulated that he be paid on a regular basis for the work done during the previous month, as certified by the company's engineer. The above is the first certificate to be issued by Henry Dennis in respect of Contract No.1.

Hitherto unknown is that, after the permanent way was laid, the road crossing at Pontfaen was to be paved with '*Glyn granite setts*' on the full width between the rails and 1ft 6in outside of the rails on each side, in true tramway fashion. The contractor was advised that the setts were obtainable from Gledrid Wharf, which indicates that the Ceiriog Granite Co. was holding stocks there.

One point to note, in respect to the contracts, is that the suppliers specified were all companies in which Henry Dennis was involved!

The contractor was given the option of making use of the rails, purchased by the GVT Co. for the new track, for his own convenience to lay temporary track for construction work on the new Pontfaen–Chirk section, with the proviso that they were cleaned after use, examined by the GVT Engineer and stacked according to his instructions. Any rails bent or damaged were to be either replaced or the value, at the rate of £5/ton, deducted from the contractor's next payment. Finally, it was stipulated that: '*no work of any kind, except in case of an emergency, shall be conducted on Sundays.*' – what a pity that we do not exercise this today!

The line rose steeply from the road at the bottom of the valley to near the top of the ridge, which flanks its northern side and close to where both the Ellesmere Canal and the Chester & Shrewsbury Railway pierce it with tunnels. Instead of a tunnel for the GVT, a deep cutting was to be excavated from which the tramway emerged to run parallel with the GWR main line to the new interchange with the GWR at Chirk station. This cutting, as mentioned, would sever one of the access roads to

Chirk Castle, which had been built as a 'new' coach road in 1767, from the Castle down to Baddy's White Gate, and thence down to the Pontfaen road.

One of the original conditions laid down by Mr Myddelton Biddulph was that in exchange for the release of land from Pontfaen to Chirk, a bridge was to be constructed across this cutting to carry his *direct and private* road to Chirk village over the tramway, on the curve close to Ty Ririd, as it turns away from the valley to run parallel with the GWR mainline at Chirk. The cost of the bridge was to be £700, which was expensive because it had to be substantial enough to cross the deep cutting on a curve. Mr Myddelton Biddulph agreed to forgo his private road when the contractor offered him £550 towards a new main drive (Hand Lane) to Chirk Castle, in lieu of the substantial road bridge over the cutting, providing that a

Lever's Bridge in May 1953, so named after a Mr Lever who was engaged in the late 1700s to make landscape improvements to the Castle grounds. Originally this was a private driveway to the Castle, but when the tramway was built it became a bridle path. The timber structure of the bridge survived until March 2011, when the Wrexham County Borough Council replaced it with a modern steel structure, totally out of keeping with a heritage site, on the grounds of the old timber structure being a Health & Safety hazard!

The late James I.C. Boyd

[5] In 1888, the famous Davies Bros. wrought iron gates were moved from their location at New Hall Lodge to their present position, at the top of Hand Lane, where they form a grand entrance to the castle.

[6] *'A History of the Parish of Chirk'* by C. Neville Hurdsman.

'horse bridge' was built instead.[5] Under an Agreement dated 20th June 1887, it was agreed that the contractor, Griffith Griffiths, would build two abutments 9ft wide by 15ft high for the horse bridge free of charge and Mr Myddelton Biddulph would pay for the construction of the bridge deck and parapets. Elias Griffith, who at that time was the Chirk Castle Agent, signed the Agreement on behalf of R. Myddelton Biddulph. When it came to the point of actually building the bridge, Myddelton Biddulph suddenly decided to refuse to pay and, in order to get the line passed by the BoT, the GVT Co. had to complete the bridge and pay for it themselves! This bridge had become known as Lever's Bridge, after a Mr Lever (not to be confused with the Mr Lever, a churchwarden at Chirk in 1840), who was engaged in the late 1700s by the Chirk Castle Estate to make landscape improvements to the Castle grounds, under the supervision of Mrs Richard Myddelton, but it later became more commonly known as 'Matchbox Bridge', because of its paling-style side rails.[6]

Tenders submitted for Contracts Nos.2 and 3 by Harry Croom Johnson of Wrexham were accepted and signed on 29th July 1887 and 23rd August 1887 respectively. The contractor was obliged *'to enter into a bond'* for a surety of £50 for Contract No.2 and £200 for Contract No.3. On 7th September 1887, Harry Croom Johnson and John Joseph Jackson, a chemist of 6 & 7 Broad Street, Hereford, signed a Bond as a surety to the GVT Co. for the sum of £250. It would appear from this that Jackson was in fact acting as a guarantor for Croom Johnson.

For Contract No.2, Croom Johnson was engaged to lay the permanent way, ballasting and packing as per normal practice, on the newly formed trackbed from Ponfaen to Chirk that had been constructed by Griffith Griffiths under Contract No.1. He was to provide all the labour, horse work, plant and tools required and the GVT Co. would supply all the materials, except the ballast, which would be supplied by Griffiths as part of his contract. The GVT Co. was to ensure the delivery of the track materials to either the Chirk station end of the new line or the Pontfaen crossing. Croom Johnson was to proceed with the work immediately or as soon as any length of trackbed, not less than 10 chains (220yds) in length, had been made ready by Griffith Griffiths. A loop at the passenger station at Chirk, new pointwork to connect with the old tramway at Pontfaen and an oak cattle guard, at the point where the tramway crossed the road at Pontfaen and entered the Chirk Castle Estate, were to be included.

The Specification for Contract No.2 stipulated that the work had to be carried out *'to the entire satisfaction of Henry Dennis Esquire of Ruabon'* and that the contractor would be paid monthly for each chain (22yds) in length of track completed. It provides a good insight into the construction of the permanent way and confirms the true gauge of the GVT, post 1888, as being 2ft 4½in:

> *'The Rails will be T Rails [flat bottom rail] 50lbs per linear yard in lengths of 28ft with about 10% of shorter lengths, to be laid on cross sleepers and fastened to them with Fang Bolts and Dogs ... The rails will be jointed with Fishplates with 4 Bolts in each joint, sufficient distance between the ends of the Rails being left for expansion. ... The Rails to be laid accurately to a gauge of 2ft 4½in ... The Rails on Curves are to be properly bent with a Screw Jack to fit the curves as required ... In laying round curves the ends of the Rails on the inner side to be cut as may be found necessary to keep the sleepers at joints square to the centre line and the requisite additional holes to be drilled for the Fish Bolts. ... The Sleepers (10ft x 10in x 5in) as supplied are to be cut in two in the middle and in all cases holes are to be bored for the Fang Bolts.'*

For Contract No.3, Croom Johnson was to provide all the tools, plant and labour required for taking up the old rails, sleepers and ballast and relaying with new rails, sleepers and ballast on the section of old trackbed between Pontfaen and Glyn Ceiriog. The GVT Co. would deliver the rails, fish bolts, fang bolts, dogs and sleepers to Pontfaen. This section included some loop lines for passing places, for which the GVT Co. would provide the necessary points and crossings.

The Specification for Contract No.3, provides further insight into the rebuilding of the tramway.

> *'The contractor is to take up the rails and sleepers of the present Tramway as the work proceeds and properly clean and stack them ... The old ballast to be removed and riddled to free it of all dirt and soil and such portions as may be found suitable may be used for bottom ballast ... The material for [new] Ballast to be provided by the [GVT] Company at the Gravel Hole near Herber or other equally convenient place [again to be riddled and this time graded, with the rough stone being used on the trackbed and the finer as top ballast].*

Probably the most significant Agreement in the lifetime of the GVT was this one, made between the company and Richard Myddelton Biddulph in 1887, which released land on the Chirk Castle Estate to enable the tramway to be rerouted to new interchange facilities with the GWR at Chirk. Other agreements released further land to facilitate an interchange with the canal at Black Park Wharf.

Collection: John Milner

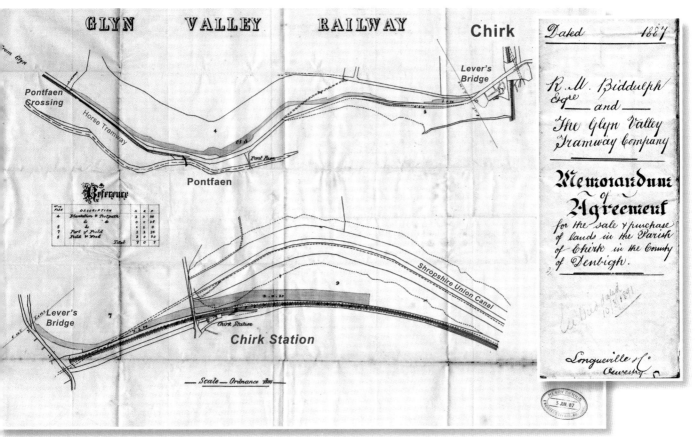

... The permanent way to be lifted and packed with Top Ballast to the proper levels and due allowance of elevation of the outer rail being made round curves ...'

Also included in this Specification for Contract No.3 is the following clause, which is of great significance, because it confirms that a steam locomotive was to be provided to assist with the rebuilding work and that the GVT Co., not the contractor, was going to provide it:[7]

'The [GVT] Company will provide a suitable Locomotive Engine, including the necessary drivers, stokers and fuel and water for the Contractor's use in hauling materials on the line. The Contractor being responsible for the carrying out of such regulations as may be necessary for the due protection of the public using the adjoining road, and to be liable for any damage or accident occasioned by the use of same. The Contractor will also be allowed the use of any of the [GVT] Company's wagons or trucks for the purposes of the Contract free of charge'

The whole of the work was to be completed and delivered up to the GVT Co. fit for traffic and in perfect working order within 5 months from date of acceptance of tender. The penalty for a delay was £5 per working day, although due allowance would be made for any severity of the weather or for delays caused by the GVT Co. not delivering materials on time.

One of H. Croom Johnson's employees, who moved into the area in 1887 specifically to work on the conversion of the tramway, was Thomas Griffiths (1871–1949). At the age of 16, he started work in September 1887 for H. Croom Johnson and was assigned as a timekeeper on the GVT contract. Griffiths later became a sales representative for the Ceiriog Granite Co., selling its 'Granomac' (tarmacadam) products. He consequently became known locally as 'Granomac' Griffiths.

In 1946, at the age of 75, Thomas Griffiths recollected a little about working on the GVT conversion:

'I remember a few scraps and scrapes among the navvies, especially in wet weather when they would go to the "fuddle" [drinking bout]. Once they were working near Pontfadog and went on the spree at the Swan Inn where several slept overnight in the coal-house and next morning turned out to work as black as the devil.' [8]

'Granomac' Griffiths
1871–1949

Thomas Griffiths started work with Croom Johnson in September 1887, as a timekeeper on the GVT contract. He later became sales representative of the Ceiriog Granite Co. selling its tarmacadam product, named 'Granomac', hence his nickname.

Collection: John Milner

Croom Johnson also employed Henry Percival Maybury as his manager in charge of the contract to build the Kerry Tramway, as well as to supervise work on the GVT. He had started his working life on the Shrewsbury & Hereford Railway before being engaged by Croom Johnson. Between 1892 and 1895 he served as engineer and surveyor of the Ffestiniog Railway. From thereon he had a distinguished career, especially during the First World War, and was later to rise through the ranks to become Brigadier-General Sir H.P. Maybury KCMG, CB, and in 1932 Director General of Roads, in the Ministry of Transport. He became a prominent figure in the Ceiriog Valley as chairman and managing director of the British Quarrying Co. Ltd, which took over the Ceiriog Granite Co. on 13th August 1929. Maybury Avenue, Glyn Ceiriog, bears his name to this day.

Griffith Griffiths, who had been awarded Contract No.1 for the earthworks from Pontfaen up to Chirk, was eager to start work immediately following the acceptance of his tender on March 23rd 1887. He began some preparatory work on the site, but had not realised that there were still legal documents to be signed and delivered to the solicitors by the GVT Co. before he could access the land and begin work. On March 26th, the Company Secretary, Edward Williams, received a letter from Potts & Roberts, Solicitors, acting for the Chirk Castle Estate, informing him that they had been told that *'sods for the line had been cut, trees were being cut at Pontfaen and that work would be started in earnest on Monday or Tuesday'* and that he had been sent the following *'wire'*:

'Glyn Valley. We are much surprised that notwithstanding the undertaking that was given, works have been commenced. Please wire at once that they will be stopped until

security we are sending tonight is completed or we must apply for an interim injunction on Monday. Potts.'

He had immediately replied: *'Works shall be stopped until security completed. Williams'.*

Once Griffith Griffiths was able to begin work on the trackbed, satisfactory progress was made and it was completed within the 5 months allowed by the contract, allowing Croom Johnson, the contractor awarded Contract No.2, to lay the track. However, elements of the contract, relating to the extensive retaining walls required on the steep slopes of the valley side at Chirk, were not completed to the satisfaction of Henry Dennis, which eventually resulted in the Griffith Griffiths' contract being terminated and, as later related, the matter ending up in court.

By the end of August, H. Croom Johnson had started relaying the track from Pontfaen to Glyn Ceiriog and, in September, Griffith Griffiths had begun work on the new bridge across the river at Dolywern. The *Llangollen Advertiser* on 7th October 1887 quoted that the foundation stone was laid on 27th September 1887 *'by Mrs Foulkes of the Queen Inn, in the presence of an intense number of spectators, which included Mr Richard Edwards, Dolywern, David Roberts, Ceiriog Cottage, John Foulkes, Queen Inn, Ruth Jones, Dolywern, Griffith Griffiths, the contractor, Mr. Davies, Clerk of the Works, etc. etc.'* and that *'the stone was set by the estimable lady amidst the tremendous cheering of those assembled'*. Initially, good progress was made with the bridge but, as the work on the line moved further up the valley, it was clear that there was going to be a serious delay with the bridges. Elements of the earthworks and the bridge abutments being built at Dolywern and Pont Bell, by Griffith Griffiths, as part of Contract No.4, had not been completed to the satisfaction of the engineer, Henry Dennis, and some rebuilding was necessary before the girder bridges could be installed to take the track over the river. The relationship between Henry Dennis and Griffith Griffiths deteriorated, with the result that they could not come to a compromise on the extra costs involved in rebuilding and eventually his contract was terminated. The outstanding work on this contract was eventually passed to H. Croom Johnson for him to complete as an 'extra' to his other contracts, to install both the girder bridges and lay the track on the diversions.

Throughout the delay, construction materials continued to arrive at Dolywern, including the girders for the two 40ft bridges and the cattle creep, which had been obtained by the GVT Co.

Brigadier-General Sir H.P. Maybury 1864–1943

Henry Percival Maybury had a very distinguished career, rising to become the Director General of Roads in the 1930s. He was employed by Croom Johnson in 1887 and had a long association with the Ceiriog Valley.

Collection: John Milner

Looking down New Road, Glyn Ceiriog, in 1887, with the Berwyn Mill on the left and, upper right, the High Street with the Wynne Slate Quarry waste tip just visible. Curving away, in the centre of the picture, from New Road to the bottom of Maybury Avenue, is the trackbed for the new station and the engine shed.

Collection: Robert Jones

from Tiddersley & Co. at a cost of £267 1s. 9d. Records of *'extra works'* undertaken by Croom Johnson, show that he had installed the bridge at Pont Bell, during the week ending December 22nd 1887, and was paid £10 for *'conveying girders from Dolywern and fixing, finding all labour and materials'*.

While the work of converting the tramway was in progress, the Directors of the Ceiriog Granite Co. agreed to work the line for a further twelve months, despite the fact that the GVT Co. had still not paid the company its operating expenses for previous years. It had little option other than to comply, in spite of the disruption caused by the conversion work on the old horse-tramway sections between Pontfaen and Glyn Ceiriog, as the tramway was the only means of transport out of the valley for its products. Passenger and parcel traffic had already ceased on 31st March 1886, but the GVT Co. Statement of Accounts for the year ending 31st December 1887 shows that the tramway continued to be busy. The receipts were from mineral traffic only but, at £875, had hardly fallen from the all-time high of £937 for minerals and merchandise in the previous year.

RAILWAY FIXED PLANT,
SWITCHES & CROSSINGS, PORTABLE RAILWAYS, &c.
HARTLEY & ARNOUX BROTHERS
ENGINEERS, STOKE-ON-TRENT.

Hartley & Arnoux Bros., of Stoke-on-Trent, were just one of a multitude of suppliers who supplied material for rebuilding the GVT. They supplied pointwork in 1888 which, when delivered, was found to be wrongly made.

For details of suppliers see Appendices 6 and 8.

Shropshire Archives
Ref: 800/44a

The main purpose of building the new line through the Chirk Castle Estate, from the valley floor at Pontfaen to rail and canal interchanges on the north side of the valley, was to provide a route with easier grades than the old horse-tramway up to the interchanges at Trehowell and Gledrid Wharf. This would enable the use of steam power and provide better interchanges with both the GWR and the SU canal. Although the cost of building all the facilities required at Chirk, other than the station platform and loop, were not included in Henry Dennis's estimate of £15,000 made on 14th September 1886, agreements had been made with the canal and railway companies and detailed planning had started.

It had been agreed, in 1884, that the GVT Co. would extend its tramway from Chirk station only as far as the entrance to Black Park Colliery canal basin and that the interchange facilities required would be built by the SUR&C Company. The basin was leased by the colliery company from Mr Myddelton Biddulph and in May 1887, the canal company began negotiating for its use as an interchange for GVT traffic. In July, plans for an additional facility at the canal edge, outside the basin area, were also approved by the SUR&C Co. Executive Committee, but it was not until late spring 1888 that all the agreements for these two interchanges were in place and construction work could begin.

Chirk station Signal Box Plan, redrawn from the original GWR drawings, as approved by Col. Rich R.E. of the Board of Trade, for the installation of the standard-gauge sidings at Chirk station for the GVT interchange wharf. Approval for the use of the sidings was given in October 1887, enabling the GVT to bring in materials direct to their site. Black Park Signal Box plan and the operational instructions for the tramway's GWR interchange sidings are shown in chapter 9 pages 230–231. Although referred to as 'Signal Box', the Chirk box carried in its early years the nameplate 'Chirk Station Signal Cabin'.

© Gordon Rushton 2010

CHIRK STATION
SIGNAL BOX
SIGNAL PLAN

To Glyn Ceiriog

DOWN LINE

To Shrewsbury   UP LINE

More urgent than the canal interchange was the construction of the rail interchange at Chirk station with which the GWR had co-operated and work on its construction had begun. The Railway Department of the BoT received a letter from the Great Western Railway Co's. General Manager, R. Beasley, on 8th October 1887 to say that it (the GWR) was in the process of installing exchange sidings to create an interchange between the GWR and the GVT, and that it was desirous of bringing these into use at once for the purpose of '*enabling materials required for the construction of the tramway*' to be conveyed down to Pontfaen by rail. The BoT appointed its inspector, Col. Rich R.E., to inspect the new GWR sidings so that they could be brought into use. He made his inspection and, although the work was incomplete in respect of signalling and interlocking, with one signal on the Shrewsbury end of the new junction in the wrong place, sanction was granted to the GWR to use the sidings subject to conditions. At the beginning of November 1887 the BoT was still voicing its concern over signalling but, by 19th November, the GWR had complied with the requirements, the new points and signals having been properly interlocked, and being operated from the 'Station Signal Box'. On behalf of the BoT, Col. Rich gave approval, stating that a further inspection would be required after the GVT Co. had completed its rail interchange wharf. This final inspection was not carried out until October 1888.

Although construction work on the conversion of the GVT line had started in the spring, by early autumn there was some dismay among shareholders, who had been led to believe that the whole length of the new line to the quarry at Hendre would be in operation before the end of 1887. It was obvious that this target date was not going to be achieved, but they were not at all sure where to lay the blame. At a meeting, it was stated that there had been no delays due to inclement weather, because it had been '*an unprecedented fine spring and summer*', the chairman insisted that it was not the fault of the Board of Directors and the engineer said that he should not be expected to take the blame, because he could not prepare final plans or start work on the line until instructed to do so. There was particular concern, not only that construction work on the extension up to the quarry at Hendre had not begun, but that the initial legal steps to obtain possession of the land had not been progressed either.

In early 1887, there had been changes in the Board Room and the directors, now R. Myddelton Biddulph (Chairman), Sir Theodore Martin, George Rooper, Henry Dennis and Elias Griffith, faced the prospect of completing the tramway by 31st July 1888, a requirement of the 1885 Act, without even the minimum finance required being immediately available. There were considerable unpaid debts and the existing agreement to purchase the £6,000 shareholding of the SUR&C Co. for a discounted sum of £2,400, before any capital expenditure was made. The latter was dealt

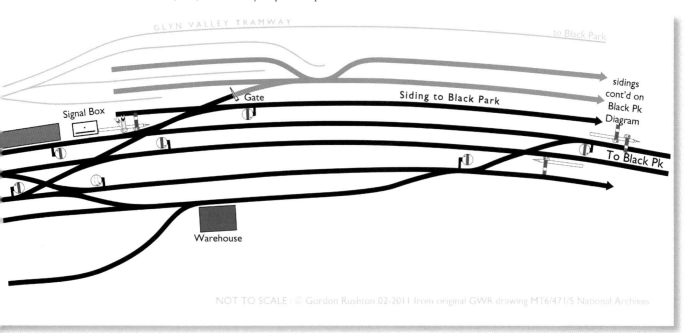

Chirk, February 23rd. 1885.

Glyn Valley Tramway Bill now in Parliament

We the undersigned undertake to purchase the shares of the Shropshire Union Railway and Canal Company (£6,000) now standing in the names of Earl of Powis, George Stanton and Richard Moon Esquires for the sum of £2400. The money to be paid on or before the works authorized by the Bill are commenced but in the event of the promoters being unable to raise the necessary capital then this undertaking becomes null and void.

R. Myddelton Biddulph
Elias Griffiths
James Coster Edwards
John Daniel Lloyd
Henry Dennis
Robert Stuart

File copy of the Promissory Note issued by promoters of the 1885 Act promising to settle the outstanding debt owing for the purchase of the GVT shares, held by the Shropshire Union Railways & Canal Co., on or before work commenced on the new tramway. The work had still not commenced by March 1887, when a new Promissory Note had been issued (file copy on opposite page), signed by the then directors, giving them a further twelve months leeway.

Collection: John Milner

with first, and on 28th March 1887, the five directors signed a Promissory Note agreeing jointly to pay for these shares in twelve months' time, should the company not be in a position to do so. It appears that, throughout the summer period, working relationships within the Board Room had been under some stress, and were rapidly deteriorating. The chairman, R. Myddelton Biddulph, was concerned because he believed that the company's engineer (Henry Dennis) and secretary (Edward Williams) were taking upon themselves *'the whole control of affairs and the construction of the line'*. He had the previous year been in favour of the appointment of a managing director, but this was overruled by the Board when he proposed that Elias Griffith who, at that time, happened to be his Agent for his Chirk Castle Estate, be appointed to the post, effectively giving him control of the tramway. Shareholders may, indeed, have got the impression that the lack of progress was due to the secretary and engineer not pushing on with the work. The reality was that the engineer could not start a new phase without proper orders from the secretary and the secretary would not issue orders for work until the company was in a position to pay for it. So, it was the overstretched company finances at the heart of the problem and these were the responsibility of the Board – a vicious circle!

It was not until late September 1887 that Edward Williams was ordered to issue the 'Notices of Intention to take Land' to the owners along the route of the extension to Hendre Quarry, and he instructed Henry Dennis to prepare detailed plans for its construction. However, it was later revealed that, in an effort to make progress, Henry Dennis had exceeded his instructions and had put the contracts for construction work out to tender, in order that the Board could consider them at its next meeting on 10th November. The contract for the earthworks, having been offered to a John Jevons & Son prior to the meeting at a contract price of £1,700, was duly ratified.[9]

[9] *Wrexham Advertizer* June 30th 1888.

During November, some of the concerned shareholders made special visits to the area to see for themselves how the work was progressing. Two of them, who between them had invested nearly £4,000, wrote to the Directors to share their disappointment. Mr Hedworth Barclay, who had

£2400. 0. 0.

28ᵗ March 1887

Twelve Calendar months after date we jointly and severally promise to pay to The Shropshire Union Railway and Canal Company or order the sum of Two thousand four hundred pounds for value received.

R. Myddelton Biddulph
Theodore Martin
George Rogers
Henry Dennis
Elias Griffith

invested almost £3,000 in the granite quarry and the railway, said that when he was in Chirk in November 1887, he was dismayed to find that the line was not completed, although he understood that it would be before the end of the year. Mr Falshaw of Leeds, who had also been induced to invest in both the GVT and Hendre Quarry and had been led to believe that the line *'would certainly be finished by the Autumn'*, said that when he was over in the middle of November, he *'was anything but satisfied with the progress: there was no sign of anything going on at the upper end and the masonry near the bridge at the lower end had fallen down'*. The directors felt obliged to call a special meeting of shareholders, because of *'a certain amount of dissatisfaction and comment in words and letters, as to the progress being made in the construction of the tramway'*. It was at this meeting that Henry Dennis reported that he been having *'difficulties with one contractor, who had not gone on as he should have done'*, but that he had *'got him in hand now'* and the company *'could make use of that portion of the line at any time. It was not finished as it should have been'*, so he had withheld payment. It is believed that he was referring specifically to the problem, reported by Mr Falshaw, of *'masonry near the bridge [having] fallen down'*. This was just one of the examples of alleged poor workmanship by the earthworks contractor, Griffith Griffiths, from whom unfinished contracts were removed, an action which he later challenged in court.

The total estimated cost for the conversion had been £15,000, and this sum was raised and available by the end of the year. Up to this time, there had been no significant overspend on any of the sections, but a shortage of available finance to fund the 'extras', which were essential to operate the line, proved to be a handicap throughout the construction period. As well as the extensive sidings and equipment required at the interchanges, these essential 'extras' included locomotives and rolling stock!

Despite the lack of capital to pay for them at the time, an order was placed in 1887 with Messrs Beyer, Peacock & Co. of Gorton Foundry, Manchester, for two new steam locomotives (Works Nos.2969 and 2970), to comply with the Board of Trade

Below: *Although there were serious allegations of poor workmanship by the GVT contractor, Griffith Griffiths, the bridge above carrying Hand Lane over the tramway at Chirk station, was extremely well finished and has stood the test of time.*

© John Milner 2010

specifications, for delivery in June 1888 at a cost of £1,150 each. With Charles Beyer having resided close to Sir Theodore Martin, it is not surprising that Beyer, Peacock & Co. was selected to build the new locomotives for the GVT.

Under Contract No.3, drawn up early in 1887, the GVT Co. had an obligation to provide a suitable steam locomotive to assist the contractor with the construction work. With the new Beyer Peacock locomotives not likely to be available until the summer of the following year, and without the capital to pay for them had they been available, the GVT Co. looked to the Snailbeach District Railways, in Shropshire, which was of similar gauge, for a solution. The ensuing co-operation enabled the Glyn Valley Tramway Co. to fulfill its contractual obligation, and led to a reciprocal arrangement with the Snailbeach District Railways Co., some years later.

Charles Frederick Beyer 1813–1876

Charles Frederick Beyer was the cofounder of Beyer, Peacock & Co. of Manchester and it was his company that was selected to build the new locomotives for the GVT. His country residence was Llantysilio Hall, nestling on the banks of the River Dee to the west of Llangollen.

Collection: John Milner

Above: *The official works photograph of the first of the GVT tram locomotives, shown painted on one side only in 'photographic grey' and posing alongside the 'white wall', specially prepared for such purposes at Beyer, Peacock & Co's. works, Gorton Foundry, Manchester.*

Left: *An extract from the specification and instructions issued to all concerned at Beyer's works, for the construction of the two GVT locomotives. Note that the names for them had already been decided.*

Collection: John Milner
Ex Beyer, Peacock & Co. – 1962

Chapter 8

The Snailbeach Connection
1887–1889

At the start of work on rebuilding the tramway, the GVT Co. was desperate to obtain temporary use of a steam locomotive, the delivery of its two new ones being more than twelve months away. It was needed in order to fulfil its obligation under Contract No.3 to: '*provide a suitable Locomotive, including the necessary drivers, stokers and fuel and water for the Contractor's use in hauling materials on the line*'. As Hendre Quarry intended to continue working during the construction period and would need to continue to send its granite down the line, it has been suggested in various reports that this provision in the contract may have been an 'umbrella' for the GVT Co. to start to use steam power to move its traffic – despite the necessary BoT permissions not being in place, other than for construction purposes.

The company did not have the finance available to purchase a second-hand engine, so there were two options open to it: either hire a suitable one from a dealer, such as Cudworth & Johnson Ltd of Wrexham, or borrow one through the goodwill of Henry Dennis and his close connection with the Snailbeach District Railways, which so happened to have 2ft 4in gauge.

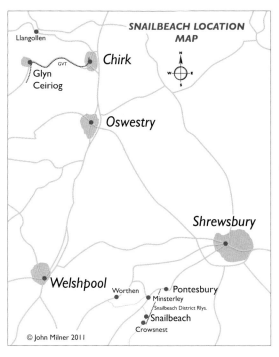

SNAILBEACH LOCATION MAP

© John Milner 2011

In the 1940s, the pioneer of narrow-gauge railway history, James I.C. Boyd, was the first person to undertake in-depth research into the history of the Welsh narrow-gauge railways, and his journeys naturally took him to the Ceiriog Valley and the GVT. He was later to record the story of the conversion of the tramway in the January 1950 issue of *The Stephenson Locomotive Society Journal*, as passed on to him by another early GVT researcher, Selwyn H.P. Higgins, who had previously interviewed many of the GVT ex-employees. The story was that two locomotives, '*Belmont*' and '*Fernhill*', had been brought from the Snailbeach District Railways, Shropshire, the gauge of which was 2ft 4in, '*along with a considerable number of wagons*', that a semi-permanent engine shed, to house two locomotives, had been built at the end of the long siding at Pontfaen (near to the road bridge) and a temporary wooden

The Snailbeach District Railways locomotive FERNHILL at Snailbeach, with a group of lead-mine workers. Its size and wheelbase illustrates why it was unable to negotiate the sharp curve on the road bridge at Dolywern in 1887.

NRM 686/94/SSPL

engine shed had been erected in the station yard, on the south side of the river, at Pontfaen station. 'Belmont' was said to have been the first locomotive to arrive and, after being unloaded from the GWR at Chirk, was transported down to Pontfaen on a flat-wagon in the charge of a traction engine.

'Fernhill', a larger locomotive, was said to have been manhandled down the road to Pontfaen on short lengths of track, in the time-honoured fashion of using two lengths of track and, as the locomotive was moved forward, taking up the length behind and placing it in front. It was said that about forty men were used to restrain the locomotive as it progressed down the hill, with the exercise taking two days! It has to be remembered that this road was not as it is today, but simply a poorly surfaced track, its rebuilding being integral with the 1887 earthworks contract for the GVT.

All plausible, and since this account was published, successive authors, including the writer, who likewise was given a similar story by the ex-GVT Company's secretary, Albert Wynn, have up to now perpetuated it, but there has always been a big question mark hanging over the accuracy of the story as told. Further research, since the last account was written in 1984 by the author, sheds new light on this event; partly dispelling some of it, but unfortunately still leaving questions unanswered.

The Snailbeach District Railways had been authorised by the Snailbeach District Railways Act 1873, which gained Royal Assent on the 5th August that year. It was built as a narrow-gauge railway of 2ft 4in gauge and ran from exchange sidings, on the GWR & LNWR joint Minsterley branch line, up to the Snailbeach lead mines. At a later date, it also served some quarries in the district. Henry Dennis was the SDR's engineer (he later became a director and chairman) and the contractor for its construction had been Elias Griffith, of Chirk. One of these quarries, Granhams Moor Quarry in Eastridge Wood, was leased on 29th September 1905 from George Montagu Bennet, 7th Earl of Tankerville, to a consortium comprising William Toye, an Inspector of Explosives of William Toye & Co.; Thomas George Marsh; Henry Dyke Dennis; Walter Pen Dennis and William Edwards, for a term of 21 years, and was operated by the Ceiriog Granite Co., forging yet another link with the Ceiriog Valley.[1,2] Opening in July 1877, the SDR was eventually to outlast the GVT by 24 years!

To work the line, the SDR Co. acquired two locomotives. One was named *'Fernhill' and* was built by Barclays & Co., Riverbank Works, Kilmarnock in 1881 (not to be confused with Andrew Barclay Sons & Co., although closely associated); it had 12" dia. x 20" stroke cylinders and 3' 0" dia. driving wheels, the centre one being flangeless. It had been purchased new by the SDR Co. in August 1881 via the agents Lennox Lange & Co. for the sum of £900. *'Fernhill'* was named after Fernhill Hall, which belonged to Thomas Heaton Lovett, who owned the Gobowen Estate, near Oswestry, and who had strong ties with Snailbeach, he being a senior proprietor of the Snailbeach Lead Mine. The other locomotive, built by Henry Hughes & Co., Loughborough, and named *'Belmont'*, had been acquired second-hand, some years previously, in 1877. Contrary to what has previously been assumed, it can only be described as being 'similar' to the Hughes' locomotives built for the Corris Railway in 1878, this having been ascertained as a result of research conducted by Nigel Taylor and Andy Cuckson. The Corris locomotives were built as 0-4-0ST types with open cabs above the waistline and roofs supported by four pillars. They were later modified to 0-4-2ST, due to the large overhang at the back, by the addition of a pony truck, and the open cabs progressively became enclosed. *'Belmont'*, however, was actually built as an 0-4-2ST, with an enclosed cab, open at the rear above the waistline, and was different in general appearance to the Corris locomotives, as well as being heavier. It had 10" dia. x 15" stroke cylinders (Corris 7" x 12") and 2' 7½" dia. driving wheels (Corris 2' 6").[3]

'Belmont' was no stranger to the Chirk area, as it had been purchased by the SDR Co. from Ifton-Rhyn Collieries Company, which had been incorporated in 1873 to extract coal from under Lord Hill-Trevor's land near Ifton, to the southeast of Chirk. The Ifton-Rhyn Co. was also considering sinking shafts on Lovett's Gobowen Estate. As related in chapter 2, Ifton-Rhyn Collieries' consultant engineer, Thomas Randolph Mellor, proposed a tramway of 2ft 4in gauge, which would connect with the GVT in order to provide the colliery with a connection to the GWR main line at Preesgweene. This never came to fruition, but a brickworks was built at the colliery and, to serve this, sand pits had been opened up next to Pentre Brook, as well as clay pits at Glynmorlas. These pits were connected to the brickworks by a 2ft 4in-gauge railway for which a locomotive, named *'Salome'*, was purchased new from Henry Hughes & Co., Loughborough. The Ifton-Rhyn Collieries Co. went into receivership in 1875, was placed into liquidation the year after, and *'Salome'* was up for disposal.

Henry Dennis, knowing Lovett and Mellor, and that the Ifton-Rhyn Collieries Co. was in liquidation, would have been well aware that *'Salome'* would be available on favourable terms. It was acquired by the SDR Co. and, on 15th February 1877, the 10-ton locomotive was loaded onto a wagon, which was then hauled by horses to the Cambrian Railways Works at Oswestry, the whole operation under the supervision of Elias Griffith, the SDR and the GVT's contractor. Here it was overhauled, repainted in red lead and given centrally mounted Cambrian Railway buffers. Its *'Salome'* nameplates were removed and the SDR Co. was credited with their scrap value. It was given a new name, *'Belmont'*, the name of Lovett's residence at Gobowen, which later became Henlle Hall. The Cambrian Railways delivered the locomotive to Pontesbury from where Elias Griffith again was engaged to move it, this time to the SDR, in readiness for its opening for traffic in July 1877.

It has now been established, from SDR Co. and other records, that *'Fernhill'* was the first locomotive to be delivered from Snailbeach on loan to the GVT. In the Snailbeach Co. draft accounts for the first half of 1888 there is a payment of £2 10s. 10d. from the GVT Co., noted as 'old', which suggests that it was owing from the previous accounting period (1887), and that it relates to the cost of transporting *'Fernhill'* from Snailbeach to Chirk. A draft summary of GVT construction expenses compiled in 1889 recorded that a sum of £2 10s. 10d. had been paid to the SDR Co. during 1888 in respect of carriage, but no other details were given. In 1935, an account of the closure of the GVT in the *Oswestry Advertizer* states that when the line was rebuilt: *'A small six-wheeled engine was provided to take the place of the horses. The first engine bought, however, proved to be unsatisfactory, and a smaller type was purchased. This worked satisfactorily until*

[1] Granhams Moor was quarried for quartzite or silica stone for road metalling, railway ballast and other uses.

[2] See also, in connection with the development of Granhams Moor Quarry, the story of the loan of *'Sir Theodore'* to the SDR in 1905, Part II of *'Rails to Glyn Ceiriog'*.

[3] For full details see *Belmont: The Snailbeach Hughes Locomotive and the Ifton-Rhyn Colliery Railway* – Industrial Railway Record 171, published by the Industrial Railway Society, December 2002, *Fernhill: The Snailbeach Barclay* – Industrial Railway Record 164, March 2001, and *'Lead Down, Coal Up'*, RCL Publications, all by Andy Cuckson.

the introduction of the first passenger engine in 1888.' Presumably, a GVT employee related this to a reporter, albeit forty-seven years after the event. The mention of the second engine being *'a smaller type'* confirms that the larger, *'Fernhill'*, was the first. The reference to *'purchasing'* these locomotives is incorrect, but mention of one with six wheels is significant. If this referred to *'Fernhill'*, which was an 0-6-0ST and weighed approximately 19 tons in working order, one would hardly call it *'small'* in narrow-gauge terms, although to newspaper reporters it may have appeared to be small in comparison with standard-gauge locomotives, with which they would be more familiar! *'Belmont'*, on the other hand, weighed approximately 10 tons and was an 0-4-2ST, which to a layman would therefore also equate to a locomotive with 'six wheels'.

present day the old tramway track can still be seen. As trade in the valley increased, a firm named Johnsons, of Wrexham, laid the present railway track. A small six-wheeled engine was provided to take the place of the horses. The first engine bought, however, proved to be unsatisfactory, and a smaller type was purchased. This worked satisfactorily until the introduction of the first passenger engine in 1888. An addition to the line from Pontfaen to Chirk was made, and there was also an addition from Glyn to the stone quarries—a distance of from three to four miles.

Part of the article in the Oswestry Advertizer 1935 relating to the use of a six-wheeled engine on the GVT.

Collection: John Milner
GVT Company Records
Courtesy: North Wales
Newspapers Ltd

[4] By the end of 1889 this had reduced to £120 17s. 1d.

[5] See chapter 7 page 191–192

Traffic on the SDR had dwindled by 1887, which was the reason why, according to Boyd's account, the company was able to release its only two locomotives to assist with the GVT conversion. However, Andy Cuckson, who has extensively researched the history of the SDR Co., advises that both *'Belmont'* and *'Fernhill'* could not have been away from Snailbeach at the same time. The SDR was still operating and employing a locomotive crew for three or four days per week, so there must have been at least one of the two locomotives in use. Unfortunately, SDR Co. pay sheets for 1887–88, which would have clarified the earlier verbal accounts, are missing from the records.

That there was a locomotive at work on the GVT sometime before the end of 1887 is confirmed by an entry in the GVT's expenditure accounts for the half-year ending 31st December 1887, under the heading 'Locomotive Power', amounting to £196 3s. 6d., suggesting that *'Fernhill'* had been at work on the GVT for some months.[4] This is further confirmed by correspondence between John Jones, of Woking, from whom the GVT Co. was purchasing 36 perches of land on the north side of the river at Dolywern, and his solicitors, Messrs Patey & Warren. On 12th April 1887, John Jones instructed them to write to Messrs Longueville & Co., the GVT Co. solicitors, to seek clarification, as he *'had been informed that Steam Power was now being used on the tramway'*. This seems to suggest that *'Fernhill'* was already on the GVT as early as April 1887.

'Fernhill' was used extensively to haul construction materials for tracklaying, by the contractor Croom Johnson, on the Pontfaen to Dolywern section of the tramway, but its performance on the old lightweight GVT horse-tramway track was not entirely satisfactory. However, a more serious problem arose because Croom Johnson was expecting that *'Fernhill'* would be able to haul the construction materials needed for the line between Dolywern and Glyn Ceiriog, across the river at Dolywern using a new bridge, which was to be built to alleviate the sharp bend over the road.[5] The building of this bridge was delayed, but construction materials continued to arrive at Dolywern. The old horse-tramway track was still in place over the Dolywern road bridge, but *'Fernhill'* was a large heavy locomotive, with a wheelbase too long to negotiate the sharp curve onto the bridge and was also deemed to be too heavy for its stone arch. The only option was to move the materials, including large quantities of rails and sleepers, in small loads using horses. Clearly this would delay progress on the line from Dolywern to Glyn Ceiriog, so a decision was made to return *'Fernhill'* to Snailbeach and replace it with the smaller and more suitable SDR locomotive *'Belmont'*.

This exchange appears to have been made in late January 1888, as the records of *'extra works'* completed on the GVT by H. Croom Johnson of Wrexham, the contractor engaged to lay the new track on the tramway, lists among other items, for the week ending 19th January 1888, *'Assisting with Locomotive'* and *'Making temporary Crossings for "Fernhill" and "Belmont" etc. etc. £6 10s. 8d.'*. These *'temporary crossings'* for *'Fernhill'* and *'Belmont'* would have been lengths of temporary track laid so that a locomotive could be run off its GWR well wagon onto the narrow-gauge GVT, and vice versa. SDR pay sheets reveal that, also in January 1888, an unnamed locomotive was dispatched, via the GWR from the SDR interchange at Pontesbury, on the Minsterley branch, to an unspecified destination. This locomotive is now believed to have been *'Belmont'*, which continued its soujourn at Chirk long after the first of the new GVT locomotives, *'Sir Theodore'*, built by the Beyer Peacock & Co., Gorton Foundry, Manchester, arrived on 17th October 1888, so that for six months or so, up to April 1889, there were two locomotives in use on the GVT.

In April 1889, a further reference to a locomotive in the SDR Co. pay sheets positively names *'Belmont'* as the locomotive that was unloaded at Pontesbury and returned to the SDR. This is the same month that the second Beyer Peacock locomotive, *'Dennis'*, was delivered to the GVT, after which the GVT had no further use for an engine on loan. As to the reference in previously published accounts to the loan of wagons from the SDR to the GVT, there is no evidence in the SDR Co. archives of wagons having been removed from Snailbeach during this period.[6] As already related, the specification for Contract No.3 clearly states that the contractor was to have the free use of the GVT Company's wagons.

[6] Snailbeach District Railways information courtesy Andy Cuckson.

'Belmont' was quite suitable for work on the GVT, although it did not comply with the BoT requirements for GVT locomotives, but this appears to have been accepted by the Board as a temporary measure. It was housed in the existing horse-tramway carriage shed on the south side of the river at Pontfaen station, which would be the *'temporary shed'* referred to by Boyd. No evidence has been found in respect of the *'temporary two-road engine shed'* erected near to Pontfaen Bridge, which he also mentioned.

In 1955, Joseph Jones, one of the GVT engine drivers who lived at 2, Ivy Cottage, Oaklands Road, Chirk Bank, related that he worked on the construction of the new line from Pontfaen to Chirk, and that he remembered that when *'Belmont'* was run a flagman would walk in front. Worthy of mention, but a very doubtful statement that possibly relates to the use of a flagman on Pontfaen crossing, Dolywern bridge before the deviation was built and wherever men were working on the track.

After returning to Snailbeach, *'Belmont'* was to visit northeast Wales once more when, in the summer of 1898, it was sent via the GWR to Cudworth & Johnson Ltd, Wrexham, for extensive repairs. It was completed and tested by February 1899 but, due to a question of liability, it was not returned until the following year.

The Snailbeach District Railways locomotive BELMONT. used on the rebuilding of the GVT, was built by Henry Hughes & Co., Loughborough, and was similar in design to the Corris Railway Hughes locomotive illustrated. Before being acquired by the SDR, it had worked on the Ifton-Rhyn Collieries brickworks tramway.

W.A. Camwell Collection
Courtesy: Stephenson
Locomotive Society

James Hughes : 16th May 1853–18th September 1933

James Hughes was loaned by the Snailbeach District Railways along with their locomotive 'FERNHILL' (later exchanged for a smaller one named 'BELMONT') to assist in the reconstruction of the Glyn Valley Tramway. After the completion of the reconstruction of the tramway he stayed to become its first engine driver. He was born at Crowsnest, near Snailbeach, Shropshire, in 1853, to Vincent Hughes, engineman, and his wife Mary.

Courtesy: Gwilym Hughes

The specification for the Croom Johnson Contract No.3 stipulated that the GVT Co. was to supply a '*suitable locomotive engine*' for use by the contractor engaged to relay the track. Construction works were still in progress when, on the 18th December 1888, the chairman of the Llangollen Highway Board sent a letter to the BoT complaining that: '*... the Glyn Valley Tramway Company are running trains loaded with granite and drawn by a locomotive, which does not consume its own smoke, at the rate of 15 or 16 miles per hour*'. The statutory speed was 8 mph. A statement made to the BoT in January 1889 by Edward Williams, who was not only secretary to the GVT Co., but the SDR Co. as well, does admit to the use of steam power '*such as has been necessitated for ballasting and other purposes in the construction of the line*'.

By this time, the first of the GVT's new locomotives, '*Sir Theodore*', had been delivered and was at work. With this being equipped with condensing gear, it is concluded that the Llangollen Highway Board's complaint refers to the use of '*Belmont*' being used to bring loads of granite down the valley; as does a later complaint by them the following year, just before '*Belmont*' was returned to the SDR in April 1889.

The home of James Hughes, No.1 Trehowell, or Trehowell Cottage as it was known, on the Quinta Estate. The garden bench can be seen in the group photograph on the next page. The photograph was taken by Caesar Hughes.

Courtesy: Gwilym Hughes

With the first locomotive from Snailbeach came James Hughes, who was born on 16th May 1853 at Crowsnest (to the south of Snailbeach). From the 1871 census records, he was listed as living at Minsterley with his parents, Vincent Hughes (a lead-mine engineer) and his wife Mary (charwoman), along with his two brothers Vincent and Caesar. He was then, at the age of 17, described as an '*engine stoker*'. By 1881, James, his wife Hannah (née Hewitt) and newly born daughter, Mary Ann, had moved to Snailbeach with his widowed mother and younger brother, who was a stationary engine driver at the lead mine. James was described as a '*railway stoker*' (fireman) at this time, presumably on the SDR. By the time of the 1891 census, James, his wife Hannah, and now increased

Alfred Hewitt, of No. 8, Snailbeach, was born in 1879 and his uncle was James Hughes. He lived all his life in Snailbeach, married a local girl in 1911, had four children and worked for the Snailbeach lead mines on surface work, including driving the winding and pumping engines. He ended his working days at Callow Hill Quarry, near to the Pontesbury end of the Snailbeach District Railways. In 1962 he related that, as a young lad, he used to cycle from Snailbeach to Trehowell to stay weekends with his uncle James. Alfred opted for surface work rather than mining because his father was permanently blinded as a result of an accidental underground explosion in 1883.

© David Ll. Davies
Collection: John Milner

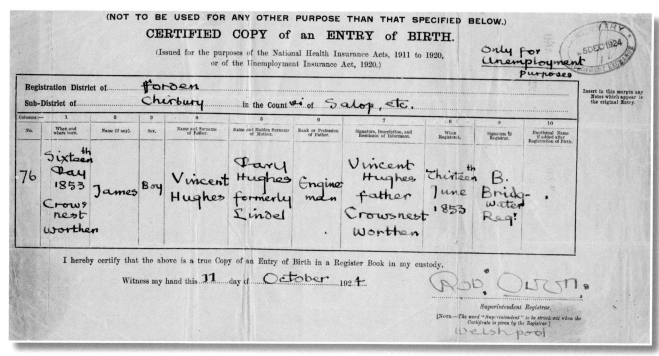

CERTIFIED COPY of an ENTRY of BIRTH.

(Issued for the purposes of the National Health Insurance Acts, 1911 to 1920,
or of the Unemployment Insurance Act, 1920.)

Only for Unemployment purposes

Registration District of .... Forden

Sub-District of .... Chirbury .... in the County of Salop, etc.

Insert in this margin any Notes which appear in the original Entry.

No.	When and where born.	Name (if any).	Sex.	Name and Surname of Father.	Name and Maiden Surname of Mother.	Rank or Profession of Father.	Signature, Description, and Residence of Informant.	When Registered.	Signature of Registrar.	Baptismal Name if added after Registration of Birth.
76	Sixteenth Day 1853 Crows nest Worthen	James	Boy	Vincent Hughes	Mary Hughes formerly Lindel	Engine man	Vincent Hughes father Crowsnest Worthen	Thirteenth June 1853	B. Bridg-water Regr.	

I hereby certify that the above is a true Copy of an Entry of Birth in a Register Book in my custody.

Witness my hand this **11** day of **October** 1924.

Rob. Owen.

Superintendent Registrar.

[Note.—The word "Superintendent" to be struck out when the Certificate is given by the Registrar.]

(Welshpool)

Top: *Copy Birth Certificate for James Hughes issued in 1924 when he was 71 years old.*

Above: *The Hughes family in the garden of No.1 Trehowell. Standing centre, James Hughes, with directly in front, his wife Hannah (née Hewitt), to the right their daughter Lily and to the left of Hannah is Eliza Hughes, wife of Caesar Hughes who took all these photographs.*

Left: *James Hughes, with arms folded, on the footplate of GLYN, photographed at Chirk. His head-gear denotes his elevated status of general foreman.*

Courtesy: Gwilym Hughes

family of four daughters and one son, were well established in a cottage, No.1 Trehowell (known as Trehowell Cottage), which was rented from the Quinta Estate. He was described as a *'railway engine driver'*, although now on the GVT and not the SDR. James and Hannah Hughes had a large family of nine children, seven of whom were living in the tiny cottage at Trehowell in 1901: Mary Ann, Lily, Dora, Vincent, James, Edward and Caesar. As far as can be established from the SDR records, James Hughes appears to have left employment with the SDR company some time in 1887, when *'Fernhill'* was loaned to the GVT but, if the newspaper reports of his death are correct, he did not move into Trehowell Cottage with his family until 1891. He stayed on with the GVT Co. after *'Belmont'* was returned to Snailbeach to become one of its permanent drivers. He had the privilege of driving the first steam passenger train to Glyn Ceiriog in 1891 and later rose to the position of general foreman in charge of the locomotive shed and other work on the tramway.

John Williams on the footplate of the third GVT locomotive GLYN and probably taken not long after it was delivered new in 1892. Standing alongside him is 'Jack' Morgan and, adjacent to the chimney, is James Hughes. Both John Williams and James Hughes moved from Snailbeach, Shropshire, to work on the GVT and were to spend their working days as devoted employees of the company.

Collection: John Milner

James Hughes was a great advocate of temperance principles and was one of the founders of the *'Sons of Temperance Friendly Society'* at Weston Rhyn, of which he was a trustee, and was one of the Patriarchs of *'The Blue Ribbon League'*, an offshoot of the *Friendly Society*. He was also a trustee of Weston Rhyn Village Institute, a member of the committee of management of the Chirk and District Co-operative Society, a member of the Parish Council for many years, a staunch worker at the Quinta Congregational Church and a prominent local preacher. With Thomas Barnes, who owned the Quinta Estate, sharing the same religious passion as James Hughes, this may account for his renting a cottage on the Quinta Estate. He died on 18th September 1934, at the age of 81. A well-attended funeral service was held in the Quinta Congregational Church after which he was interred in his wife's grave.

Previous accounts relate that John Williams, born 1866, also came from Snailbeach with James Hughes, but he did not do so until sometime after April 1891, as he was then still residing in Snailbeach with his parents George Williams, who was listed as being an *'engine driver, stationary'*, and his wife Mary. Interestingly, in the 1881 census he was recorded as still being a *'scholar'* at the age of 15 – most boys from working-class families were at work before that age. Unlike James Hughes, John Williams had not worked for the Snailbeach District Railways and his occupation is first recorded, at the age of 25, as a *'stationary engine driver'* at the Snailbeach lead mines, although it is known that at one time he was working for the LNWR for a short period.

In 1894 he married Mary Jane Edwards, who was born in Worthen, near Snailbeach, and their first child was born at Weston Rhyn the following year. This suggests that he must have moved from the Snailbeach district to the Ceiriog Valley sometime between 1891 and 1895; probably shortly after April 1891 when the GVT steam service was getting under way and an extra driver was needed. He would almost certainly have been recommended for the position by James Hughes, who would have known him at Snailbeach. John Williams lived at Bron-heulog Cottage, Castle Mill with his family which, in 1901, comprised his three sons and mother-in-law, Margaret Edwards, who had come from Worthen to live with them. There were no demarcation lines on the GVT and employees were expected to undertake whatever was required of them. One of John Williams' not-too-frequent 'special' tasks was seeing to any boiler retubing that was required.

In 1962, Alfred Hewitt of Snailbeach related that apart from James Hughes and John Williams, who left the district with their families to work on the Glyn Valley Tramway, a third person, Joseph Evans, who was a carpenter, followed in their footsteps.

With the return of *'Belmont'* to Snailbeach the relationship between the two railways was only temporarily over as, in 1905, the GVT was to return the favour and loaned *'Sir Theodore'* to the Snailbeach District Railways; a story that will be related in Part 2 of this work.

Chapter 9

The Company in Turmoil
1888

By the beginning of 1888, relationships between the directors had degenerated to such an extent that the business of the company was being conducted in an atmosphere of complete mistrust.

The special meeting of shareholders, called because of the widespread dissatisfaction, was held on 27th January 1888, by which time they had become very uneasy, because the promises that the line would be completed by the end of 1887 had not materialised. They suspected that they were not being kept fully informed and were anxious to know when they could expect to see a return on their investments. Many of these shareholders had also invested in Hendre Quarry and were concerned that a serious delay in constructing the tramway extension would have a deleterious effect on the proposed developments there. One of them, Mr Falshaw of Leeds, said that he '*was up at the Glyn on the previous day and found that no arrangement had been made, even for the purchase of land*', which was '*very wrong, unpardonably wrong*', and he questioned whether there were '*any financial difficulties*'.

The Chairman, Mr R. Myddelton Biddulph, acknowledged that there had been delays, but reported that '*latterly much more effective progress had been made*' and that the directors hoped that the line would be partially opened by the end of March. The Secretary said that, with '*a very trifling exception*', all monies due from shareholders had been paid and explained that the delay in purchasing the land for the extension was due to the claims of the landowners being '*so exorbitant, that the directors have not been able to deal with them*'; however, at their meeting held earlier that day, they had agreed that the best way forward was to inform the landowners that, unless they appointed an arbitrator, the company would apply for a Board of Trade valuer, and '*pay the amount of the valuation into the Bank of England and take possession of the land*'. The shareholders agreed that the following motion be put to the meeting: '*That it be an instruction to the directors that unless the land from the New Inn, Glyn Ceiriog* [to Hendre], *can be arranged for by private contract on satisfactory terms within the next fortnight, an application shall be made to the Board of Trade for a valuer.*' The motion was carried.

In his report on progress to date, Henry Dennis said that the Section No.1 contracts down from Chirk station to Pontfaen were complete, but the line from Chirk station to Black Park canal basin had not been started, because it had not been included in the original estimate. The Section No.2 contract, for taking up the old and laying down the new track from Pontfaen to New Inn, Glyn Ceiriog, '*was going forward fast*' and there remained only about 20 chains to finish. The embankments and masonry for the bridges required for the two diversions, which made up Section No.3, were complete, and contracts for '*making and fixing the girders were entered into*'; he expected that

'the work would be done within a fortnight'. The contract for the earthworks for Section No. 4, from the New Inn to Hendre Quarry, had been agreed at £1,700, and all the material for this extension was on the ground and paid for, but work could not start until the company had legal possession of the land. However, he was hopeful that before the end of another ten days the company would have possession of sufficient land to start the contractor.

Each of the eleven different owners along the route had been issued with a 'Notice of Intention to take Land', inviting them to make a claim for compensation. In 1886, when preparing the Plans and Sections for the extension and having been advised that the land there was worth about £25 per acre, Henry Dennis estimated that it should cost no more than £500 in total, which was a generous average of about £50 per acre. In the event, some of the owners lodged considerably higher claims, with the total in excess of £2,500. In its dismay, the GVT Co. had responded by making offers totalling about half this sum, some of them considerably lower than the valuations made by the professional land valuer engaged by the company. However, this meeting on 27th January 1888 was a turning point, as the threat made by the company to apply for a Board of Trade valuer had an immediate effect, an owners' solicitor suggesting that *'arrangements should be made as to letting the two values meet, instead of going to the Board of Trade'.* Within days, those owners who were in serious disagreement about the value of their land had appointed arbitrators to settle the purchase price, and within a few weeks arrangements

Richard Myddelton Biddulph 1837–1913

Richard Myddelton Biddulph changed the fortunes of the GVT by allowing the tramway to be rerouted through his Chirk Castle Estate.

Oil on canvas portrait painted in 1901 by Robert Brough (1872–1905).

Private Collection/ Photo © Christie's Images/ The Bridgeman Art Library HOU410996

had been made to allow the GVT Co. access to the land and the contractor to start work.

As part of the agreements, the GVT Co. was to erect iron fencing (hurdles) painted in a dark colour on the extension boundaries, to provide level crossings with proper approaches and gates for those owners whose access to their fields had been severed and to maintain all the existing drainage and water supplies. Lengthy negotiations on such details led to delays in drawing up the conveyance documents so that, in some cases, the tramway was built and in operation before they had been formally signed.

The Plans and Sections produced by Robert H.F. Stuart for the 1885 Bill show that he had envisaged this extension starting from the horse-tramway terminus at the New Inn. However, his generous 'Limits of Deviation' on the plans allowed Henry Dennis to plan a route out of Glyn Ceiriog alongside the river, passing first through land on which would be built a locomotive shed, passenger station and a coal wharf. The horse-tramway warehouse and crane on the New Inn site were to be kept in use and the track serving these, as was that to the Cambrian incline, would continue to be worked by horses.

About three-quarters of an acre of land, valued at £230, was required for the site of the passenger station and locomotive shed, for which the owner, David Jones (a retired farmer, formerly of

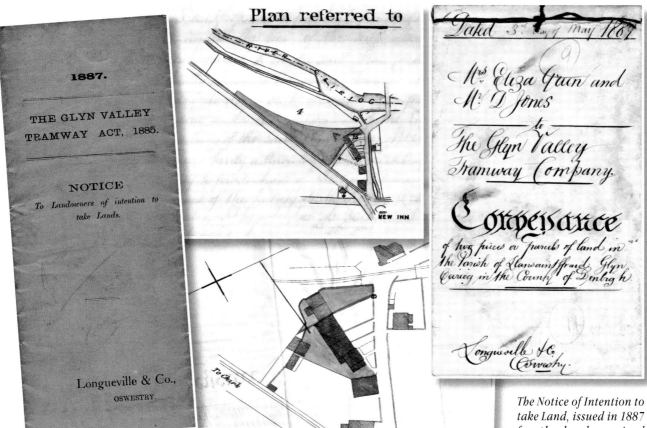

Plan referred to

1887.

THE GLYN VALLEY
TRAMWAY ACT, 1885.

NOTICE
To Landowners of intention to
take Lands.

Longueville & Co.,
OSWESTRY.

The Notice of Intention to take Land, issued in 1887 for the land required for the new station and engine shed site, with the Conveyance and drawing, finally agreed between the parties in May 1889. The lower drawing shows, in red, the later acquisition from David Jones, in March 1892, of the two cottages next to the station.

Collection: John Milner

Hafodygynfor Farm), claimed £567. The GVT Co. offered only £200, so the matter was referred to arbitration with Thomas Whitfield of Oswestry acting on behalf of the GVT Co. and James Davies, also of Oswestry, acting for David Jones. These arbitrators appointed Thomas Richard Wynne, land agent of Corwen, to be the umpire and, on 14th February 1888, he gave his decision that David Jones was entitled to £455. Although the award was made to David Jones, the conveyance for the land, dated 3rd May 1889, shows that this sum was paid directly to Eliza Green, widow, because she had a large long-standing mortgage debt owing to her on the Hafodygynfor Farm lands.

From the station, the tramway was to run close to the river where a wide strip of land, measuring about two acres and valued at £395, was required for a coal wharf. It included half the riverbed and was owned by Thomas Allen Hughes who claimed £747, but had been offered only £350. This claim too went to arbitration using the same arbitrators. The umpire's award of £620, was paid into the bank on 18th February and the GVT Co. was given immediate possession. By April, Mr Hughes was complaining that due to '*trespass and default of* [the] *Engineer*', a considerable quantity of his land '*had been taken outside the limits agreed*', which resulted in the GVT Co. eventually having to pay an extra £50.

Mr Hughes had not been happy with the choice of the route alongside the river. He had been willing to '*accept a smaller sum, if the line was made at the upper end of the field*' opposite the New Inn, from where it would not interfere with water being drawn from the river by the tenants and occupiers of the several dwelling houses on his lands. He insisted that if their access to the river was to be severed by the tramway, then they were to be given '*the rights of full and free access to cross the GVT line … for the purpose of taking water from the river*'. The company had to agree to build a tramway crossing and maintain a length of river walling, incorporating steps down to the river. In addition, '*irrigation works*' consisting of a culvert '*under the line to carry water from the River to the remaining parts of the field*' had to be built and forever maintained, to supply water for cattle.[1]

[1] The culvert, as built, was an 18-inch pipe that received river water held back by a weir opposite Upper Mill. The stone walling is still partly in situ today.

We the within named Thomas Whitfield and James Davies in pursuance of the directions of the Lands Clauses Consolidation Act 1845 in this behalf Do by this writing under our hands made before we have entered upon the matters within referred to us nominate and appoint Thomas Richard Wynne of Corwen in the County of Merioneth Land Agent to be Umpire to decide upon such in case we shall differ As witness our hands this tenth day of February One thousand eight hundred and eighty eight—

Thos Whitfield –

James Davies

I Thomas Richard Wynne of Corwen in the County of Merioneth Land Agent Do Hereby solemnly and sincerely declare that I will faithfully and honestly and to the best of my skill and ability hear and determine the matters referred to me under the Glyn Valley Tramway Act 1885

Made and published in the presence of

J. R. Wynne.

Top: *The Agreement between Thomas Whitfield, Arbitrator for the GVT Co. and James Davies, acting on behalf of Thomas Allen Hughes, in respect of the purchase of the land for the coal yard at Glyn Ceiriog, to appoint Thomas Richard Wynne of Corwen as Umpire.* Middle: *The award made by T.R. Wynne for the land required for the station and engine shed site.* Bottom: *The award made to Thomas Allen Hughes for the purchase of the coal yard land.*

Collection: John Milner

The process of statutory land acquisition

The GVT Acts of Parliament granted the GVT Co. the rights of compulsory purchase of land required within the deviation limits set in the deposited Plans & Sections. The stages of the process were:

1. The purchaser issues a 'Notice of Intention to take Land' to the landowner, giving details of the land to be taken and inviting a claim for compensation.

2. The purchaser considers the claim and, if it is unacceptable, makes a counter-proposal.

3. Should the parties not agree, each engages an arbitrator to continue the negotiations. The arbitrators jointly appoint an umpire to make the award, should they not be able to agree.

4. If either of the parties refuses to accept the decision of the umpire, the matter goes to litigation and is placed before a judge.

If any landowner had refused to enter into negotiations with the GVT Co., the company could have applied for a BoT valuation, paid the money into the Bank of England and taken possession of the land.

Arbitration

between

The Glyn Valley Tramway Co.

and

Mr. Thomas Allen Hughes.

After inspecting this piece of Ground and carefully hearing and considering all matters connected with and bearing upon the case, I have come to the conclusion that Mr. Thomas Allen Hughes is entitled to and I award him the sum of Six hundred and twenty pounds (£620.)

J. R. Wynne.

Arbitrator

Corwen
14th February 1888.

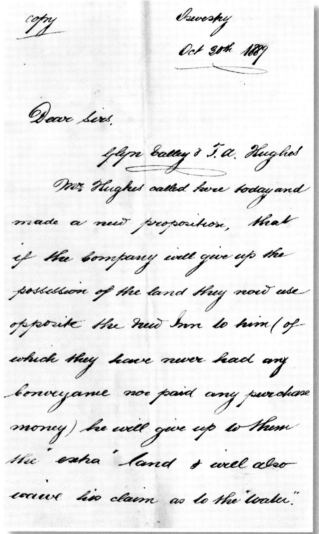

After passing through the Thomas Allen Hughes land, the tramway route moved away from the river to follow Robert Stuart's proposed route across a string of fields, which had formerly belonged to the Coed y Glyn Estate. In August 1876, the New Cambrian Slate Company had purchased nineteen acres of the estate but, by 1879, this company was in financial difficulties and started selling them off. One purchaser was the Cambrian Slate Quarry manager, Robert Roberts Thomas, at that time living at The Laurels, Glyn Ceiriog, who later sold a strip across four of his fields to the GVT Co. for £110. The adjacent field was owned by a Samuel Edwards, who was offered £15 for the strip required. The route then continued across two fields purchased from the Slate Co. by Thomas Williams in 1879, which had been passed on to his daughter, Catherine Evans, wife of John Evans of Southport, as *'tenant for life'*, which the arbitrators agreed was worth £55 6s. 3d. The remaining field in this group was still owned by the New Cambrian Slate Co. but, for some unknown reason, *'occupied for the time being'* by Henry Dennis and Samuel Smith of Chester who, in 1890, purchased it from the liquidator of the Slate Company. Valuation tables show that the arbitrators valued the strip at £40, but a draft conveyance to the GVT Co. was not prepared until 1896.

The route continued up the valley crossing several fields belonging to Dolhir Farm, which was held in trust for the Corwen College Charity. The charity, set up in 1750 with money from the estate of William Eyton of Plas Warren, Ellesmere, had converted Corwen College, situated in the town of Corwen and a former lodging house for priests, into almshouses for the accommodation of *'six widows of poor clergymen'* from parishes within Merionethshire. The Dolhir lands were purchased with the remainder of the money, to provide an income to support the widows. The

Trustees held no Deeds, but made a solemn declaration that Dolhir Farm and lands had been in the possession of the Charity from before 1755.

The strip of land required (valued at about £124) measured about one and a half acres, which included a small stretch on the other side of the river. This extra land was required because the river needed to be moved several yards to the east, in order for the line to squeeze around the steep escarpment. The trustees put in a claim for £250, but the GVT Co. offered only £120. There was an extra claim of £400 compensation for the buildings and farmyard at Dolhir, which were described as being *'contiguous to the proposed tramway and situated so close to the line as to be uninsurable'*. This *'would necessitate their removal or the payment of such a sum by the company as would recoup the landlord and tenant in case of fire'*. The College Trustees agreed to arbitration and appointed Richard Charles Butler Clough, land agent and valuer of Denbigh, to act on their behalf. Thomas Whitfield of Oswestry again acted for the GVT Co. and on 10th March 1888, they agreed to *'the sum of £205 in respect of land taken and severance damage only'*; there was no mention of compensation for the farm buildings. Henry Dennis was to be given access from 7th April and the purchase was to be completed by 1st November 1888.

At the far end of the College lands the strip fanned out, and Henry Dennis chose not to continue to follow the route proposed by Robert Stuart, which was to have crossed over the Ceiriog at this point to pass through the then disused Lower Pandy Quarry. When the Ceiriog Granite Co. became the operator of the quarry, this crossing point was used to build a bridge to connect the quarry to the GVT.

The main line carried on along the west bank, over several fields belonging to Messrs Agostino and Stefano Gatti, both of the Royal Adelphi Theatre in London. It reached a small plot of land adjacent to the river in Pandy, for which the GVT Co. offered £40 to the owner, a William Parry. Here, it was to cross the river on a bridge with a 40ft span before continuing across further fields belonging to the Gatti brothers and rejoining the Robert Stuart proposed route.

The Gatti brothers were Anglo-Swiss entrepreneurs in the West End of London, with a string of successful business interests, mainly theatres and café-restaurants, but which also included the Charing Cross and Strand Electricity Supply Corporation Ltd. In May 1881, they had purchased a large expanse of land in the Pandy area, including farms, cottages and woodland, with a total area of about 250 acres, from Edward Levy Lawson, at a cost of £48,557 16s. 0d. Some of these were ancient freeholds, but others had been common and waste lands allotted to Frederick West by the Inclosure Act 1846 and included Pen-y-Craig, Tyn-y-Berllan, Coed-y-Glyn Ucha, Coed-y-Glyn Issa and Gelli.

Plans show that just before the line reached Pandy, a short strip of land was required to provide access to the GVT from the Llanarmon–Glyn Ceiriog Road. The purpose of this was not recorded, but it may have been required because the Gatti brothers appear to have had ideas of developing the valley as a tourist area. Their solicitor's records of the 1887 transactions state that there was *'no objection to a station'* being built at Pandy and that, on February 1st 1888, Elias Griffith had *'seen the vendors in London… as to their building an Hotel on a portion of their property'*. No further references to such developments have been found.

About two and a half acres of Gatti land, valued at £177 10s. 0d., were required, but the company had offered only £150 and the matter was referred to arbitrators. Messrs Gatti appointed Mr Jenkins of Ruthin who agreed a price of £225 with Thomas Whitfield, acting for the GVT Co., but before the negotiations were finalised, Henry Dennis asked for an additional piece for which the company was willing to pay an extra £8 6s. 8d., making the total paid £233 6s. 8d.

The line finally had to pass across four fields belonging to Cwm Clyd Farm owned by Thomas Jones of Oswestry, before reaching the entrance to Hendre Quarry at the end of the extension. As it approached, the strip required ran along the riverbank but, at one point, the river had to

Agostino and Stefano Gatti, who were Anglo-Swiss entrepreneurs in the West End of London and owned theatres, including the Royal Adelphi, café-restaurants and even an electricity company, had purchased about 250 acres of land at Pandy, through which the GVT was to run. The documents relating to the purchase of land by the GVT Co. reveal that, with the arrival of the tramway, they were planning to build a hotel to be served by a passenger station at Pandy.

Collection: John Milner

Purchase of Land for the GVT Extension Glyn Ceiriog–Hendre

	Field Numbers	Location/Situation	Area			Cost of Land			Source Document	Document Date	Purchase Date
			a	r	p	£	s	d			
Eliza Green / David Jones	4, 15	Engine Shed Site	0	3	1	£455	0	0	Umpire award	14 02 1888	03 05 1889
Thomas Allen Hughes	27, 29–32	Glyn Coal Wharf	1	3	33	£670	0	0	Henry Dennis letter	30 04 1890	07 10 1890
Robert Roberts Thomas	36–37, 53 & 55	These four pieces of land in Glyn Ceiriog Parish were formerly owned by the Cambrian Slate Company.	0	2	0	£110	0	0	Agreement	02 07 1888	Unknown
Samuel Edwards	54		0	1	2	Offer by GVT = £15			Corrected plan	10 10 1887	Unknown
Catherine Evans, life tenant	56 & 57		0	1	19	£55	6	3	Agreement	20 07 1888	15 03 1889
Henry Dennis / Samuel Smith	58		0	1	2	Arbitrator award £40			Draft conveyance	1896	18 11 1896
Corwen College (Trustees)	61, 63–65 & 67–69	Glyn Ceiriog Parish	1	2	6	£205	0	0	Agreement	04 10 1888	01 11 1888
	9	Llangollen Parish	0	0	14						
William Parry	92	Next to Pandy bridge	Unknown			Offer by GVT = £40			Valuation table	1888	Unknown
Messrs A & S Gatti	70–71,78–79,84–86	Pandy, Glyn Ceiriog Parish	2	2	20	£233	6	8	Agreement & Plan	28 04 1888	01 06 1888
	21–22, 24a	Pandy, Llangollen Parish									
Thomas Jones	25, 27 & 29–30	Llangollen Parish	1	3	0	£200	0	0	Agreement	13 03 1888	25 03 1888
Edward Roberts (Trustees)	17	Llansilin Parish	0	0	26	GVT valuation = £15			Notice of Intention	12 10 1887	Unknown

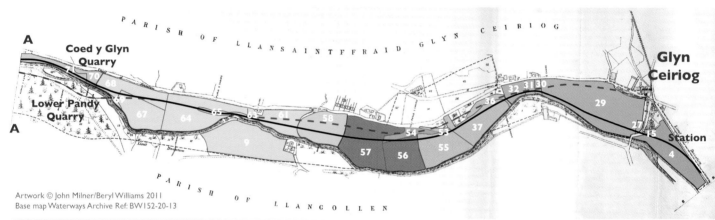

Artwork © John Milner/Beryl Williams 2011
Base map Waterways Archive Ref: BW152-20-13

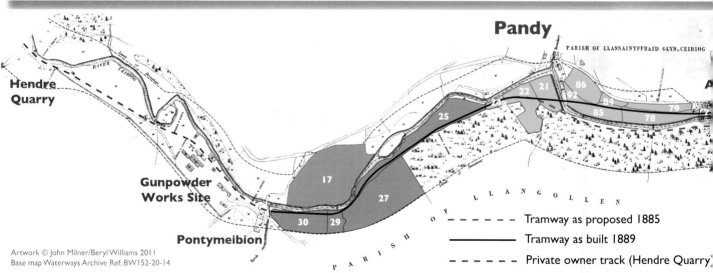

Artwork © John Milner/Beryl Williams 2011
Base map Waterways Archive Ref: BW152-20-14

A strip of land, almost two miles long, was required for the GVT extension to Hendre Quarry. The GVT Act 1885 had given the company the power to compulsorily purchase this land from within the strict 'Limits of Deviation' shown on the Plans and Sections, drawn up by the then engineer, Robert H. F. Stuart, who had proposed a route starting at the New Inn. When Henry Dennis took over, he amended this route to start closer to the river. During 1887, the eleven different owners of the lands over which the track was to be built, all received formal 'Notices of Intention to take Land' and an invitation to enter into negotiations with the GVT Co. on price. Many of them appointed arbitrators to negotiate on their behalf. The table has been compiled using evidence from many different documentary sources and, in many respects, is still incomplete.

be moved over several yards to the west, in order to create the trackbed. A retaining wall was necessary and a small piece of land, valued at £15, had to be taken from the field on the opposite side of the river, which was owned by the Trustees of Edward Roberts (who had died on 24th March 1887). Their claim was for £40, but neither the GVT Co. offer, nor the final purchase price agreed is known.

For the land to be taken from Cwm Clyd Farm, measuring about one and a half acres and valued at £132, Thomas Jones claimed £464, but the GVT Co. offered only £120. Part of this strip included half the river bed. A document dated 19th March 1888, shows a purchase price of £200 had been agreed. However, Thomas Jones made allegations that Henry Dennis had taken land outside the agreed boundaries, which resulted in a further agreement being made on 25th August 1888, stating that the GVT Co.:

> *'shall be allowed to continue their line of Tramway over and upon the land of the said Thomas Jones ... and shall complete the same as soon as possible. After the expiration of two months from this date, it shall be ascertained whether the said Company have taken land belonging to the said Thomas Jones other than that comprised in ... the plan and if it is ascertained that they have done so they shall forthwith pay to the said Thomas Jones a sum calculated at the same price ...'.*

The matter was not finally settled until 17th January 1890, when arbitrators were appointed. James Davies of Oswestry acting for Thomas Jones and Richard Wilson for the GVT Co., agreed that the measurement of the total land taken was in total one and three-quarter acres and not one and a half.

At the Annual General Meeting of GVT shareholders, held in Oswestry on 13th March 1888, there was no quorum and, because no business could be transacted, it was adjourned until 29th May 1888. The directors considered that, by the end of May, they would be able to present *'a more agreeable report'*, but the choice of this much later date suggests that at that time, in March, progress on the line was again in danger of faltering and the directors were reluctant to face the shareholders until some significant progress could be reported.

A year earlier, on 28th March 1887, the directors, Robert Myddelton Biddulph, Sir Theodore Martin, George Rooper, Henry Dennis and Elias Griffith, had given a joint Promissory Note to the SUR&C Co. in respect of the purchase of the latter's £6,000 shareholding, for the sum of £2,400 payable at the end of twelve months from the date of the Note. These were Ordinary Shares, which carried voting rights, and it was expected that by March 1888 the company would have funds available to pay for them.

A resolution had been passed at a Directors' Meeting on 26th January 1888 to sell the £6,000 worth of SUR&C Co. shares, once purchased, at 50% discount, thus making the GVT Co. a profit of £600. Edward Williams, the GVT Company's Secretary, had been authorised by the directors to proceed with either finding the money or a purchaser. By the time March arrived, the finance raised by the company for this purchase had already been used to pay for work on the line. To resolve this, it had been agreed at a meeting of the Board that the money could be found by deferring certain payments over the next eighteen months. However, Robert Myddelton Biddulph and Elias Griffith refused to sign an authority to defer these payments. With the Note being due, Edward Williams, the GVT Company's Secretary, knowing that the company had no other way to raise the funds, paid the SUR&C Co. the £2,400 (the agreed price for the shares valued at £6,000) from his own pocket and in his own name, unwittingly giving him control of the company. However, Williams had offered to transfer the canal company shares, in equal proportions, to the five directors who had signed the Promissory Note, but that offer was refused by Biddulph and Griffith, who took immediate legal action to prevent the SUR&C Co. from transferring the shares to Williams, despite the fact that they had endorsed the purchase of the shares by Williams in the first place. It appears that Mr Myddelton Biddulph and Elias Griffith were disgruntled, because they had not realised that the Preference Shares they held did not have any voting rights![2]

[2] The Terms & Conditions on the rear of Preference Share Certificates clearly state that: *'No person is entitled to vote at Meetings of the Company in respect of the Shares included in this Certificate'.*

In a letter to a later meeting of shareholders Sir Theodore Martin made the comment that: '*Mr Williams relieved us* [the directors] *and the company from the difficulty, and I certainly hold him to be entitled to our warmest thanks for having done so.*' He also stated that: '*those who refused to sign want to get the shares into their hands for some other purpose than the mere desire to have votes*'.

At the adjourned shareholders' meeting, held on 29th May 1888, it soon became clear that relationships within the Boardroom were continuing to deteriorate. With this meeting being an adjournment of the Annual General Meeting, before any business could be transacted the register of shareholders had to be sealed by the chairman. When the secretary laid the register before Mr Myddelton Biddulph for his signature, there was immediately an objection from Elias Griffith that the register was not complete, as it did not state '*the proper number of shares*' that he held. The chairman said that '*in face of the protest*' he could not sign the register. Heated arguments followed, because unless the register was signed, all business transacted at the meeting would be declared null and void. In spite of the protestations from both fellow directors and the shareholders, the chairman continued to refuse to do so. It became apparent that the £6,000 worth of canal company shares had not been listed anywhere in the register and this was the root of this particular problem.

It was reluctantly accepted by the meeting that '*it would be illegal to authenticate the list with omissions in it*'. The ordinary shareholders, having already been persuaded to accept a reduction in the total value of their Ordinary Shares, from £17,610 to £8,205, had become highly suspicious of the move to have the SUR&C Co. shares, purchased by Williams, reallocated to the GVT Co. directors, and after more than an hour or so of more wrangling, much of it concerning the voting rights of preferential shareholders, it was agreed that as no business could be done that day, the register would be authenticated at a later date and the present meeting adjourned. In the lull, which occurred while a suitable date was being discussed, Henry Dennis reminded the meeting that the locomotives were to be ready for delivery about 25th June and the sum of £2,300 would have to be found to pay for them before they were delivered. He said that he, for one, was prepared '*to find £1,000 of that money, more if necessary, in order to complete the line and provide rolling stock*'. He tried to continue and make his formal report, but failed, amid cries of '*The chairman*', '*The chairman*' as shareholders demanded to hear from the chairman first. Then '*a scene of much excitement ensued*' as Mr Dennis persisted in his attempts to continue, but '*the uproar became very great, nearly all those present being on their feet and making a great noise*': a situation which continued until Mr Dennis gave way to the chairman. The meeting was formally adjourned until 29th June 1888, but it was agreed that reports and statements could be read for the benefit of those present. Throughout the reading of these, the atmosphere remained unstable, derogatory remarks continued to be made, and personal insults exchanged.

The chairman, Mr Myddelton Biddulph, was asked to present the Report of the Directors and to approve the Statement of Accounts up to 31st December 1887, both of which should have been presented at the Annual General Meeting in March of which this meeting was an adjournment. His enigmatic response was that '*The report of the directors was sent to the Chairman for his signature, but the Chairman has not attached it. The Statement of Accounts was not forwarded, and the signature was not attached for that reason.*' However, he was allowed to make a statement in which he explained that, as chairman, he had refused to sign the report prepared by a majority of the directors, because it contained statements that he considered were too optimistic. He had also refused to approve the accounts, because they contained '*items of indebtedness of which he had no knowledge*'. He continued his statement by saying that if he had known that preference shareholders would not be entitled to vote, then '*Neither his money, nor those important sums subscribed by his friends, amounting to about two-thirds of the preference shares, would ever have been subscribed, nor would his land have been cut up by this hideous railway.*'

A letter from Sir Theodore Martin, a respected director who was unable to be present, was read out by Mr George Rooper, in which Sir Theodore offered to find £500 towards the purchase of

[No. 5.] **Details of Capital Expenditure.**
FOR YEAR ENDING 31ST DECEMBER, 1887.

	£	s.	d.
On Lines in Course of Construction :—			
Purchase Money for Land.........	392	0	0
Construction of Way and Stations, including Rails, Chairs, Sleepers, &c.	7075	1	1
Parliamentary Deposit	502	13	0
Paid on account of obtaining Act of 1885	71	0	0
Engineering and Surveying	300	0	0
Plant	641	6	0
Mr. Biddulph for Bridge over Railway near Lever's House	550	0	0
General Charges	43	14	6
	£9575	**8**	**7**

[No. 6.] **Return of Working Stock.**

[No. 7.] **Estimate of further Expenditure on Capital Account.**

	£	s.	d.
Amount due to Ceiriog Granite Co.	2,000	0	0
Messrs. Martin & Leslie, Messrs. Longueville & Co., Mr. Dennis, and Mr. Griffith's debt	2,000	0	0
Messrs. Longueville & Co.'s Costs from 1884 to 1887	555	16	6
Do their Payments.........	163	11	6
Mr. Dennis' Estimate of further Expenditure, including cost of Locomotives, extra to the Balance of the £15,000 Preference Capital to be paid up	7,000	0	0
Messrs. Martin & Leslie's Costs of Act of 1885	775	4	0
	£12,494	**12**	**0**

locomotives and rolling stock, adding that '*others, no doubt, will come forward with the money and so save the credit of the Company*'.

Finally, just before the end of the meeting, which had already lasted over two and a half hours, the engineer, Henry Dennis presented a short report, in which he reminded shareholders that his original estimate of £15,000 had not included the line from Chirk station to Black Park canal basin, which would cost an additional £2,000, nor the necessary sidings at Chirk station, and that £2,300 was also required for the two new locomotives. He reported that the purchase of land for the extension up to Hendre Quarry, for which he had estimated £500, had already cost £1,500.

At the next Directors' Meeting, held on 8th June 1888, the matter of the SUR&C Co. shares should have been resolved when Edward Williams agreed to dispose of the shares that he had purchased, on receipt of the certificates, at the discretion of the Directors, but there was no resolution because, at this point, Mr Myddelton Biddulph and Mr Griffith departed from the meeting, Mr Myddelton Biddulph stating that he did not see that his further presence during the deliberations of the Board would be to any advantage.

The Meeting continued with Sir Theodore Martin in the Chair and an examination of the company's liabilities revealed that a further £7,000 was immediately required to '*complete the contracts for work, land, locomotives etc*'. There was no other course open but to make a further issue of £10,000 in preference shares. In the event, only forty shares at par value were applied for, and during the remainder of 1888 the directors were forced to cover the capital requirements of the company themselves. In desperation they resorted to a 50 per cent discount issue, but again without success. The problems with the conversion of the tramway, as were those of the original horse tramway, were due to the total construction cost having been grossly under-estimated. This was especially so with regard to the purchase of land for the extension from Glyn Ceiriog to the granite quarry at Hendre.

Extract from the annual accounts for the year ending 31st December 1887, showing the details of capital expenditure and the estimated further expenditure required to complete the tramway – as it turned out it was being a little economical with the truth!

Collection: John Milner

GLYN VALLEY TRAMWAY COMPANY.

Further issue of 1,000 Five per cent. Preference Shares of £10 each.

Payable £1 per Share on application, £1 per Share on Allotment, and the remainder by Calls at no less interval than 3 Months at £1 per Share.

SIR,

It will be seen from the Resolutions, copies of which will be found on the other side, we are instructed by the Directors to inform you that further Capital is required to complete and stock the Line, and that it is necessary to issue more Preference Shares to raise the amount required.

The new Shares will be entitled to a cumulative preferential dividend of £5 per cent. per annum, on the amount from time to time called and paid up thereon respectively out of the net revenue of the Company, in priority to any dividend on the Ordinary Shares of the Company, and payable half yearly. No person will be entitled to vote at Meetings of the Company in respect of these new Shares.

The Preference Shareholders will further be entitled to participate equally with the Ordinary Shareholders in the division of profits which may remain after the Ordinary Shareholders have been paid a cumulative Five per cent. dividend.

We shall be obliged by your informing us on or before Saturday, the 23rd instant, how many of the new Shares you will take.

By Order of the Board,

LONGUEVILLE & Co.,

SOLICITORS.

OSWESTRY, 13th June, 1888.

The adjourned meeting of the shareholders was resumed on Friday 29th June 1888, at the Hand Hotel, Chirk, with Mr Richard Myddelton Biddulph in the chair, together with a large attendance of shareholders. He stated that he could only hope that the meeting would be an orderly one, and that every person who wished to speak would be allowed to do so without interference – wishful thinking!

Sir Theodore Martin, who again was unable to be present, had forwarded a very long letter to be read to the shareholders, in which he clearly summarised the situation regarding shares and explained why the Preference Shares carried no voting rights. As related earlier, he was in wholehearted support of Mr Williams, the Company Secretary, and his action in purchasing the SUR&C Co. shares and said that he '*could only conclude that those who refused to sign want to get the shares into their hands for some other purpose than the mere desire to have votes*'. He

The Hand Hotel (left) in Chirk, coaching inn on Telford's road to Holyhead, was the venue for the infamous meeting of GVT shareholders, on 29th June 1888, chaired by Richard Myddelton Biddulph. The proprietor was Elias Griffith, who had been the contractor to the GVT in 1872 and was chairman of the Board 1886–87.

Collection: John Milner

Notice sent out by the GVT Co. secretary, Edward Williams, reconvening the adjourned Annual General Meeting of shareholders.

Collection: John Milner

continued with a vehement attack on the conduct of Elias Griffith and then accused him of stealing rail from the tramway for use in Hendre Quarry, of which he was the manager.

'I need not characterise conduct of this kind. I leave the shareholders to form their own opinion of members of a Board who decline to be governed by the decisions of the majority of that Board; and one of whom, I mean Mr [Elias] Griffith, repudiates the action taken upon a resolution, of which he not only approved, but was indeed the chief instigator, and yet to which he afterwards informed our Chairman he had never assented. I need not say how painful it must be to every honourable man to sit upon the same Board with one who acts in this way. ... ...

At a meeting of the Board, at which Mr Griffith was present, tenders for the purchase of the Company's old rails were considered. One of the tenders was for the entire quantity at a satisfactory price. It was accepted, Mr Griffith assenting. Judge of the astonishment of my brother directors and myself on a letter being received from the purchaser, stating that a considerable portion of these rails had, subsequently to the acceptance of his tender, been removed to the granite quarries of which Mr Griffith is manager, and calling on the Board immediately to replace them and to pay him damages. These rails are still retained at the granite quarries, and we are at this moment threatened with an action of damages in consequence of their removal – an act done, I need not say, without the sanction or cognisance of the Board. These are the facts; let Mr Griffith reconcile them, if he can, with his duty to his brother Directors, or to the Company, whose interest, as their director and trustee, he was bound to protect.'

Sir Theodore then broadened his attack to include the Chairman, Mr Myddelton Biddulph:

'Without more money the line cannot be completed or put into efficient working order. Where is that money to be got? We turn in vain for assistance to Mr Griffith and the gentlemen with whom

Oswestry, 21st June, 1888.

Dear Sir,

The adjourned Annual General Meeting of the Shareholders of the Glyn Valley Tramway Company will be held at the Hand Hotel, Chirk, on Friday, the 29th instant, at Eleven o'clock.

Yours faithfully,

EDWARD WILLIAMS,

Secretary.

219

The summary of a detailed breakdown of capital expenditure for 1887 and up to the 5th December 1889. Of interest is the entry for 'girders', which were the bridge girders for the river bridges supplied by Tiddesly & Co. for £267 1s. 9d., and the entry for coal used during construction, which came from the Ruabon Coal & Coke Co. (a Henry Dennis company) and Trehowell Colliery. See Appendix 6.

Shropshire Archives Ref: 800/44A

he acts. The Chairman and he declined even to join in the deliberations of the Board, as to what had best be done toward finding the additional capital. The ship is drifting on the rocks, and they will not lift a hand to save it from ruin. In these circumstances the rest of the Board have had to cast about and see what can be done in this emergency.'

As Sir Theodore approached the end of his letter, he issued a warning, followed by some words of encouragement: *'Internal discord is ruin to any undertaking. There ought to be none in our Company. If we all work together with genuine regard only to the welfare of what I believe, once fairly launched, will be a most successful enterprise, we shall do well.'*

Immediately the letter was read, Henry Dennis rose to make his reply to the statement made by the chairman, Mr Myddelton Biddulph, at the last meeting, which he considered was *'a public attack on the Board over which he presides'*, as well as an attack on him personally as the engineer. He intended to refute the chairman's misstatements of facts and put before the shareholders the full particulars of expenditure in relation to his estimate that was accepted at the meeting held on 14th September 1886. He produced documents to show how the work had been divided into four sections. The estimates for each section were very detailed and specified the materials to be used. The total estimate was for the line only, as it was considered that more shares would be issued to raise the capital required for *'the locomotives, tram cars, station shed, offices, rolling stock and the like'*. It appears that there had been no significant overspend on any of the sections, except for land for the extension to Hendre.

Henry Dennis then explained how the extortionate cost of land had increased the cost per mile of line:

'When it is considered that nine miles of railway, laid with a 50lb steel rail on sleepers 4ft 6in by 10in by 5in, and six bridges, three of which are over the river Ceiriog, are made for a sum of £15,610, or £1,734 a mile, or to put it in another way, deduct the amount paid for land, £2,248, the cost of the railway pure and simple is but £1,485 per mile. I feel sure that practical men acquainted with the cost of railway construction cannot from these figures fail to come to the conclusion that considerable economy has been used. In my own experience I have never yet heard of such a length, with so substantial a permanent way, having been made for anything like the amount.'

To date, the additional costs included £1,040 spent upon the extension to the canal, £110 for rails to Great Western sidings, £644 paid to the Granite Co. on account of rolling stock, and £573 spent on the Parliamentary deposit and other expenses. There were also railway freight accounts, advertising and sundry other payments, outside of the original estimate that had been incurred from time to time in carrying out the orders of the Board.

One of the shareholders returned to the accuracy of the Register of Shareholders, which had caused such a problem at the last meeting. He drew the attention of the meeting to the £2,400 Shropshire Union shareholding, which had been entered in the register as £6,000 to balance the books, and that there were errors in the numbers of shares held by certain individuals. Furthermore, he pointed out that the directors had entered the reduced value of the Ordinary Shares (now valued at £8,205) as £11,810. He also objected because, since the adjourned meeting, the names of 29 new shareholders had been added to the register, who appeared to be either *'Mr Williams' clerks or Mr Dennis' employees'*. Up to this point in the meeting, Henry Dennis had been enjoying a lot of support from shareholders, until it was revealed that he had sold a block of his own shares in the GVT Co. to his own employees and associates, in order to swell support at the meeting. This he refuted and insisted that the new shareholders present were not his employees, but his *'brother workers'* – to which a heckler jeered *'Same thing'*!

From this lengthy meeting, it became apparent that the directors were trying to better their own individual causes as well as trying to cover up their mismanagement of the company's affairs;

blaming each other as each point was raised by the shareholders. A *'stormy scene'* ensued, following which the chairman, Myddelton Biddulph, made a statement in which he said that he *'regretted to think that be could not continue to act in harmony with the GVT Board, nor did he see any possibility of agreeing with them'*. He *'declined any longer to sit on the Board with Mr. Dennis or Mr. Williams'* and *'resigned his chairmanship'*.

One local preference shareholder, a Mr. John Thomas from Chirk said:

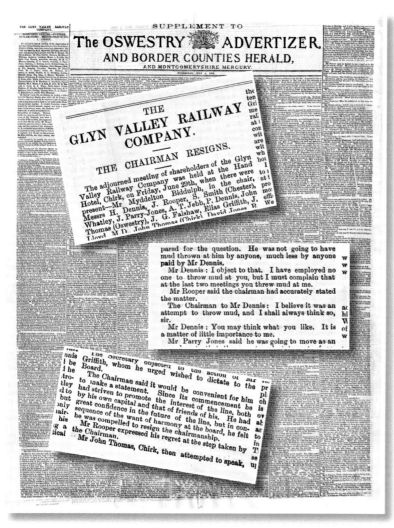

'I am sorry I have no vote, but the way the line has been made is a disgrace. First of all, the time the work has taken is ridiculous. We were promised the complete line in November, then in March, then in May. I want to show that the money spent on it has been spent very foolishly,' to which Mr Dennis replied: *'Go on, say what you like, I take no notice; it makes no difference in the world to me.'* Mr Thomas responded: *'If you do not, perhaps others will. You are not a creator, unless it is a creator of faggot votes. How do you like that?'*

Mr Thomas then went on to criticise the bridge that had been built over the line by Chirk station, saying that it *'might have been built by a common navvy at half of the money it cost'*, at which point *'a storm of noise and excited gesticulations broke out amidst cries of "Sit down" and counter cries'*. Mr Thomas went on to describe the bridge near Mr Lever's house as a *'horse box rather than a bridge'*. The storm continued and Mr Myddelton Biddulph left the meeting with a band of his followers, along with Elias Griffith.

Following the departure of the dissidents the meeting continued under the chairmanship of Mr George Rooper, who in 1883 had taken over the Wynne Slate Quarry from The Wynne Slate Quarry Co. Ltd, and was obviously keen to see the GVT operational, so that he could transport his slate out of the valley.

Both the Oswestry Advertizer and the Wrexham Advertizer, felt that the wranglings of the of the GVT Co. directors and shareholders was too good to miss and they published an almost verbatim account in the form of a supplement.

Collection: John Milner
Courtesy: NWN Media Ltd

As this meeting was the second adjournment of the Annual General Meeting, which should have been held in March, the final business was the re-election of the two retiring directors, Henry Dennis and Elias Griffith, both of whom had offered themselves for re-election. One of the shareholders, a Mr Thomas of Oswestry, said that it appeared to him that *'Mr Dennis was in a dual capacity as Director and Engineer'*, and thought that these *'positions were incompatible'*. However, it was confirmed that Mr Dennis had written a letter of resignation from his office as engineer earlier in June and this resignation had been accepted. Mr Thomas was satisfied and Henry Dennis was duly proposed, seconded and re-elected as a director. It was also proposed and seconded that Elias Griffith be re-elected to the Board, but there was some hesitation and discussion before the vote was taken, when it was pointed out that he had been a *'disturbing element'* in the recent problems and that his behaviour would lead to *'a Board which, divided against itself, would carry them all on the rocks on which they should be stranded'*. When the motion was eventually put to the meeting, there was not one vote for it and accordingly Elias Griffith was declared not being re-elected.

The conflicts within the company, and especially this three-hour-long meeting, drew a great deal of attention, which undoubtedly did much harm to the reputation of an already ailing GVT Company. The local press deemed it to be of sufficient public interest for the publication of a special supplement, with the *Oswestry Advertizer & Border Counties Herald*, the *Montgomeryshire Mercury* and the *Wrexham Advertiser* reporting all the proceedings almost verbatim. This was not, however, the end of the matter, as legal wrangles followed between the individuals concerned, with regard to accusations made at the meeting, but still the directors pursued a policy of misleading the shareholders with regard to the true operational state of the tramway. The matter of the SUR&C Co. shares was eventually resolved in the High Court, with three of the directors, plus Mr Myddelton Biddulph and Mr Griffith, each receiving one-fifth of the shares.

While the battles were going on in the boardroom, work was progressing with the tramway conversion, with a deadline for completion of 31st July 1888, this being the date required by the 1885 Act. However, at this date, although the track from Chirk station to Glyn Ceiriog was all laid, several elements of the earthworks contracts, awarded to Griffith Griffiths, had not yet been completed, neither had the facilities at the interchanges at Chirk station and Black Park Basin. The contractors, John Jevons & Son had been at work on the Hendre extension since late February and had made good progress and the track laying by Croom Johnson was already well advanced, although it was not expected to be finished to Hendre Quarry, at the far end, for some time.

Although no specific details had been disclosed at the shareholders' meetings held earlier in 1888, difficulties had arisen during the execution of the contracts to construct the earthworks for the new line up the steep bank from Pontfaen to Chirk station and the embankments for the diversion at Dolywern. Griffith Griffiths, the contractor, had started work on the trackbed up to Chirk at the end of March 1887 and, as work progressed, had received a monthly payment for work completed. The whole of the work for this contract should have been completed within five calendar months but, although the trackbed appears to have been finished within that time, difficulties had been encountered in stabilising the steep slope of the valley-side into which it was cut. The use of retaining walls and embanking a short section of the Chirk to Pontfaen road had been necessary, which had led to delays. On 22nd August 1887, some elements of the contract remained unfinished, but although the GVT Co. had the power to take the contract away from Griffiths, he was allowed to continue, consequently incurring the penalty stipulated in the contract of £5 per day!

During this period, there appears to have been a complete breakdown in communication between Henry Dennis and this particular contractor. It was not until the 20th September 1888 that the company eventually acted and '*took the work out of his hands*', by which time it claimed that '*there was due* [from Griffiths] *a sum of £5 for each day in respect of 332 working days for non-completion of the works, amounting in all to the sum of £1,660*'. Griffiths had received stage payments totalling £1,890 for work completed, but the GVT Co. had withheld from him a sum of £661 18s. 6d., which it said was '*necessary by reason of negligent and defective workmanship*' and had further demanded an additional sum of £637 12s. 3d., in order to complete the works. This last sum included £250 for 2,000 yards of fencing, £220 for remedial work on the Chirk to Pontfaen road, £146 for work on the slopes and embankments and £18 for walling.[3] Taking into account a smaller sum of £5 12s. 8d., that had been overcharged for extra ashlar stone, the GVT Co. was claiming a total of £2,451 18s. 3d., which was about 85% of the total value of the two Griffith Griffiths contracts which amounted to £2,877.

[3] The figure of £146 included additional work on the embankments on the deviation at Dolywern.

Griffith Griffiths disputed this sum and refused to settle, taking the matter to the High Court, Queen's Bench Division. Papers, referenced '1888 G. No.2511' that were deposited on 24th April 1889, show that his case was based mainly on the lack of formal communication from Henry Dennis, as he had not been given the required written notices that his work was unsatisfactory, nor written instructions '*to make more rapid progress*', as the company was required to do by the contract. He alleged that he '*was wrongly prevented from proceeding with the work with due diligence and from completing the same*' and that '*Henry Dennis ... wrongfully refused to certify work or measure or value work after a reasonable time*' as stated in the contract and he claimed that, by not doing so, the company *'had waived'* this requirement. The £1,660 which had accrued from the £5 per day penalty was challenged on the grounds that the company *'had sustained no damage by the alleged delay'*. He stated that his work was complete and that it had been *'completed to the satisfaction of Henry Dennis'* adding that *'if in any respects it remained incomplete, it was only in some trivial and unimportant details, which did not entitle the company to object that he had not proceeded with due diligence or had not completed the work within the meaning of the contracts'*.

The outcome was that, on 18th May 1889, the Court ordered that the whole of the matters in the case should be referred to George Robert Jebb Esq, civil engineer, of Birmingham, to make an Award.[4] On 31st July 1889, Jebb, *'having duly weighed and considered the several allegations of the said parties and the evidence tendered by them'*, published his findings:

'I award and adjudge that the defendants [GVT Co.] were and are indebted to the plaintiff [Griffiths] … in the sum of one thousand, two hundred and one pounds, two shillings and seven pence [£1,201 2s. 7d.] … and I further award and adjudge that the plaintiff was and is indebted to the defendants … in the sum of three hundred and ninety eight pounds, seven shillings and one penny [£398 7s. 1d.]…'

The case had been taken to the High Court by Griffith Griffiths, because the GVT Co. was claiming a total of £2,451 18s. 3d. from him but, although some of his work may have been *'defective in trivial ways'* and had not been finished on time, Jebb considered that most of it had been completed *'within the meaning of the contracts'* and he was due a further payment of £800 or so, on which sum the company was to pay interest at 4% per annum from the date of the writ, until it was paid off. This result must have come as a great disappointment to the GVT Co., which was still in severe financial difficulties, and also to Henry Dennis who, on 8th July 1889, in a private letter to Alexander Mackintosh, engineer to the Great Western Railway, had confidently written *'I have been all day on the ground and in the office and have come to the conclusion that the whole of our claim ought to be allowed by the Arbitrator.'*

This episode must have reflected very badly on the GVT Co., but more so on the working practices and judgement of its engineer Henry Dennis, who had failed to communicate with a contractor in the manner specified in the contracts and also failed to realise that his allegation that the work completed by Griffith Griffiths was not in accordance with the contracts, would not withstand the scrutiny of an engineer appointed by the High Court.

In contrast to Griffith Griffiths, whose work was not completed and whose contracts No.1 and No.4 for earthworks were terminated, Croom Johnson finished his tracklaying contracts No.2 and No.3, to the satisfaction of the engineer, Henry Dennis, and appears to have been further engaged to undertake most of the extra works required outside the main contracts. This work included elements of earthworks contracts and building interchange facilities, as well as the rest of the tracklaying for the line. He completed the outstanding work on the deviations and installed the girder bridges, as *'extras'* to his No.2 contract, which was for laying the track from Pontfaen to Glyn Ceiriog.

On 23rd March 1888, the Llangollen Advertiser reported the good news that:

'After a full year of slow progress, we are glad to inform readers that the first two sections extending from Chirk station to the New Inn at Llansantfraid [Glyn Ceiriog] are nearly completed. Also the Queen Bridge constructed over the Ceiriog at Dolywern is finished. This bridge is 40 foot span and the structure itself is a firm, well executed work. The steam engine [BELMONT] made its first passage over it on the 14th inst, with a long train of ballast trucks to the great satisfaction of the onlookers, who had provided a number of fog signals to welcome the advent of the "fire horse" for the first time to the Glyn valley. The other bridge near the middle factory [Pont Bell] is fast approaching completion. This

Copy of the Award made by George Robert Jebb on 31st July 1889, under the jurisdiction of the High Court, in settlement of the dispute between the GVT Co. and its contractor Griffith Griffiths.

Collection: John Milner

[4] This is the same George Robert Jebb who, as engineer to the SUR&C Co., had been responsible for building the GVT horse tramway in 1872/3.

This is named the Jubilee Bridge and is in the style similar to the latter excepting that it is of shorter span. When this is finished, with a few extras in additions, the line will be completed as far as the New Inn, and we are anxiously looking forward to the first of May which we hope, will be the opening day for passenger traffic. In the meantime two stations should be erected at Dolywern and Llansantfraid [Glyn Ceiriog] *respectively. The third or upper section has been contracted for by Mr Jellop a spirited contractor from Dudley* [This is a bit of misreporting, as the contractor was Jevons & Son of Dudley] *who has already commenced operations and promises to have his portion completed in 3 months hence.'*

An account, dated 26th May 1888, shows that the work of installing the girder bridges comprised *'fixing Girders & Cross Girders ... supplying and fixing 6" Decking, supplying & fixing 12" X 8" balks to carry permanent way, supplying Ballast Boards, bolts, rivets etc.'* at a total cost of £137. On the same date, Croom Johnson made a request for £30 *'on a/c of walling'* at Pont Bell Bridge, and an account he submitted on June 16th 1888 lists a culvert that he rebuilt at Dolywern for £3 10s. 0d., several instances of wall demolition and rebuilding, hedge removal, hedge planting and the erection of iron hurdle fencing at various locations. He also raised the embankment at Dolywern at a cost of £5 and laid 13 chains of the track over this deviation for the sum of £10 1s. 6d.

Croom Johnson was also engaged to undertake *'extra works'* and tracklaying for the extension from the rail interchange at Chirk station to the canal interchange planned at Black Park. As agreed with the SUR&C Co., and laid down in the 1885 GVT Act, the GVT line was to extend to a point on the canal towing path, just short of the entrance to Black Park Colliery Basin, where a canal-side granite wharf was to be built, which would be the extremity of locomotive working.

A letter from Croom Johnson to Henry Dennis, dated 27th March 1888, advising him that the bridges at Dolywern and Berwyn (Glyn Ceiriog – Pont Bell) were completed and requesting a stage payment.

Shropshire Archives
Ref: 800/44B

The cost of construction of this extension from Chirk station to Black Park and the provision of facilities for the canal-side interchange had not been included in the 1886 estimate of costs prepared by Henry Dennis; nevertheless, in spite of its financial difficulties the GVT Co. was obliged to provide this interchange, as part of the agreement to give equal facilities to the canal Co. and the GWR, which was made before the Bill for the 1885 Act was presented. If the canal interchange was not built, the tramway company would not be able to use its rail interchange at Chirk, which was, by this time, almost complete and there would have been no satisfactory means of moving granite and slate brought down the valley, out of the Chirk area.

The tramway extension from Chirk to Black Park was to be about ³/₄ mile long, about half its length passing through a wooded area that had to be cleared. The first work on the site was undertaken by the contractors John Morris & Company. Details of the contract have not been found but the work would have been of a preparatory nature, including clearing the ground of trees and scrub ready for the earthworks. John Morris was paid a total of £110 4s. 4d., having begun work early in 1888, receiving his first staged payment on March 3rd and his last on May 3rd.

John Morris was closely followed on site by Croom Johnson, who submitted accounts, dated May 26th and June 17th 1888 for 'Work done in Connection with Extension to Canal', which included detailed items, such as: excavating, making formation for line of Railway etc.: £151 13s. 0d., laying Permanent Way, from points near Slate Wharf (at Chirk station) to Canal Basin: £46 2s. 3d., Taking down and re-fixing iron hurdle fencing etc.: £8 6s.0d., cutting down large tree, lopping same and filling up hole: £2 15s. 0d. Also mentioned were items for the GWR interchange facilities: 'Platform Wall, Tipper, etc.'

Although the SUR&C Co. Executive Committee had approved plans in July 1887 for the agreed canal interchange, it was March 1888 before it finally approved the construction of a new 170ft-

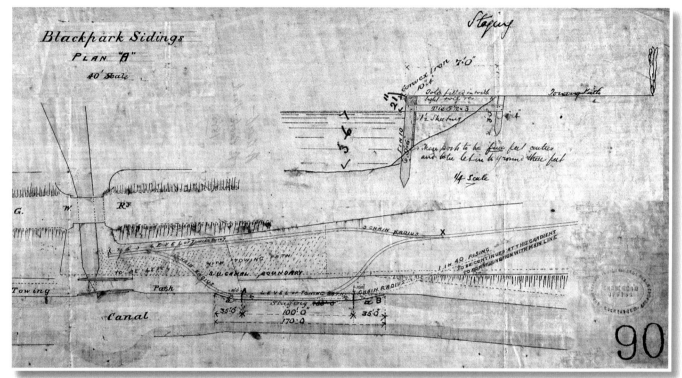

Above: *In 1888 the Engineer's Office of the SUR&C Co. produced two schemes for a new wharf alongside the canal at Black Park. Plan 'A' (above) was to provide enough storage space for 2,271 tons of granite setts stacked 6ft high (cross-hatched on plan) and Plan 'B', not shown, for 834 tons. By about 1904 the production of granite setts had given way to gravel for road works and the wharf was redesigned to handle this new traffic.*

Shropshire Archives Ref: SA-IMG16819

Right: *An extract redrawn from the GVT Plans & Sections 1885 showing, in red, the limit of the GVT locomotive working for the new canal-side wharf. Pencilled in on the original plan is the suggestion of extending the tramway under the GWR bridge to the main basin, which was done at a later date.*

The Waterways Archive Ref: BW152-20-17 (part)

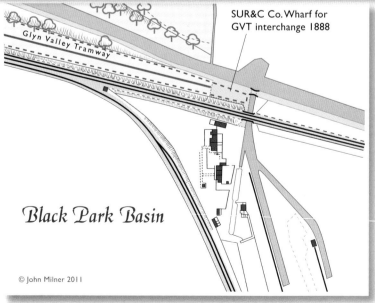

Shropshire Union Railways and Canal.

(93 Memo.)

Memo. *from the* ENGINEER,

New Street Station,

_____ 188   **BIRMINGHAM.**

To _____

Glyn Valley Railway
Proposed Sidings at Black Park for SU Co.
Estimated Cost of
Sidings Warehouse Crane   £670 . 0 . 0

W.4/28.

Shropshire Union Railways and Canal.

(93 Memo.)

Memo. *from the* ENGINEER,

New Street Station,

_____ 188   **BIRMINGHAM.**

To _____

Black Park Sidings
Area of ground enclosed by lines of Sidings & which
will be available for storing setts closely packed say 6ft high

Plan "A"   757 Sup. Yds.   = 2271 Tons of Setts
*   "   "B"   278   "   "   =   834   "   "   "*

Note- Area taken out from line one yard clear of rails all
round)

W.4/28.

Memos from the SUR&C Co.'s Engineer. Top: *The estimated cost of providing the new sidings, a warehouse and a crane.* Bottom: *Details of the storage capacity provided by each of the two proposals for the new wharf.*

The Waterways Archive
Gloucester
Licence No.: 0609 JM
Ref: BW152-20-2a and 2c

long wharf, with timber staging, directly on the canal edge, between the statutory end of the GVT and the canal entrance to Black Park Basin, with a loop and storage area on an adjacent area of widened towpath . There is later evidence of a crane and a stable being sited on this new wharf.[5]

The line was further extended along the towing path under the GWR main line, to make full use of the facilities at the colliery basin. This short section of tramway had to be horse-worked, because of the sharp curve in the track and the low bridge carrying the GWR over the entrance. By an agreement made before the Bill for the 1885 Act was presented, the facilities at the basin had been provided by the SUR&C Co. and, while the GVT Co. agreed to the connection, it was certainly not favourable to the SUR&C Co.'s later suggestion that the tramway company should work it free of charge! The construction work progressed well and at the July 1888 meeting of the SUR&C Co. Executive it was reported that small amounts of traffic were being transshipped between the GVT and the canal and vice versa.

The tramway was inspected by Major-General Hutchinson of the BoT, the GVT seeking his official approval, not just for the operation of steam power, but for the reintroduction of passenger traffic from Chirk to Glyn Ceiriog. However, he considered the tramway too incomplete for a certificate to be issued and the matter was left in abeyance by the GVT Co., so deferring capital expenditure on passenger coaches. By this time, the company was more interested in resolving

[5] This canal-side wharf underwent major alterations in 1905 when a high-level ramp was built, with a wagon tippler and chute, built specifically for loading granite into the boats.

what were becoming long-term financial problems, by concentrating on installing all the necessary interchange facilities at Chirk to encourage continued investment in the quarries up the valley, which would be its main source of revenue.

In December 1888, R. Lloyd Williams, the surveyor for the newly formed Denbighshire County Council, wrote direct to the BoT to lodge a complaint that: *'Much of the work on this line has been done in anything but a satisfactory manner, without due regard to the ordinary rules of construction, and not well calculated to stand the vibration, which is constantly going on with a line of this sort.'* He carried on to say that the safety of those travelling on the road had been entirely neglected, which was an accident waiting to happen, and that considerable expense would become necessary to prevent the road (Pontfaen–Chirk), where it has been altered, from slipping and collapsing.

The directors, in their report at the end of 1888, had to admit that, although the tramway had been relaid, it was, in fact, far from complete in operational terms:

> *'The cost of so far completing the railway has in several particulars exceeded the amount originally estimated ... Very considerable expense has become necessary in providing Wharfage and Storage Accommodation, both at Chirk station and the Black Park terminus, to facilitate the exchange of traffic both with the Great Western Railway and the Shropshire Union Canal. Substantial iron rail fencing has been insisted on for long lengths of line ... In order to develop the trade, both in slate and granite, immediate additions have been essential to the stock of trucks and wagons ... to ensure easy and safe working, Brake Vans have also had to be ordered, and special cars for the passenger traffic ... The Engine Shed at Chirk and Booking Offices at the termini; as well as an Office for the Company, are also indispensable.'*

Estimates for 1888 had included two tipplers for the loading bank at Chirk station, passenger cars, forty wagons, repairs to the landslide at Pontfaen, weighing machines, new workshops and a goods shed and coal wharf at Chirk. Also included were new sidings at Pontfaen, Dolywern, New Inn and Pandy, and further extensions of the standard-gauge exchange sidings at Chirk, but none of these, in total requiring an additional capital expenditure of £3,500, were yet in place.

All the 'additional' requirements were fundamental to the operation of the tramway, taking into account the anticipated traffic portrayed in the prospectus, but funding had not been included in the 1886 estimate, because it had been planned to raise the additional capital required for *'the locomotives, tram cars, station shed, offices, rolling stock and the like'* by a further share issue. In the event, this failed, so the company found itself, as it did after laying the original horse tramway, without the funds to make a newly built line fully operational. In reality, the tramway was nowhere near to being fully operational as a mineral line, nor anywhere near ready to open for passenger traffic, as had been anticipated by the directors.

To further exacerbate the situation, Messrs Beyer, Peacock & Co. had refused to deliver the two new steam locomotives until they had been paid for. However, this was partly resolved, probably by way of directors' loans and, on 17th October 1888, the first of the new GVT locomotives, *'Sir Theodore'*, had arrived from the Gorton Works of Beyer, Peacock & Co., Manchester, to join *'Belmont'*, the locomotive previously brought in on loan from Snailbeach to help with the construction work.

However, in spite of all the problems, at long last, after many years of battles on all fronts, the Ceiriog Valley had its steam-operated tramway, thus providing the industries of the valley with an efficient means of conveying their output to the rest of the country. The track had been relaid between Pontfaen and Glyn Ceiriog, with two new bridges over the river, a new line had been built between Pontfaen and Chirk, which would provide interchanges with both the GWR and the SU canal, and it was expected that the track for the extension to Hendre Granite Quarry and other outstanding work would soon be complete.

The new canal-side wharf at Black Park, taken in 1904, showing that the track had been extended to serve the main basin. A boat awaits loading with granite chippings. Note the crane chain and hook above the page header.

Unknown Wrexham photographer. Collection: David Ll. Davies

The towpath bridge over the entrance to Black Park basin, which passes underneath the Great Western Railway, with a rare view of part of the basin – a boat is moored at the wharf and in the background is the old Ceiriog Granite Co. slab works. The wharf in the top photograph is to the right of the bridge.

Courtesy: Ian L. Wright
Ex. Derek Chaplin

The appendix to section 14 of GWR service timetables for 1st January 1935 includes working instructions for the GVT main line private sidings at Chirk. These would have altered little, if at all, over the years.

Courtesy: Bob Pearman

Shunting in Glyn Valley Sidings.

The normal position of the hand points leading from Machine Siding to Middle Road and Tip Road at the Black Park end, and from Machine Siding to Tip Road and Machine Siding to Middle Road at the Chirk end, is for the Machine Siding, and these three pairs of points must always be set for the Machine Siding and locked by pin, cotter and padlock, except when shunting operations by G.W. engine are being carried out in the Middle Road and Tip Road. The key of the padlocks is in the custody of the Glyn Valley Company.

Before shunting operations are commenced the Glyn Valley Company's representative must, before unlocking the hand points, satisfy himself that the Middle Road and Tip Road are clear of any road vehicles, and he will be responsible for preventing any road vehicles entering upon those sidings until the shunting is completed and the three hand points are locked in the normal position.

Clearances Glyn Valley Stone Siding.

Notice Boards worded as under :—
    "Engines must not go beyond this point"
have been fixed at each end of the wharf on the Glyn Valley stone siding, and engines working on the siding must not pass beyond the points referred to.

Black Park Signal Box plan, drawn from the original GWR drawings, as approved by Col. Rich R.E. of the Board of Trade, showing the two GVT standard-gauge private sidings where they rejoin the Down main line. Approval for the use of the sidings was given in October 1887, enabling the GVT to bring in materials direct to their site for the reconstruction and afterwards to provide an interchange for traffic. Chirk Signal Box plan is shown in chapter 7 page 192–193.

© Gordon Rushton 2010

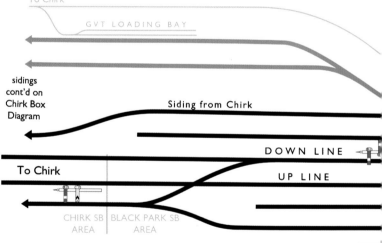

CHIRK AND BLACK PARK.

Black Park Down Refuge Siding.

This siding is accessible from the Down main line at Black Park and from the Up main line at Chirk. It is 506 yards long, and will hold a train of 72 wagons. Guards of Down trains shunted into this siding must be careful not to allow their trains to back foul of the Glyn Valley Sidings at the Chirk end.

It is available from the Black Park end during the time Black Park box is open, and from the Chirk end on weekdays only, whilst Chirk box is open.

The hand points leading from the refuge siding to the Glyn Valley Sidings at the Black Park end are secured by bolt and padlock, and the key is kept in Black Park Signal Box.

When the Shunter requires to use the points leading into the Glyn Valley Sidings, he must obtain the key from the Signalman, and during the time the key is out of his possession the Signalman at Black Park must not shunt a second train into the refuge siding, or accept a train from Chirk to run over the siding to Black Park.

The Shunter will be responsible for securing the points by locking them in their normal position, and he must return the key to the Signalman as soon as the work is completed.

Wagons deposited in the Glyn Valley Sidings must be left clear of the refuge in all cases.

Before a train or portion of a train is allowed to enter the refuge siding at the Chirk end, the Chirk Signalman must obtain the permission of the Black Park Signalman on the telephone, and should the train be withdrawn he must advise the Black Park Signalman accordingly. Particulars must be entered in the train register books at Chirk and Black Park and the times recorded.

In the event of there already being a train on the siding at the Black Park end, the Chirk Signalman must verbally instruct the Guard that the refuge is occupied and the Guard must remain in his van and signal the Driver back so that he may stop clear of the other train. The Chirk Signalman must also exhibit a caution signal to the Driver as he passes the box.

During the time that a train is on the siding at the Chirk end and the Black Park Signalman requires to shunt a train he must advise the Chirk Signalman and satisfy himself that there is sufficient room to hold the train, and before he allows the train to set back he must verbally instruct the Guard that there is another train on the siding. He must also exhibit a caution signal to the Driver as he passes the box. The Guard must remain in his van and signal the Driver back so that he may stop clear of the other train.

During fog or falling snow, only one train must occupy the refuge siding at a time.

BLACK PARK
SIGNAL BOX
SIGNAL PLAN

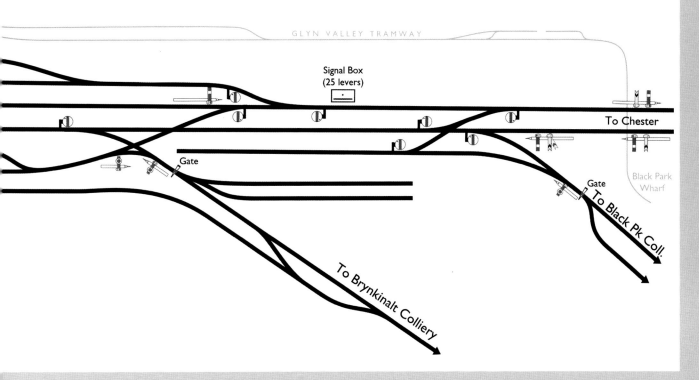

GLYN VALLEY TRAMWAY

Signal Box
(25 levers)

To Chester

Gate

Black Park Wharf

Gate

To Black Pk Coll.

To Brynkinalt Colliery

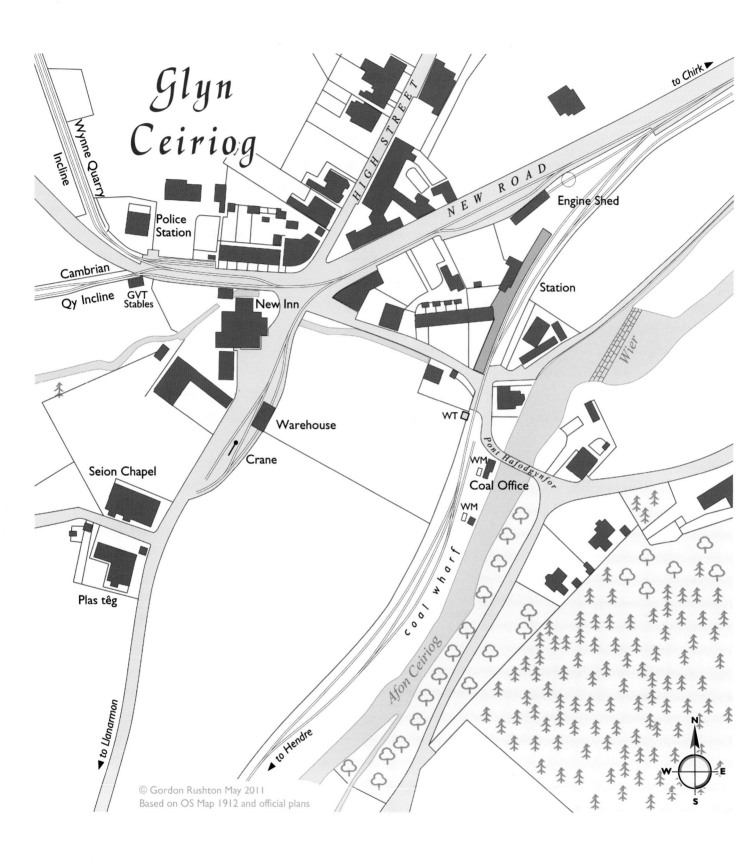

Glyn Ceiriog

Incline

Wynne Quarry

Police Station

Cambrian

Qy Incline

GVT Stables

New Inn

Warehouse

Crane

Seion Chapel

Plas têg

to Llanarmon

to Hendre

HIGH STREET

NEW ROAD

to Chirk ▶

Engine Shed

Station

Wier

WT

Pont Halodgynfor

WM

Coal Office

WM

coal wharf

Afon Ceiriog

N
W   E
S

© Gordon Rushton May 2011
Based on OS Map 1912 and official plans

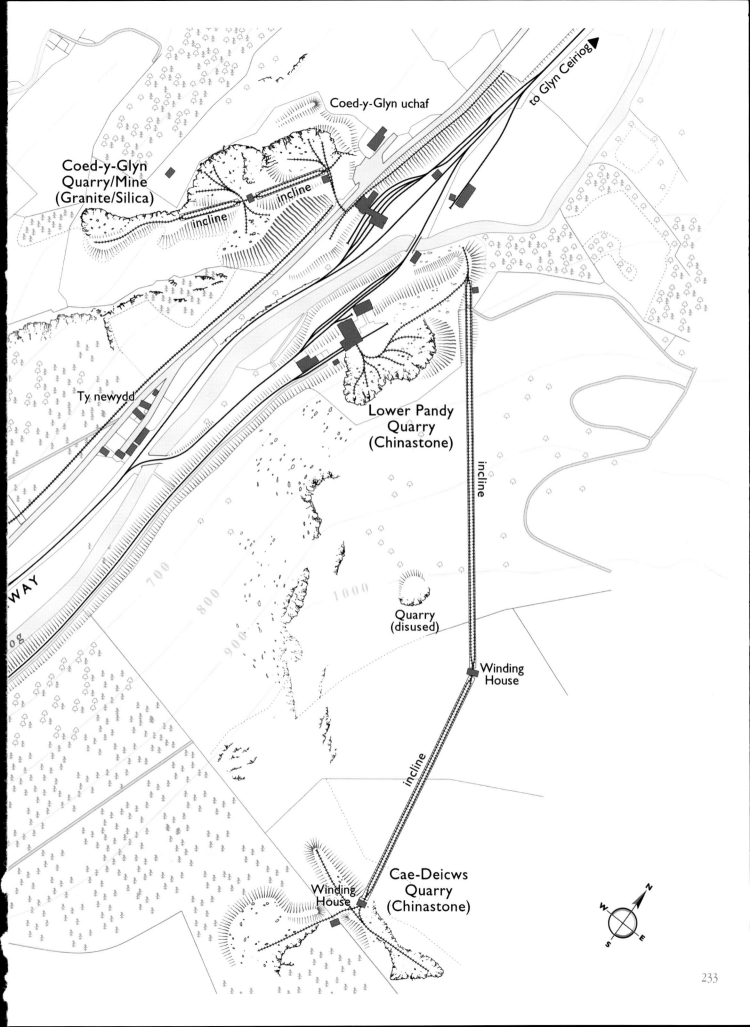

Coed-y-Glyn uchaf

Coed-y-Glyn
Quarry/Mine
(Granite/Silica)

incline

incline

to Glyn Ceiriog

Ty newydd

Lower Pandy
Quarry
(Chinastone)

incline

700

800

900

1000

Quarry
(disused)

Winding
House

WAY

0g

incline

Winding
House

Cae-Deicws
Quarry
(Chinastone)

N
W   E
S

233

Chirk Station

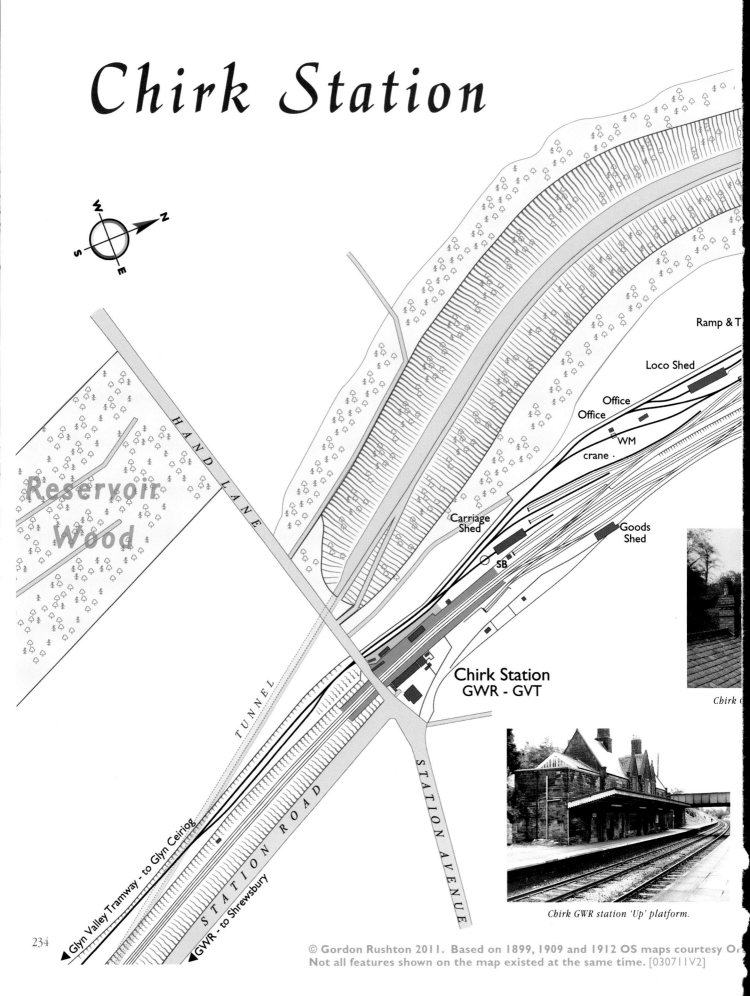

Reservoir Wood

HAND LANE

TUNNEL

STATION ROAD

Glyn Valley Tramway - to Glyn Ceiriog

GWR - to Shrewsbury

STATION AVENUE

Ramp & T

Loco Shed

Office

Office

WM

crane

Carriage Shed

Goods Shed

SB

Chirk Station
GWR - GVT

Chirk G

Chirk GWR station 'Up' platform.

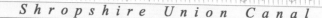

Shropshire Union Canal

SB

Carriage
Shed

Stores

Smithy

Carpenters

Repair
Shop

pplers

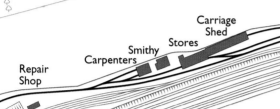

Chirk GVT station, looking towards Hand Lane Bridge and the GWR on the left.

GVT station (left) and GWR station (right).

GVT engine shed and (right) the granite loading ramp.

GVT smithy.

GVT station carriage shed.

GVT engine shed and coaling stage.

GVT yard carriage shed.

nance Survey, and other sources.

Photographs: H.C. Casserley, David Ll. Davies, H.G.W. Household, WRRC and collection John Milner.

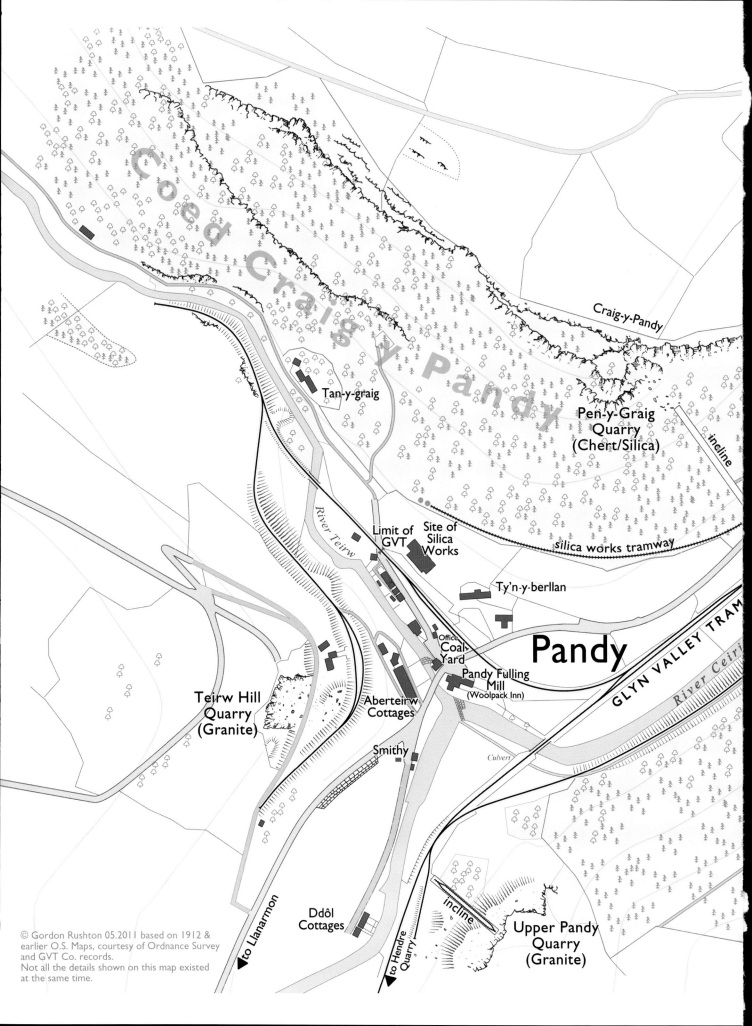

Coed Craig y Pandy

Craig-y-Pandy

Tan-y-graig

Pen-y-Graig
Quarry
(Chert/Silica)

incline

River Teirw

silica works tramway

Limit of
GVT

Site of
Silica
Works

Ty'n-y-berllan

Pandy

GLYN VALLEY TRAM

River Ceiri

Office
Coal
Yard

Teirw Hill
Quarry
(Granite)

Aberteirw
Cottages

Pandy Fulling
Mill
(Woolpack Inn)

Smithy

Culvert

incline

to Llanarmon

Ddôl
Cottages

to Hendre Quarry

Upper Pandy
Quarry
(Granite)

Hendre Quarry

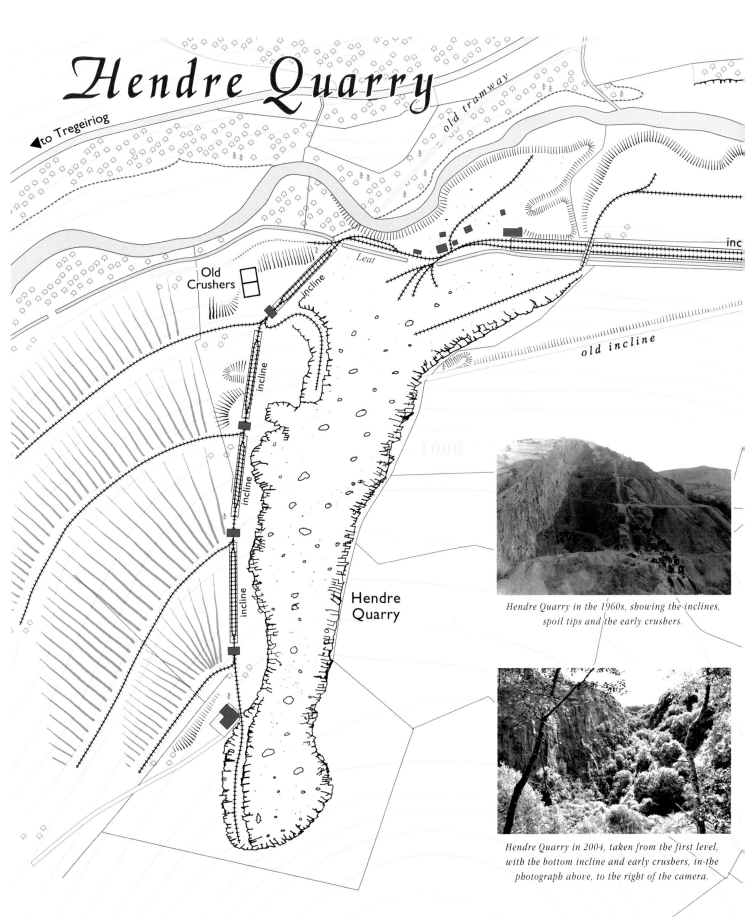

to Tregeiriog

old tramway

inc

Leat

Old
Crushers

incline

incline

old incline

incline

incline

1000

incline

Hendre
Quarry

*Hendre Quarry in the 1960s, showing the inclines,
spoil tips and the early crushers.*

*Hendre Quarry in 2004, taken from the first level,
with the bottom incline and early crushers, in the
photograph above, to the right of the camera.*

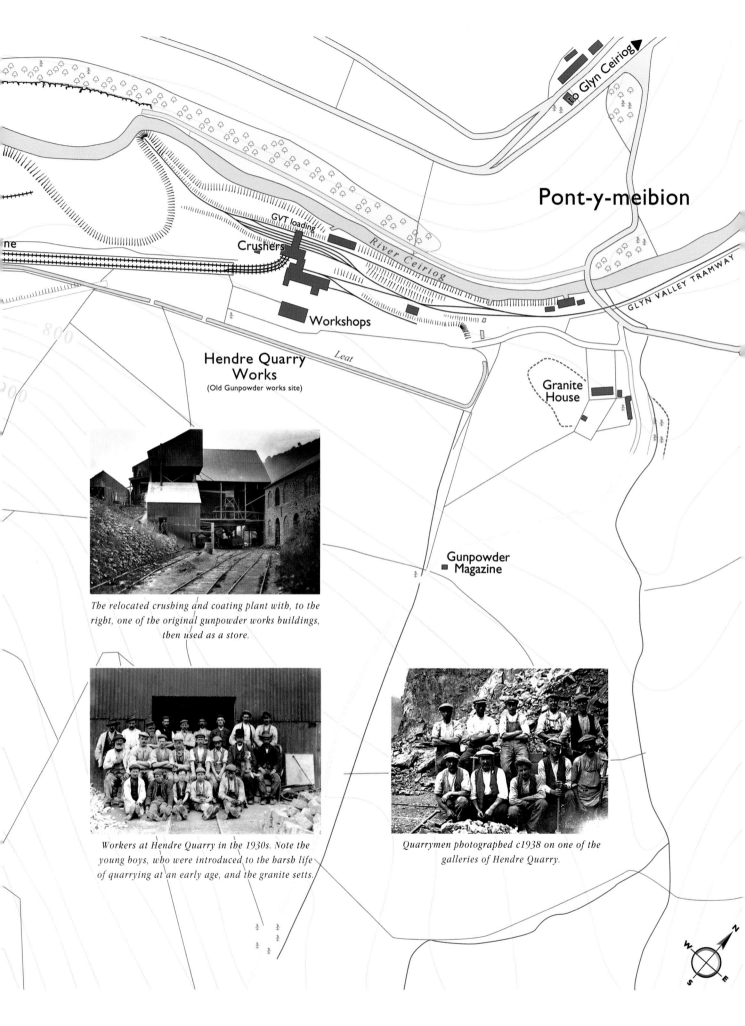

to Glyn Ceiriog ▶

Pont-y-meibion

GVT loading

Crushers

River Ceiriog

GLYN VALLEY TRAMWAY

Workshops

Hendre Quarry Works
(Old Gunpowder works site)

Leat

Granite House

800

900

Gunpowder Magazine

The relocated crushing and coating plant with, to the right, one of the original gunpowder works buildings, then used as a store.

Workers at Hendre Quarry in the 1930s. Note the young boys, who were introduced to the harsh life of quarrying at an early age, and the granite setts.

Quarrymen photographed c1938 on one of the galleries of Hendre Quarry.

Chapter 10

The Final Drive Forward
1889–1890

The main traffic expected on the converted GVT was 'Down' traffic of stone and slate from the quarries, but provision also had to be made to re-establish and expand the 'Up' traffic of coal, grain, building materials and general goods. By the beginning of 1889, agreements were in place for the GVT Co. to purchase extra land to provide *additional sidings for coal and other traffic … at various points on the line*' and, by the end of March that year, Sir Theodore Martin was able to state in his Chairman's Report that: *'Land has now been obtained, sufficient for sidings and wharfage accommodation … and this item of expense has now been closed.'*

At Pontfadog, a strip of land situated between the road and the river, measuring about half an acre, had been purchased from Richard Lewis of Tynyfron for £57 10s. 0d. to enable a long siding to be built, and at Dolywern, the triangular plot measuring about a quarter of an acre, at the junction of the Llwynmawr road with the main road, had been obtained for £55 from Samuel Hughes, to enable the company to provide a small goods yard.

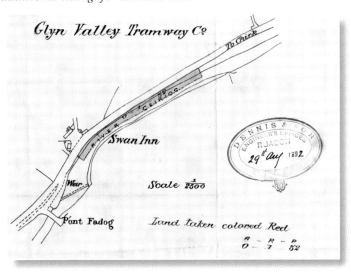

Plan dated 1892 showing the land purchased at Pontfadog for the construction of a siding. This was eventually converted to a loop.

Collection: John Milner

A coal yard was planned at Pandy, which would not only serve the local community, but also the two villages higher up the valley, Tregeiriog and Llanarmon Dyffryn Ceiriog. The yard was to be reached by a short spur (150yds) from the tramway to the Llanarmon road, which it crossed on a level crossing, and entered land belonging to Tyn-y-Berllan Farm opposite the Woolpack Inn, formerly Pandy Mill. An Agreement dated 1st January 1889 shows that the additional one and a half acres of land required for the spur and coal yard was to be purchased from Messrs Agostino and Stefano Gatti of the Royal Adelphi Theatre, London.[1] One of the conditions of purchase was that, on the boundary between the coal yard and the farmland, the GVT Co. would *'forthwith erect and for ever hereafter maintain a good and substantial stone or brick wall of the height of five feet six inches from the surface of the ground'*. This wall was built of stone and some lengths still stand. The purchase price of £150 included another half acre or so of steeply sloping land between the main road and the tramway extension, about a quarter of a mile down river, which was required by the developers of Coed-y-Glyn Quarry for loading hoppers. Where the spur joined the extension main line, a storage loop was installed and, at the coal yard end, it was later connected (c1892) to the Teirw Hill Roadstone Quarry's own tramway, which accessed the quarry via a bridge over the River Teirw and a 'Z' reverse up the steep side of the valley.

[1] See chapter 9 for details of the Gatti brothers and their involvement at Pandy.

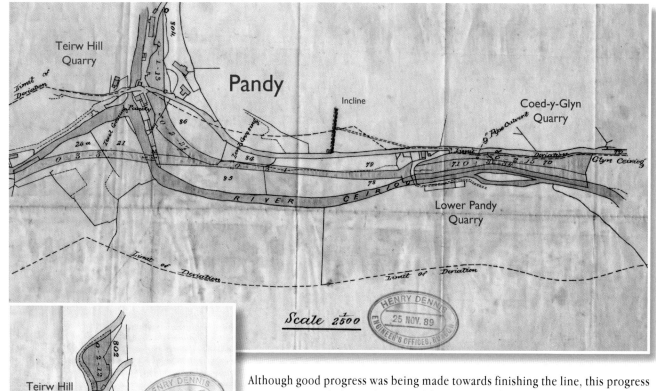

Top: *The extent of the land purchased by the GVT Co. from the Gatti brothers for the tramway, as built through Pandy, including the spur to the coalyard and its connection to Teirw Hill Quarry.* Below: *Extra land was purchased by Henry Dennis on behalf of the Teirw Hill Roadstone Co. Ltd to link the spur with the quarry tramway.*

Collection: John Milner

Although good progress was being made towards finishing the line, this progress was continuously being hampered by a string of complaints arising from the close monitoring of the works by local inhabitants, including complaints passed on to the BoT that steam locomotives were being used for unlicensed traffic. In response to enquiries from the Board, the GVT Company's secretary, Edward Williams, stated on the 4th January 1889 that steam power was being used for construction purposes only and took the opportunity to request a further inspection of the tramway:

'I am desired by my Directors to state that up to the present no passenger traffic has taken place on the Glyn Valley Tramway and that, although steam power has been used, such has been necessitated for ballasting and other purposes in the construction of the line, which is now rapidly approaching completion. I am further requested by my Directors to request that your Board will kindly allow one of your inspectors to pay the line a visit with a view to making his report and they would respectfully suggest a day not earlier than the 19th inst. be selected for the purpose.'

However, the company found that it still had to satisfy a series of demands from the local authorities, as well as those from the BoT, before a full licence to operate a passenger service would be granted.

Following the complaint made by the Surveyor of Denbighshire County Council to the BoT in December 1888, about the way in which the tramway had been constructed, in particular, where the alignment of the road had been altered between Pontfaen and Chirk, John Jackson of Caeangwynion, Chirk, who was the Surveyor for the Parish of Chirk, had also complained to the BoT. He had gone one stage further and served Notice on the GVT Co., giving it fourteen days to respond to his request for the erection of a screen between the tramway and the road, along the upper section of the Pontfaen–Chirk bank, to prevent horses being frightened, which in turn posed a danger to *'passengers on the Glyn Valley Highway'*. Jackson, who had described himself as: *'a large farmer'* who knew *'horses and their habits well'*, was aggrieved by the fact that the GVT Co. secretary had issued but a simple acknowledgement of his Notice and that the company had chosen to ignore it.

In respect of horses being frightened by the engines, Major-General Hutchinson of the BoT informed the GVT Co. in March that it was essential that the new highway from Chirk–Pontfaen should be adequately fenced along its southern side, so as to prevent frightened horses being driven over the edge and down the steep slope into the valley below, along with their drivers and load. The GVT Co. secretary was quick to point out that the fencing of this length was nothing to do with the company, as it was the responsibility of the highway authority. Ordnance Survey maps of the period show that the Wem & Bronygarth Turnpike Trust had never fenced this particular length of its road.

Hutchinson recommended a screen of 90ft in length, with a height of not less than 5ft 6in above track level, between the tramway and the road at the point where the tramway, hidden from view, gradually emerged to run level with the top of the retaining roadside wall, and that wherever practicable shrubs should be planted to screen the tramway from the road. He considered that, in view of the GVT speed restriction on the GVT of 8 miles per hour, a screen was not necessary along the whole length of the upper portion of the Chirk–Pontfaen road, because it would create a further danger, as the engine driver would then be unable to see the horses on the road!

The Llangollen Highway Board and the Chirk Parish Road Authority eventually accepted the responsibility for the erection of the fencing on the roadway. The former fulfilled its obligation during 1889, but the latter did not, refusing to do so until the GVT Co. erected the screening to its satisfaction. The Chirk Authority's refusal to act was to cause even bigger problems when Denbighshire County Council later took over its responsibilities for the road.

At this time, the GVT Co. was still in serious financial difficulties, with many outstanding debts and liabilities. A list of these, compiled at the end of January 1889 and confirmed as correct by Mr Dennis and Mr Williams on the 15th February, amounted to £12,726 12s. 8d. This included £657 required to complete work on the two unfinished Griffith Griffiths contracts, £300 owed to Jevons & Son for work already completed on the extension to Hendre, £250 for extra works still to be done and there was still £411 16s. 0d. due for interchange facilities already installed at Chirk and Black Park. The list contained the names of more than 20 suppliers of construction materials and equipment with outstanding invoices, totalling in excess of £600.[2] Croom Johnson was still owed £40 for *'pulling up old rails'* and £100 for removing the workshops from Pontfaen. Rolling stock on order, included 20 wagons (£400), 2 brake vans (£106),

The Agreement between the GVT Co. and the Gatti brothers, of the Adelphi Theatre, London, for the sale of the additional land required for the spur and coal yard at Pandy.

Collection: John Milner

[2] See Appendices 6 and 8 for details of suppliers.

Looking along the road towards Pontfadog, this postcard illustrates the uniqueness of the Glyn Valley Tramway; very much a 'railway' in its own right, apart from the fact that it ran alongside the road, flanked on the other side by the picturesque River Ceiriog.

Collection: Graham Greasley

2 passenger cars (£150), as well as the second locomotive at £1,150. Solicitors and land valuers were due in excess of £3,800, some of it for work done in 1887, and the extra land required to build the Pandy spur, valued at £150 had yet to be paid for. The debit on the company's capital account at the bank was £1,300 and a debt to the Ceiriog Granite Co. of £2,000 for operating the line was still outstanding.

On 18th February 1889, a circular had informed shareholders that *'a sum off £9,000'* was immediately required *'to pay off a sum of £2,000 due to the Ceiriog Granite Co. and other liabilities to complete the line and fit the same with a second engine and rolling stock to carry both passengers and goods'*. The directors were proposing *'to raise the same by issuing the remainder of the 5 per cent. Preference Shares at par, and the Ordinary Shares at 50 percent discount'*.

When the locomotive builders, Beyer, Peacock & Co. wrote to the company's secretary in March 1889, demanding payment for the locomotive *'Dennis'*, which was already six months overdue, and claiming interest accordingly, the GVT Board replied saying that the directors *'declined to entertain it'*. However, the matter was soon resolved, as *'Dennis'* was delivered to Chirk the following month.

The GVT now had its two new tram locomotives, which, as has already been related, enabled *'Belmont'* to be released from duties and returned to Snailbeach. However, expecting the tramway to handle the traffic anticipated with just two locomotives was a little ambitious, and resulted in a third one being purchased three years later.

In April 1889, the Secretary of the Llangollen Highway Board yet again complained to the Board of Trade about the loads of granite that the GVT Co. was moving over the tramway:

'The trains of granite so brought down during the last winter and spring are more than the Engine can control, or pull up in case of horses being frightened.'

He requested that the Board of Trade ensure that the public was amply protected from any dangers caused by the tramway.

Major-General Hutchinson re-inspected the GVT line later that month and his internal report at the BoT was detailed, there being numerous defects that he needed to see rectified before he could recommend to the BoT that the tramway was certified as fit for use. In the meantime, he permitted the use of the tramway for goods traffic only, subject to the following list of requirements being attended to as soon as possible:

1. Wing walls to be built either side of Lever's Bridge [their addition is clearly visible today].

2. A shelter for passengers to be provided on the GVT platform with access to the 'Down' platform of the GWR.

3. The road crossing at Dolywern to be provided with proper gates, to be kept closed across the tramway, other than when a train was due to cross.

4. Cattle stops to be provided where the tramway passes from private land to a public road.

Letter sent out by the GVT Co. secretary inviting potential investors to take up a new share issue in the company, in the hope of raising the extra capital required to pay off debts and complete the tramway.

Collection: John Milner

Glyn Valley Tramway Co.

DEAR SIR,

To pay off a sum of £2,000, due to the Ceiriog Granite Company, and other liabilities to complete the Line, and fit the same with a second Engine and Rolling Stock to carry both Passengers and Goods, a sum of £9,000 is immediately required. Your Directors propose to raise the same by issuing the remainder of the 5 per cent. Preference Shares at par, and of the Ordinary Shares at 50 per cent. discount.

I am requested by my Directors to ask how many Shares you will take, and whether Preference or Ordinary.

I shall be obliged by an answer by the 25th inst., that I may lay the same before my Board, who meet on the 26th.

I remain,

Your obedient Servant,

EDWARD WILLIAMS,

Company's Offices,   SECRETARY.

Upper Brook Street, Oswestry,

18th February, 1889.

5. *Longitudinal timbers to be fitted on all bridges and the track ballasted to protect the timber bridge decking from fire.*

6. *The decking over cattle creeps to be closed in and similarly ballasted.*

7. *Several sections of fencing, absolutely necessary for the safety of the public driving along the highway, in case of horses being frightened by the passage of engines, to be erected to the satisfaction of the highway authorities.*

On the operational side, he specified that trains must come to a complete stop at the Pontfaen, Pontfadog and Dolywern road crossings and the speed was not to exceed 4 miles per hour at the road junctions at Castle Mill and Roberts' Flannel Factory. During his inspection, Major-General Hutchinson had checked all the bridges with a test load and his verdict was that they were satisfactory and had minimal deflection under load.

Following the receipt of Hutchinson's inspection report, and with the objective of addressing the inspector's requirement to provide a shelter for passengers, the GVT Co. secretary, Edward Williams, had in May 1889 approached the GWR Co. to discuss the possibility of erecting a *joint Shelter Shed*, probably with the idea of persuading the GWR Co. to share the cost. No further action appears to have been taken and the GVT Co. eventually built its own waiting room with an attached office on the GVT platform.

Much of the outstanding work required was completed in June and on 4th July the GVT Co. secretary further advised the BoT that '... *the Glyn Valley Tramway will, in the opinion of the Directors of the said Tramway Company, be sufficiently complete for the safe conveyance of passengers on the fifth day of July*'.

Above: The Second Notice, sent by the GVT Co. secretary to the BoT, advising that the tramway would be 'sufficiently completed' for the carriage of passengers by 5th July 1889 – or so he thought!

Left: A GVT Co. cheque made out to Messrs Kerr, Stuart & Co., which was cancelled, perhaps due to the shortage of funds. What the GVT Co. purchased from Kerr, Stuart & Co. is not recorded, but it may have been for the two locomotive turntables.

Collection: John Milner

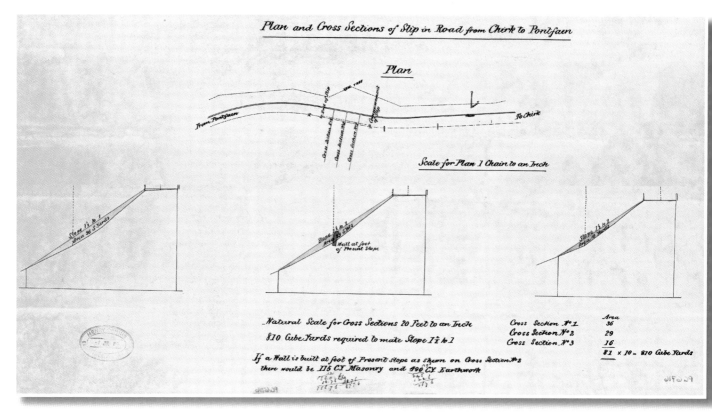

Plan and Cross Sections of Slip in Road from Chirk to Pontfaen

Plan

Scale for Plan 1 Chain to an Inch

Natural Scale for Cross Sections 20 Feet to an Inch

810 Cube Yards required to make Slope 1½ to 1

Cross Section Nº 1	Area 36
Cross Section Nº 2	29
Cross Section Nº 3	16
	81 × 10 = 810 Cube Yards

If a Wall is built at foot of Present Slope as shewn on Cross Section #2
there would be 115 CY Masonry and 490 CY Earthwork

The plan produced by Henry Dennis and dated 8th July 1889 showing the retaining wall and earthworks required to stabilise the slip that occurred below the Pontfaen–Chirk road, resulting in the road dropping where it had been modified as part of the GVT contract with Griffith Griffiths.

National Library of Wales
P782 – Robertson Map No.128

[3] Henry Dennis blamed the landslide on the poor workmanship by the contractor Griffith Griffiths, which was strongly disputed. Griffiths had taken the matter to the High Court, Queen's Bench Division in April 1889.

The tramway was duly inspected again that month but, yet again, the BoT withheld the certificate, this time until iron hurdle railings had been erected along certain lengths of the tramway and the abutments at Lever's Bridge on the Chirk Castle Estate had been put in good order. Furthermore, the BoT would not permit the carriage of passengers until a suitable passenger carriage had been provided. Drawings and specifications for *Tramway Passenger Cars* had been submitted to the BoT at the end of May 1889 and approved. The BoT were informed that carriages had been ordered and were now in the course of construction, although neither the quantity nor a date for delivery was stated. It appears that the GVT Co. was hoping to make use of the old horse-tramway open 'toastracks' and the Astbury closed coach for the time being, to postpone any outlay of capital on new carriages.

One problem, which had occurred at the end of 1888, of which both the GVT Co. and the road authority were fully aware, and for which the tramway company had included a sum for repairs in its estimate of capital expenditure for the year 1889/90, was a landslide on the embankment on the south side of the Chirk–Pontfaen road, at a location just to the Pontfaen side of the water trough, with the result that the road had also dropped.[3] It was urgent that the slope was stabilised and the road repaired.

The improvements and alterations to the road had been the contractor's responsibility under the earthworks contract for the new line from Pontfaen–Chirk, but Griffith Griffiths had had his contract terminated in September 1888, before the landslide had occurred, and was in dispute with the GVT Co. by the time remedial work was urgently required. Henry Dennis' solution was to build a retaining wall part way down the slope, top up the soil and raise the road level back to where it was. A 'hump' in the embankment on the valley side of the road, about halfway down the road from Chirk to Pontfaen, indicates where this wall was built. The drawing for the remedial work, prepared by Henry Dennis and dated 8th July 1889, indicates that apart from a retaining wall to stabilise the steep slope, an additional 810 cub.yds of soil was needed to lessen the steepness of the embankment. The road slip caused by the landslide was not the only problem on these steep slopes, because in January 1890 it was reported to the GVT directors that much subsidence was occurring on the embankments at Pontfaen because of the extra weight of soil due to the wet weather, which was also blamed on the failure of Griffith Griffiths to stabilise the steep slopes, as required by his contract.

The GVT Co. was still struggling to raise the finance to provide the facilities which were essential for its operation, and to further exacerbate the company's problems its bankers, The Old Bank, Oswestry, wrote to the secretary on 3rd August 1889 reminding him that the company's account was overdrawn to the extent of £2,870 and saying: *'We should be glad to hear from you and your Directors to what extent this account is likely to be overdrawn and for how long?'* At the Directors' Meeting on 10th September it was resolved to make a request for a £4,000 overdraft facility, which appears to have been granted, as the company proceeded with the purchase of additional equipment and the erection of buildings at Chirk.

Despite all the earlier arguments with regard to retaining the old portion of the tramway from Pontfaen to Trehowell for use by the colliery and brickworks on the Quinta Estate, this section of track fell into disuse during 1889, as a result of both these establishments having been closed down earlier that year.

Back in December 1888, Thomas Barnes had concerns about the profitability and the future prospects of the Trehowell Colliery and the brickworks, so had commissioned Nathaniel R. Griffith, mining engineer, of Westminster Chambers, Wrexham and Plasnewydd, Ruabon, to advise. The coal seams were exceptionally thin, less than 2ft in places, and sandwiched between beds of fireclay up to 6ft thick and the coal was described as being of *'very inferior quality'*. At the time, the colliery's

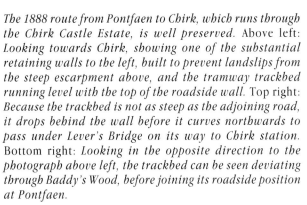

The 1888 route from Pontfaen to Chirk, which runs through the Chirk Castle Estate, is well preserved. Above left: *Looking towards Chirk, showing one of the substantial retaining walls to the left, built to prevent landslips from the steep escarpment above, and the tramway trackbed running level with the top of the roadside wall.* Top right: *Because the trackbed is not as steep as the adjoining road, it drops behind the wall before it curves northwards to pass under Lever's Bridge on its way to Chirk station.* Bottom right: *Looking in the opposite direction to the photograph above left, the trackbed can be seen deviating through Baddy's Wood, before joining its roadside position at Pontfaen.*

output was about 135 tons of coal and 150 tons of fireclay per week, the latter being mostly used by the brickworks on site. Of the brickworks, Nathaniel Griffith reported that it was not being run at full capacity and was capable of producing 40,000 bricks per week, although these and other products, such as drainpipes and floor tiles, were '*not of the best quality*' and would not '*command either a high price or a ready sale*'. Nathaniel Griffith concluded his report by saying that about £3,000 would have to be spent on the colliery and brickworks in order to boost production, and even then there would be no probability of this capital outlay being recouped. Also, he was of the opinion that Barnes would be unlikely to find a tenant for either the colliery or the brickworks. This report had given Barnes little encouragement to spend money on the concerns, so they were closed down and the plant and equipment sold at auction on 23rd May 1889.[4] At a GVT Co. Directors' Meeting in November 1889 of that year, it was resolved that the track on the Trehowell branch should be lifted, and 10 tons of the rail sold to Mr F.E. Rooper, of the Wynne and Cambrian Slate Quarries, at market price.

[4] Nathaniel Griffith Report – Hawarden Record Office Ref. D/DM/832/18

By the end of 1889, a decision had been made about providing the buildings and additional equipment and facilities that were immediately essential to the operation of the tramway. This enabled a detailed list of the company's liabilities to be drawn up by Henry Dennis on 5th December 1889, which totalled £2,937 8s. 6d. and showed that very little had been paid out for buildings and equipment during the previous year. The list revealed that most of the new buildings to be built at Chirk station were to be constructed from materials reclaimed from present buildings serving the horse tramway, perhaps accounting for the fact that the buildings at Chirk were an odd selection of architectural styles. Estimates were also included for the planting of trees along the new route from Pontfaen to Chirk, and for building a retaining wall along part of the same section, both of these having been requested by Major-General Hutchinson.

Additional comments, written in by Henry Dennis, included a request that the warehouse and 2-ton crane at Gledrid should be immediately moved to Chirk:

> '*This is required at once,*' he stated; '*we are much inconvenienced now with groceries, flannel, and much like damageable goods. This traffic is increasing.*'

The crane from Gledrid was moved to Chirk, but the warehouse was not moved in its entirety, because the bottom of the timbers was rotten, having been buried in the wet ground at Gledrid instead of being sat above ground level on a stone or brick foundation, as is traditional. It is likely that only those wooden side panels that were still in good condition were removed for use in buildings at Chirk, as the framework and the remaining timber side-panelling were later salvaged and reused in a building that survives in part to this day.

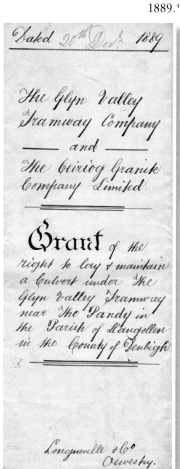

The Grant made by the GVT Co. to the Ceiriog Granite Co. giving it the right to build a culvert under the tramway at Pandy, for a leat to Lower Pandy Quarry – 20th December 1889.

Collection: John Milner

Traffic was on the increase and prospects for the tramway, as well as the valley community, looked very good indeed! There were plans for major developments at many of the quarries, both large and small, which would produce a significant increase in 'Down' traffic for the GVT, as well as regular employment for men in the valley. At the end of 1889, the former chinastone quarry at Pandy was reopened by the Ceiriog Granite Co. where the waste chinastone was to be crushed for use as railway ballast. The GVT Board agreed to install two turnouts in the extension to facilitate rail access into the quarry. On the opposite side of the valley, the newly formed Glyn Stone Company (taken over by the Glyn Granite Co. Ltd in 1894) had plans to develop Coed-y-Glyn Quarry and arrangements were being made with Francis Rooper, one of the proprietors, to provide GVT loading sidings. Further up the valley, land was being purchased on Teirw Hill, above Pandy, where a roadstone quarry was planned with a tramway down to connect with the GVT Pandy spur. Developments were also taking place above Glyn Ceiriog, where the Rooper partnership was opening up new slate beds in both the Cambrian and Wynne Slate Quarries, and installing modern machinery to increase output and once again provide the tramway with regular slate traffic. In anticipation of the increase in traffic from all these quarry developments, the

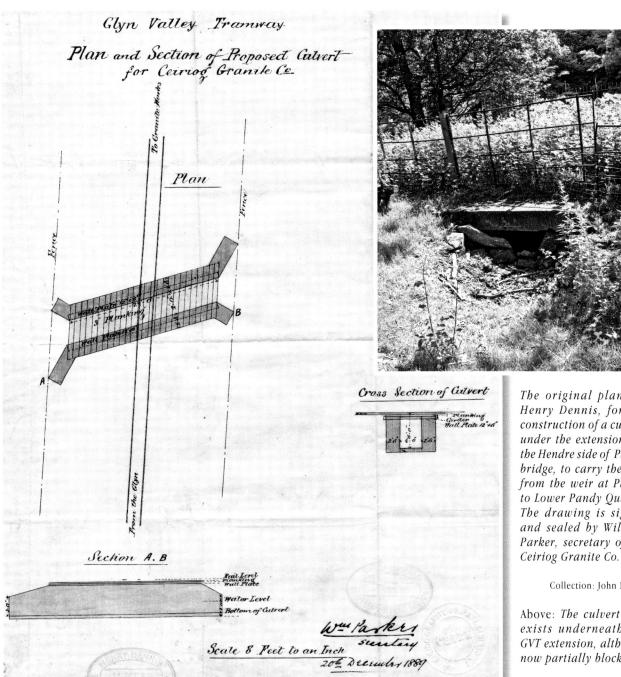

Glyn Valley Tramway.

Plan and Section of Proposed Culvert for Ceiriog Granite Co.

Plan

Cross Section of Culvert

Section A.B

Scale 8 Feet to an Inch
20th December 1889

The original plan, by Henry Dennis, for the construction of a culvert under the extension, on the Hendre side of Pandy bridge, to carry the leat from the weir at Pandy to Lower Pandy Quarry. The drawing is signed and sealed by William Parker, secretary of the Ceiriog Granite Co.

Collection: John Milner

Above: *The culvert still exists underneath the GVT extension, although now partially blocked.*

© John Milner 2010

GVT Co. agreed to increase its rolling stock by purchasing forty new wagons, from the Midland Railway Carriage & Wagon Co. Ltd.

In connection with its development of Lower Pandy Quarry, the Ceiriog Granite Co. requested the construction of a culvert under the extension, close to the Hendre side of the tramway bridge at Pandy. The culvert was to carry a leat from the existing weir in the River Ceiriog, which had served the former fulling mill (by this time converted to the Woolpack Inn), to Lower Pandy Quarry. The granite company was to be responsible for its construction and was to ensure that the tramway remained operational while it was being built. It was also to maintain it in perpetuity. The design for the culvert, dated 14th October 1889, had been drawn by Henry Dennis and, as with all structures on the GVT, it was well constructed:

With the GVT extension to Hendre Quarry at long last becoming reality, turnouts were installed to enable the Ceiriog Granite Co. to lay a loop line with sidings and reopen Lower Pandy Quarry, the then redundant chinastone quarry.

Collection: John Milner

'Side walls to be built of good sized local stones in mortar made with the best lias lime ... the bottom to be pitched with good flat stones ... wall plates to be of best pitch pine 12 inches by 6 inches ... to be fixed to the Masonry with good holding down bolts every six feet ... Planking to be of three inches thick of best Red Deal ... Two girders to be three lengths of Rails 75 lbs to the linear yard riveted together 10 feet long and well fixed on 4 good dimension stones at least 2 feet 6 inches by 12 inches by 12 inches each.'

William Parker, Secretary of the Ceiriog Granite Co. had signed the Agreement for the culvert on 20th December 1889, but the construction work did not start until the following summer. Today, the entrances to the culvert can be found among the vegetation covering the sides of the former trackbed and its route northeast across the adjoining land is still visible.

Throughout the rebuilding period, the accounts show little variation in receipts illustrating that the tramway continued to carry goods and minerals. In fact, there was an upward trend, which no doubt pleased the directors and shareholders alike, or at least distracted them from the other financial problems for a while. The quarries were now using the GWR line to transport their goods from Chirk, and a proportion of the incoming goods also came by rail. How the company managed to continue to operate the tramway while the reconstruction work was in progress, is an interesting logistical question!

The goods interchange at Black Park Basin had been in operation since July 1889 and, although some 300 to 400 tons of incoming goods for the valley were being transshipped to the GVT each month, outgoing goods traffic was only a small fraction of this, which led the SUR&C Co. to complain

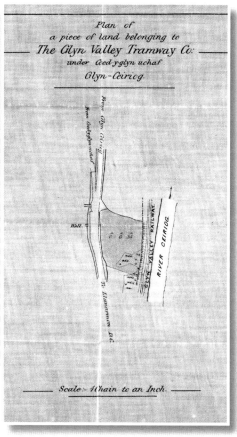

that the GVT Co. was favouring the GWR with its traffic. No evidence has been found of the granite wharf alongside the canal being in operation at this time. The concern of the SUR&C Co. is understandable because, at this time, canal companies throughout the national network were suffering fierce competition from the railways; their profits were falling and there was a general decline in waterways traffic. The adverse weather during the winter of 1889–1890 reduced tramway traffic and GVT Co. receipts, when work in the Ceiriog Valley granite and slate quarries had to be suspended.

The Annual Return for 1888 had listed one passenger coach, which is assumed to have been the closed Astbury one from the horse tramway.[5] In January 1889 two new coaches had been ordered from the Midland Railway Carriage & Wagon Co. Ltd, Shrewsbury, at a total cost of £150 and the Returns confirm that these had been delivered by the end of that year, increasing the number to three. The first of these new coaches was a 4-wheel centre-door clerestory saloon and the second a similar one, without the clerestory. A further coach, again from the MRC&W Co., Shrewsbury, was ordered by the end of 1891, this time being a narrow open one with end balconies and somewhat continental in style. It was possibly a cancelled order that the carriage company was prepared to offer to the GVT Co. at a cost of £85 12s. 0d. After 1891, the GVT Co. was to purchase a fleet of more conventional open and closed carriages for the tramway.

At the end of 1889, a List of Liabilities on the capital account up to December that year was compiled by the company secretary. This appears to be a list of unpaid bills, mainly from suppliers of materials and equipment, totalling £1,098 17s. 1d., to which has been added sums owing to Elias Griffith (£500), Ceiriog Granite Co. (£2,000) and the Old Bank (£4,000), as well as the sum of £3,000 calculated by Henry Dennis, on December 5th 1889, as the approximate total cost of works, materials and equipment immediately required to be paid for, in order to complete the conversion. The total of about £10,600 was offset by sums due from calls on shares, arrears of

A memorandum and plan from Francis Rooper to Sir Theodore Martin in respect of acquiring a piece of 'waste boggy hillside', opposite his Coed-y-Glyn granite mine, for the purpose of building a crushing and loading plant, which would give the mine direct access to the GVT for transporting its output.

Shropshire Archives
Ref: SA-IMG 46900-01
and 800/44C

[5] No Annual Returns for rolling stock were submitted by the GVT Company prior to 1888, the responsibility for so doing being that of the Shropshire Union Railways & Canal Co. up to 1881 and then the Ceiriog Granite Co. 1881–1885, both as operators of the tramway.

Over: *The second locomotive from Messrs Beyer, Peacock & Co., appropriately named DENNIS after Henry Dennis, was delivered in April 1890 and is here photographed later in life at Chirk.*

© Gwilym Hughes ex Caesar Hughes

Photo: © Gwilwym Hughes

The new station at Glyn Ceiriog not long after its completion, with the Wynne Slate Quarry in the background. The engine shed, large enough to house two locomotives, looks pristine, as does the station with its attractive platform lamps, paling fencing, nameboard and seat. To the left-hand side is the old ticket office from the New Inn terminus. Behind the station building is a string of bolster wagons with some rather long tree trunks on them, standing on roadside.

Collection: John Milner

[6] See page 220

[7] Ref. 'The Glyn Valley Tramway' by David Llewelyn Davies. Oakwood Press 1991.

calls and a deposit owing, in all totalling £475, indicating that the company was still short of more than £10,000 to pay for the conversion. A Summary of Capital Expenditure from March 1887 shows that £29,048 7s. 0d had already been paid out by December 1889.[6]

Passenger traffic on the horse tramway had ceased on 31st March 1886, but it was to be five years before the GVT Co. officially re-introduced the service. In the annual report for 1889, presented in March 1890, the chairman was optimistic about receiving BoT approval for its introduction, saying that following the opening of the service in the summer, he expected that passenger traffic '*may reasonably be expected to be not inconsiderable*'. However, his optimism was unfounded, as the company did not obtain the authorisation it required from the BoT, due to failure of the local road authority to erect some 200 yards of fencing along a length of the Chirk–Pontfaen road. This was the fencing that the BoT had deemed essential to prevent any horse that had become unsettled by the close presence of a steam locomotive, from going over the edge of the road and tumbling down the steep side of the valley.

In spite of the GVT Co. not having the certification from the BoT, some unofficial passenger working is said to have been operated during that summer of 1890![7] As the company had not yet taken delivery of any of the new coaches on order, the old ones from the horse tramway (the open toastracks and the closed coach) were probably used. None of these had been approved nor were they suitable for steam operation, although there is indisputable photographic evidence of the horse-tramway coaches being used at the time of the reopening in 1891. It is also possible that passengers were carried in open wagons with temporary seats fitted, as had been the practice in the early horse-tramway days and on other narrow-gauge railways in Wales.

The summer season was over before the BoT was able to authorise the carriage of passengers and, by this time, the GVT Co. itself decided it would be prudent to delay the reopening. The explanation given by the chairman in the Directors' Report for 1890, presented in March 1891, being that the company '*did not deem it advisable to open for Passenger traffic during the winter months* [1890–91], *as it would have been impossible to work much traffic except at a serious loss'*. The timetable/poster, announcing the opening of the tramway for passenger traffic, had been printed in anticipation of opening in November 1890, but the space for the actual day and date had been left blank – this was reused the following year with 'November' being crossed out and 'March', with the day and the date, written in.

During the early months of 1890, work had continued on the construction of buildings and facilities, at Chirk and elsewhere, in preparation for the opening of the line. The minutes of a committee meeting, held on 29th May 1890, confirm that it was resolved that the *'shed'* (presumably the old carriage shed) be removed from Pontfaen to Chirk and likewise, those on 12th July, that the company's stables from the New Inn, Glyn Ceiriog, be incorporated into new buildings at Chirk station. Both of these had been built for the horse tramway and were of typical SUR&C Co. construction, consisting of timber units that could easily be dismantled, moved and reassembled.

Despite unease in the boardroom, the Directors had no option but to move forward and provide the facilities and service that their customers required, even though the capital available was limited.

The GVT Co. had gradually been acquiring the additional rolling stock that it would need. In January 1889, twenty new wagons had been ordered at a cost of £400, along with two brake vans at £106 from the Birmingham Railway Carriage & Wagon Co., the first brake van having been delivered in June 1890. Earlier in the year, the same company had supplied five tar wagons at a cost of £19 10s. 0d. each, which would be used to carry tar from Chirk to the Ceiriog Granite Co., for the manufacture of tarmacadam.

During this time, the inhabitants of Tregeiriog, realising that the tramway was not being extended from Hendre up to their village, as authorised by the GVT Acts 1878 and 1885, were supporting complaints made by Denbighshire County Council against the GVT Company, in order to win support for their own cause. However, because of the shortage of capital, the GVT Co. was not in a position to extend the line further, but neither had it the authorisation to raise additional capital until after the tramway had opened for passenger traffic, so by supporting the County Council, which was delaying the opening of the line, the inhabitants of Tregeiriog, were effectively acting against their own interests and the whole situation became gridlocked.

Handwritten notices were sent out for GVT board or committee meetings. This example, sent to Samuel Smith, Town Clerk of Chester City Council, on 25th October 1890, was one of the last before the GVT Co. started issuing more formal printed notices for meetings.

Collection: John Milner

The completed tramway was almost a mile short of its authorised termination at Tregeiriog and the inhabitants, in true Ceiriog Valley style, had formed a committee that sent a petition to the Rt. Hon. the President of the Board of Trade in June 1889, signed by most of the population of Tregeiriog, Llanarmon and the surrounding area. The main grievance was that the GVT Co. had the authority to build the line to Tregeiriog, which would benefit an additional *'700 inhabitants'*, who were being deprived of a means of reaching Chirk station; they had also complained that they were being inconvenienced by the GVT Co. having rendered the road down the valley impassable.

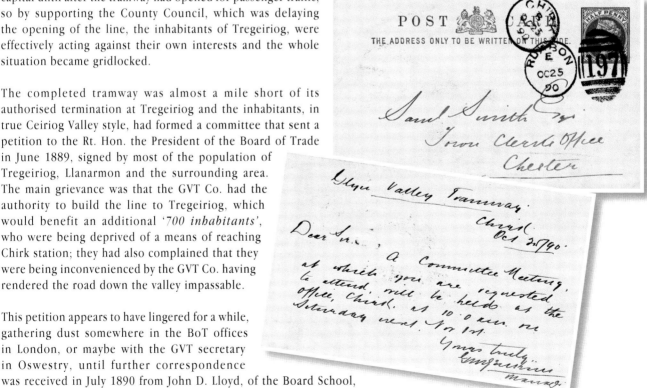

This petition appears to have lingered for a while, gathering dust somewhere in the BoT offices in London, or maybe with the GVT secretary in Oswestry, until further correspondence was received in July 1890 from John D. Lloyd, of the Board School, Llanarmon D.C., on behalf of the committee, complaining that the Ceiriog Granite Co. was the only beneficiary of the GVT line up the valley. In a letter dated 30th July, the GVT secretary, Edward Williams, advised the BoT that the GVT Co. was '*however prepared to extend it* [the tramway] *as soon as the people who say they want the line contribute the necessary funds*', adding that '*none of the Petitioners have contributed anything to the Company's funds*'. This sparked off some interchanges and finally an official response, from the GVT Co. secretary, on 11th August 1890:

> '*The complaint of the Committee of the inhabitants of Llanarmon Dyffryn Ceiriog ... is wholly without justification. No promise to take the Tramway to Tregeiriog was ever made by my Company, although they would have been quite ready to extend the line to that point if they had received any support from the district towards the expense. Not one shilling, however, has been locally subscribed, or any offer made of the necessary land upon reasonable terms. The Company have, with difficulty, obtained the capital to complete the line to its present terminus, and cannot undertake fresh obligations until the development of traffic on the line encourages them to extend it.*'

There was also unease at Glyn Ceiriog and, on the 21st July 1890, a public meeting of the inhabitants of Glyn Ceiriog and the neighbouring Parish of Glyntraian was held at the National Schoolroom, Glyn Ceiriog, to discuss the delay in opening the tramway for passenger traffic. The meeting was so well attended that the doors of the hall had to be opened to enable those outside, who were not able to get in, to hear the proceedings. All classes of society were represented from the clergy and ministers (all denominations), landowners, quarry owners, farmers, mill-owners and shopkeepers, down to the artisan and members of the labouring classes.

The meeting was chaired by Mr Francis Edward Rooper, of the Cambrian and Wynne Slate Quarries, who lived on-site at the Wynne Quarry from where he was responsible for the day-to-day running of these two quarries and was in the process of opening the Coed-y-Glyn stone quarry further up the Ceiriog Valley. He was the youngest son of George Rooper, a London solicitor, who was a GVT Co. director and the major shareholder of the Pant Glâs Slate & Slab Quarry Co. Ltd, who had recently come to the aid of the ailing Cambrian and Wynne Slate Quarries, injecting the finance that had been lacking to develop them into productive slate mines. He opened the meeting by stating that:

**Francis E. Rooper
1858–1939**

Owner of the Cambrian and Wynne Slate Quarries, the Coed-y-Glyn granite mine and, in 1900, the New Inn, which was renamed the Glyn Valley Hotel.

Courtesy: Angela James

Looking towards Chirk, the screening erected on the Pontfaen–Chirk section of the tramway as a compromise to satisfy the requirements of the BoT and the highways authorities. The telegraph poles alongside the road can just be seen beyond the fencing.

Collection: John Milner

The Ceiriog Valley at its very best. The Glyn Valley Tramway had left its dreary roadside existence and was diverted at Dolywern to cross the River Ceiriog on a new bridge, appropriately named The Queen Bridge, and enter the new station, which served both the local community and the Queen's Hotel, before returning to the roadside. On 14th March 1888, 'BELMONT', with a long train of ballast wagons accompanied by the crack of fog signals placed on the line, was the first steam locomotive to cross the bridge to the great satisfaction of the onlookers. The formation, the bridge and the station building all survive as a reminder of the days when this tranquil scene was disturbed by the regular rumbling of a train passing over the bridge.

© John Milner 2010

Right: *Plan of the land purchased from Thomas Allen Hughes, dated 11th December 1889. Note that the GVT Co. was obliged to install an 18" pipe from the river above the weir into the field, for watering livestock.*

Below: *This view of Glyn Ceiriog, taken from the Wynne Quarry, shows the Upper Mill (flannel). now demolished, and in front of it the GVT coal yard and the track sweeping away up the valley. In the foreground are the Glyn Valley Hotel (New Inn) and its stable yard. On Quarry Road (bottom right) empty GVT slate wagons await their 'elevation' to the quarries and further wagons can be seen standing at the old New Inn terminus. c.1900.*

Collection: John Milner

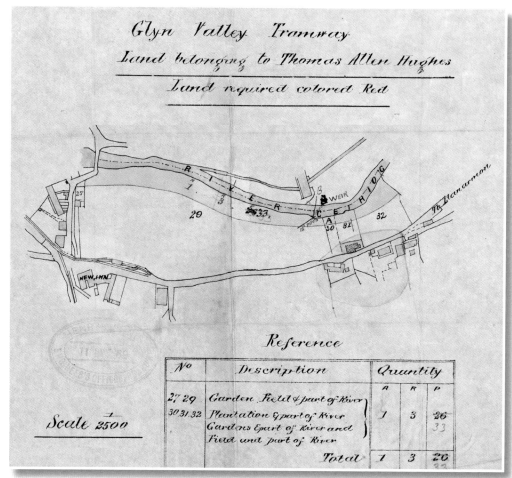

Glyn Valley Tramway
Land belonging to Thomas Allen Hughes
Land required colored Red

Scale 2500

Reference

No	Description	Quantity		
		A	R	P
27.29 30.31.32	Garden Field & part of River Plantation & part of River Gardens & part of River and Field and part of River	1	3	26 33
	Total	1	3	26 33

'We are not met here tonight in the interests of the Tramway Company, but in those of the inhabitants of the Glyn Valley generally and of these two parishes in particular. We have all heard the question constantly asked, and have asked the same thing ourselves, "Why is the tramway not carrying passengers?" and "When is it going to be opened for passenger traffic?" At last we determined to ascertain the facts, and these facts I now beg to lay before you.'

He explained that the reason for the delay was the failure of the Chirk Parish Road Authority in the execution of its obligations, which in turn was preventing the BoT from issuing the certificate for the carriage of passengers – much akin to present-day bureaucracy! He said that Major-General Hutchinson had inspected the line, but had withheld the certificate until the road between Pontfaen and the top of the ascent to Chirk was properly fenced on the side that dropped away into the valley below, as there was concern that horses on the road could be frightened by the appearance of a train and would bolt over the unfenced side of the road, plunging them into the valley below. At the time of the meeting there were some 200 yards still unfenced, which was the responsibility of the Chirk Highways Authority. Rooper told the meeting that: *'Two hundred yards of post and rail fencing, which at the outside would not cost more than half-a-crown a yard has stopped this line being opened for something like a year – (Cheers) – and it is that which is stopping the line from being opened at the present time.'* *'Shame, and hear, hear'* was the immediate response.

The Chirk Parish Road Authority was refusing to do this work until the GVT Co. had erected a screen between the tramway and the road, the argument being (as previously related) that if the horses could not see the locomotive then they would not be frightened by it. Major-General Hutchinson had been consulted and while he generally objected to any such screening, on the grounds that it was far more dangerous, as the horses would not be able to see the engine or understand where the noise was coming from, he did however propose a short length as a compromise. The GVT Company had erected this, but it had failed to satisfy the Chirk Parish Road Authority.

To make matters worse, the jurisdiction for the road had recently been transferred from the Chirk Parish Road Authority to the Denbighshire County Council, which had decided in its wisdom that a committee should be appointed to consider the problem – as County Councils often do! The committee duly decided that, irrespective of the Board of Trade Inspector's recommendation, an additional 690ft of the GVT section of track, from Pontfaen to Lever's Bridge, should be screened from the road, along with the implementation of a number of other requirements (all of which were later withdrawn). The response to the recommendation was blunt and to the point: *'We admit it is our business to fence the road, no one can, however, compel us to do so, and unless you erect this screen we shall not erect this fence, and you cannot open the line,'* to which the Tramway Company responded: *'A screen is not necessary, and the Government Inspector not only does not require it, but objects to it.'*

When the GWR branch was built from Gobowen to Oswestry in 1848, there had been a similar problem to that now faced by the GVT Co. The line leaves Oswestry on a high embankment running parallel to the road and the authorities there had insisted on a screen being erected, so that trains could not be seen from the road by horses. This was soon taken down, because the horses on the road were startled by the noise, but could not make out from where it was coming.

London barristers had been consulted by the GVT Co. over the question of whether or not they were obliged to provide the screening and it was their opinion that if neither the Act of Parliament nor the Board of Trade required such a screen, but the local authority wanted it, then the local authority was responsible for its erection and costs.

Also present at the meeting in Glyn Ceiriog was Mr John Davies, bailiff to Sir Theodore Martin, representing his master's interests, who said:

'If it had not been for Sir Theodore's pluck, perseverance, and money, the line would have gone to smash long ago – (Cheers); and if Sir Theodore was a bit disgusted and tired of

spending so much money on what he considered an ungrateful country they could hardly be surprised. They all there knew Sir Theodore, and what a liberal kind-hearted landlord he was. ... and though Sir Theodore was made a better offer pecuniarily for the [Cambrian] quarry he satisfied himself that his [the Chairman's] firm were the most likely people to carry it on, and to do good to the district – (Loud Cheers).'

Francis Rooper's concluding speech at this public meeting was befitting that of any Statesman and throughout he carried the support of the meeting with him:

'The shareholders have done nothing but quarrel between themselves. ... We know that if properly managed the line has a great future before it, but it is written in the oldest and best book ever written [the Holy Bible], "A house divided against itself shall never stand." We venture to advise the Glyn Valley Tramway Shareholders to peruse that book before their next meeting – (Laughter). This tendency to quarrel has, I fear, extended beyond the shareholders. However, we have nothing to do with all that, we who are chiefly concerned

With the extension to Hendre Quarry having been completed by the end of 1889, the GVT was now able to carry minerals direct from the quarries in the upper reaches of the Ceiriog Valley to the railhead and canal at Chirk. Long 'Down' trains were traditionally split at Pontfaen and brought up to Chirk in two sections. These two rare photographs show the two sections of a granite train, with SIR THEODORE in charge, climbing up through Baddy's Wood on the Chirk Castle Estate and heading for Chirk. Photographed in the latter years of the GVT.

Ken Nunn Collection
The Locomotive Club of
Great Britain

want the line opened for passenger traffic, and we will have it – (Loud cheers). There is one force we must all sooner or later bow to, a force that is greater than Statesmen or Parliament, greater than County Councillors or Tramway Directors, the force of public opinion. That force we must now bring to bear. We, in fact, say to all concerned, cease your bickerings and quarrellings, or, at any rate, if you can't cease from them, don't let them interfere with our interests. Consider a moment. Suppose the line was stopped, what would become of this beautiful valley. The Quarries would, of course, have to stop work, a very large sum now paid away in cash every month in wages would also cease. This money not only benefits this valley, but a great deal of it finds its way to Llangollen, Oswestry, and other neighbouring towns. Wales is often called a poor country. I say Wales is one of the richest countries in the world – (Cheers). Look around you; you all know the enormous amount of mineral wealth lying waiting to be realised in this valley. To get it capital is required. Now the long delay in opening this line has done an enormous amount of harm to this valley and to this district. People who invested capital up here have been disheartened and disgusted, and it can hardly be expected, after the treatment they have met with, that they will invest more here; others were ready to invest capital here, but they were not going to do so till they saw whether the tramway would continue working or not, and until it was passed for passenger traffic there was no certainty about its going on. This valley, if the line were stopped, would be like a big man with his throat stopped, it would soon be dead, so to speak. In conclusion, let me urge you all, wherever the good and prosperity of this valley are concerned, to let no difference, political, religious, or otherwise, divide you, but in all matters concerning the good of the place, pull together for the common good. If you do this in the future as in the past, and as you have done tonight, there is, I am sure, a great and prosperous future for the Glyn Valley and its inhabitants – (Loud Cheers).'

Glyn Ceiriog,

Llangollen,

22nd July, 1890

GLYN VALLEY TRAMWAY.

———

Sir,

In pursuance of a resolution passed at a Meeting of the inhabitants of the parishes of Llansaintffraid-Glyn-Ceiriog and Glyn Traian, of which I was Chairman, I beg to forward you a Report of the Proceedings containing the resolutions passed.

I am, Sir,

Your obedient Servant,

FRAS. E. ROOPER.

This was, and still is to this very day, the great spirit of the Ceiriog Valley!

Francis Rooper, as one of the principal industrialists in the Ceiriog Valley, was of course perhaps more concerned than most!

A motion was put to the meeting by a Mr David Roberts who said:

'The delay in opening the Glyn Valley Tramway for passenger traffic is most injurious to the interests of the inhabitants of the Glyn Valley and of the parishes of Llansantffraid-Glyn-Ceiriog and Glyn Traian and this meeting strongly urges upon all concerned to do all they can to enable this to be done without further delay – (Cheers)'. Speaking in Welsh, Mr Roberts said that he was *'old enough to have attended meetings for thirty years about a railway to the Glyn. The first thing for which they had agitated, was a road up the valley; they got it, and next they got a tram, and that night they were met to agitate for a passenger carrying tram. For thirty years he had been living in hopes of being carried to Chirk by rail – (Laughter)'.* Mr Jacob Morris, in seconding the motion, commented that: *'No visitor ever came to the Glyn without falling head over ears in love with it, and if visitors only had the opportunity of getting there, the Glyn would rival Llandudno and Llanrwst – (Cheers) – but now it was a kind of paradise lost.'*

The day after the meeting of the residents of Glyn Ceiriog and Glyn Traian held on 21st July 1890, Francis Rooper, who acted as chairman, sent a report on the proceedings to Denbighshire County Council, the directors of the GVT Co. and others, urging them to settle their differences and get on with opening the tramway for passenger traffic.

Collection: John Milner

The author endorses this sentiment, but as for Glyn Ceiriog being a rival to Llandudno, well, that is another matter. George Evans, Quarry Manager, expressed his view that perhaps once the tramway was open for passenger traffic, then '*People would not find it necessary to go to the môr* [sea] *when they could get at the moors in the neighbourhood of the Glyn – (Cheers).*'

The motion was carried more than unanimously, as some people put both hands up!

A Report of the meeting was forwarded the next day to the Denbighshire County Council, the tramway directors and others concerned. Ultimately the County Council had to comply, but not before causing extensive delays and expenditure to the GVT Co., and damage to the industries in the valley. To add to the strife, the County Council also complained to the BoT that there was no check on the speed of the trains being run, as the engine driver was able to override the automatic speed control fitted '*... as was done on the occasion of General Hutchinson's visit*'.

While all this was going on, Francis Rooper and his fellow quarry owners were incurring heavy transport costs, because the tramway facilities were still not complete and were unable to cope with the demand. He argued that if the GVT Co. reduced its tariff by 6d. per ton then that would release a huge sum of money for reinvestment in the quarries. There was also concern that the GVT Co. was not providing a reliable service, a local builder, Ellis Hughes, complaining that he had to pay three or four men to stand idle, because the GVT had not delivered materials on time.

Whether or not public opinion had any influence on events we may never know, but by the end of 1890 the problems of previous years were resolved and the Directors were now, at long last, working in harmony under the chairmanship of Sir Theodore Martin. In his report for 1890, presented in March 1891, he was able to advise the shareholders that the Board of Trade had finally given its consent to the opening of the Glyn Valley Tramway for passenger traffic. The past year showed a credit balance of £271 12s. 8d. on the net revenue account, which must have been a little encouragement to those who invested in the tramway. Early in 1891, an issue of £8,300 in 5 per cent Debenture stock successfully cleared the debt to the bank and provided some additional capital required to complete the work.

Although much criticism had been made of Henry Dennis, it has to be recognised that, had it not been for his continuous financial support and his services as its engineer between 1886 and 1890, the Glyn Valley Tramway would have been in the hands of the Official Receiver long before the latter date. This fact was recognised by the GVT Board and, at their meeting in March 1891, it was resolved that:

> '*The sum of £1,000 to be voted to Mr Henry Dennis, in recognition of his important service to the Company, and in re-payment of the outlays incurred by him on their account as Managing Director from 1st October 1886 to July 1890.*'

As a retiring director, he was unanimously re-elected at the Annual General Meeting of Shareholders which followed, having relinquished his managerial responsibilities to George Morse Jenkins, who had been engaged to fill the post of joint Company Secretary and Manager of the tramway, at a salary of £140 18s. 0d. for 1891.

After this, all the bickering and arguing gradually settled down for the time being. The industries in the valley, at long last, had a steam-operated means of transport, which was about to open for passenger traffic as well, but that was not all, as the valley was given another means of communication. Early in 1890, Denbighshire County Council had given the Postmaster General its consent for the erection of '*a line of poles and wires along the Glyn Valley main road*' from Chirk to Glyn Ceiriog; the valley was entering the new world of telecommunication, albeit telegraph at this time, as the telephone did not arrive in the valley until c1920, with the exception of an internal system installed in the slate quarries by the Glyn Slate Co. in 1899![8]

8 See '*Slates from Glyn Ceiriog*' by John Milner. Ceiriog Press 2008.

Chapter 11

Reopening for Passenger Traffic
1891–1903

With the Annual General Meeting of the Glyn Valley Tramway Company due to take place on 24th March 1891, the Directors were conscious that they could not again face the shareholders and make excuses for not having the tramway open for passenger traffic. Every effort was made to provide the minimal facilities necessary to start the service, and on 11th March of that year, a notice appeared in the local press:

'The Glyn Valley Tramway will be opened for passenger traffic on Monday next [16th March]. With the exception of Sundays, when there will be no trains, there will be four Up trains, and three Down trains daily. On Wednesdays, however, a special train will take the place of one of the ordinary trains, and run somewhat later both ways.' [1]

[1] Wednesdays have always been the traditional market days in Oswestry.

In its 18th March 1891 issue, *The Oswestry & Border Counties Advertizer* gave a full account of the grand opening:

OPENING OF THE GLYN VALLEY TRAMWAY

'After anxiously looking forward for so many years, fraught with alternate hopes and disappointments, and almost despair, to the opening for passenger traffic, of a steam tramway from Chirk to Glyn Ceiriog, the good people of Chirk and neighbourhood and of the pretty valley, in which the winding waters of the Ceiriog pursue their way, have now reason to be thankful for what is undoubtedly to them an inestimable boon. The advancing claims of civilisation, in respect of more rapid, cheaper, and altogether more convenient methods of conveyance, to and fro, in Welsh country districts, have as far as this part of the principality is concerned, been met in a very advantageous and practical manner, and there is now no reasonable doubt of the success of the policy promoted by the Directors. On Monday, when the line was opened, there were abundant and striking evidence of the feelings of lively satisfaction with which the railway is welcomed. Running from the siding adjoining the Great Western Main Line at Chirk, the route of the tramway is practically the same as that of the old horse tram. There are five Up trains, and four Down trains, with slight provisional alterations, all of which stop at each of the stations, which number three, irrespective of Chirk and Glyn Ceiriog stations, and are Castle Mill, Pontfadog, and Dolywern.

The fares are as follows: Between Chirk and Castle Mill; single fare 3d., double fare 6d.; between Chirk and Pontfadog; 6d. and 10d.; between Chirk and Dolywern; 8d. and 1s. 2d.; and between Chirk and Glyn Ceiriog; 10d. and 1s. 6d. Trains do not stop to pick up

Photographed at Glyn Ceiriog by Lettsome & Sons, on the day that the tramway reopened for passenger traffic, is locomotive DENNIS with the new clerestory centre-door saloon coach, behind which is the horse tramway closed coach and what appears to be a 'home-made' open coach with pew-like seats. On the footplate James Hughes (left) from Snailbeach. Note that the engine shed had not yet been built.

Collection: John Milner

GLYN VALLEY TRAMWAY
COMPANY.

IMPORTANT NOTICE.

Opening OF THE Line for Passenger Traffic.

ON *Monday, March 16t.*

The above Line will be opened for the conveyance of Passengers, between

CHIRK AND GLYNCEIRIOG,

And on and from that date (Sundays excepted), the following Trains to and from Chirk, in connection with the Great Western Railway Company's Trains will be run:---

FROM	UP TRAINS. Times.					FROM	DOWN TRAINS. Times.			
	A.M.	A.M.	P.M.	P.M.	P.M.		A.M.	P.M.	P.M.	P.M.
CHIRK, arr. from Chester	...	9 28	1 30	...	5 15	GLYNCEIRIOG ... dep	8 0	4 45	4 55	7 10
" " "	...	9 46	...	...	...	DOLYWERN ... "	8 10	4 55	5 5	7 20
" " Shrewsbury	.	9 8	1 37	3 47	5 58	PONTFADOG ... "	8 20	5 5	5 15	7 30
						CASTLE MILL ... "	8 35	5 20	5 30	7 45
CHIRK ... ... dep.	6 55	10 0	2 0	3 55	6 10	CHIRK	8 50	5 35	5 45	8 0
CASTLE MILL ... "	7 10	10 15	2 15	4 10	6 25					
PONTFADOG ... "	7 25	10 30	2 30	4 25	6 40	CHIRK dep. for Chester...	9 8	5 58	5 58	9 37
DOLYWERN ... "	7 35	10 40	2 40	4 35	6 50	" " Shrewsbury	9 28	7 7	7 7	10 16
GLYNCEIRIOG ... arr.	7 45	10 50	2 50	4 45	7 0					

The following Fares will be charged :

		Single Journey.	Double Journey.
Between CHIRK and CASTLE MILL	..	3d.	6d.
" " PONTFADOG	..	6d.	10d.
" " DOLYWERN	..	8d.	1/2
" " GLYNCEIRIOG	..	10d.	1/6

Children over Three years of age and under Twelve, Half-price.

Passengers intending to travel by any of the above Trains, must join at one of the places named, as the Trains will not be stopped between Stations to pick up or set down Passengers.

Each Passenger will be allowed to convey 60lbs. weight of personal luggage only, free of charge—**the same not being merchandise or other articles carried for hire or profit**; any excess above this weight will be charged. For the protection of their luggage, Passengers are requested to have their names and destination clearly stated upon, and properly fastened to each article. Notice is hereby given, that the Company will not be responsible for the care of the same unless fully and properly addressed with the name and destination of the party, nor for any article conveyed inside the carriages. The Company will not be responsible for articles left in any of their offices for the convenience of the owners, unless deposited in the booking office, and the fixed charge of twopence per package paid.

NOTICE.—Passengers should be at the Station five minutes before the time fixed for the departure of the trains. The times shown on this bill are the times at which the trains are intended to arrive at and depart from the several Stations, but the Company cannot guarantee these times being kept under any circumstances, nor be responsible for delay. The times of other Railways are inserted for the convenience of the public, but the Company do not guarantee their correctness, and does not hold itself responsible for any delay, detention, or other loss or injury whatsoever, arising off its line, nor for the arrival of this Company's trains in time for the nominally corresponding trains of any other Company.

March
Chirk, November, 1890.

G. M. JENKINS,
MANAGER.

T. OWEN, PRINTER, THE LIBRARY, OSWESTRY.

The Notices announcing the opening of the line for passenger traffic, were originally printed in anticipation of Board of Trade giving the GVT Co. approval to open the tramway in November 1890. Approval was not forthcoming and the Notices were manually amended for use in 1891.

Collection: John Milner

passengers between the stations, and any pedestrians who wish to join the train must do so at one of the stations mentioned. Each passenger will be allowed 60lbs weight of personal luggage only, free of charge, the same not being merchandise or other articles carried for hire or profit. The time occupied in running the train from Chirk to Glyn Ceiriog is 50 minutes, at the rate of eight miles per hour. There are two substantially built engines to be used on the line, manufactured by Messrs Beyer, Peacock & Company, of Manchester, and they have been christened 'Sir Theodore', and 'Dennis'. Sir Theodore Martin being the Chairman of the Board of Directors, and Mr Henry Dennis, New Hall, Ruabon, the Managing Director. It would at first appear that some difficulty might be experienced with regard to passing animals, such as horses and cattle on the highway, but the care exercised on Monday by the driver, Thomas [James] Hughes, and the fireman, John Morgan, when several horses were both met and overtaken, was sufficient to show that no danger is to be apprehended in this respect, and certainly not under ordinary circumstances.

The exact length that the trains run for passenger traffic is 6^1/$_2$ miles, but it is hoped that in time to come there will be an extension to Pandy, which will mean an addition of a mile.^{2} The Company have Parliamentary power to extend, also, to Tregeiriog, but we understand this step is not yet contemplated. The gauge is 2ft 4^1/$_2$ inches, and the travelling is accomplished with remarkable ease and comfort, there being a total absence of jolting except when the driver is suddenly compelled to moderate the speed. One of the new coaches, used on Monday, together with one of the old ones and an open car, was manufactured by the Midland Carriage & Wagon Company, Shrewsbury, and is of neat design and construction. The interior is nicely fitted up, and contains sitting accommodation for twelve persons. There are none of the divisions of Classes, first, second, and third, all parts of each coach being open for the use of everybody. In the summer we understand it is the intention of the Company to use low uncovered cars, with side doors, and these will form very comfortable means of conveyance to and fro. The tickets from picking-up stations to the intermediate stations can be obtained from the van at the rear of the train.

^{2} See chapter 9 page 212

There has already been a considerable amount of traffic in stone along the route, the tonnage being between 70 and 80 tons, and sometimes more, per day, and there is little doubt that with the development of the slate trade, the railway will become a busy and profitable commercial undertaking. The railway is within easy reach of the Chinastone and Granite Quarries at Glyn and Glyn Slate Quarry. An unloading wharf has been erected at Black Park, and the stone can either be brought from Glyn and transshipped on to the Great Western Railway or loaded on to the canal boats, and then carried to the intended destination. Thus it will be seen that an important connection will be formed between the well-known quarries and the commercial centres of the north.

On Monday, the first train being rather early, 6.35 a.m., did not carry many passengers, but the Up train at two o-clock and the other trains in both directions were extensively patronised. Amongst the early passengers were the courteous manager Mr G.M. Jenkins, Mr John Jones (Buenos Ayres), Mr John Clarke, Mr G.T. Allen, Ponsonby Arms, [Llangollen] and Mr Pryce Evans, Llangollen, Mr Oswald Fox (representing Mr Edward Williams, Oswestry), Mr David Roberts, Dolywern and a representative of the [Oswestry] Advertizer. When the two o-clock train left Chirk, there was an explosion of fog signals. At Pontfadog, the train was met by the Glyn Brass Band, and the musicians had some difficulty in finding sitting room, which was at length obtained in the slate trucks, much to the amusement of the passengers. At Dolywern there was a gathering of quite a hundred people, and the train became crowded to its utmost. When the train arrived at the Glyn, there was a large assembly of people, old men and women, young men and maidens and children, who hailed with expressions of great delight the first crowded train on the new system. The scholars from the National Schools, numbering 400, marched in procession to the little station near the New Inn, to meet the train, under the care of Messrs Hughes and Davies. When the passengers had alighted, the band struck up a merry tune, and led a long procession, which made its way into a spacious field alongside the main road, which was kindly lent for the occasion by Mr Jones, Hafod-y-gynfor. When passing into the field each scholar received an orange and a bun, the distribution of which was carefully undertaken by Mr Wynn, New Hall, Miss Hughes, Glanywern, and Mrs Jones, Hafod-y-gynfor. Cannon firing took place, and there was a little display of bunting. Sports, including races and football contests, were very much enjoyed, during which the band played a selection of music. The Committee who organised the rejoicing in such a successful manner consisted of Messrs D. Foulkes, the New Inn, Chairman, T. Allen Hughes, Post Office, Treasurer, T. Morris, Temperance Hotel, Secretary, D. Jones, T. Morris, New Mills, R. Edwards, William Edwards, Smithy, and R. Thomas. Before the 4.45 p.m. train left the Glyn, the train and its occupants were photographed by Messrs Lettsome and Sons, of Llangollen, Photographers to the Queen.

There will be no running of trains on Sundays. On Good Friday a special train will leave Chirk at 11.30 a.m. and will return from the Glyn at 4.35 p.m. in connection with the Eisteddfod to be held there that day.'

At the Annual General Meeting, just one week later, Sir Theodore Martin (chairman) was thus able to report that, to the satisfaction of the directors, the tramway had been opened at last, and was now fully operational. Although mention was made that further capital expenditure was required, to the extent of an estimated £3,500, it was not pointed out that the rolling stock and facilities of the tramway were still far from being adequate to operate a reliable and profitable service.

This early postcard, of about 1905, with its incorrect photo tint interpretation of the colours of the coaches, van and locomotive SIR THEODORE, shows a mixed train bound for Glyn Ceiriog standing at Pontfaen halt, having just crossed the road from Baddy's Wood. This new location was much less convenient for the residents of Pontfaen than the old horse-tramway station. They now had to walk down to the road bridge, cross the river and then up the valley towards the Chirk fish hatchery. Below are typical tickets of the steam era (a comprehensive selection is to be found in Part 2 of this work).

Collection: John Milner

The following extract from the Traffic Receipts provides a summary of the level of passenger, goods and mineral traffic for one week ending 10th April 1891, shortly after the tramway was opened for passenger traffic:

Passengers from Chirk		68
" " New Inn		79
" " Intermediate Stns.		89
Total for Week		**236**
Revenue		£7 3s. 10½d.
Total Goods/Mineral Traffic 'Up'		30 tons
Total Goods/Mineral Traffic 'Down'		326 tons

Having finally opened the line for passenger traffic, the GVT Co. faced obstruction from its neighbour, the Great Western Railway. The latter had erected a barrier between their respective platforms at Chirk *'causing great inconvenience to GVT passengers wishing to transfer to and from the GWR trains'*. It had been a requirement of the BoT that the GVT platform had direct access to the 'Down' platform of the GWR, for the convenience of passengers changing at Chirk. The GVT Co.'s secretary made representation to the GWR Co. and the matter was resolved, the barrier being removed and replaced by a gate.

Just over a month after the grand opening, the GVT was to become entwined in a drama more befitting Pinewood Studios than the peaceful Ceiriog Valley, and it is worthy of being related in full, as written in the *Llangollen Advertiser* dated 1st May 1891:

'GLYNCEIRIOG – Exciting Capture of Card Sharpers.

On Wednesday evening, April 22nd, the village and neighbourhood was considerably excited by the capture here of a gang of gamblers by the Oswestry police. The 7.10. Down train had left the station in proper time, but about twenty minutes later considerable alarm was caused on hearing the engine whistle and the train coming backwards with the guard's van first. Crowds of people collected immediately in the station, to discover to their surprise that one of the carriages of the newly arrived train was occupied by a posse of police in charge of several strangers. It appears that the prisoners had induced Mr. Evan Evans, Derwenlas, Isygarreg, near Machynlleth, when travelling on the GWR between Wrexham and Ruabon, to lay money on the three-card trick, and in a very short time pocketed the sum of £7 2s. 0d. of his money. At Ruabon, Evans changed his compartment, and at Gobowen the prisoners left the train and proceeded in the direction of Selattyn, while Evans informed a policeman, who happened to be on the platform, of the circumstances. The officer took the train immediately for Oswestry, and reported the case to Supt. Langford who, with P.S. Perry and another officer, gave chase, and at Gobowen came upon the track of the tricksters, who had gone up the Ceiriog Valley. They found them waiting for the train at the Queen Inn [Dolywern], but did not arrest them until they were seated in the railway carriage, when a scuffle took place, and the assistance of the engine-driver and a bystander was demanded in the Queen's name. The Mêlée, as might be imagined, caused considerable alarm to a female – the only other occupant of the carriage – whose screams brought out the village squire of Dolywern who, with promptitude came to the rescue with an old constable's staff and handcuffs, which had done duty under his great-grandfather. Having succeeded in handcuffing the prisoners together, Supt. Langford got the train to steam back to Glyn, in order to get assistance of P.C. Morris. From there they took the train to Oswestry, where, on Friday, the prisoners were charged before magistrates, but were dismissed, the offence having taken place outside the jurisdiction of the court. They were, however, immediately re-arrested, conveyed to Wrexham and on the following day charged with fraudulently obtaining £7 2s. 0d. by means of the three-card trick. Two of the prisoners were discharged, and on Monday the others, who gave the names of John Williamson, baker, Liverpool, and John Willey, nut hawker, Birmingham, were committed to the Quarter Sessions for trial. Mr R.H. Ellis, of Oswestry, appeared for the prisoners.'

It had been reported in the *Llangollen Advertiser*, on the 20th September 1889, that '*a granite quarry of great dimensions and of superior quality has been found on the land of the Venerable Archdeacon Thomas of Meifod*'; this land was situated on the opposite side of the valley to Hendre Quarry, just south of the River Teirw. The report said that a line for a tramway had been marked out up to the quarry and that construction of this from the GVT at Pandy coal yard was expected to start at an early date. In order to make the connection the quarry tramway had to cross the Pandy–Nantyr road, pass over land owned by Messrs Agostino and Stefano Gatti and then over the River Teirw. On June 2nd 1890, on behalf of the promoters of a company to be formed to work the quarry, Henry Dennis had purchased about half an acre from the Gatti brothers for the sum of £39 13s. 6d., to enable the connection to be made with the GVT line at the coal yard.

The Teirw Hill Roadstone Company Ltd. was incorporated on the 9th July 1891 (No. 34395) and was promoted by Sir Theodore Martin KCB and Henry Dyke Dennis (son of Henry Dennis), along with George E. Woodford, an accountant from Ruabon; William Edwards, a mining engineer of Oswestry; Harry Croom Johnson, the railway contractor of Wrexham, who had undertaken the track-laying for the recent conversion of the GVT line to steam; and Frederick Starr, a waterworks engineer of The Groves, Chester.

The line was built and quarrying on Teirw Hill was started, employing a handful of men but, for some unknown reason, the enterprise was not a success. A Notice published in the *London Gazette* on December 13th 1895 reported that an Extraordinary Resolution had been passed at a meeting of The Teirw Hill Roadstone Company on 11th December that: '*It has been proved to the satisfaction of the Company that the Company cannot, by reason of its liabilities, continue its business … and that the Company be wound up voluntarily.*' The GVT Co. was able to obtain the small plot of land adjacent to the river Teirw, for the sum of £25, at an auction held at the Hand Hotel, Chirk on 11th February 1896. The rails, which were the property of the GVT Co., were still in situ.

On 8th September 1891, an Extraordinary General Meeting of GVT Co. shareholders was held at the offices of Sir Theodore Martin, 27 Abingdon Street, Westminster, London, to approve the raising of further capital of £5,000 by way of either loans or 5% Debentures. However, before proceeding, there was a legal issue to settle, because the balance of the authorised and, as yet, unissued Preference Shares had to be taken up first. To enable the capital to be raised, the directors agreed to take up this balance between them, which meant that the company had now created or sanctioned all the capital authorised under its Acts of Parliament (1870 & 1885), leaving no further balance available.

The title page of the Memorandum of Association for the Teirw Hill Roadstone Co. Ltd at Pandy.

Collection: John Milner

By the end of 1891, traffic had increased from a modest 6,013 tons in 1888 to a total of 28,039 tons, of which 27,392 tons was mineral traffic from the quarries. The following year, 1892, saw a massive 75 per cent increase in this tonnage, to a total of 49,022 tons, but this high level was not to be reached again until 1901. At the same time, passenger figures had steadily increased from 13,020 in 1891 to 15,623 in 1892. The GVT issued its first two season tickets in 1892, but they were never in great demand.

The year 1891 proved to be a successful one for the GVT Company, and must have encouraged the Directors and shareholders alike, as the Chairman's Report, dated March 1892, would suggest:

'We have the satisfaction of reporting that the steady increase of traffic during the past year encourages us to anticipate that this line will at no distant date yield a satisfactory return to the Shareholders, while proving, as it has already greatly proved, an increasing boon to the Proprietors and Inhabitants of the whole Valley.

The Roadstone Quarries, which at present are the chief traders on the line, have by the excellent quality of their Stone already secured a very extensive trade. Such is the demand for stone of this quality that it seems to admit of almost indefinite expansion. Another Quarry [Teirw Hill], close to the terminus of the line, is now being opened, and from this also a considerable increase of traffic may be expected. The growing use by the Railway Companies of Granite broken small, as ballast for their permanent way, may be looked to as a source of large traffic. We have for some months been carrying a supply of stone for this purpose to the Great Western and London & North Western Joint Railway Companies, from the Ceiriog Granite Quarry [Hendre], part of a current contract for twenty thousand tons.

The Cambrian Slate Quarries, where much has been done in the way of opening fresh chambers and providing improved machinery, are steadily increasing, and that company's slates are finding their way into the best markets. From this source increased traffic has arisen, and more may be expected.

The Passenger Traffic upon the line has already exceeded our most sanguine anticipations, even although it has been carried on under great disadvantage, our stock of Passenger Cars being at times quite unequal to the demands upon it. This defect is now being remedied by the construction of additional carriages, which will be ready to meet the certain large increase of visitors to the Valley by excursion trains and otherwise, when the fine weather sets in.

It has been necessary to meet the large and rapid development of traffic by ordering a new locomotive [GLYN], to be delivered this month. Thirty new coal and granite wagons have been bought during the year, and thirty more have been ordered, and also several passenger cars. The line has also been extended to the Pandy, where a depot for coal, grain, stone and other traffic will be established.

The siding space at Chirk has become quite inadequate for the accommodation of the traffic and its interchange with the Great Western Railway, and for this purpose more land will have to be purchased, which by our arrangement with Mr Myddelton Biddulph, we are entitled to acquire. Coal wharves and sidings, it has been found, must be provided at Pontfadog and the New Inn, and Waiting Rooms for passengers at the several stations on the line.

All these things, which cannot be delayed, involve an immediate outlay, which the company is now in a position to meet by the further issue of Debentures. Your Directors are confident

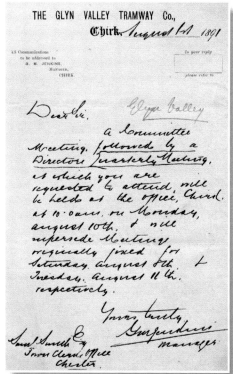

Up to 1892 either the GVT Co. secretary or manager laboriously handwrote notices for committee or board meetings but, with the tramway now settled down, printed notices of meetings for the year were issued.

Collection: John Milner

267

A third locomotive was ordered by the GVT Co. in December 1891 from Beyer, Peacock & Company (Order No.3500) and this was delivered in March 1892. Unlike the other two locomotives, it was supplied with a fully enclosed front spectacle plate and the foootplate was lengthened by 1ft to provide more room, no doubt as a result of operating experience with the first two locomotives.

Courtesy: John Amlot and Jonathan Clay

that the traffic, which will thus be brought upon the line, will yield a satisfactory return upon the expenditure.

It will be seen from the accounts that the revenue available for dividend, after paying Interest on the Debentures and all expenses of working for the last year, is £1,233. 18s. 0d. inclusive of the balance of £271. 12s. 8d. carried over from 1890. It is proposed, with the approval of the Shareholders, to apply £550. 3s. 7d. of this sum to the extinction of arrears of interest on the Preference Stock up to the 31st December, 1888, and to carry over the balance to the next Account.'

Theodore Martin
Chairman

As related in Sir Theodore Martin's report to the shareholders, the increase in traffic necessitated the purchase of a third locomotive. Appropriately to be named '*Glyn*', an order had been placed with Beyer, Peacock & Co. of Manchester (Order No.3500) in December 1891, for delivery by March 1892. It was similar to the first two locomotives, but was slightly modified and lengthened to give more footplate room.

Extra wagons had been needed to cope with the increased granite traffic from Hendre. At this time there was a growing use by the main-line companies of good-quality granite for ballasting their track, and the Ceiriog Granite Co. was currently supplying an order for 20,000 tons of ballast to the Great Western and the London & North Western Joint Railway Companies. As well as the thirty new coal and granite wagons mentioned in the report, three passenger coaches had been delivered during the last year and, in order to cope with the predicted further increase in traffic, thirty more wagons and four more passenger carriages were on order.

This second batch of thirty wagons was specifically required to cater for the expected traffic from the Teirw Hill Roadstone Quarry at Pandy, which was due to open in early 1893. An additional capital requirement of £2,500 to cover these, together with the building of waiting rooms for passengers, and coal wharves and sidings at Pontfadog, New Inn and Pandy, as well as the extension of the standard-gauge sidings at Chirk, was raised by issuing additional debentures.

By March 1892, the company realised that more land would soon be required for sidings and facilities at the Chirk interchange with the GWR, and it was agreed that it should take advantage of an agreement that was already in place with Mr Myddelton Biddulph, to purchase the adjacent field, situated between the GVT station site and the canal. This 5-acre field was conveyed on 10th November 1892, at a cost of £957, but the expansion of the GVT operation into it did not take place.

During 1891, the GVT Co. had made arrangements to obtain possession of the two end cottages, with their gardens, of the terrace (formerly known as Penybont Cottages) adjacent to the station site, which, at that time, were occupied by a David Davies and a Robert Edwards. The conveyance, dated 24th March 1892, shows that they were purchased from David Jones, a retired farmer, formerly of Hafod-y-gynfor, for the sum of £250. This row of cottages and the road soon became known as Railway Terrace and today is still referred to as such by the older generation. In c1923, Sir Henry Maybury who, as a young man, had worked as a manager for the GVT Co.'s contractor, H. Croom Johnson, and was by then the Director-General of Roads (Ministry of Transport), formally named the road Maybury Avenue.[3]

[3] see chapter 7 page 190

During 1892, the facilities for waiting passengers were enhanced when four small waiting rooms were built in traditional Ruabon red brick at Chirk, Pontfadog, Dolywern and Glyn Ceiriog, to cater for the comfort of passengers. Those at Pontfadog and Dolywern were each a single room, but those at Chirk and Glyn Ceiriog stations included both a waiting room and booking office accommodation. Each was furnished with bench seating around the walls and also had a fireplace.

The waiting rooms at Pontfadog and Dolywern survive to this day, as a reminder of the tramway, and together with the engine shed at Glyn Ceiriog, they were given Grade 2 Listed Buildings

The new locomotive GLYN standing alongside the unfinished platform and station building at Glyn Ceiriog in the summer of 1892. The train was made up of the two centre-door saloons, the 'narrow' open coach and two of the new closed coaches. To the right of the photograph is James Hughes.

Courtesy: WRRC
Ref: MML0625

Apart from the waiting rooms built at Chirk and Glyn Ceiriog stations, a further two were built at Dolywern (above) and Pontfadog (right). Both survive to this day and are registered as Grade II listed buildings. The Dolywern building has been minus its chimney for some time but, apart from some 'modern' rendering, it is still intact with its original bench seating and fireplace. The Pontfadog one is preserved by the New Glyn Valley Tramway & Industrial Heritage Trust and houses a display of photographs of the tramway. Note the differences in the architecture of the two buildings.

The date of construction is inscribed in a brick on the now rendered gable end of Dolywern waiting room.

status in 2003. Strangely, the waiting rooms at Pontfadog and Dolywern, although of similar size and configuration, varied in their architectural design. The station building at Glyn Ceiriog still stands and has been converted into a house, but the one at Chirk was demolished along with all the other tramway buildings on the site. In neither case was the small plot of land, on which the small waiting rooms at Pontfadog and Dolywern were built (each less than one perch in area), formally conveyed to the GVT Company! Legal possession was established by default, in 1936 for the one at Pontfadog and 1937 for Dolywern, in each case the company having to provide a statutory declaration of enjoying more than 12 years' undisturbed possession of the building and the land on which it was built.

The waiting room at Pontfadog was sold in 1936 by the GVT Co. liquidator to Robert William Ellis, of Pontfadog Post Office, and over the years has been used for a variety of purposes. Significantly, it is preserved for posterity as it was purchased on 12th January 1989 for £3,250 by the GVT Group, predecessor of the New Glyn Valley Tramway & Industrial Heritage Trust. It is now fully restored and houses a small exhibition of photographs and other documentation relating to the tramway. The NGVT&IH Trust is also in the process of restoring the engine shed at Glyn Ceiriog, with the intention of converting it into an industrial heritage centre. The waiting room at Dolywern, which was purchased by Denbighshire County Council from the GVT Co. liquidator in 1937, also remains intact and is now in private ownership.

An exciting event, as far as the employees of the GVT and inhabitants of Dolywern were concerned, occurred on the 5th January 1893. Some 23 men were invited (wives in those days were simply not invited to such functions) by Messrs Richard Edwards and David Roberts, of Dolywern, to a Christmas supper to '*mark the occasion of the completion of the pretty and convenient little station erected at Dolywern and as expression of gratitude to the proprietors and their employees*'. Guests arrived at 7 p.m. in '*Special*' trains from Glyn Ceiriog and Chirk and were treated to a supper of roast beef and plum pudding. Due to the station being far too small Richard Edwards gave the

Locomotive No.3 GLYN standing at the platform at Chirk station, not long after its delivery in 1892. On the footplate is John Williams, standing next to him 'Jack' Morgan and adjacent to the chimney James Hughes. Coupled to the engine are two of the new Midland Railway Carriage & Wagon Co. coaches. The sign just visible in the top right-hand corner is advertising the Queen's Hotel, Dolywern.

Collection: John Milner

SIR THEODORE with a train of empty 4-ton granite wagons having just left the river bridge at Pandy and heading for Hendre Quarry. Centre page is the old Pandy fulling mill (At that time The Woolpack Inn and today the Pandy Mill Glass Studio & Gallery), to the left is Aberteirw Terrace and above it the Teirw Hill Roadstone Quarry. Running parallel to the river and fenced off from the field is the leat, fed from the weir near Pandy Mill, which ran through a culvert under the GVT track and on to Lower Pandy Quarry to power the stone crushers. The Pandy spur to the coal yard can just be seen in the centre right-hand side of the picture. Photographed by John Thomas c1900.

Llyfrgell Genedlaethol Cymru
The National Library of Wales
Ref: (WlAbNL)00331774
Image: jth00486

The second locomotive to be delivered from Messrs Beyer, Peacock & Co. was appropriately named DENNIS after Henry Dennis. Here, it is seen at Chirk between the station and the engine shed. With there being no obvious sign of the engine being in steam, this may well be a photograph taken shortly after its delivery in April 1889.

The wavy pattern on the paintwork, was produced by cleaning down the paintwork with paraffin, coating it with tallow and wiping it over with a rag in an artistic fashion.

Collection: Dewi Parry Jones

GLYN VALLEY TRAMWAY.

Chirk Station, May 12th 1893

In your Reply, please give this Reference

The amount shown at the foot hereof stands to your debit in our Books; and as the Company require a prompt settlement of all sums due for carriage, I shall feel obliged by a remittance in course of post.

Messrs Brynkinalt Coll Co.

Chirk

I am, your obedient Servant, *S. M. Jenkins* fur J⁰ Owen.

Woodall, Minshall, and Co., Caxton Press, Oswestry

Date of Delivery.	Delivered Station from 2	Quantity and Description of Goods.	WEIGHT.				RATE.	PAID ON.			TOTAL CHARGE.		
			Tons	cwts.	qrs.	lbs.		£	s.	d.	£	s.	d.
May 10	Pant Glas Co	Coal	6				2/1						16	8

Paid May 24 G M Jenkins pro GVT

A GVT Statement in respect of the delivery of coal from Brynkinalt Colliery, Chirk, to the Pant Glâs Slate & Slab Co. Ltd at the Wynne Quarry, Glyn Ceiriog, on 10th May 1893.

Collection: John Milner

use of his kitchen for the event, after which they returned to the station where they were further treated to hot punch, beer and tobacco. Mr D. Roberts, who was elected chairman for the occasion, proposed a toast to '*The Queen*' and '*success to the GVT and to Mr Dennis the chief proprietor*' coupled with further toasts to Mr Jenkins, manager, and Mr Hughes, the senior engine driver.

The first two years of the new passenger service had shown that there was a good demand for it, but this was not the only herald of success. Apart from an increase in mineral traffic, there had also been a steady increase in the carriage of general merchandise, both up and down the valley, which included coal, farm supplies, beer for the local inns, building materials and general supplies for shops and private individuals. Although there was no arrangement for the collection and dropping off of goods at intermediate halts, parcels could be left at the end cottage at Castle Mill, once an Inn, only a few feet from the tramway. Most supplies were easily transported in open wagons, but it soon became apparent that more suitable vehicles were required to carry the more delicate and perishable goods, which needed protection from the elements. In 1889, tarpaulins had been purchased from

As a result of a steady increase in the carriage of general merchandise, both up and down the valley, the GVT Co. had two 4-ton vans built by the Midland Carriage & Wagon Co. of Shrewsbury at the end of 1893.

Collection: John Milner

a J. Marsden, at a cost of £24 8s. 11d., but these would not have provided guaranteed protection for the most vulnerable of the merchandise carried. To cater for this trade, two four-wheel closed vans were ordered from the Midland Railway Carriage & Wagon Co. and these were delivered in 1893. The amount of general merchandise carried in 1893 amounted to 1,370 tons in total, representing just over 3 per cent of the total freight carried. It is interesting to note that despite extensive hill farming in the Ceiriog Valley, no attempt was ever made by the company to carry livestock, which were predominately sheep and traditionally taken by road to Oswestry market, although the official GVT Returns for 1891 had a column headed '*Goods & Cattle General Account*'.

The directors were no doubt relieved to be able to report to their shareholders, at the Annual General Meeting in March 1893, that:

> '*We have the satisfaction to report such a steady increase in traffic during the past year, as fully confirms us in the anticipation expressed in our last report, that the line will at no great distance of time yield a satisfactory return to the Shareholders.*'

With the total expenditure on the Glyn Valley Tramway from its inception to date being £61,157, the shareholders were, no doubt, very relieved to hear that they might, at long last, expect a return on their investments. The only problem was that the revenue that was to become available for the payment of dividends was about to be wiped out by the settlement of arrears of interest on preference shares and debentures, most of which were held by the directors!

The encouraging upturn in mineral traffic of 1892 was suddenly dampened during 1893. Although the output of the slate quarries was on the increase and, to meet this extra traffic, six new slate wagons were ordered, overall there was a modest drop of 4,228 tons from the previous year's total of 47,990 tons, with the result that revenue had fallen. A decrease in traffic from the Ceiriog Granite Co., due to keen competition from quarries in areas closer to the user destinations, forced the GVT Co. to reduce its carriage rates in order to assist the granite company in its plight. The tramway company hoped that, by doing so, the CG Co. would be able to reduce the price of granite, making it more attractive to its distant customers. This was a gamble for the GVT Co., because an increase in its own revenue was dependent on the quarry attracting new customers and increasing its output.

The deviation and station at Dolywern showing the line protected by a cattle grid as it leaves the road from Chirk (top right), passing over a cattle creep (not visible) and sweeping around on an embankment in order to cross the new river bridge. Upon the insistence of the Board of Trade, gates were installed across the track next to the Waiting Room and all trains were obliged to stop before crossing the Llwynmawr road. Note the coal yard (bottom left), with a weighbridge and buffer stop, the latter probably from the old horse-tramway siding.

© Gwilym Hughes

While there had been a fall in mineral traffic during 1893, the passenger traffic was to increase steadily and, by the end of the year, the company had provided twelve new carriages, including one with First Class accommodation. This carriage was a somewhat extravagant item of capital expenditure on the part of the GVT Co. directors, as an average of only eight passengers per week throughout the life of the tramway ever travelled First Class! The passenger traffic had increased as a result of extensive advertising by the company, which had realised that as well as a need for a local service the valley also had a tourism potential.

However, it became apparent that in spite of the success of the passenger service, the survival of the tramway was dependent on the traffic generated by the granite quarries. The new-found enthusiasm of the GVT Co. directors in 1892 slowly evaporated, until, at the Annual General Meeting on 20th March 1894, Sir Theodore Martin announced that:

> 'The result of last year's working has, to some extent, disappointed our expectations. After paying the interest on Debentures, the Balance available for dividend is £1,376 13s. 1d. This compares unfavourably with the £2,191 19s. 7d. available last year for the same purpose.'

To reassure shareholders that it was not all bad news, Sir Theodore concluded his report saying that: 'The prospects of the undertaking, despite the abnormal decline of last year, are, in our opinion, most satisfactory.'

However, not only had the tonnages passing down the valley from the quarries fallen, but the quarry companies were not paying their dues. The GVT Co. was alerted to the worsening situation by way of a letter, dated 18th March 1895, from its accountant, G.H. Haswell, Chester, who wrote:

'We ought to point out to you that the Traffic Outstandings [Overdue customer accounts] *are somewhat abnormal. The following debts were owing at 31st December 1894 ex. Ceiriog Granite Co. £525 6s. 0d., Teirw Hill Granite Co. £210. 4s. 6d., Glyn Slate Co. £35. 8s. 9d., Glyn Granite Co. £80. 16s. 01d. and F.E. Rooper £0. 6s. 11d.'*

At that time, the Ceiriog Granite Co. had a maximum credit of £300.

Severe winter weather at the beginning of 1895 had added to the problems, completely closing all the quarries during January and February. The Ceiriog Granite Co., the GVT Co.'s major customer, was still experiencing particular difficulties due to the growing competition in the stone trade, and the GVT Co. was forced to further reduce the carriage rate on all tarmacadam sent out from Hendre Quarry to places thirty miles distant and upwards from Chirk, in the hope that this would stimulate an increase in this traffic. This action produced no result other than to further reduce revenue. In order to ameliorate its deteriorating financial situation, the GVT Co. had to continuously raise additional loans and debentures to continue operations, although modest dividends were paid to the Preference Shareholders.

The Ceiriog Granite Co.'s Hendre Quarry, as did some of the mills in the valley, relied heavily on water from the River Ceiriog to drive its machinery. As well as during the winter, the weather could also have an adverse effect on the quarries' production in the summer months, when, during a drought, water-powered machinery ground to a halt if there was a shortage of water in the river. The extremely dry summer of 1896 was no exception, as related in Sir Theodore Martin's report presented at the company's AGM on 2nd March 1897:

> *'... Our hopes* [of a large increase in traffic] *were disappointed, owing to the extremely dry weather during the months of June, July and August, which caused a great scarcity of water in the River Ceiriog, and had the effect of partially stopping operations at the Ceiriog Granite Company's Quarry, as that Company is dependent upon water power for working their machinery.'*

Visitors to Glyn Ceiriog today, and indeed the younger members of the community, have little realisation that had they been walking down New Road in the early 1900s they could have been confronted by a hissing monster, SIR THEODORE, trundling its way along the road, with its rake of little carriages and empty wagons. This photograph was taken c1920.

Collection: John Milner

Locomotive GLYN with a train consisting of the narrow open coach, two of the new open ones and the clerestory centre-door saloon, stands in Glyn Ceiriog station ready to depart for Chirk with what looks like a party in their 'Sunday best' who are having a special trip for the day.

Denbighshire Record Office
Ref. DD/WL/309/2 (39)

The prospectus of 1885 had estimated that ultimately the mineral and general goods traffic carried would reach 90,000 tons, producing £9,250 gross receipts per annum. It predicted the payment to shareholders of a dividend in excess of 10 per cent. Not surprisingly, the performance of the company was never able to reach these estimated figures. The finances were very finely balanced, with an average of 60 per cent of traffic receipts being from the carriage of granite. Thus the tramway company was heavily reliant upon the Ceiriog Granite Co., needing to carry a minimum of 50,000 tons of granite per annum, in order to break even and maintain a service – a vulnerable position for any company that relied heavily on one major customer. However, the next decade proved that this could be done but, even if foreseen in the 1890s, it would have been of no comfort to the disappointed shareholders of that time.

Although the GVT Act of 1885 had made provision for the conveyance of mail, '*as Her Majesty's Postmaster-General may from time to time require*', it was not until March 1898 that an arrangement was made whereby the company undertook to convey the whole of the mail between Chirk and Glyn Ceiriog. This resulted in a revised timetable, and an improved service in winter months. The Postmaster General paid the GVT Co. a fixed fee of £80/annum for the carriage of the Mail and, surprisingly, the rate was not to be revised for about sixteen years – try telling that to Royal Mail in 2011! The new timetable started in 1898 and at the end of that year the GVT Co. received the sum of £67 9s. 8d. for the carriage of mail on the tramway.

The conditions laid down by the Postmaster-General within the 1885 Act stipulated that any mail carried in a passenger carriage must not exceed the maximum weight allowed for the luggage of *ordinary* passengers, and that passengers must not be inconvenienced. To allow the carrying of unaccompanied letter mail in a carriage shows that there was not much concern for its security, but goods and parcels did have to be '... *in charge of an officer of the Post Office travelling as a passenger*', if they were not secured in the brake van. The same conditions that appertained to the main line railway companies for the carriage of mail were to apply to the tramway company. In practice, all the mail was actually conveyed securely in the brake van.

Because seven years had passed since it had received its full BoT licence to operate both the passenger and goods service, Spring 1898 was a critical time for the GVT Co. The tramway was due for its inspection by the BoT, due every 7 years, to ensure that all aspects of the infrastructure and mode of operation still complied with the regulations stipulated and conditions under which the original licence was granted – if not, then it would not be renewed until a further inspection had shown that all recommendations had been heeded.

Edmundson tickets were issued throughout the life of the GVT and there was a comprehensive range to cover all eventualities. Not even the Postmaster-General was able to escape!

Collection: John Milner

On 18th March 1898 Col. Yorke R.E. inspected the tramway, accompanied by George Morse Jenkins, the GVT Company's secretary and manager, W. Griffiths, chairman of Chirk District Council, and Mr Davies, the Council's surveyor. Highly unusual for the GVT, the report of the inspection was very positive. No complaints had been made and Col. Yorke was able to report to the BoT that: '*The permanent way, engines and rolling stock are in good order, and all the conditions relating to the traffic upon the line are the same now as when the tramway was last inspected ... I can recommend to the Board of Trade to authorise the use of*

GLYN at the new Glyn Ceiriog station with one of the new coaches (this one designated 'Smoking' and numbered '4' on the soleplate). James Hughes is in the centre on the platform. The gentleman in the coach seems determined that the photographer should get a good shot of him and has framed himself neatly in the door droplight! Note that the platform fencing has not yet been erected.

Collection: John Milner

steam power for a further period of 7 years.' Jenkins was quick to seize upon this positive response from the BoT and on 21st March he wrote to them, saying that in view of the GVT having worked the line safely for the past seven years, now was the opportune time for the Board to sanction an increase of the statutory speed limit of trains along the roadside from 8 to 10 mph, and to 12 mph where running off the highway. He further requested that the company be permitted to dispense with the level crossing gates at Dolywern station, replacing them with cattle grids. However, he did say that if, subsequently, there were any public objections, then the company would reinstate them.

Denbighshire County Council considered the GVT proposal to raise the speed limit and on 22nd April wrote to the BoT to say that they had no objection. By the 26th April the GVT had received its licence renewal for the use of steam for a further 7 years, but no response from the BoT in respect of raising the speed limit or removing the crossing gates at Dolywern. However, an internal BoT memo, dated 4th May, shows that it was prepared to grant the increase in speed, but that such increase of speed would: *'render the abolition of the gates at Dolywern station undesirable'*. The increase in speed was duly granted.

The concern of employers for the welfare of workers in the 19th century was very much a voluntary affair. Some employers took great care of their employees who, after all, were the backbone of the business but, by the end of the century, employers were starting to feel the brunt of the heavy hand of the law with claims resulting from injuries sustained at work. Colliery owners in the area, including Henry Dennis with his Ruabon Coal & Coke Co. Ltd., became increasingly concerned about their liabilities in respect of the welfare of their workers and the fact that they could face claims resulting from injuries at work. On the 2nd June 1898, the North Wales Employers' Mutual Indemnity Co. Ltd. was registered *'to indemnify members of the Company against proceedings, claims from employees etc.'*. Henry Dennis became the chairman. On the 11th July that year the GVT Co. was accepted for membership, making a subscription of £9. 13s. 4d.

The original horse-tramway terminus opposite the New Inn, in the early 1900s, which by then had been renamed the Glyn Valley Hotel. The hotel no longer had a passenger service to its door and guests with their luggage had to be transported to and from the new station at the bottom of Station Avenue. Note the trap outside the hotel with the luggage on it and across the road the box-like structure, which is the weighbridge.

Collection: John Milner

By early 1899, when Sir Theodore Martin presented the chairman's report for 1898, the difficulties of the early 1890s were all but forgotten, as he predicted a brighter outlook for shareholders with the news that revenue from both goods and passenger traffic was increasing. Also, the company was now in a position to pay the arrears of the 4% owing on Preference Shares for the half-year ending June 30th 1893. However, there was no good news, yet, for the Ordinary Shareholders, who still had to wait for a return on their investments.

Revenue from goods traffic had increased from £2,687 2s. 7d. in 1897 to £2,878 3s. 5d. in the following year and likewise passenger traffic from £590 12s. 5d. to £691 8s. 7d. The latter, Sir Theodore commented: *'may, no doubt, have been due in some measure to the fine weather; but the more the valley becomes known, the more its attractions will be appreciated, and a steady improvement in the number of passengers may fairly be anticipated'*.

By 1900, the traffic receipts showed an increase of 5% over the previous year, but the operational costs had risen by 16%. The reason for this sharp increase in costs was explained by Sir Theodore Martin in his report to the shareholders at the 1901 Annual General Meeting, who stated that: *'The cost of working has been considerably higher owing to the increased price of coal, coke, etc. A sum of £314 7s. 1d. had also to be paid in settling a claim for injury sustained by Mrs Parker of Chirk, through being thrown out of a Trap in passing over the Company's level crossing at Glyn.'* The GVT Co. had considered Mrs Parker's issue to be a little doubtful, but had decided to settle out of court, possibly aware that the crossing in question might not have always been conscientiously maintained for the safe passage of road traffic. Which crossing it was is not stated.

In the following year both passenger and granite traffic continued to show a steady and promising growth. This was sustained and in 1902 the mineral traffic on the GVT reached a peak of 59,525 tons. To cater for further growth in passenger and granite traffic, the company purchased another

The uppermost level of the Coed-y-Glyn granite mine, started by Francis Rooper for the Glyn Stone Co. in 1891. It was transferred to the Glyn Granite Co. Ltd in 1894 and became a vast network of huge caverns on several different levels, hewn out of solid granite. The output from this level was sent down an incline and across the Glyn Ceiriog–Llanarmon Road to crushers high above the GVT tracks and from where the screenings were despatched. In 1911, the Glyn Silica Co. took over the lease of the mine.

Collection: Angela James

The New Inn, which had become a well-known hostelry since the arrival of the first passengers on the Glyn Valley Tramway outside its doors in April 1874, was taken over in 1900 by a consortium headed by Francis Rooper. They formed The Glyn Valley Hotel Co. Ltd, which purchased the New Inn from the then owner, Thomas Allen Hughes, and from whom a mortgage was also arranged. Its name was changed to the Glyn Valley Hotel. Note the track in the bottom right-hand corner of the photograph, which is the link between the tramway on New Road and the quarry inclines up Quarry Road.

Collection: John Milner
(Documents courtesy Miss Einwen M. Jones)

two third-class closed coaches and twenty new granite wagons, at a total cost of £789 10s. 0d., from the Midland Railway Carriage & Wagon Company. These brought the fleet of coaches up to 14 and that of granite wagons to 205, there being no further additions during the rest of the tramway's life. In comparison with the number of granite wagons, the GVT had but a modest 26 slate wagons. However, although passenger numbers had continued to increase, reaching 33,127 in 1903, the expected increase in mineral traffic did not materialise and, instead, started to go into a decline that lasted for nine years.

By this time Francis Edward Rooper, who had arrived in the valley in the early 1880s, had become a well-established figure in the locality and was a respected member of the community. Slate traffic from Glyn Ceiriog had all but ceased when his father, George Rooper, had taken over both the Wynne and Cambrian slate quarries and Francis had been given the day-to-day responsibility of running both of them, living with his family at *Bronydd*, a house built for him on the Wynne Quarry site. By the early 1900s, the open quarries had been successfully developed into mines and together employed about 140 men, sending out on the GVT to Chirk in excess of 4,000 tons of slate annually. Francis had also taken over the development of the defunct Coed-y-Glyn granite mine, which was now employing about 40 men, and he was making moves to form a company to purchase the New Inn at the heart of Glyn Ceiriog. The New Inn was not only a reputable establishment for weary travellers, but was the terminus of the GVT up to 1888. By early 1900, its name had been changed to The Glyn Valley Hotel.

Francis Rooper was the major promoter of The Glyn Valley Hotel Company Limited, which was incorporated on May 3rd 1900 with capital of £5,000 divided into 5,000 shares of £1 each, for the purpose of acquiring '*as a going concern the business of Hotel Keepers and the other businesses (if any) now carried on at the Glyn Valley Hotel (formerly the New Inn) Glyn Ceiriog*'. The other promoters all had Chester addresses and included: Charles George Haswell, chartered accountant, Thomas Harris, merchant; George Herbert Reynolds, solicitor; Edward Povey, gentleman; Arthur Montfort Archer, surgeon; and R. Cathcart Smith, gentleman.

The New Inn and much of the land around it was owned by Thomas Allen Hughes, of *The Mount*, Glyn Ceiriog, shopkeeper, and it was conveyed to the Glyn Valley Hotel Co. Ltd on 27th December 1905, for the price of £6,000. The schedule with the conveyance shows that in 1853 the property had been in multi-ownership which had included the Wynne sisters: Sarah Roberts, Mary Bibby and Elizabeth Teece, and had come to Thomas Allen Hughes via Thomas Hughes. On the next day, Francis E. Rooper and C.G. Haswell signed, as Directors of the Glyn Valley Hotel Co., for a mortgage of £4,500 from Thomas Allen Hughes.

The GVT terminus at Glyn Ceiriog, somewhat in line with its big brothers the main-line railways, from 1891 boasted a post and telegraph office, as well as a hotel, all owned by Thomas Allen Hughes. The post office is shown between the New Inn (to right) and its stables (to left). High above the roofline can be seen the waste tips of the Wynne Slate Quarry with 'Bronydd' on the left and the quarry smithy on the right.

Collection: John Milner

River Ceiriog

•

Friend

The Chirk Fishery Company Ltd was registered in 1900 and built a fish hatchery alongside the river between Pontfaen and Castle Mill for the breeding of trout, which were despatched via the GVT to Chirk and thence by the GWR to destinations all over the country. The fish hatchery, under new ownership, is today still a thriving concern.

Collection: John Milner

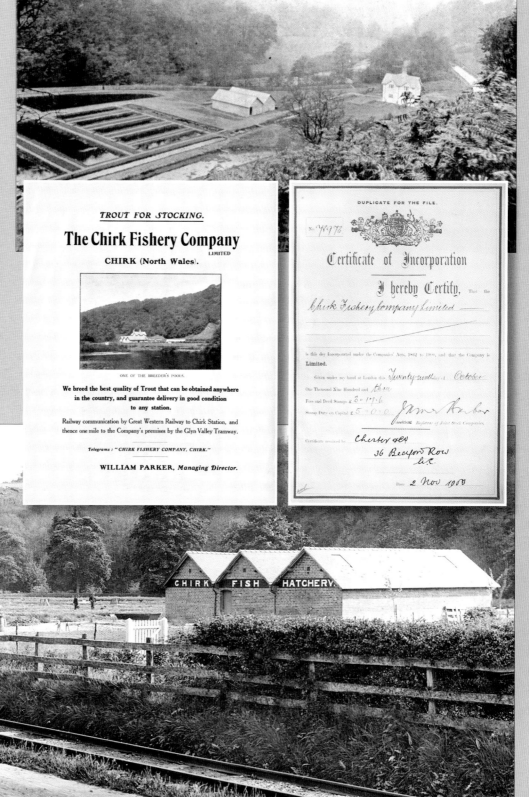

TROUT FOR STOCKING.

The Chirk Fishery Company
LIMITED

CHIRK (North Wales).

ONE OF THE BREEDER'S POOLS.

We breed the best quality of Trout that can be obtained anywhere in the country, and guarantee delivery in good condition to any station.

Railway communication by Great Western Railway to Chirk Station, and thence one mile to the Company's premises by the Glyn Valley Tramway.

Telegrams : " CHIRK FISHERY COMPANY, CHIRK."

WILLIAM PARKER, Managing Director.

DUPLICATE FOR THE FILE.

No. 96973

Certificate of Incorporation

I hereby Certify, That the

Chirk Fishery Company Limited

is this day Incorporated under the Companies' Acts, 1862 to 1900, and that the Company is Limited.

Given under my hand at London this *Twenty ninth* day of *October* One Thousand Nine Hundred and *three*
Fees and Deed Stamps £ *3 . 17 . 6*
Stamp Duty on Capital £ *5 . 0 . 0*

James Farrer
Assistant Registrar of Joint Stock Companies

Certificate received by *Chester & Co 36 Bedford Row W.C.*

Date *2 Nov 1900*

CHIRK FISH HATCHERY.

River Ceiriog
•
Foe

On 1st January 1902, the swollen waters of the River Ceiriog washed away a substantial section of the road and tramway on the bend between the turning for Talygarth Ucha and Felin Newydd, Glyn Ceiriog. A note in the GVT Departure/Arrival Record Book records the incident and shows that the tramway was closed until 22nd January. Note the wagonloads of granite being unloaded on the opposite bank and the schoolchildren surveying the scene. The breach was duly repaired and a substantial retaining wall was built, in which there is a plaque to mark its erection by the County Council.

Collection: John Milner
Plaque photograph: © Robert Jones

This enterprise appears to have been a complete failure because on 30th December 1913, the '*said sum of £4,500 with an arrears of interest was still due to Thomas Allen Hughes*', who exercised his power of sale and agreed to sell '*the Glyn Valley Hotel with the outbuildings, stables, premises and several pieces or parcels of land*' to Edward Hughes of the Llwynmawr Hotel, Dolywern, for the sum of £3,000.

The river has always been popular for its trout fishing and, in 1901, a fish hatchery was built by the Chirk Fishery Co. Ltd, approximately halfway between Pontfaen and Castle Mill. William Parker, agent to the Chirk Castle Estate, became managing director. To serve the construction of the hatchery, a short siding was installed, costing the hatchery company £15 15s. 9d., and this remained in situ until the tramway closed. A brochure of the time boasts that the hatchery was established to '*breed the best quality of Trout that can be obtained anywhere in the country, and guarantee delivery in good condition to any station*', and visiting the hatchery was described as a novel experience derived from a run upon the Glyn Valley line, the '*Toy Railway*', to the fish hatchery premises. Although not an official stopping place, presumably the GVT Co. had entered into an arrangement to stop trains there, to set down and pick up passengers. Live trout were despatched from the fish farm in water-filled milk churns, via the GVT to Chirk and thence by the GWR to destinations such as Liverpool, Manchester and the West Midlands, thereby ensuring that the fish were fresh on arrival.

The River Ceiriog was both a friend and a foe of the Glyn Valley Tramway; friend in the sense that many of the industries that provided goods for the tramway to carry depended upon the powers of its water to drive their machinery, and foe when its flood torrents washed away the track, bringing the tramway to a grinding halt.

Such an event happened during the night of the 1st January 1902, when a substantial section of the road, its retaining wall and the tramway were washed away on the bend between the turning for Talygarth Ucha and Felin Newydd, just east of Pont Bell, Glyn Ceiriog. The train record book records that the line was closed '*Owing to floods having washed away the line in several places*' and that it was not reopened until 22nd January.

Traffic on the tramway was further affected in 1903 because of a reduction in the output from the quarries, but even worse was a disastrous flood that occurred on 26th October 1903, when Nant Lafar washed away portions of the incline to the Cambrian Slate Quarry as well as '*... further great damage to the river wall between Castle Mill and Pontfadog, and at other places*'. The damage to the Cambrian Incline did not please the GVT Co., as it carried responsibility for its maintenance and had only just incurred a large expenditure on other repairs to it. By April the following year, the incline was still not operational and this was causing a big problem for the Cambrian Quarry, as it had to resort to transporting its slate down to Glyn Ceiriog by road, thus involving additional transshipment and costs. Despite all the disruption in 1903, the GVT Co. only saw a minor drop in its total revenue for the year, from £4,518 to £4,401.

The company had, by 1903, spent £63,681 on the construction of the tramway and the provision of facilities, but that figure did not include the expenditure incurred and ultimately written off by the Shropshire Union Railways & Canal Co. when it took over the horse tramway. The cost per mile computes to £7,278 which, in comparison, is over three times the cost of the Talyllyn Railway (1865) which involved some major engineering and ground work, but it is only marginally over that for the Snailbeach District Railways (1877).

The Ceiriog Granite Company was proving to be a successful and ambitious company. From the late 1880s onwards it had been acquiring lands with quarrying rights, on both sides of the stretch of the valley served by the GVT extension, for the purpose of reopening former quarries and developing new ones. As well as various forms of granite, mainly used for roadstone and ballast, the company quarried chinastone and silica rock for the pottery industry. These 'new' quarries worked in conjunction with Hendre and, where appropriate, with the company's tarmacadam plant.

One of the first of the granite company's acquisitions was the former Lower Pandy chinastone quarry, where the company built a substantial crushing facility driven by water power from a leat that carried water from the River Ceiriog at Pandy. Access from the GVT was provided by a line that left the GVT extension on the north side of Coed-y-Glyn Ucha, crossed the river into the quarry, ran under the loading hoppers of the crushing plant and rejoined the GVT extension via another bridge over the river to the south of Coed-y-Glyn Ucha. Later, the Ceiriog Granite Co. built a new line starting from a junction with the GVT extension at a point just to the Hendre side of the GVT bridge over the river at Pandy, from where it followed the course of the leat to terminate above the crushing plant.[4]

Close by, high up the escarpment above the GVT, just to the south east of Pandy, the Ceiriog Granite Co. also opened a new granite quarry in 1902, appropriately named Upper Pandy Quarry. A single siding ran from the GVT extension to the foot of the incline that served the quarry, from where stone was loaded into wagons either to be sent to the crushers or transported out of the valley via the GVT. The only tangible evidence on the provision of this siding is an Agreement that was made, on 12th February 1902, between a John Evans and the Ceiriog Granite Company *'in respect of the construction and use of a tramway siding'* on his land. This quarry was short-lived and was the scene of a fatal accident involving several quarrymen.

About 1900, the Ceiriog Granite Co. purchased a small outside-cylinder 0-4-0T locomotive, which had been built by the Lilleshall Co. of St. George's, Oakengates, Shropshire. The locomotive carried maker's plates that were inscribed *'Lilleshall Company – Engineers – Shropshire – 1880'*. The Lilleshall Company had been established in 1764 and specialised in the manufacture of blast engines (for furnaces) together with winding and pumping engines. It started building steam locomotives in the early 1860s.

The precise history of the Ceiriog Granite Company's 'Lilleshall' locomotive is a little inconclusive owing to specific records not being available. According to original despatch records kept by a

A view of Pandy looking towards Llanarmon. On the left can be seen Upper Pandy Quarry (1902–1908), with its gated siding and a rake of granite wagons on the GVT extension line; moving to the right are the Woolpack Inn (the former Pandy fulling mill), Aberteirw Terrace and the GVT coal yard. The area in the foreground to the right is the site of the later Silica Works.

Collection: John Milner

[4] See fold-out map page 233.

The diminutive 'Lilleshall' locomotive, purchased c1900 by the Ceiriog Granite Co. for work in Hendre and Lower Pandy Quarries, is photographed standing on the private siding that ran from near the tramway bridge at Pandy to the upper level of Lower Pandy Quarry. Running alongside is the leat from the weir at Pandy to the quarry. Note the lightweight track, and the loaded quarry tipper wagon with its maker's name burnt on it – 'The Wigan Wagon Company Ltd' – and the Woolpack Inn on the left.

Collection: John Milner
Ex F. Moore

Mr Hoggins, who worked for the Lilleshall Company from c1885 and who eventually rose to the position of Engineers' Accountant, the company had built a narrow-gauge 0-4-0T locomotive No. 331, named *'Laura'*, which was supplied new to the Heyford Iron Co., Northamptonshire. The Lilleshall company's locomotive numbers ran consecutively with its order numbers for all products and appear to have never been carried on the maker's plates. It has not been possible to confirm the precise date of the order. It is thought to have gone for use on the 2ft 8in gauge line at the Heyford Co.'s ironworks, either charging the furnaces or removing slag to the tips. The ironworks closed during the depression of the 1890s and the locomotive was sold to C.D. Phillips & Co., dealers, of Newport.

The Phillips Machinery Register for 5th June 1900 carried details of a 2ft 8in locomotive for sale: *'Lilleshall Iron Co., 2ft 8in gauge, new copper box, perfect condition. £180'* and, on the 6th October 1900, another advert (Anon) appeared: *'Wanted – Loco. 2ft 4½in gauge or one that can easily be altered to that gauge'*. The advert would suggest that the most likely destination, with a specific gauge of 2ft 4½in, was Hendre Quarry. Because it had inside frames, it would have had to have undergone substantial work to re-gauge it to 2ft 4½in. Phillips may have been delighted to find a customer and may have undertaken necessary alterations to get rid of it – but why the '1880' maker's plates remains a mystery.

The main use made of the 'Lilleshall' was working between Hendre and Lower Pandy Quarries. It was initially used to convey chinastone waste from Lower Pandy Quarry up the valley to the crushers at Hendre using the lower-level GVT line, but after a coating plant for the manufacture of tarmacadam was installed at Lower Pandy Quarry in 1908, it was used to bring crushed stone down the valley from Hendre Quarry to the Lower Pandy Quarry to be coated with tar for tarmacadam, using the granite company's high-level line from Pandy. As GVT rails were used for part of both these journeys, the Ceiriog Granite Co. must have had an agreement in respect of running rights over them, but no record of such has so far been traced nor is there mention of any payments for such in the GVT Co. accounts.

The 'Lilleshall' was taken out of use about 1926, when the tarmacadam coating operation was transferred back to Hendre Quarry. Dick Morris, a Hendre employee, was officially listed as an 'Engine Driver' in the official returns dated 1927, so he was obviously the one who looked after the 'Lilleshall' up to that date, bearing in mind that the returns would be twelve months behind.

In 1942, railway historian and friend of the author's, Selwyn H.P. Higgins, was stationed with the Royal Engineers at Nesscliffe Camp, near Oswestry, and he approached the British Quarrying Co. Ltd at its Head Office in Shrewsbury, asking if he could acquire the maker's plates from the 'Lilleshall' engine at Hendre. Previously, he had made efforts to save the engine for preservation, but to no avail – sadly it was another nine years before the railway preservation era was to start. However, he did received a response, dated the 8th October 1942, saying that:

> *'We are offering the loco as it stands, and if we dispose of it, we will advise you immediately of the purchaser. In the meantime we will have to leave the plates in position, as we have no other warranty as to manufacture and date. In the event of its being sold as scrap, the plates will be taken off and forwarded to you. We anticipate disposing of it this month or early November.'*

There were no buyers, regrettably, and it was cut up for scrap in 1944, although the author found various parts from it still on site in 1955, including the cab and bunker. Selwyn Higgins did indeed acquire the plates and when he died these were transferred to the National Railway Museum with most of his collection. What a pity this interesting little locomotive was never preserved for posterity!

With the Glyn Valley Tramway now successfully operating in the 20th century, this is an appropriate time to conclude Part 1 of *'Rails to Glyn Ceiriog'* and what, for the authors, has

The 'Lilleshall', still displaying its maker's plates, in a forlorn state at Hendre Quarry in October 1942. It was cut up in 1944 and parts of the cab were still lying around in 1955. The nameplates were salvaged by Selwyn H.P. Higgins and are now in the National Railway Museum. The plate shown above is a replica cast from the original.

Collection: James I.C. Boyd
Ex S.H.P. Higgins

Plate courtesy: Keith Buckle

been a *taith ar antur anhygoel* (an extraordinary journey of adventure), unearthing the mysteries of the early history of this gem of a Welsh narrow-gauge railway, much of which has previously gone unrecorded or has been incorrectly interpreted.

The story, so far, has touched upon the early history of the Ceiriog Valley, including the arrival of the canal and the main-line railway at Chirk, the industries in the valley, which were desperate to have an efficient means of transport to connect their businesses to these national networks, as well as an account of the early pioneers and the various schemes promoted to build a railway up the Ceiriog Valley, all of which were destined for failure for one reason or another. That was until circumstances led to the adoption of a plan proposed by Henry Dennis, who became the GVT company's engineer, to build a roadside horse-drawn tramway. This plan was the basis of the GVT Act 1870 for the building of a tramway along the turnpike road and with steep gradients up from the valley bottom to reach the canal and railway interchanges, which made it highly inefficient and expensive to operate. The period of construction, the Board Room battles and the trials and tribulations of the early years, have all been covered in some detail, culminating in the tramway's triumphal days when it was converted to steam operation.

Part 2 of this work continues with the history of the tramway from 1904, its further developments, the disruption caused by World War I, the proposal by Warrington Corporation to flood the upper reaches of the valley and the competition from road transport, not only for passengers but for the carriage of goods and minerals. This competition resulted in the tramway's closure for passenger traffic on 6th April 1933, with its final demise to all traffic on 6th July 1935. Its route and operation are described in detail with a wealth of illustrations, together with full details of the locomotives and rolling stock, supported by super-detailed, specially commissioned drawings, all researched from primary sources.

Trên Bach y Glyn
Little Train of Glyn

Selected Bibliography

Printed Sources:

Baker & Civil   *Bagnalls of Stafford* Phyllis Rampton NGR Trust
Borrow, George   *Wild Wales* William Collins, Sons & Co. 1862
Boyd, J.I.C.   *Narrow Gauge Rails in Mid-Wales* Oakwood Press 1952, 1965 and 1970 editions
Bradley, V.J.   *Industrial Locomotives of North Wales* Industrial Railway Society 1992
Cozens, Lewis   *The Van & Kerry Railways with the Kerry Tramway* 1953
Davies, D.Ll.   *The Glyn Valley Tramway* Oakwood Press 1962
"   "   *The Ceiriog* Published by author 1963
Davies, Alfred, Sir   *Evicting a Community* 1923
Davies, Walter   *A General View of the Agricultural and Domestic Economy of Wales* 1810
Hadfield, Charles   *The Canals of the West Midlands* 1966
"   "   *Thomas Telford's Temptation* 1993
Hurdsman, C.N.   *A History of the Parish of Chirk* Bridge Books 1996
"   "   *A History of the Parishes of St. Martin's & Weston Rhyn* Bridge Books 2003
Jones, Jane A.L.   *The History of Llanarmon Dyffryn Ceiriog and Tregeiriog* Herald Printers 2000
Jones, D.P. & R.O.   *100 Years in the Valley Vol. I & II* Ceiriog Press
Jones, G.P.   *The Extent of Chirkland 1391–1393* The University Press of Liverpool 1932
Lerry, G.G.   *Collieries of Denbighshire* 1968
Lewis, Samuel   *Topographical Dictionary of Wales* 1849
Lindsay, Jean   *History of the North Wales Slate Industry* David & Charles 1974
MacKay, J.C.   *Light Railways* Crosby Lockwood & Son 1896
Milner, John   *The Glyn Valley Tramway* Oxford Publishing Co. 1984
"   "   *Slates from Glyn Ceiriog* Ceiriog Press 2008
Morris, Richard K.   *Canals of Shropshire* 1991
Parry, Edward   *The Railway Companion from Chester to Shrewsbury* 1849
Pennant, Thomas   *Pennant's Tours in Wales* H. Humphreys 1883
Quenby, Ron   *Thomas Telford's Aqueducts on the Shropshire Union Canal* 1992
Richards, Alun   *Gazetteer of the Welsh Slate Industry* Gwasg Carreg Gwalch 1991 & 2007
"   "   *Slate Quarrying in Wales* Gwasg Carreg Gwalch 2006
Rolt, L.T.C.   *Landscape with Machines* Longman 1971
Roscoe, Thomas   *Roscoe's North Wales* 1836
Tonks, E.S.   *Snailbeach District Railways* 1950
Wrexham C.B.C.   *Pontcysyllte Aqueduct & Canal Heritage Site Nomination for World Heritage Site status*

Wilson, Edward   *The Ellesmere and Llangollen Canal 1975*
Wright, Ian l.   *Canals in Wales* 1977
   Beyer-Peacock Quarterly Review
   Railway Magazine 1902
   Llangollen Advertiser
   Oswestry & Border Counties Advertizer

National Archives:

   Board of Trade records
   Shropshire Union Railways & Canal Company – Executive Committee Minutes 1872–1891
   Companies House records including:
     Ellesmere and Glyn Valley Railway Company 1867
     Glyn Valley Tramway Company
     Records of Ceiriog Valley quarry companies

Denbighshire Record Office:

   Ellesmere & Glyn Valley Railway records
   Glyn Valley Tramway records
   Wem & Bronygarth Turnpike Trust records
   George Rooper records

Flintshire Record Office:

   Nathaniel R. Griffiths Reports
   Cullimore Collection

National Library of Wales:

   W.R. Jones Papers (Gwenith Gwyn)
   Longueville Papers
   Chirk Castle records

Shropshire Archives:

   Ellesmere & Glyn Valley Railway records
   Glyn Valley Tramway records
   Longueville Papers
   Shrewsbury & Chester Railway records
   Shropshire Union Railways & Canal Co. records

John Milner Collection (Private):

   Ceiriog Press photographic collection
   David Llewellyn Davies collection of GVT research
   J.I.C. Boyd collection of GVT research
   S.H.P. Higgins collection of GVT research
   GVT Company surviving records
   GVT Company liquidator's records
   Angela James Collection (Custodian of)

Beryl Williams Collection (Private):

   Canal, Ceiriog Valley and industrial records

Appendix 1

Currency and Units

Monetary values are quoted throughout the book in pre-decimal currency (converted 1971) and all units are British Imperial.

Currency

12 pence (written 12d.) = 1 shilling (written 1s. or 1/-)
20 shillings = £1 (a shilling was also known as a 'bob')
1 guinea = £1 1s. 0d. or 21 shillings

A half-penny (pronounced *hay-p'ny*) is written ½d.
A quarter-penny (called a farthing) is written ¼d.

Length

1 inch or 1" or in. = 25.4 millimetres
12 inches = 1 foot
1 foot (1' or ft) = 30.48 centimetres
3 feet = 1 yard or yd = 0.914 metre
22 yards = 1 chain = 20.12 metres
10 chains = 1 furlong = 201.17 metres
8 furlongs = 1 mile = 1,760 yds = 1.61 kilometres

Area

144 sq. inches = 1 sq. foot
9 sq. feet = 1 sq. yard = 0.836 sq. metre

Land measurement

40 perches = 1 rood
4 roods = 1 acre = 0.40 hectare

Weight

16 ounces (oz) = 1 pound (lb) = 0.454 kilogram
14 pounds (lb) = 1 stone
2 stones = 1 quarter
4 quarters = 1 hundredweight (cwt)
20 cwt = 1 ton = 1.016 tonnes

Liquid

2 pints = 1 quart = 1.136 litres
4 quarts = 1 gallon = 4.546 litres

Appendix 2

Welsh Place Names

Bronygarth	*Bron* – 'breast', *garth* – 'ridge'; top of ridge.
Bryn	A 'hill' or 'mount', as in *Brynkinalt*.
Ceiriog	Derivation unknown.
Chirk	Possibly the English corruption of *Ceiriog*.
Coed	'Wood', as in *Coed-y-Glyn*.
Dolywern	'Meadow of the alder trees'.
Glyn	'Glen' or 'deep valley', as in *Glyn Ceiriog*.
Hendre	'Established habitation'.
Llan	A 'place with a church', as in *Llangollen*. The only two villages in the valley with ancient churches are both prefixed *Llan*. A place or village without a church is *Pentre*.
Llanarmon Dyffryn Ceiriog	There are several Llanarmons in Wales, and the last two words distinguish this particular village.
Llwynmawr	'Big grove' or 'bush', *Mawr* being 'great' or 'big'.
Melin	'Mill', as in *Melin y Castell* or 'Castle mill'.
Nant	'Brook' or 'ravine', as in *Nantydramwys*.
Pandy	A 'fulling mill'. This is a place where cloth is scoured and thickened. The earth used by a fuller to full or bleach cloth absorbed grease, and is still known by its former usage.
Pont	'Bridge', as in *Pontfadog* (Madoc's bridge). This is one of the relics of the Roman occupation, as the Welsh absorbed several Latin words.
Santffraid	'Saint Bride, Ffraed or Brigit', a Celtic goddess adopted by Christianity, as in *Llansantffraid*.
Tre	'Homestead' or 'hamlet', as in *Tregeiriog*.
Y or yr	Definitive article 'the', as in *Pont-y-Blew*, becomes 'yr' before a vowel, as in *Craig-yr-Oryn* (*Craig*, a 'crag' or 'rock').

As with Cornish and Breton, Welsh was one of three languages that developed out of an ancient British tongue. It had become recognisably Welsh by AD 550.

Courtesy: David Ll. Davies

Appendix 3

Industries of the Ceiriog Valley

Served by the Glyn Valley Tramway from 1873 to 1935

Industry	Works	Location	Employees	Dates
Slate	Wynne Quarry/ Mine	Glyn Ceiriog	81 in 1904	1750–1928
	Cambrian Quarries/Mine	Glyn Ceiriog	134 in 1929	1790–1947
	Craig-yr-Oryn Quarry	Nr. Llwynmawr	5 in 1891	1824–1903
	Nantyr Quarry	Nantyr	<10	1832–1876
Granite	Hendre & Upper Pandy Quarries	Hendre & Pandy	115 in 1928	1874–1953
	Coed-y-Glyn Quarry/Mine*	Coed-y-Glyn Ucha	46 in 1897	1890–1907
	Teirw Hill Quarry	Pandy	7 in 1895	1892–1895
Chinastone	Craig-y-Pandy Quarry*	Pandy	25 in 1911	1865–1920
	Lower Pandy Quarry	Opposite Coed-y-Glyn Ucha	<20	1865–1904
	Caedeicws Quarry	Caedeicws	35 in 1902	1900–1903
Silica	Silica Works	Pandy	<20	1911–1922
Lime	Bronygarth Lime Works	Castle Mill (Bronygarth)	<20	1770–1920
Coal	Quinta & Trehowell Collieries	Trehowell	>250	1860–1889
Kiln goods	Trehowell Brickworks	Trehowell	<20	1860–1889
Flannel	Gynfor Upper Mill	Glyn Ceiriog	<40	1815–1951
	Berwyn Lower Mill	Glyn Ceiriog	<40	1818–1923
	Felin Newydd	Glyn Ceiriog	30 in 1881	1880–1898
Gunpowder	Hendre Powder Works	Pont y Meibion	<20	1874–1879
Fish	Chirk Fish Hatchery	Chirk	<5	1901 – Extant
* Also silica deposits				

Selected Industries in the Valley pre-dating, or not served by, the Glyn Valley Tramway

Slate	Tŷ Draw Quarry	Glyn Ceiriog	–	1529–1740
Lead	Lead Levels	Teirw Valley	Exploratory only	1850s
Lime	Penissa Glyn Lime Works	Herber	–	?–c1870
Iron	Pont-y-Blew Forge	Pont-y-Blew	20 in 1795	1640–1870
Silica	Bryn Quarry	Selattyn Road	<20	1917–1922
Coal	Brynkinalt Colliery	Chirk	>900	1840–1928
	Collieries at Chirk Bank	Chirk Bank	–	1775–1839

Many of the undertakings worked spasmodically. The comparative size of the various operations can be deduced from
the numbers of employees listed which, where possible, have been quoted from documentary sources.
In some instances, the start and end dates shown are approximate.
See rear endpaper for further details of the location of the industries listed and other quarries and collieries.

Appendix 4

Glyn Valley Tramway – Horse-drawn era
Additional Expenditure Required 1873

		£	s.	d.
1.	Pontfaen station	176	0	8
2.	Pontfaen siding	2	0	0
3.	Pontfaen stables	110	0	0
4.	Pontfaen turntable	16	15	11
5.	Pontfaen siding	8	12	5
6.	Pontfaen machine house	60	14	8
7.	Roadside siding extension	6	16	10
8.	Gledrid canal basin	5	0	0
9.	Gledrid canal bank towing path	24	14	0
10.	Gledrid siding	176	4	1
11.	Gledrid warehouse	166	10	5
12.	Gledrid lift-up bridge	35	3	9
13.	Cambrian canal-side slate wharf	18	3	0
14.	Herber Tollhouse window alteration	1	0	0
15.	Herber gravel pit siding	25	6	6
16.	Pontfadog siding	24	14	6
17.	Dolywern Queen's Inn siding	64	5	2
18.	New Inn siding	164	0	8
19.	New Inn coal wharf	181	5	9
20.	New Inn walling	132	7	0
21.	New Inn warehouse	165	18	2
22.	New Inn stables	219	10	9
23.	New Inn ticket office	7	2	0
24.	Cambrian incline second track *	555	14	7
	* The main contract for building the tramway had included a single track incline			

Because the Glyn Valley Tramway Company had initially experienced difficulty in raising the finance to build the tramway, many essential buildings, items of equipment and works required were not included in the original downward-revised estimate of £10,000. The above items appeared on a list compiled c1873, by the first operator of the tramway, the Shropshire Union Railways & Canal Company, which had been forced to provide, or pay for, these necessary 'extras' that had not been included in the main contract for the construction of the tramway which had been awarded to Elias Griffith.

Appendix 5

Traffic Figures: 1888–1903

| Year | Passengers (in numbers) | | | | Goods (in tons) | | | Train Miles |
	First Class	Third Class	Total	Seasons	Minerals	General Merchandise	Total	Totals
1888	–	–	–	–	6,013	–	6,013	20,400
1889	–	–	–	–	13,795	–	13,795	10,134
1890	–	–	–	–	19,648	677	20,325	20,385
1891	–	13,020	13,020	–	27,392	647	28,039	18,149
1892	–	15,623	15,623	2	47,990	1,032	49,022	24,988
1893	87	20,820	20,907	3	43,762	1,370	45,132	27,439
1894	325	21,642	21,967	2	39,198	1,017	40,215	28,746
1895	241	24,726	24,967	5	33,628	344	33,972	31,252
1896	227	25,266	25,493	3	41,582	788	42,370	35,547
1897	293	24,848	25,141	2	37,292	994	38,286	33,227
1898	513	28,887	29,400	2	38,695	1,240	39,935	35,544
1899	301	29,900	30,201	5	36,912	1,282	38,194	36,639
1900	493	31,042	31,535	5	43,080	1,461	44,541	25,556
1901	566	30,957	31,523	6	49,528	1,183	50,711	25,425
1902	565	30,557	31,122	2	58,057	1,468	59,525	26,178
1903	623	32,504	33,127	1	55,680	1,271	56,951	26,501

For traffic Figures 1904–1935 see *Rails to Glyn Ceiriog* Part 2

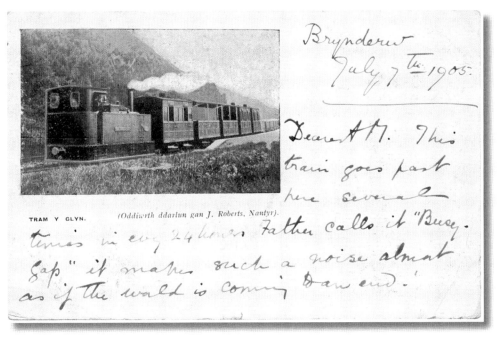

TRAM Y GLYN. *(Oddiwrth ddarlun gan J. Roberts, Nantyr).*

Brynderw
July 7th 1905.

Dearest M. This train goes past here several times in every 24 hours. Father calls it "Busy Gap" it makes such a noise almost as if the wald is coming to an end.

Even though the Glyn Valley Tramway passed close to several homes, making 'such a noise almost as if the world is coming to an end', there was an element of local pride and affection for it. This privately printed postcard, dated 1905, written at Brynderw, a house sandwiched between the GVT extension and Llanarmon Road, on the outskirts of Glyn Ceiriog, illustrates this sentiment. The writer has felt it appropriate to use a postcard illustrated with 'Tram y Glyn', by J. Roberts, Nantyr.

Collection: John Milner

Appendix 6

Extracts from the Summary of Capital Expenditure 1887–1889

(Breakdown of expenditure summarised on page 220 chapter 9)

	Date	Supplier	Material	£	s.	d.
		Axles, Fishplates, Girders, etc.				
1.	19.10.1887	Bayliss & Co.	bolts	440	2	6
2.	19.10.1887	Tiddesly & Co.	girders	267	1	9
3.	19.11.1887	Bayliss & Co.	bolts	185	10	8
4.	19.11.1887	Reynolds & Co.	drilling machine	6	1	6
5.	12.12.1887	Brymbo Steel Co.		17	8	8
6.	27.01.1888	Bayliss & Co.	bolts	19	0	0
7.	27.01.1888	John Taylor & Sons	engine pump	3	17	5
8.	03.03.1888	Brymbo Steel Co.		6	6	9
9.	03.03.1888	Edward Thomas & Co.		6	4	1
10.	03.03.1888	Thomas Edwards (blacksmith), Chirk	iron	2	10	0
11.	03.03.1888	Baker Bros.		27	10	0
12.	02.05.1888	Hartley, Arnoux & Fanning & Co.		71	19	8
13.	27.07.1888	Hartley, Arnoux & Fanning & Co.		80	0	0
14.	02.08.1888	Ruabon, Coke & Coal Co.		16	15	10
15.	03.09.1888	Hadfields		100	0	0
16.	06.11.1888	Hadfields		155	0	0
17.	23.11.1888	Brymbo Steel Co.		3	11	9
18.	15.12.1888	Bayliss & Co.		33	7	9
19.	15.12.1888	Hartley, Arnoux & Fanning & Co.		86	16	6
20.	12.03.1889	Cudworth & Johnson		52	10	0
21.	12.03.1889	R.H. Mason		17	8	8
		TOTAL for AXLES, FISHPLATES, GIRDERS, etc.		£1,599	2	10

	Date	Supplier	Material	£	s.	d.
		Iron Hurdles etc.				
1.	22.10.1887	J.C. Gittens, Wrexham	iron fencing	60	18	9
2.	27.01.1888	J.C. Gittens, Wrexham	iron fencing	64	13	3
3.	18.09.1888	J.C. Gittens, Wrexham	iron fencing	300	0	0
4.	21.11.1888	J.C. Gittens, Wrexham	iron fencing	265	16	9
5.	18.06.1889	Thomas Edwards (blacksmith), Chirk	iron gates	17	4	8
		TOTAL for IRON HURDLES etc.		£708	3	5

	Rails and Related Carriage						
	Date	Supplier	Carriage	Material	£	s.	d.
1.	21.05.1887	Guest & Co.		rails	87	5	10
2.	17.06.1887	Guest & Co.		rails	174	6	0
3.	15.07.1887	Guest & Co.		rails	381	7	7
4.	15.07.1887		SUR&C Co. carriage		29	4	8
5.	10.08.1887	Guest & Co.		rails	299	11	5
6.	10.08.1887		carriage		40	9	11
7.	19.10.1887	Guest & Co.		rails	378	0	2
8.	02.11.1887		GWR carriage		110	9	0
9.	19.11.1887	Guest & Co.		rails	128	5	11
10.	19.11.1887		GWR carriage		69	14	3
11.	12.12.1887	Guest & Co.		rails	232	3	7
12.	28.12.1887		carriage		33	19	2
13.	02.01.1888	Guest & Co.		rails	654	13	3
14.	27.01.1888	Guest & Co.		rails	218	8	1
15.	27.01.1888		GWR carriage		14	1	4
16.	29.01.1888		SUR&C Co. carriage		24	12	9
17.	03.03.1888	Guest & Co.		rails	28	6	0
18.	02.05.1888	Guest & Co.		rails	218	6	8
19.	18.09.1888	Guest & Co.		rails	519	14	6
20.	15.12.1888		GWR carriage		114	1	3
21.	22.01.1889	Guest & Co.		balance	217	18	10
			TOTAL for RAILS (including CARRIAGE)		£4,186	16	4

	Sleepers and Timber					
	Date	Supplier	Material	£	s.	d.
1.	08.03.1887	R. Grandidge, Chester	sleepers	600	0	0
2.	21.03.1887	R. Grandidge, Chester	sleepers	300	0	0
3.	17.06.1887	R. Grandidge, Chester	sleepers	300	0	0
4.	18.06.1887	E. Meredith Jones	timber	4	0	0
5.	28.09.1887	Mr. Thomas	timber	55	0	0
6.	02.12.1887	Jenkins & Jones	timber	58	13	3
7.	03.03.1888	William Griffiths, Rhosweil	timber	13	7	8
8.	18.09.1888	William Griffiths, Rhosweil	timber	35	9	7
9.	23.11.1888	Jenkins & Jones	timber	35	0	0
10.	01.12.1888	R. Grandidge, Chester	sleepers	175	0	0
		TOTAL for SLEEPERS and TIMBER		£1,576	10	4

RAILS TO GLYN CEIRIOG

Engines, Trucks, etc.

	Date	Supplier		£	s.	d.
1.	10.09.1888	Beyer, Peacock & Co.	locomotive	1,150	0	0
2.	16.04.1889	Beyer, Peacock & Co.	locomotive	1,150	0	0
3.	21.05.1889	Samuel Lloyd, Chirk	pipe	1	3	9
4.	21.05.1889	Wilson & Co.	tippler	33	0	0
5.	21.05.1889	Birmingham Wagon Co.	wagons	214	10	0
6.	24.10.1889	Birmingham Wagon Co.	wagons	175	10	0
7.	24.10 1889	Kerr, Stuart & Co., Stoke	turntables	129	4	0
			TOTAL for ENGINE, TRUCKS, etc.	£ 2,853	7	9

Various Supplies

	Date	Supplier		£	s.	d.
1.	January 1888	Light & Co.		9	19	8
2.	January 1888	Parker	sundries		5	2
3.	January 1888	J.J. Ward		4	19	6
4.	26.03.1889	R.J. Roberts (ironmonger)		7	5	3
5.	18.06.1889	Sothen		1	7	6
6.	18.06.1889	Groom & Sons, Wellington		2	0	0
7.	18.06.1889	Haldern & Co.		1	7	0
8.	18.06.1889	Ernest Reynolds		1	13	0
9.	05.11.1889	W.H. Read		6	16	6
10.	05.11.1889	Ceiriog Granite Co.	macadam	39	0	4
			TOTAL	£74	13	11

Remaining Lists in the Summary of Capital Expenditure 1887–1889

	Date from	Date to	Heading	Comments	£	s.	d.
1.	15.02.1887	29.11.1889	Wages	fortnightly totals, no other details	1,240	5	5
2.	01.07.1887	02.12.1889	Advertising etc.		93	7	1
3.	02.12.1887	23.01.1889	Solicitor costs etc.	mainly relating to land purchase	221	17	8
4.	–	–	Paid to revenue	cash	101	17	5
5.	31.01.1887	–	Ceiriog Granite Co.	for plant + interest	691	0	0
6.	09.02.1887	28.02.1889	Costs of Act 1885 etc.	fees & parliamentary deposit etc.	3,643	0	8
7.	28.09.1887	31.05 1887	R.M. Biddulph Esq.	includes rent charge	803	16	10
8.	22.08.1887	26.07.1889	Purchase of land	including valuation etc.	2,754	0	8
9.	16.08.1887	21.11.1888	Postage & general	via Elias Griffith at Hand Hotel	253	5	6
10.	21.03.1887	05.11.1889	Carriage of materials	GWR, SUR&C Co. & Roberts, including SDR	229	16	7
11.	13.05.1887	24.10.1889	Paid to contractors	including Griffith Griffiths award	7,929	8	3
12.	09.02.1887	15.12.1888	Commission etc.	commission & interest	33	12	11
13.	03.03.1888	15.12.1888	Coal in construction etc.	from local collieries	53	13	4

Appendix 7

Estimates for Expenditure immediately Required at Chirk
Extracted from 1889 Lists of Liabilities

			£	s.	d.
1.	Chirk	Tippler & fixing	40	0	0
2.	Chirk	Water tank fixed	15	0	0
3.	Chirk	2 turntables fixed	150	0	0
4.	Chirk	Raising wings to GWR bridge	46	16	0
5.	Chirk	1 weighing machine fixed	60	0	0
6.	Chirk	Removing warehouse from Gledrid & fixing crane	100	0	0
7.	Chirk	1 locomotive	1,150	0	0
8.	Chirk	20 wagons	400	0	0
9.	Chirk	2 brakevans	106	0	0
10.	Chirk	2 passenger cars	150	0	0
11.	Chirk	Removing workshops from Pontfaen	100	0	0
12.	Chirk	Sundries for platform etc.	200	0	0

Appendix 8

Other Suppliers Extracted from the 1889 Lists of Liabilities

		£	s.	d.
Dennis & Co.	building stone	£22	2	5
W.H. Hughes, Plaskynaston		£50	10	8
Marsden, Manchester	tarpaulins	£24	8	11
Ruabon Water Co.	water pipes	£70	0	0
Midland Railway Carriage & Wagon Co.	coach	£85	12	0
Ruabon Coal & Coke Co.	points, crossings, etc.	£49	19	5
J.E. Powell, Wrexham	bar iron etc.	£13	0	1
Charles Wade & Co., Birmingham	lamps	£4	14	5
G.E. Woodford, Ruabon		£7	9	2
Thomas Owen			12	0
Ruabon Glazed Brick Co.		£9	15	11

Index

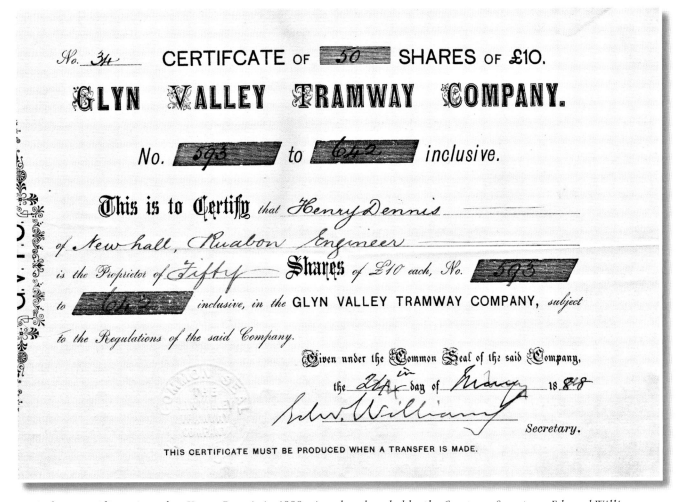

No. 34 CERTIFCATE OF *50* SHARES OF £10.

GLYN VALLEY TRAMWAY COMPANY.

No. *593* to *642* inclusive.

This is to Certify that *Henry Dennis*

of *New hall, Ruabon Engineer*

is the Proprietor of *Fifty* Shares of £10 each, No. *593*

to *642* inclusive, in the GLYN VALLEY TRAMWAY COMPANY, subject

to the Regulations of the said Company.

Given under the Common Seal of the said Company,

the *24th* day of *March* 18*88*

Edw. Williams

Secretary.

THIS CERTIFICATE MUST BE PRODUCED WHEN A TRANSFER IS MADE.

A share certificate issued to Henry Dennis in 1888, signed and sealed by the Company Secretary, Edward Williams of Oswestry.

Collection: John Milner

Below: *GLYN with its skirt just skimming the grass on the side of the track in 1933, not long before the tramway was to close and somewhat reminiscent of the 1960s character Dougal in the Magic Roundabout!*

Courtesy: Rev. J.R. Simpson

Y Diwedd

The Glyn Valley Tramway

and the industries of the Ceiriog Valley

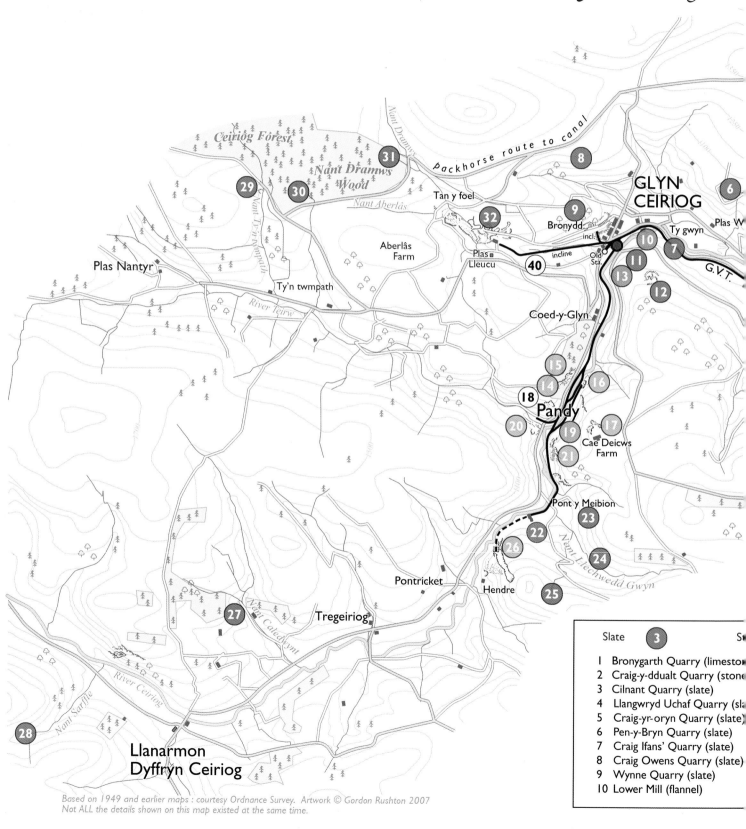

Ceiriog Forest

Nant Dramws Wood

Nant Dramws

packhorse route to canal

Nant Aberlâs

GLYN CEIRIOG

31

29

30

8

6

Tan y foel

32

9

Bronydd

Plas W

Aberlâs Farm

incl.

10

Ty gwyn

Plas Nantyr

Plas Lleucu

incline

40

Old Sta.

7

G.V.T.

Ty'n twmpath

11

13

River Teirw

Coed-y-Glyn

12

Ty'n twmpath

15

14

16

18

Pandy

20

17

19

Cae Deicws Farm

21

Pont y Meibion

23

22

26

Nant Llechwedd Gwyn

24

Pontricket

Hendre

25

Nant Caledlyyn

27

Tregeiriog

Nant Sarflle

River Ceiriog

28

Llanarmon Dyffryn Ceiriog

Based on 1949 and earlier maps : courtesy Ordnance Survey. Artwork © Gordon Rushton 2007
Not ALL the details shown on this map existed at the same time.

Slate	3	S
1	Bronygarth Quarry (limeston
2	Craig-y-ddualt Quarry (stone
3	Cilnant Quarry (slate)
4	Llangwryd Uchaf Quarry (sla
5	Craig-yr-oryn Quarry (slate)
6	Pen-y-Bryn Quarry (slate)
7	Craig Ifans' Quarry (slate)
8	Craig Owens Quarry (slate)
9	Wynne Quarry (slate)
10	Lower Mill (flannel)